CINEMA NOW

CINEMA NOW

Author Andrew Bailey
Editor Paul Duncan

TASCHEN

HONG KONG KÖLN LONDON LOS ANGELES MADRID PARIS TOKYO

Contents — Inhalt — Sommaire

DVD Contents — Inhalt DVD — Contenu DVD

Preface — Vorwort — Préface

One of the great 'movie' movies of the last decade is Taiwanese director Tsai Ming-liang's *Goodbye, Dragon Inn* (*Bu San*, 2003). A romantic rumination on the dying art of moviegoing, it is set on the closing night of a cavernous old Taipei movie palace where the 1966 King Hu swordplay classic *Dragon Inn (Long men ke zhen)* unspools to a smattering of patrons. Ghosts and the living alike prowl the aisles and restrooms in search of human connection. Hu's *Dragon Inn* remains immortal thanks to the likes of Quentin Tarantino and Ang Lee, who have fetishized it for international audiences in the form of *Kill Bill Volumes 1* and *2* (2003, 2004), and *Crouching Tiger, Hidden Dragon* (*Wo hu zang long*, 2000). These latter movies briefly enchanted audiences on multiplex screens, before quickly settling into permanent residency on cable and DVD, to be enjoyed anew in the digital home.

As for Tsai's haunting gem, finding an audience in this day and age isn't so simple. I was lucky to see *Goodbye, Dragon Inn* on a screen in the cavernous basement multiplex of a Pasadena shopping mall on the last day of its Los Angeles theatrical engagement, with a midweek matinee audience of myself and a pair of dowagers (who were asleep at the twenty-minute mark). I don't think I could have enjoyed it any more than I did, not that this bodes well for the future exhibition of Tsai's films in my country. One year later, *Goodbye, Dragon Inn*'s North American distributor, Wellspring, shuttered its New York-based theatrical division, thus ending an era of art films in America.

The truth is that when it comes to territories and distribution rights, the only profitable outlet for a small company releasing foreign and art films lies in ancillary markets like DVD – which is how most people in the world will discover the majority of the works described in this book, including *Goodbye, Dragon Inn*.

The experience of seeing films on the home screen is not altogether a bad thing. It is easier to be intimate with a movie on one's own, like reading a book, which is why the emergence of the so-called "fourth screen," bringing together the once-separate worlds of movies, television and personal computers, is transforming the entertainment business. Today's affordable high-definition television sets with state-of-the-art surround sound mean picture quality at home is sharp and clear, and sound is often better because you are not disturbed by crunching popcorn, nattering patrons, and mobile phones.

With competition for discretionary income at its most frenzied, with Internet surfing, video games (increasingly cinematic and narrative-driven) and other media competing with theatrical motion pictures for the global attention span, with the online blogosphere diluting the value of film criticism via egalitarian prognostication by rank amateur critics, how does the discriminating cineaste determine whether or not a film is worth seeing?

Film culture has always promoted the beautiful and talented celebrity faces on the screen. But up until the mid-1970s the print media also gave space to the budding auteurs *behind* the camera – making mavericks like Terrence Malick and the late, great Robert Altman as celebrated as their films. Since then celebrity gossip, box office figures for the latest blockbuster film and awards-season prognostication have driven movie news, regardless of the quality of the films or their place in our society. The auteurs have had to find alternative means of promotion, embracing the digital datastream of the Internet, where the next wave of film culture thrives.

Some serious academic film magazines survive, including *Cahiers du cinéma*, *Sight and Sound* and *Film Comment*. Each of these publications now routinely features major celebrities on its covers, while still pushing an art-house agenda. Youthful upstarts made in their image, like Canada's quarterly *CinemaScope* – the print publication *du jour* that best represents the aims of the *Cahiers* generation – struggle to compete with frequently updated movie blogs organized like magazines, containing in-depth features and late-breaking news within the same publication. Who wants to wait for a Cannes recap in *Film Comment* when you can get your information instantly?

More than ever (and for better or worse) it is Internet bloggers who drive film culture, breaking new names and heralding hot titles months in advance of their film festival premieres or theatrical and DVD releases. Bloggers like Todd Brown, at his *Twitch* website, cultivate instant word of mouth for new films and filmmakers in every corner of the world. *Twitch* introduced Russian upstart Pavel Ruminov to film fanatics in their living rooms. Ruminov's brilliant Internet marketing campaign for his baroque Russian horror film *Dead Daughters* (*Myortvye docheri*, 2006) includes a series of web-only teasers that created an eerie mythology for the film months before it entered post-production.

What today's cinephile requires is a filter system to help distil the valuable from the passable and the downright useless. In *Cinema Now* we present the recent works of international filmmakers we think are among the most exciting in the world today. Enamored as we are of the art film and its contribution to film culture over the years, we've made a selection that speaks both to the general moviegoer and the discerning cinephile. We love a decent genre movie like Neil Marshall's *The Descent* (2005) – and *The Descent* is as artful as popular filmmaking gets – as much as we admire the latest uncompromising work of an auteur working with Hollywood money, like Alexander Payne, Spike Jonze and David O. Russell, the heirs to the maverick filmmakers of the 1970s.

We also have a soft spot for the international underdog whose primary means of discovery remains film festival premieres and the DVD market, which is why we're pleased to include in *Cinema Now* a few names you've probably never heard of before, including Portugal's João Pedro Rodrigues, Hungary's György Pálfi, Thailand's Apichatpong Weerasethakul and the aforementioned Tsai Ming-liang, whose follow-ups to *Goodbye, Dragon Inn,* the outrageously inventive comedy-musical *The Wayward Cloud* (*Tian bian yi duo yun*, 2004/05) and *I Don't Want to Sleep Alone* (*Hei yan quan*, 2006), were both criminally undistributed in many parts of the world, including North America.

One drawback in putting together a book like this is that no matter how many people you want to include, there are always another hundred or more terrific directors who we couldn't reach, or were too busy filming, or were separated from us by language barriers. If you think you belong in future editions of this book, e-mail us at cinemanow@taschen.com and we'll see if Mr. Taschen will be kind enough to let us do another volume.

Until then, dive in and enjoy the myriad works of sixty great directors working around the world right now.

Andrew Bailey

January 8, 2006, San Francisco, California

Zu den bemerkenswertesten „Filmfilmen" der letzten zehn, fünfzehn Jahre zählt sicherlich *Goodbye, Dragon Inn* (*Bu San*, 2003) des taiwanesischen Regisseurs Tsai Ming-liang. Schauplatz dieses romantischen und nachdenklichen Werks über das Dahinsiechen der Kinokultur ist ein weitläufiger alter Filmpalast in Taipeh, in dem sich ein paar alte Stammkunden zur letzten Vorstellung von King Hus Kampfkunstklassiker *Die Herberge zum Drachentor* (*Long men ke zhen*, 1966) zusammenfinden. Im Verlauf des Films streifen sowohl Geister als auch Gäste auf der Suche nach zwischenmenschlichem Kontakt durch Gänge und Toiletten.

Unsterblich geworden ist Hus *Die Herberge zum Drachentor* vor allem dank seiner Verehrer Quentin Tarantino und Ang Lee, die ihren persönlichen Kult mit *Kill Bill – Volume 1* und *2* (2003, 2004) und *Tiger & Dragon* (*Crouching Tiger, Hidden Dragon / Wo hu zang long*, 2000) zum Ausdruck brachten und auf ein internationales Publikum übertrugen.

Für Tsais meisterliche Gespenstergeschichte ein Publikum zu finden ist nicht so einfach. Ich hatte das Glück, *Goodbye, Dragon Inn* noch am letzten Tag seiner Laufzeit in den Kinos von Los Angeles auf der Leinwand eines riesigen Multiplex im Untergeschoss eines Einkaufszentrums in Pasadena sehen zu können. Es war eine Vorstellung mitten in der Woche, und unter dem spärlichen Matinee-Publikum saßen abgesehen von mir nur noch ein paar alte Damen (die schon nach 20 Minuten eingeschlafen waren). Trotzdem habe ich den Film sehr genossen – was allerdings für die künftige Präsentation von Tsais Filmen in meinem Heimatland nicht zwangsläufig Gutes verheißen muss.

Ein Jahr später stellte Wellspring, die in New York ansässige nordamerikanische Verleihfirma für *Goodbye, Dragon Inn*, genauer gesagt, die von Harvey und Bob Weinstein geführte, neu geordnete Muttergesellschaft Weinstein Company, ihre Vertriebsaktivitäten ein. So endete eine Ära der Filmkunst in Amerika, in deren Anfangsjahren sich die Weinsteins mit dem Aufbau von Miramax als Pioniere profiliert hatten.

Tatsache ist: Ein kleines Unternehmen, das sich für ausländische und künstlerisch anspruchsvolle Filme einsetzt, findet im Rahmen der regionalen Vertriebsrechte die einzigen profitablen Absatzmöglichkeiten auf Nebenmärkten wie dem Verkauf von DVDs – und nur auf diesem Weg wird weltweit das Publikum die meisten der in diesem Buch beschriebenen Filme, darunter auch *Goodbye, Dragon Inn*, entdecken können.

Das Erlebnis, sich Filme zu Hause anschauen zu können, ist an sich keine schlechte Sache. Auf sich alleine gestellt, ist es einfacher, sich intensiv auf einen Film einzulassen, so, wie man ja auch ein Buch alleine liest. Deshalb wird das Aufkommen jener „vierten Generation bewegter Bilder", die die einst getrennten Welten von Film, Fernsehen und PC zu einer einzigen vereint, die Unterhaltungsbranche verändern. Da neuerdings hochauflösende Fernseher mit perfektem Raumklang zu erschwinglichen Preisen zu erwerben sind, kann man nun zu Hause ein scharfes, klar gezeichnetes Bild und oft auch einen besseren Sound genießen, denn man wird weder von knisterndem Popcorn-Gemampfe noch von labernden Besuchern, Schlürfgeräuschen oder Handys mit unerträglichen Klingeltönen genervt – es sei denn, das eigene bimmelt.

Wie soll ein anspruchsvoller Cineast, der sich dergleichen einigermaßen leisten kann und die Sache mit Enthusiasmus angeht, bei all den Verlockungen des Internets, dem stetig anwachsenden Angebot an (zunehmend filmisch aufbereiteten und einen Erzählstrang verfolgenden) Videospielen und anderen Medien, die mit Kinofilmen um die Aufmerksamkeit eines globalen Publikums wetteifern, und angesichts von Online-Blogs, in denen Amateurkritiker schön gleichberechtigt ihre Einschätzungen und Wertungen kundtun und eine qualifizierte Filmkritik verwässern, herausfinden, ob es sich wirklich lohnt, diesen oder jenen Film anzuschauen?

Die Filmkultur hat die schönen und talentierten Leinwandgesichter immer schon zu Berühmtheiten aufgebaut. Doch bis Mitte der 1970er-Jahre haben die Printmedien auch den aufstrebenden Filmautoren *hinter* der Kamera Raum gegeben und so dafür gesorgt, dass selbst Einzelgänger wie Terrence Malick und der späte, grandiose Robert Altman genauso berühmt wurden wie ihre Filme. Seither beherrschen – ungeachtet der Qualität der Filme und ihrer gesellschaftlichen Bedeutung – Klatschspalten über Prominente, Box-Office-Zahlen der neuen Blockbuster und Spekulationen über anstehende Preisverleihungen die Nachrichten zum Thema Kino. Die Filmemacher mussten alternative Promotionsmöglichkeiten finden und so nutzen sie nun auch die digitalen Datenströme des Internets, in dem eine neuartige Filmkultur gedeiht.

Einige der seriösen Filmmagazine mit intellektuellem Anspruch wie *Cahiers du cinéma*, *Sight and Sound* und *Film Comment* haben bislang überlebt. Jede dieser Publikationen widmet ihren Titel inzwischen ganz selbstverständlich herausragenden Persönlichkeiten, pflegt jedoch weiterhin die redaktionelle Auseinandersetzung mit Filmkunstwerken. Junge Neugründungen, die diesen Vorbildern nacheifern, wie die kanadische

Preface — Vorwort — Préface

Vierteljahresschrift *CinemaScope* – ein angesagtes Printmagazin, das die Zielsetzungen der *Cahiers*-Generation am besten repräsentiert –, müssen sich allerdings gegen ständig auf den neuesten Stand gebrachte Film-Blogs behaupten, die wie Zeitschriften aufgebaut sind und in ein und derselben Ausgabe sowohl ausführliche Artikel als auch hochaktuelle Nachrichten bieten. Wer hat schon Lust, auf eine Einschätzung des Festivals von Cannes in *Film Comment* zu warten, wenn er alle interessanten Informationen auch viel früher abrufen kann?

Häufiger denn je sind es Internet-Blogger, die der Filmkultur einen Schub verpassen, mit neuen Namen aufwarten und schon Monate vor Uraufführungen auf Filmfestivals, Kinostarts oder DVD-Veröffentlichungen auf Geheimtipps hinweisen. Blogger wie Todd Brown auf seiner Web-site *Twitch* kultivieren das Lancieren von Mundpropaganda für neue Filme und Filmemacher aus jedem Winkel der Welt. *Twitch* hat Filmverrückte in ihrem Wohnzimmer mit der russischen Neuentdeckung Pavel Ruminov bekannt gemacht. Zu Ruminovs brillanter Internet-Marketingkampagne für seinen barocken russischen Horrorfilm *Dead Daughters* (*Myortvye docheri*, 2006) gehört eine Reihe von Teasern, die nur im Web zu sehen sind und den Film schon Monate vor der Postproduktion mit einem unheimlichen Mythos umgaben. Durch jene Website kam schließlich sogar ein Vertrag mit Sony über ein englischsprachiges Remake zustande – noch bevor der Film überhaupt in Russland angelaufen war.

Was der Cinephile heute braucht, ist eine Art Filtersystem, das ihm hilft, das wirklich Gute vom Akzeptablen und vom schlicht Entbehrlichen zu unterscheiden. In *Cinema Now* präsentieren wir die jüngsten Werke internationaler Filmemacher, von denen wir meinen, dass sie zu den weltweit aufregendsten Regisseuren unserer Tage zählen. Da wir uns dem künstlerischen Film und seinem Beitrag zur Entwicklung der Filmkul-tur leidenschaftlich verbunden fühlen, haben wir für unsere Auswahl Werke berücksichtigt, die sowohl den normalen Kinobesucher als auch den kritischen Cinephilen anzusprechen vermögen. Wir schätzen ausgesprochene Genrefilme wie Neil Marshalls *The Descent – Abgrund des Grauens* (*The Descent*, 2005) – und *The Descent* ist sowohl kunstvoll als auch unterhaltend –, doch wir bewundern ebenso die neuen kompro-misslosen Werke von Filmemachern wie Alexander Payne, Spike Jonze und David O. Russell, die sich zwar von Hollywood finanzieren lassen, aber als Erben der eigenwilligen Filmemacher der 1970er-Jahre gelten können.

Wir hegen auch eine gewisse Vorliebe für jene internationalen Underdogs, die außer bei Uraufführungen auf Filmfestivals und auf dem DVD-Markt kaum eine Chance haben, wahrgenommen zu werden. So freuen wir uns, dass wir in *Cinema Now* manchen Namen aufnehmen konn-ten, den der Leser zuvor vermutlich noch nie gehört hat – zum Beispiel den Portugiesen João Pedro Rodrigues, den Ungarn György Pálfi, den Thailänder Apichatpong Weerasethakul und den bereits genannten Tsai Ming-liang, dessen zwei nach *Goodbye, Dragon Inn* entstandenen Filme, die außergewöhnlich erfindungsreiche Musical-Komödie *The Wayward Cloud* (*Tian bian yi duo yun*, 2004/05) und *I Don't Want to Sleep Alone* (*Hei yan quan*, 2006), von Filmvertrieben in vielen Ländern der Welt, auch in Nordamerika, sträflich vernachlässigt wurden.

Ein Buch wie dieses zusammenzustellen hat einen Nachteil: Gleichgültig, wie viele Filmemacher man aufnimmt, es bleiben immer zahl-reiche großartige Regisseure unberücksichtigt, die wir nicht kontaktieren konnten, die mit Dreharbeiten beschäftigt oder aufgrund von Sprach-barrieren für uns unerreichbar waren. Wenn Sie meinen, Sie sollten in Nachfolgebänden berücksichtigt werden, schicken Sie uns bitte eine E-Mail an *cinemanow@taschen.com*. Dann werden wir sehen, ob Herr Taschen so freundlich ist, uns eine nächste Ausgabe zu ermöglichen.

Bis dahin aber lassen Sie sich auf die unzähligen Werke dieser sechzig bemerkenswerten Regisseure ein, die in unseren Tagen überall auf der Welt an ihren Œuvres arbeiten. Viel Vergnügen.

Andrew Bailey   **8. Januar 2007, San Francisco, Kalifornien**

Le cinéaste taïwanais Tsaï Ming-liang est l'auteur de l'un des très grands films consacrés au cinéma ces dix dernières années, *Goodbye Dragon Inn* (*Bu San*, 2003). Méditation romantique sur le déclin de l'art d'aller voir un film au cinéma, ce film se déroule lors de la dernière séance d'un vieil et immense palais du cinéma de Taïpei, où l'on projette à un public fort clairsemé *Dragon Inn*, classique du film de sabres réalisé par King Hu en 1966. Fantômes et vivants hantent les allées et les toilettes, en quête de rapports humains.

Le *Dragon Inn* de Hu conserve son immortalité grâce à des cinéastes comme Quentin Tarantino et Ang Lee qui en ont fait un objet fétiche pour le public du monde entier dans ses deux volets de *Kill Bill* et *Tigre et Dragon*.

En revanche, notre époque n'aide guère le bijou obsédant de Tsaï à trouver son public. J'ai eu la chance de voir *Goodbye Dragon Inn* sur un écran de l'immense multiplex situé au sous-sol d'un centre commercial de Pasadena, le dernier jour de son exploitation à Los Angeles. Pour cette projection d'un après-midi de semaine, j'étais en compagnie d'un duo de douairières, endormies dès la vingtième minute. Je ne peux avoir plus apprécié ce film que ce jour-là, même si cela n'augure rien de bon pour les projections futures des films de Tsaï dans mon pays.

Un an plus tard, Wellspring, distributeur nord-américain de *Goodbye Dragon Inn*, fermait son département distribution de New York. Ou plutôt, il était fermé par sa maison mère, la toute nouvelle Weinstein Company, propriété de Harvey et Bob Weinstein. Ainsi s'achevait toute une époque du cinéma d'auteur en Amérique, dont les frères Weinstein avaient été l'origine, aux débuts de Miramax.

À vrai dire, en ce qui concerne les territoires cinématographiques et les droits de distribution, le seul débouché rentable d'un petit distributeur de films étrangers et de films d'auteur réside dans l'exploitation des films en édition DVD. C'est d'ailleurs par ce biais que la plupart des spectateurs du monde découvriront la majorité des films évoqués dans ces pages, notamment *Goodbye Dragon Inn*.

Voir un film sur son petit écran n'est pas un mal en soi, en dépit des nombreuses sources de distraction. Il est même plus facile d'être en intimité avec un film quand on est seul, comme lorsqu'on lit ; c'est pourquoi l'émergence du « quatrième écran », qui réunit les univers jadis séparés du cinéma, de la télévision et de l'ordinateur, est en train de transformer l'industrie du spectacle. Grâce aux téléviseurs à haute définition et son *surround*, devenus abordables, l'image disponible chez soi est précise et claire, et le son souvent meilleur, car on n'est plus dérangé par le bruit du pop-corn, des spectateurs bavards et des téléphones portables aux sonneries insupportables – sauf, quand c'est le sien.

La course aux recettes nettes est désormais effrénée : l'exploitation en salles est en concurrence avec Internet, les jeux vidéo (de plus en plus cinématographiques et narratifs) et d'autres médias pour attirer l'attention du public mondial. La blogosphère dissout la valeur de la critique cinématographique dans le pronostic égalitaire de critiques grossièrement amateurs. Alors comment le cinéphile averti peut-il décider qu'un film mérite ou non d'être vu ?

La culture cinématographique a toujours mis en avant les visages célèbres, beaux et talentueux, du grand écran. Mais, jusqu'au milieu des années 1970, la presse audiovisuelle ouvrait ses colonnes aux auteurs naissants, *derrière* la caméra. Des esprits libres, comme Terrence Malick ou le grand et regretté Robert Altman, recevaient autant d'éloges que leurs films. Depuis, commérages, résultats commerciaux du dernier *blockbuster* et pronostics fleurissant avant la saison des récompenses occupent les pages des revues, quelle que soit la qualité des films ou leur place dans notre société. Contraints de trouver d'autres moyens de promotion, les cinéastes-auteurs doivent se jeter dans le flux des données numériques d'Internet, vivier de la nouvelle vague de la culture cinématographique.

Il existe encore des revues de cinéma sérieuses comme les *Cahiers du Cinéma*, *Sight and Sound* et *Film Comment*. Elles arborent désormais régulièrement des célébrités sur leurs couvertures, tout en favorisant le cinéma d'auteur. De jeunes revues faites à leur image, comme le trimestriel canadien *CinemaScope* – publication la plus en vue et celle qui reprend le mieux le flambeau des *Cahiers* – ont bien du mal à survivre face aux blogs fréquemment mis à jour, organisés comme des magazines, qui comprennent à la fois des articles de fond et des brèves. Pourquoi attendre un compte rendu du festival de Cannes dans *Film Comment* quand on peut obtenir l'information en temps réel ?

Plus que jamais (pour le meilleur et pour le pire), la culture cinématographique vit grâce aux internautes qui révèlent de nouveaux noms et annoncent les films-vedettes plusieurs mois avant leur présentation en festival ou leur sortie en salles ou en DVD. Par exemple, Tod Brown et son site « Twitch » entretiennent le bouche-à-oreille instantané à propos des nouveaux films et cinéastes des quatre coins du monde. C'est Twitch qui a présenté aux cinéphiles en pantoufles Pavel Ruminov, l'étoile montante du cinéma russe. Ruminov a orchestré sur Internet une campagne très réussie pour la promotion de son film d'horreur baroque *Dead Daughters* (2007), en proposant une série d'extraits uniquement visibles sur la Toile. Ce film a ainsi acquis un étrange statut mythique plusieurs mois avant le début de la postproduction. Le site a suscité la conclusion d'un accord avec Sony pour la réalisation d'un remake en anglais, avant même que le film ne sorte en Russie.

Le cinéphile d'aujourd'hui a besoin d'un filtre pour faire le tri entre ce qui est valable, passable ou carrément médiocre. *Cinema Now* présente les œuvres récentes de cinéastes du monde entier que nous considérons parmi les plus enthousiasmants. Passionnés par le cinéma d'art et essai et par sa contribution historique à la culture cinématographique, nous avons établi une sélection qui s'adresse aussi bien au grand public qu'au cinéphile averti. Nous adorons les films de genre de qualité, comme *The Descent* de Neil Marshall (2005) – preuve que le cinéma populaire peut aussi être artistique –, comme nous admirons la dernière œuvre sans concession d'auteurs financés par Hollywood, tel Alexander Payne, Spike Jonze ou David O. Russell, héritiers des cinéastes indépendants des années 1970. Nous avons également un faible pour les laissés-pour-compte du cinéma mondial dont la découverte se fait avant tout dans les festivals et sur le marché du DVD. Nous sommes donc très heureux d'ouvrir ces pages à quelques noms dont vous n'avez sans doute jamais entendu parler, comme le Portugais João Pedro Rodrigues, le Hongrois György Pálfi, le Thaïlandais Apichatpong Weerasethakul et le susnommé Tsaï Ming-liang. De ce dernier, les suites de *Goodbye Dragon Inn* que sont *La Saveur de la pastèque* (2005), comédie musicale d'une inventivité extravagante, et *I Don't Want to Sleep Alone* (2006), ont été scandaleusement ignorées par les distributeurs de nombreuses régions du monde, dont l'Amérique du Nord.

L'ennui avec ce genre d'ouvrage, c'est que l'on a beau y inclure un grand nombre de personnalités, il reste toujours une centaine de cinéastes admirables que nous n'avons pas pu contacter ou qui étaient en tournage, ou que la barrière des langues nous a empêchés de rencontrer. Si vous estimez que vous aussi vous devriez figurer dans les prochaines éditions de ce livre, envoyez un courriel à cinemanow@taschen.com et nous verrons si M. Taschen veut bien nous laisser publier un nouveau volume.

En attendant, laissez-vous guider par ce joli bouquet d'œuvres réalisées par soixante grands cinéastes d'aujourd'hui.

Andrew Bailey   **8 janvier 2007, San Francisco**

DIRECTORS

The volatile German-Turkish romantic drama *Head-On* (*Gegen die Wand*, 2003/04), the fourth feature by the young Hamburg-born writer-director Fatih Akin, snapped up the Golden Bear at the 2004 Berlin Film Festival and riveted audiences the world over with its tempestuous portrait of lovers torn apart by cultural differences, hard living and psychological illness both real and imagined. Cahit (Birol Ünel), a rough-hewn German prone to bouts of drinking, fighting and womanizing, meets Sibel (Sibel Kekilli), a delicate Turkish refugee, in a Hamburg psychiatric ward after respective suicide attempts. His is real, hers is faked, to escape a marriage arranged by her devout Muslim family. Sibel begs Cahit to marry her to win back her family's esteem; Cahit agrees, believing the sham marriage will repair his wrecked life. The couple share an apartment and little else – he's a slob with a temper; she's a demure neat freak with a heart of gold. When they find themselves falling in love, it's with the brute force of a sucker punch to the gut. Akin employs dark comedy and tragedy to marvelous effect in *Head-On*, showing the messiness of romantic love in all its ragged, terrible glory. Akin elicits remarkable performances from Ünel, who starred in the director's first feature, *Short Sharp Shock* (*Kurz und schmerzlos*, 1997/98), and newcomer Kekilli, an office worker discovered in a Cologne shopping center. The film's soundtrack pulsates with cross-pollinated fare, including traditional Turkish songs by Romany musicians, a subject Akin returned to in the documentary *Crossing the Bridge: The Sound of Istanbul* (2004/05).

Das romantische deutsch-türkische Drama *Gegen die Wand* (2003/04), der vierte Spielfilm des jungen, in Hamburg geborenen Autors und Regisseurs Fatih Akin, heimste bei der Berlinale 2004 den Goldenen Bären ein und fesselte das Publikum weltweit mit seinem ungestümen Porträt zweier Liebender, die durch kulturelle Unterschiede, schwierige Lebensumstände und wirkliche oder auch eingebildete psychische Probleme auseinandergerissen werden. In einer psychiatrischen Klinik in Hamburg trifft Cahit (Birol Ünel), ein ungehobelter Kerl, der zu Saufgelagen, Schlägereien und Frauengeschichten neigt, auf Sibel (Sibel Kekilli), eine empfindsame junge Türkin, die wie er einen Selbstmordversuch

Gegen die Wand

Head-On / Head-on

"The role of the 'lost soul' Cahit [in *Head-On*] was closely adapted to Birol Ünel – even though it contains many of my own longings and my desire to break through the norms. He celebrates poetic self-destruction, like Kurt Cobain and Jim Morrison."

„Cahits Charakterisierung als ‚verlorene Seele' [in *Gegen die Wand*] war auf Birol Ünel zugeschnitten –
auch wenn in dieser Rolle viele meiner eigenen Sehnsüchte und Bedürfnisse, Normen zu durchbrechen, enthalten sind.
Wie Kurt Cobain und Jim Morrison huldigt er einer poetischen Selbstzerstörung."

« Le rôle de Cahit [dans *Head-on*], le paumé, était fait pour Birol Ünel, même s'il est
nourri de mes propres envies de faire exploser les normes. Il glorifie l'autodestruction poétique,
comme celle de Kurt Cobain et de Jim Morrison. »

A sham marriage becomes a tumultuous love affair between two wounded souls in the German art-house hit, featuring a Greek chorus of Turkish musicians.

In diesem Film, der mit großem Erfolg in deutschen Arthouse-Kinos lief, wird die Geschichte zweier verletzter Seelen erzählt, zwischen denen sich aus einer Scheinehe eine turbulente Liebesaffäre entwickelt. Türkische Musiker kommentieren das Geschehen wie ein Chor in einer griechischen Tragödie.

Un mariage blanc se transforme en histoire d'amour tumultueuse entre deux âmes blessées dans ce succès du cinéma d'auteur allemand, avec un groupe de musiciens turcs faisant fonction de chœur grec antique.

Crossing the Bridge:
The Sound of Istanbul

Fatih Akin, born in Germany to Turkish immigrants, set off for the East-West cultural nexus of Istanbul to examine street rap, Romany instrumentals and Kurdish slow burns in his vibrant, soulful music documentary.

Fatih Akin, als Sohn türkischer Einwanderer in Deutschland geboren, machte sich nach Istanbul auf und dokumentierte die Musikszene dieses west-östlichen Schmelztiegels der Kulturen in einem lebendigen, mitreißenden Film, dessen musikalisches Spektrum vom Straßenrap über Roma-Instrumentalklänge bis zu kurdischen Klageliedern reicht.

Né en Allemagne d'immigrés turcs, Fatih Akin s'est rendu au carrefour culturel entre Orient et Occident qu'est Istanbul, pour entendre de plus près le rap local, la musique instrumentale traditionnelle et les excentricités kurdes pour ce documentaire musical plein de vie et de sentiment.

PEDRO ALMODÓVAR

Born 24 September 1949 in Calzada de Calatrava, Spain

Riding a crest of outstanding works that began with *All About My Mother* (*Todo sobre mi madre*, 1999) and continued up to *Volver* (2006), the legend from La Mancha began 2007 on a wave of glory that confirmed his status as the world's most beloved auteur. For Almodóvar – our modern master of movie melodrama – the resplendent *Volver*, with its ensemble cast of women learning to live without men, might have constituted his finest hour, as so many fans and critics insisted. But that's what they said about his film noir *Bad Education* (*La mala educación*, 2004), his doomed romance *Talk to Her* (*Hable con ella*, 2002) and his motherhood opus that initiated one of the greatest runs in movie history – not that *Live Flesh* (*Carne trémula*, 1997) or *The Flower of My Secret* (*La flor de mi secreto*, 1995) were anything to complain about. Almodóvar's gift is his deep appreciation for women in every conceivable form and phase of life, including the feisty transsexual Agrado (Antonia San Juan) in *All About My Mother*, the sultry drag queen Zahara of *Bad Education*, played by Gael García Bernal, or the heart-tugging airport janitress Raimunda, embodied with saucy exuberance by Penélope Cruz in *Volver*. And let's not forget the Almodóvar stock players that came before them: Maura, de Palma, Paredes – legends all. What Almodóvar has achieved through his ravishing work is a kind of liberation for us all. He stuck a frock on his native Spain when it needed it the most, transforming a country and then the movies with a spritz of glamour for which Hollywood misplaced the recipe ages ago.

Nach einer Reihe herausragender Werke, die von *Alles über meine Mutter* (*Todo sobre mi madre*, 1999) bis zu *Volver – Zurückkehren* (*Volver*, 2006) reicht und dem Spanier den Status eines eigenwilligen und weltweit bewunderten Filmautors einbrachte, surft die Legende aus der Mancha gegenwärtig auf die Woge des Erfolgs. Folgt man den Reaktionen zahlloser Fans und Kritiker, könnte der brillante Film *Volver* mit seinem Darstellerensemble aus Frauen, die lernen, ein Leben ohne Männer zu führen, für Almodóvar, unseren modernen Meister des melodramatischen Films, den Höhepunkt markieren. Doch einhellige Begeisterung gab es auch schon für seinen Film noir *La Mala Educación – Schlechte Erziehung* (*La mala educación*, 2004), die schicksalhafte Romanze *Sprich mit ihr* (*Hable con ella*, 2002) und für sein Mutterschaftsopus *Alles über meine Mutter* (*Todo sobre mi madre*, 1999), das in den Kinos zu einem der größten Dauerbrenner der Filmgeschichte avancierte – ganz abgesehen davon, dass *Live Flesh – Mit Haut und Haar* (*Carne trémula*, 1997) oder auch *Mein blühendes Geheimnis* (*La flor de mi secreto*, 1995) alles andere als schlecht waren. Almodóvars besondere Gabe ist sein tiefgründiges Verständnis für alle Facetten des Weiblichen, ob für den resoluten Transsexuellen Agrado (Antonia San Juan) in *Alles über meine Mutter*, die von Gael García Bernal dargestellte sinnliche Dragqueen Zahara in *Schlechte Erziehung* oder die von Penélope Cruz mit frecher Ausgelassenheit verkörperte, herzergreifende Flughafenputzfrau Raimunda in *Volver*. Und nicht zu vergessen: Maura, de Palma, Paredes – allesamt Legenden, die früher schon zu Almodóvars Frauenriege gehörten. Mit seiner hinreißenden Arbeit hat Almodóvar uns alle auf irgendeine Weise befreit. Er putzte sein heimatliches Spanien heraus, als es am nötigsten war, und trug zur Veränderung des Landes und zur Erneuerung des Kinos bei, dem er einen Hauch jenes Glamours verpasste, dessen Ingredienzen Hollywood seit ewigen Zeiten nicht mehr finden kann.

Après des œuvres admirables, de *Tout sur ma mère* (*Todo sobre mi madre*, 1999) à *Volver* (2006), l'homme de La Manche entame l'année 2007 sur la crête d'une vague de gloire qui confirme son rang d'auteur le plus apprécié au monde. Pour nombre de critiques et d'admirateurs, le resplendissant *Volver* est peut-être la plus belle œuvre du maître du mélodrame, avec son cercle de femmes qui apprend à vivre sans les hommes. Mais c'est aussi ce que l'on dit de son film noir *La Mauvaise Éducation* (*La mala educación*, 2004), de l'histoire d'un amour condamné dans *Parle avec elle* (*Hable con ella*, 2002) et de l'ode à la maternité, qui a battu des records de longévité à l'affiche. Sans parler de l'excellent *En chair et en os* (*Carne trémula*, 1997) et de *La Fleur de mon secret* (*La flor de mi secreto*, 1995). Almodóvar a le don de comprendre la psychologie féminine quelles que soient les formes et les phases de la vie, que ce soit avec Agrado (Antonio San Juan), la fougueuse transsexuelle de *Tout sur ma mère*, avec Zahara (Gael García Bernal), la sensuelle drag queen de *La Mauvaise Éducation*, ou avec Raimunda, l'attachante femme de ménage, interprétée avec une exubérance coquine par Penélope Cruz dans *Volver*. Citons également les comédiennes légendaires et fétiches du cinéaste qui les ont précédées, Maura, de Palma, Paredes. Avec une œuvre captivante, Almodóvar est parvenu à nous offrir une sorte de libération. Il a donné de nouveaux habits féminins à son Espagne natale au moment où elle en avait le plus besoin. Il a transformé un pays *et* le cinéma avec ce zeste glamoureux dont Hollywood a perdu depuis longtemps la recette.

SELECTED FILMS →
1991 *Tacones lejanos (High Heels)* **1993** *Kika*
1995 *La flor de mi secreto (The Flower of My Secret)* **1997** *Carne trémula (Live Flesh)*
1999 *Todo sobre mi madre (All About My Mother)*
2002 *Hable con ella (Talk to Her)*
2004 *La mala educación (Bad Education)*
2006 *Volver*

SELECTED AWARDS →
1988 *Mujeres al borde de un ataque de nervios:* Best Young Film, European Film Awards; Golden Osella (Best Screenplay), Venice Film Festival
1999 *Todo sobre mi madre:* Best Director, Cannes Film Festival
2000 *Todo sobre mi madre:* Best Director, Goya Awards; Best Foreign Film, César Awards **2003** *Hable con ella:* Best Original Screenplay, Academy Awards; Best Film not in the English Language, Best Screenplay, BAFTA Awards; Best European Union Film, César Awards

Todo sobre mi madre

All About My Mother / Alles über meine Mutter / Tout sur ma mère

Theatricality, artifice and the transformative power of acting compete with motherhood, bereavement and rehabilitation in what many Almodóvar fans maintain is his most heartfelt, emotionally complex achievement.

Theatralik, Raffinesse und die Verwandlungskunst der Schauspieler auf der einen, Mutterschaft, Trauer um einen Verlust und die Rückkehr ins gesellschaftliche Leben auf der anderen Seite – viele Fans von Almodóvar halten diesen Film für sein anrührendstes, emotional vielschichtigstes Werk.

La théâtralité, l'artifice et la magie du jeu d'acteur rivalisent avec la maternité, le deuil et la réinsertion dans ce que les admirateurs d'Almodóvar tiennent pour son chef-d'œuvre de sincérité et de complexité émotionnelle.

"Already when I was very young, I was a *fabulador*.
I loved to give my own version of stories that everybody already knew.
When I got out of a movie with my sisters, I retold them the whole story.
In general they liked my version better than the one they had seen."

„Schon in sehr jungen Jahren war ich ein Fabulierer. Ich liebte es, meine eigene Version von Geschichten zum Besten zu geben,
die eigentlich jeder kannte. Wenn ich mit meinen Schwestern aus dem Kino kam, erzählte ich ihnen die gesamte Geschichte des Films nach.
Meist fanden sie meine Version spannender als die, die sie gerade gesehen hatten."

«Tout petit, j'étais déjà conteur. J'adorais raconter à ma manière des histoires que tout le monde connaissait déjà.
Quand je sortais d'un film avec mes sœurs, je leur racontais toute l'histoire. En général, elles préféraient
ma version à celle qu'elles avaient vue.»

Penelope Cruz (above) is a nun suffering from AIDS and Cecilia Roth (left) is a grieving mother reeling from the death of her son – quintessential Almodóvar heroines who find transcendence amid hardship.

Penélope Cruz (oben) spielt eine aidskranke Nonne und Cecilia Roth (links) eine trauernde Mutter, der der Tod ihres Sohnes schwer zu schaffen macht – typische Almodóvar-Heldinnen, die in der Auseinandersetzung mit ihrem Elend Transzendenz gewinnen.

Penélope Cruz (ci-dessus) interprète une infirmière malade du sida et Cecilia Roth (ci-contre) une mère qui porte le deuil de son fils, archétypes des héroïnes d'Almodóvar transcendées par l'adversité.

Hable con ella

Talk to Her / Sprich mit ihr / Parle avec elle

In an about-face for the typically female-centric Almodóvar, the lives and loves of men take center stage in this romantic tragedy about two women in comas and the two men who love them.

In dieser romantischen Tragödie über zwei Frauen im Koma und die beiden Männer, die sie lieben, stehen – eine Kehrtwende für Almodóvar, dessen Filme sonst stets um Frauen kreisen – die Lebens- und Liebesgeschichten der Männer im Mittelpunkt.

Délaissant les histoires de femmes, Almodóvar raconte les amours et les existences de deux hommes dans une tragédie romantique consacrée à deux femmes tombées dans le coma et aux hommes qui les aiment.

Javier Cámara (above) is so obsessed by ballet dancer Leonor Watling (right) that he spies on her, and becomes her nurse when she falls into a coma. Almodóvar frames him behind glass and windows to show his distance from the other characters.

Javier Cámara (oben) ist von der Balletttänzerin Leonor Watling (rechts) so besessen, dass er ihr nachspioniert. Als sie ins Koma fällt, pflegt er sie sogar. Almodóvar zeigt ihn immer wieder hinter Glasscheiben und in Fenstern stehend und unterstreicht so die Distanz dieser Figur zu den anderen.

Javier Cámara (ci-dessus) est obsédé par la danseuse interprétée par Leonor Watling (ci-contre), au point de l'espionner et de devenir son infirmier lorsqu'elle tombe dans le coma. Almodóvar le cadre derrière une fenêtre pour souligner sa distance à l'égard d'autrui.

La mala educación

Bad Education / La Mala Educación – Schlechte Erziehung / La Mauvaise éducation

Past and present collide with devastating force in Almodóvar's lush, heartbreaking glimpse at a pedophile priest scandal and its effect on two young victims.

In Almodóvars sinnlicher, herzergreifender Rück- schau auf einen Skandal um einen pädophilen Priester und die Auswirkungen seiner Taten auf zwei jugendliche Opfer prallen Vergangenheit und Gegenwart mit zerstörerischer Wucht aufeinander.

Télescopage brutal entre le passé et le présent dans cette enquête déchirante aux images léchées sur le scandale d'un prêtre pédophile et de ses deux jeunes victimes.

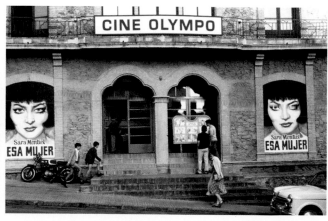

Mining such disparate topics as romantic obsession, male beauty and the nurturing power of cinema, *Bad Education* evokes film noir and the doomed romance of Hitchcock's *Vertigo* as only Almodóvar can.

La Mala Educación – Schlechte Erziehung, der aus so unterschiedlichen Themen wie romantischer Obsession, männlicher Schönheit und der ermutigenden Macht des Kinos schöpft, erinnert in typisch Almodóvar'scher Weise an Traditionen des Film noir und die zum Scheitern verurteilte Liebe in Hitchcocks *Vertigo*.

Œuvre puisant dans l'obsession romantique, la beauté masculine et la force pédagogique du cinéma, *la Mauvaise Education* évoque le film noir et l'amour maudit de *Sueurs froides* d'Hitchcock, comme seul en est capable Almodóvar.

Overleaf: Pedro Almodóvar (left) directs Gael García Bernal (right).

Folgende Doppelseite: Pedro Almodóvar (links) gibt Gael García Bernal (rechts) Regieanweisungen.

Pages suivantes : Pedro Almodóvar (à gauche) dirige Gael García Bernal (à droite).

Volver

Volver – Zurückkehren

Penelope Cruz returns in this bittersweet comic melo-drama as yet another heart-wrenching Almodóvar heroine; waitress, laundress, caterer, janitor, mother, daughter and singer.

In diesem bittersüßen, komischen Melodram ver-körpert Penélope Cruz wiederum eine von Almodó-vars herzzerreißenden Heldinnen: Sie ist Kellnerin, Wäscherin, Essenslieferantin, Hausmeisterin, Mutter, Tochter und Sängerin zugleich.

Dans cette comédie mélodramatique douce-amère, Penélope Cruz joue une nouvelle héroïne poignante d'Almodóvar : serveuse, blanchisseuse, concierge, femme de ménage, mère, fille et chanteuse.

Featuring a coterie of women navigating bereavement, singlehood and self-sufficiency with grace and aplomb, *Volver* could be rechristened 'Women on the Verge of a Nervous Breakthrough'.

Mit seiner Riege von Frauen, die ihr durch Verluste, Single-Dasein und Selbstgenügsamkeit gekennzeichnetes Leben mit Anmut und Souveränität meistern, könnte auch *Volver* den Titel „Frauen jenseits des Nervenzusammenbruchs" führen.

Portrait d'un groupe de femmes naviguant avec grâce et aplomb entre deuil, célibat et autonomie, *Volver* pourrait aussi s'intituler «Femmes au-delà de la crise de nerfs».

A consummate director of women, Almodóvar fills *Volver* with a wide range of winsome female characters spanning three generations – including a mother and daughter played by returning muses Carmen Maura and Penelope Cruz.

Almodóvar, der so geschickt wie kaum ein anderer Regisseur Frauen zu führen weiß, bietet in *Volver* eine Vielfalt einnehmender weiblicher Charaktere auf, die drei Generationen repräsentieren. Auch seine beiden Musen Carmen Maura und Penélope Cruz sind wieder dabei und spielen Mutter und Tochter.

Passé maître dans l'art de diriger les femmes, Almodóvar a rempli *Volver* de personnages féminins attachants, appartenant à trois générations, dont une mère et sa fille, Carmen Maura et Penélope Cruz, muses almodovariennes.

ANDREA ARNOLD

Born 5 April 1961 in Dartford, UK

Arnold won the Academy Award for Best Live Action Short Film for her harrowing 25-minute drama *Wasp* (2003), about a poor single mother who leaves her four children outside a Glasgow pub while she drinks away the hours with a former boyfriend. Demonstrating a keen flair for working-class realism in the spirit and tone of Mike Leigh, Arnold revisited the same bleak milieu for her feature debut *Red Road* (2006), a voyeuristic psychodrama that won the third-place jury prize at the Cannes Film Festival in addition to the prestigious Sutherland Trophy at the London Film Festival. Newcomer Kate Dickey stars as Jackie, a widowed surveillance-camera monitor on a decaying north Glasgow housing estate who begins stalking the parolee (Tony Curran) who was complicit in the mysterious deaths of her husband and child. Sexually charged and fraught with suspense, the gritty, provocative *Red Road* – shot on high-definition video blown up to 35mm, and co-starring up-and-coming actors Martin Compston and Nathalie Press – marked the debut of a confident storyteller whose sharply observed working-class characters engulfed in miserable surroundings threaten to return in two upcoming features. Co-produced by Lars von Trier's Zentropa Productions, *Red Road* was the first in the Advance Party projected trilogy of films – a sort of Dogme 95 for the screenwriting set – in which three filmmakers write and direct separate stories set in Scotland featuring the same core group of nine characters created by Zentropa regulars Lone Scherfig and Anders Thomas Jensen.

Mit dem erschütternden 25-Minuten-Drama *Wasp* (2003), das von einer mittellosen, alleinerziehenden Mutter handelt, die ihre vier Kinder vor einem Pub in Glasgow zurücklässt, während sie ihr tristes Dasein mit einem ehemaligen Freund im Alkohol ersäuft, gewann Arnold den Academy Award für den besten Live-Action-Kurzfilm. Ihr Spielfilmdebüt *Red Road* (2006), ein voyeuristisches Psychodrama, das beim Filmfestival von Cannes mit dem Jury-Preis geehrt und beim London Film Festival mit der angesehenen Sutherland Trophy ausgezeichnet wurde, ist im gleichen trostlosen Milieu angesiedelt. Darin beweist Arnold – im Geiste und Tonfall eines Mike Leigh – ihr klares Gespür für ein realistisches Bild der Arbeiterklasse. Newcomerin Kate Dickey spielt die verwitwete Jackie, die Aufzeichnungen von Überwachungskameras der Stadt Glasgow auswertet. Als sie Aufnahmen von einer verwahrlosten Hochhaussiedlung an der Red Road studiert, entdeckt sie den auf Bewährung entlassenen Clyde (Tony Curran), der in den geheimnisvollen Mord an ihrem Mann und ihrem Kind verwickelt war. Das sexuell aufgeladene, spannungsreiche und provokative Werk – gedreht auf hochauflösendem Video und besetzt mit jungen, vielversprechenden Schauspielern wie Martin Compston und Nathalie Press – ist das Debüt einer selbstbewussten Geschichtenerzählerin, deren scharf gezeichnete und in elenden Verhältnissen hausende Working-Class-Charaktere wohl in zwei weiteren Filmen wiederkehren werden: Der von Lars von Triers Zentropa Productions koproduzierte *Red Road* ist nämlich der erste Film einer Trilogie des Advance-Party-Projekts – einer Art Dogma 95 für Drehbuchvorlagen –, bei dem drei Filmemacher drei unterschiedliche, in Schottland angesiedelte Geschichten verfassen und verfilmen, die jeweils um die gleiche von den Zentropa-Mitstreitern Lone Scherfig und Anders Thomas Jensen entwickelte Kerngruppe von neun Charakteren kreisen.

Wasp (2003) est l'histoire d'une mère célibataire et pauvre qui passe son temps à boire avec un ancien amant, laissant ses quatre enfants devant un pub de Glasgow. Les 25 minutes poignantes de ce film ont valu à Arnold de remporter l'oscar du meilleur court métrage. Douée pour le réalisme ouvrier dans l'esprit d'un Mike Leigh, la cinéaste situe dans le même milieu sombre l'intrigue de son premier long métrage *Red Road* (2006), psychodrame voyeuriste, lauréat du prix du jury à Cannes et du prestigieux trophée Sutherland au Festival de Londres. Jackie (incarnée par Kate Dickie, pour la première fois à l'écran), jeune veuve, contrôleuse des caméras de surveillance d'une cité du nord de Glasgow, se met à suivre l'homme (Tony Curran), en liberté conditionnelle, mêlé au décès mystérieux de son mari et de son enfant. Riche de sensualité et de suspense, cru et provocateur, tourné en haute définition et gonflé en 35 mm, *Red Road* marque les débuts prometteurs des comédiens Martin Compston et Nathalie Press, et d'une réalisatrice dotée d'une grande assurance dont les personnages englués dans un environnement sinistre réapparaissent dans deux autres films. Coproduit par Zentropa Films, la société de Lars von Trier, *Red Road* (2006) est le premier volet d'une trilogie réalisée dans le cadre du projet Advance Party, l'équivalent de Dogma 95 pour les scénaristes : trois cinéastes écrivent et mettent en scène des récits indépendants, se déroulant en Écosse avec le même groupe de neuf personnages, créés par Lone Scherfig et Anders Thomas Jensen.

FILMS →
2003 *Wasp* [short]
2006 *Red Road*

SELECTED AWARDS →
2005 *Wasp:* Best Live-Action Short Film, Academy Awards
2006 *Red Road:* Jury Prize, Cannes Film Festival; Best Film, Best Director, BAFTA Scotland Awards; Sutherland Trophy, London Film Festival

Wasp

In her award-winning short film, Arnold – and her set photographer Holly Horner – examined working-class woes through the eyes of four unsupervised children and their unfit mother.

In ihrem preisgekrönten Kurzfilm widmete sich Arnold – gemeinsam mit ihrer Set-Fotografin Holly Horner – den Nöten der Arbeiterklasse aus der Perspektive von vier sich selbst überlassenen Kindern und ihrer unfähigen Mutter.

Dans son court métrage primé, Arnold et sa photographe de plateau Holly Horner scrutent les malheurs de la classe ouvrière, à travers les yeux de quatre enfants, négligés par une mère incapable de les élever.

Red Road

Set amid a crumbling housing project, Arnold's feature debut, an atmospheric revenge drama, pulls no punches in its depiction of the grim, paranoid machinations of modern urban life on a Glasgow council estate.

Arnolds Spielfilmdebüt, ein atmosphärisch dichtes Rachedrama, dessen Schauplatz eine verwahrloste Hochhaussiedlung ist, beschreibt gnadenlos die trostlosen, paranoiden Machenschaften, die das städtische Sozialwohnungsmilieu im heutigen Glasgow beherrschen.

Histoire de vengeance dans une cité délabrée de Glasgow, le premier long métrage d'Arnold est une description implacable des sombres machinations paranoïaques de la vie urbaine moderne.

"I do not choose the ideas for my films – they choose me.
They present themselves when I am least expecting them, mostly
in everyday situations, like when I am walking my dog or chopping onions.
They usually start as images that will not go away and I am compelled
to deal with them. It's as if I don't have a choice in the matter."

„Ich suche mir die Ideen für meine Filme nicht aus – sie suchen mich aus. Sie tauchen genau dann auf,
wenn ich es am wenigsten erwarte, meist in Alltagssituationen, zum Beispiel, wenn ich gerade meinen Hund ausführe oder Zwiebeln schneide.
Gewöhnlich sind es zuerst Bilder, die mir nicht mehr aus dem Kopf gehen. Ich bin also gezwungen, mich mit ihnen zu beschäftigen.
Es ist, als hätte ich gar keine andere Wahl."

«Je ne choisis pas mes idées de films, ce sont elles qui me choisissent. Elles se présentent à moi quand je m'y attends le moins,
surtout dans des situations quotidiennes, quand je promène mon chien ou quand j'épluche des oignons.
Ce sont des images qui persistent et il faut que je m'y attelle. Comme si je n'avais pas le choix.»

Kate Dickey makes her film debut as Jackie, a surveillance camera operator who obsessively tracks an ex-con across a bleak north Glasgow council estate, resulting in psychosexual intrigue.

In ihrer ersten Kinorolle spielt Kate Dickie eine für Überwachungskameras zuständige städtische Angestellte, die wie besessen einem in einer öden Sozialwohnungssiedlung im Norden Glasgows hausenden Exsträfling nachspioniert – bis die Geschichte in einer psychosexuellen Intrige gipfelt.

Dans ce thriller psychosexuel, Kate Dickie fait ses débuts au cinéma dans le rôle de Jackie, contrôleuse de caméras de surveillance, obsédée par un ancien détenu, dans une cité sinistre du Nord de Glasgow.

DARREN ARONOFSKY

Born 12 February 1969 in Brooklyn, USA

The metaphysical thriller *Pi* (1996/97) interwove dashes of chaos theory, fuzzy math, the Kaballah and paranoid conspiracy for the mind-bending account of a numbers-obsessed genius barricaded in his New York City apartment in search of the mathematical key to the universe. The startling debut feature, which won the Directing Prize at the Sundance Film Festival, introduced a Harvard-educated young master of complex and grandiose ideas who wasn't about to make his brainy thrillers easy to digest. For his second feature *Requiem for a Dream* (2000), Aronofsky examined addiction in its various forms, employing restless crosscutting techniques, split screens and a downward spiral effect operating on both rhythmic and visual levels, making this adaptation of Hubert Selby's 1978 novel a harrowing experience – the proverbial bad trip as film art. Aronofsky's third, most ambitious feature was the psychedelic science-fiction historical romance *The Fountain* (2006), again juggling multiple themes, ideas and story lines in a triptych spanning 1,000 years about the interplanetary pursuit of eternal life in the form of a magical tree. Starring Hugh Jackman as a 16th-century Spanish conquistador, a 21st-century neurologist and a space traveler in the distant future, each fighting to save his beloved from certain death, *The Fountain* melded the biblical tree-of-life story from *Genesis* with Bowie's Major Tom narrative and a metaphysical through line involving neuroscience and Spanish conquistadors that earned the film comparisons to *2001: A Space Odyssey* (1968). With its stunning cinematography by Matthew Libatique and a score by the Kronos Quartet with Clint Mansell, the *Pi* helmer solidified his status as a visionary purveyor of dense cinematic headtrips.

Der metaphysische Thriller *Pi – Der Film* (*Pi*, 1996/97) verknüpfte Elemente der Chaostheorie, abgehobene Mathematik, die Kabbala und paranoide Verschwörungsfantasien zu einer alle Vorstellungen sprengenden Filmerzählung über ein in seiner New Yorker Wohnung verschanztes zahlenbesessenes Genie auf seiner Suche nach der mathematischen Formel für das Universum. Dieses beim Sundance Film Festival mit dem Regiepreis ausgezeichnete, aufsehenerregende Spielfilmdebüt machte einen Harvard-geschulten jungen Künstler bekannt, der mit seiner komplexen und grandiosen Fantasie kopflastige Thriller hervorbringt, die nicht eben leicht verdaulich sind. In seinem zweiten Spielfilm *Requiem for a Dream* (2000) widmete sich Aronofsky mit unablässigem „cross cutting", geteilten Bildern und einem abwärts führenden Spiraleffekt sowohl auf rhythmischer wie auch auf visueller Ebene der Sucht in ihren unterschiedlichsten Erscheinungsformen und schuf mit der Adaption von Hubert Selbys 1978 erschienenem Roman ein qualvolles Filmerlebnis – buchstäblich den schlechten Trip als Kinokunst. Aronofskys dritter und ambitioniertester Spielfilm ist *The Fountain* (2006), eine psychedelische Science-Fiction-Lovestory, die wiederum mit verschiedenen Motiven, Vorstellungen und Erzählsträngen jongliert. In der Form eines 1000 Jahre umspannenden Triptychons erzählt der Film von der interplanetarischen Jagd nach dem ewigen Leben, dessen Geheimnis mit einem Zauberbaum verbunden ist. Hugh Jackman spielt darin sowohl einen spanischen Konquistadoren des 16. Jahrhunderts als auch einen Neurologen des 21. Jahrhunderts und einen Weltraumreisenden in einer fernen Zukunft. Alle drei wollen ihre Liebste vor dem sicheren Tod retten. In *The Fountain* verschmilzt die biblische Genesisgeschichte des Lebensbaums mit Bowies Erzählung von Major Tom, wobei sich Neurobiologie und spanische Konquista als roter Faden durch die Story ziehen. Kein Wunder, dass der Film mit *2001: Odyssee im Weltraum* (*2001: A Space Odyssey*, 1968) verglichen wurde. Die überwältigende Kameraführung von Matthew Libatique und eine Filmmusik, die das Kronos Quartett und Clint Mansell zusammenführt, trugen das ihre dazu bei, dass der Schöpfer von *Pi* seinen Status als visionärer Lieferant anspruchsvoller filmischer Kopftrips festigen konnte.

Histoire hallucinante d'un génie obsédé par les nombres, barricadé dans son appartement new-yorkais à la recherche d'une clé mathématique de l'univers, *Pi* (1996/97) est un thriller métaphysique où s'entremêlent théorie du chaos, mathématiques fumeuses, kabbale et complot parano. Cet étonnant premier film, prix de la mise en scène au Festival Sundance, révèle un jeune cinéaste, ancien de Harvard, maniant idées complexes et grandioses sans l'intention de faciliter la tâche du spectateur. Dans son deuxième film, *Requiem for a Dream* (2000), Aronofsky s'intéresse à la dépendance sous ses diverses formes, utilisant d'incessants va-et-vient dans le temps, des écrans divisés et un effet de spirale descendante à la fois rythmique et visuelle, qui font de cette adaptation du roman de Hubert Selby Jr (1978) une expérience très prenante – le *bad trip* élevé au rang d'art. Film de science-fiction, *The Fountain* (2006), sa troisième œuvre et la plus ambitieuse aussi, est une histoire d'amour historique et psychédélique qui jongle avec des thèmes, des idées et des intrigues multiples, dans un triptyque se déroulant sur 3 000 ans, quête interplanétaire de la vie éternelle sous la forme d'un arbre magique. Hugh Jackman y interprète un conquistador espagnol du XVIe siècle, un neurologue du XXIe siècle et un voyageur spatial d'un avenir lointain, chacun d'eux devant arracher sa bien-aimée à une mort certaine. *The Fountain* emprunte à l'arbre de vie de la *Genèse*, comme à *Major Tom* de David Bowie, selon un fil conducteur métaphysique réunissant neurosciences et conquistadors. On l'a comparé à *2001, l'odyssée de l'espace*. Avec une image splendide due à Matthew Libatique et une partition composée par le quatuor Kronos avec Clint Mansell, le réalisateur de *Pi* confirme son statut de pourvoyeur visionnaire d'intenses voyages mentaux.

FILMS →
1996/97 *Pi*
2000 *Requiem for a Dream*
2006 *The Fountain*

SELECTED AWARDS ›
1998 *Pi*: Dramatic Directing Award, Sundance Film Festival; Open Palm Award, Gotham Awards
1999 *Pi*: Best First Screenplay, Independent Spirit Awards
2001 Franklin J. Schaffner Award, American Film Institute

The Fountain

The stunning camerawork of cinematographer Matthew Libatique brings to life this epic romance spanning the centuries, including the 16th-century Spanish court ruled by the queen of Spain, played by Rachel Weisz.

Die überwältigende Kameraarbeit Matthew Libatiques verleiht dieser viele Jahrhunderte überspannenden epischen Romanze Lebendigkeit. So spielt die Geschichte auch am spanischen Hof des 16. Jahrhunderts. In der Rolle der Königin: Rachel Weisz.

La splendide photographie de cette épopée sentimentale à travers les siècles est due au chef-opérateur Matthew Libatique; ici au XVIᵉ siècle, avec Rachel Weisz en reine d'Espagne.

In one of three disparate roles, Hugh Jackman stars as the Spanish conquistador Tomás, sent to the New World by the queen of Spain to locate the biblical tree of life.

Einer der drei völlig unterschiedlichen Filmparts von Hugh Jackman ist der des spanischen Konquistadoren Tomás, den die Königin von Spanien beauftragt, in der Neuen Welt den biblischen Baum des Lebens zu suchen.

Dans l'un de ses trois rôles, Hugh Jackman incarne Tomás, conquistador espagnol envoyé dans le Nouveau Monde par la reine à la recherche de l'arbre de vie biblique.

"Filmmaking is an exercise in paranoia. When one writes, the goal is to relate every scene to your main character, to your theme. That's exactly how paranoid schizophrenics look at the world. They believe everything in the universe revolves around them. So in effect, all characters in a film would only be truly conscious if they were paranoid."

„Filmemachen ist eine Übung in Paranoia. Bei der Abfassung des Drehbuchs versucht man, jede Szene auf die Hauptfigur zu beziehen, auf das Thema der Geschichte. Genauso sehen paranoide Schizophrene die Welt. Sie glauben, alles im Universum drehe sich um sie. Alle Charaktere eines Films hätten demnach nur dann das richtige Bewusstsein, wenn sie paranoid wären."

«Le cinéma, c'est l'expérience de la paranoïa. Quand on écrit, on cherche à rapporter toutes les scènes à son personnage principal, à son propre thème. Telle est la vision du monde des schizophrènes paranoïdes, persuadés que l'univers entier tourne autour d'eux. Si bien que tous les personnages d'un film ne seraient vraiment conscients que s'ils étaient paranoïaques.»

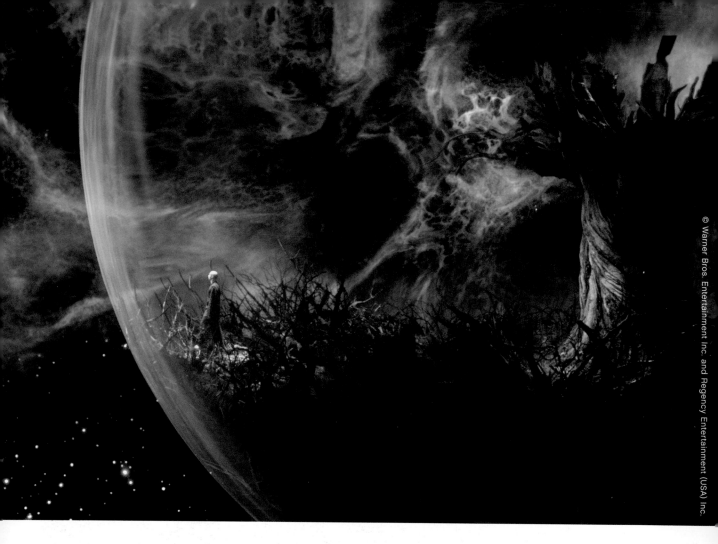

An art and visual effects department comprising nearly one hundred technicians created the mesmerizing look and feel of 26th-century space travel in the third triptych of Aronofsky's *The Fountain*.

Der dritte Teil von Aronofskys Triptychon *The Fountain* zeigt eine Weltraumreise, die im 26. Jahrhundert unternommen wird. Ein Team von fast hundert Technikern erarbeitete die Spezialeffekte, die für faszinierende Bilder und eine packende Atmosphäre sorgen.

C'est à une centaine de techniciens-décorateurs et aux effets visuels que l'on doit l'ambiance hypnotique d'un voyage spatial au XXVIᵉ siècle, dans le troisième volet de *The Fountain* d'Aronofsky.

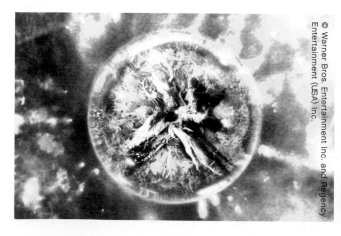

The French writer-director of the international hit thriller *The Beat That My Heart Skipped* (*De battre mon cœur s'est arrete*, 2004/05) is the son of noted screenwriter and director Michel Audiard, whose sartorial-minded police procedurals of the 1960s and 1970s featured the matinee idols Alain Delon and Lino Ventura. Specializing in a stylish new breed of French crime thriller that updates the hardboiled chic of his father's era, the Parisian native Jacques Audiard, with script collaborator Tonino Benacquista, creates tough-as-nails screen characters that don't require hip-hop and Glocks to let the world know they mean business. As the thuggish Parisian real-estate 'enforcer' Thomas Seyr in *The Beat That My Heart Skipped*, a remake of James Toback's 1977/78 thriller *Fingers* that swept France's César awards, the previously unkempt actor Romain Duris underwent a sartorial makeover that put him in the company of the fashionable heroes populating Audiard *père*'s policiers. That same gritty elegance was in abundance throughout Audiard's previous thriller, *Read My Lips* (*Sur mes lèvres*, 2001), starring Emmanuelle Devos – in another César-winning turn for an Audiard player – as a deaf-mute secretary who finds herself transformed after descending into the Parisian crime underworld with a co-worker. Audiard and Benacquista concoct superior thrillers that keep an audience basking in style and grasping in the dark for what might happen next.

Der französische Drehbuchautor und Regisseur des international erfolgreichen Thrillers *Der wilde Schlag meines Herzens* (*De battre mon cœur s'est arrêté*, 2004/05) ist der Sohn des vor allem als Drehbuchautor bekannten Michel Audiard, in dessen Kriminalgeschichten der 1960er- und 1970er-Jahre elegante Topstars wie Alain Delon und Lino Ventura die Hauptrollen spielten. Der in Paris geborene Jacques Audiard entwickelte einen neuartigen Stil des französischen Kriminalthrillers, der den abgebrühten Chic der Ära seines Vaters zu einer neuen Aktualität verhilft. Gemeinsam mit Co-Autor Tonino Benacquista zeichnet er knallharte Leinwandcharaktere, die weder Hip-Hop noch dicke Knarren benötigen, um der Welt zu zeigen, dass sie es ernst meinen. Für seine Rolle als rüpelhafter Pariser Immobilienhai Thomas Seyr in *Der wilde Schlag meines Herzens*, einem Remake von James Tobacks 1977/78 entstandenem Thriller *Finger – Zärtlich und brutal (Fingers)*, wurde der sich sonst eher nachlässig gebende Schauspieler Romain Duris so herausgeputzt, dass er den schicken Polizeihelden der Filme von Audiard senior in nichts nachstand. Die gleiche offenkundige Eleganz prägte bereits Audiards vorherigen Thriller *Sur mes lèvres* (2001), in dem Emmanuelle Devos – auch sie eine César-gekrönte Audiard-Darstellerin – eine taubstumme Sekretärin spielt, die von einem gemeinsam mit einem Kollegen unternommenen Ausflug in die Pariser Unterwelt wie verwandelt zurückkehrt. Audiard und Benacquista hecken erstklassige Thriller aus, die ihr Publikum stilvoll verwöhnen und stets gefangen halten, indem sie es immer über das, was als Nächstes geschieht, im Dunkeln lassen.

Thriller qui a séduit les publics du monde entier, *De battre mon cœur s'est arrêté* (2004/05) est l'œuvre du fils du célèbre scénariste et dialoguiste Michel Audiard, dont les films policiers des années 1960 et 1970, aux personnages élégamment vêtus, étaient interprétés par les vedettes Alain Delon et Lino Ventura. Jacques Audiard s'est spécialisé dans un nouveau genre policier très stylisé qui donne un coup de jeune aux héros chics, mais rudes, du temps de son père. Avec le scénariste Tonino Benacquista, il crée des durs à cuire qui ne prennent pas de gants pour faire comprendre qu'ils ne plaisantent pas. Dans *De battre mon cœur s'est arrêté*, remake de *Mélodie pour un tueur* (James Toback, 1977/78) et lauréat de plusieurs césars, Romain Duris quitte sa dégaine négligée pour incarner Thomas Seyr, «justicier» de l'immobilier parisien un peu voyou, et rejoint la galerie de héros chics qui peuplent les films d'Audiard père. Le précédent film d'Audiard, *Sur mes lèvres* (2001), regorge de la même élégance rude. Emmanuelle Devos (autre lauréate d'un césar grâce à ce film d'Audiard) interprète une secrétaire sourde, transfigurée par une descente dans les enfers de la pègre parisienne, en compagnie d'un collègue. Audiard et Benacquista savent concocter des thrillers au style achevé et au suspense imparable. Le dernier film en date du duo, *Les Disparus* (2007), réunit Juliette Binoche et Daniel Auteuil, le couple de *Caché* de Michael Haneke, cette fois dans le rôle de parents affolés à la recherche de leurs enfants adolescents enlevés par le milieu parisien.

FILMƮ →
1993/94 *Regarde les hommes tomber*
(See How They Fall) **1996** *Un héros très discret*
(A Self-Made Hero) **2001** *Sur mes lèvres*
(Read My Lips) **2004/05** *De battre mon cœur
s'est arrêté (The Beat That My Heart Skipped)*
2007 *Les Disparus (The Disappeared)*

ƮELECTED AWARDƮ →
1995 *Regarde les hommes tomber:* Best First Film, César Awards
1996 *Un héros très discret:* Best Screenplay, Cannes Film Festival
2002 Emerging Masters Showcase Award, Seattle International Film
Festival **2002** *Sur mes lèvres:* Best Writing (with Tonino Benacquista),
César Awards **2006** *De battre mon cœur s'est arrêté:* Best Director,
Best Film, Best Writing (Adaptation, with Tonino Benacquista),
César Awards; Best Film not in the English Language, BAFTA Awards

Sur mes lèvres

Read My Lips

"(My father) often said that filmmakers were idiots.
He didn't see cinema as a true art form.
That was the atmosphere I grew up in as a child."

„[Mein Vater] meinte oft, Filmemacher seien Idioten.
Er betrachtete den Film nicht als ernst zu nehmende Kunstform.
In einer solchen Atmosphäre wuchs ich auf."

«[Mon père] disait souvent que les réalisateurs étaient des imbéciles.
Pour lui, le cinéma n'était pas un art. C'est dans cette ambiance que j'ai grandi.»

A romanticist par excellence of the Parisian under-belly, Audiard makes riveting cinema out of a love affair between petty criminal Vincent Cassel and deaf secretary Emmanuelle Devos.

Wie kaum ein anderer Regisseur vermag Audiard die Schattenseiten von Paris zu verklären. Aus einer Liebesgeschichte zwischen einem kleinen Gauner (Vincent Cassel) und einer schwerhörigen Sekretärin (Emmanuelle Devos) macht er großes Kino.

Passé maitre dans la représentation romanesque de la pègre parisienne, Audiard captive le spectateur avec cette histoire d'amour entre un petit malfrat (Vincent Cassel) et une secrétaire sourde (Emmanuelle Devos).

De battre mon cœur s'est arrêté

The Beat That My Heart Skipped / Der wilde Schlag meines Herzens

At once elegant and hardboiled, Audiard's contemporary spin on James Toback's crime thriller *Fingers* helped elevate lead actor Romain Duris to the front rank of young European male actors.

Audiards elegantes und zugleich abgebrühtes Remake von James Tobacks Kriminalthriller *Finger – Zärtlich und brutal* (*Fingers*, 1977/78) beförderte den Hauptdarsteller Romain Duris in die erste Reihe junger europäischer Schauspieler.

À la fois rude et élégant, ce remake contemporain de *Mélodie pour un tueur* de James Toback a propulsé Romain Duris au premier rang des jeunes comédiens européens.

SIDDIQ BARMAK

Born 7 September 1962 in Panjshir, Afghanistan

In the audaciously titled *Osama* (2003), the first feature film to emerge from Afghanistan after the fall of the Taliban, a young girl attempts to pass as a boy in an effort to support her widowed mother and grandmother, their spouses having perished in the decades of war that ravaged the country in the years between the Soviet invasion in 1979 and the defeat of the Taliban in November 2001. Barmak was no stranger to the fascistic actions of the famously repressive religious police that eradicated centuries of Afghani culture during its despotic reign – including two of Barmak's short films and much of the Afghani National Film Archive. After living in exile from 1996 to 2001, Barmak returned to Kabul to head the Afghan Film Organization, determined to restore his native film culture to prominence. With funding and an Arriflex camera courtesy of Iranian director Mohsen Makhmalbaf, Barmak filmed *Osama* in the streets of Kabul, casting street kids and locals in key roles. Lead actress Marina Golbahari was a beggar discovered at age twelve outside a local cinema. Grim and unrelenting in its depiction of the mullahs' savagery towards woman and children, *Osama* was rife with unforgettable imagery: a fallen burqua flowing down a muddy street as mullahs disperse crowds of women with a hose; young males rocking in tandem with their rote recitations of the Koran; and, most disturbing of all, women and children stored in cramped holes in the ground by their treacherous mullah husbands. Barmak's second feature is *Opium War* (2006/07), the story of two American soldiers wounded in the Afghanistan desert – one black, one white – who stumble across a Russian tank occupied by a family of Afghani opium growers.

In Barmaks kühn *Osama* (2003) betitelten ersten Spielfilm, der nach dem Sturz der Taliban in Afghanistan entstanden war, versucht ein Mädchen, als Junge durchzukommen, weil es Mutter und Großmutter versorgen muss – beides Witwen, die ihre Männer in den Jahren zwischen der sowjetischen Invasion 1979 und der Niederlage der Taliban im November 2001, als Krieg das Land verwüstete, verloren haben. Als Betroffener hat Barmak die faschistischen Aktivitäten der berüchtigten Religionspolizei miterlebt, die während ihrer despotischen Herrschaft Jahrhunderte afghanischer Kultur vernichteten – darunter auch zwei Kurzfilme von Barmak und große Teile des nationalen Filmarchivs Afghanistans. Nach Jahren im Exil kehrte er schließlich nach Kabul zurück, um den afghanischen Filmverband zu leiten und der Filmkultur seiner Heimat wieder Geltung zu verschaffen. Mithilfe von Spenden und einer Arriflex-Kamera, die ihm der iranische Regisseur Mohsen Makhmalbaf zur Verfügung stellte, drehte er *Osama* in den Straßen von Kabul. Die Hauptrollen besetzte er mit Straßenkindern und Ortsansässigen. Seine Hauptdarstellerin Marina Golbahari entdeckte er, als die 12-Jährige vor einem Kino der Stadt bettelte. Konsequent und unerbittlich führt *Osama* in unvergesslichen Bildern die Brutalitäten der Mullahs gegen Frauen und Kinder vor Augen: eine verlorene Burka, die eine schlammige Straße hinabtreibt, nachdem Mullahs eine Frauenmenge mit einem Wasserschlauch auseinandergetrieben haben; junge Männer, die ein zuckelndes Gespann fahren und dabei auswendig gelernte Koranverse aufsagen, und – besonders verstörend – Frauen und Kinder, die von ihren treulosen Mullah-Ehemännern und -Vätern in engen Erdlöchern gehalten werden. Barmaks zweiter Spielfilm *Opium War* (2006/07) erzählt die Geschichte von zwei amerikanischen Soldaten – einem Schwarzen und einem Weißen –, die in der afghanischen Wüste verwundet werden und auf einen russischen Panzer stoßen, den eine Familie afghanischer Opiumbauern in Beschlag genommen hat.

Film au titre audacieux, *Osama* (2003) est le premier long métrage réalisé en Afghanistan après la chute du Taliban. Une adolescente tente de se faire passer pour un garçon afin de subvenir aux besoins de sa grand-mère et de sa mère, devenues veuves après avoir perdu leurs époux pendant la guerre qui a ravagé le pays après l'invasion soviétique de 1979 jusqu'à la défaite du Taliban en novembre 2001. Barmak a lui-même subi la répression fasciste de la police religieuse qui, durant son règne despotique, a anéanti des siècles de culture afghane, dont l'essentiel des archives nationales du film, et parmi elles, deux de ses courts métrages. Après un exil au Pakistan de 1996 à 2001, Barmak revient à Kaboul pour diriger l'Organisation du cinéma afghan, bien décidé à redonner à la culture cinématographique nationale toute son importance. Grâce au soutien financier du cinéaste iranien Mohsen Makhmalbaf, qui lui donne aussi une caméra Arriflex, Barmak tourne *Osama* dans les rues de Kaboul, attribuant les rôles principaux à des enfants des rues et à des Kaboulis. À 12 ans, Marina Golbahari, interprète du rôle féminin, mendie devant un cinéma de quartier. Portrait sombre et implacable de la sauvagerie des mollahs à l'égard des femmes et des enfants, *Osama* regorge d'images inoubliables : une burqa projetée dans la boue, tandis que des mollahs dispersent une foule de femmes à coups de jet d'eau ; des jeunes hommes en transe en récitant le Coran ; et, plus dérangeant encore, femmes et enfants confinés dans des trous creusés dans la terre par leurs maris mollahs. *Opium War* (2006/07), le deuxième film de Barmak, raconte l'histoire de deux soldats américains – l'un noir, l'autre blanc – blessés dans le désert afghan, qui découvrent un char russe occupé par une famille d'Afghans, producteurs d'opium.

FILMS →
2003 *Osama*
2006/07 *Opium War*

SELECTED AWARDS →
2003 *Osama:* Golden Camera – Special Mention, Cannes Film Festival; New Currents Award – Special Mention, PSB Award, Pusan International Film Festival; Sutherland Trophy, Best Film, London Film Festival **2004** *Osama:* Golden Globe, Best Foreign Language Film, Golden Globes USA

Osama

"In *Osama*, most of the actors were street kids in real life. My belief is that we can also find some great future filmmakers among these children. We're trying to teach them, to provide facilities, encourage them to develop their ideas, to make documentaries and short films."

„Die meisten Darsteller in *Osama* waren im wirklichen Leben Straßenkinder.
Ich bin davon überzeugt, dass auch unter diesen Kindern der eine oder andere wichtige Filmemacher der Zukunft zu entdecken ist.
Wir versuchen, sie zu unterrichten, ihnen Möglichkeiten zu bieten, sie zu ermutigen, ihre Ideen zu entwickeln,
sich mit Dokumentationen und Kurzfilmen zu erproben."

«Dans *Osama*, la plupart des comédiens sont des enfants des rues.
Je suis convaincu qu'il est aussi possible de trouver de futurs grands cinéastes parmi ces enfants.
Nous essayons de leur apprendre le cinéma, de leur fournir du matériel, de les encourager à faire naître leurs
idées, à faire des documentaires et des courts métrages.»

With a face to melt hearts and a quiet desperation resulting in wrenching cinematic suspense, young Marina Golbahari, unprofessional until discovered in the streets of Kabul, helps turn *Osama* into a movie for the ages.

Mit ihrem anrührenden, von stiller Verzweiflung erfüllten Gesicht vermag die junge Marina Golbahari, eine in den Straßen von Kabul entdeckte Laiendarstellerin, eine filmische Spannung zu provozieren, die herzzerreißend wirkt und dazu beiträgt, aus *Osama* ein zeitloses Filmkunstwerk zu machen.

Un visage à fendre le cœur, un désespoir tranquille débouchant sur un suspense poignant: la jeune Marina Golbahari, actrice amateur jusqu'à sa découverte dans les rues de Kaboul, fait d'*Osama* un film intemporel.

MATTHEW BARNEY

Born 25 March 1967 in San Francisco, USA

The mind-blowing installations of the visual artist and filmmaker Matthew Barney fuse elements of sculpture, performance, architecture, set design, video art and special effects to create a mesmerizing film universe. Structured as ritualistic actions shot at site-specific locations and often involving large quantities of molten petroleum jelly, Barney's films are typically inscrutable affairs that stand out as highly accomplished, rigorously conceived productions from a master of visual and kinetic invention. *Drawing Restraint 9* (2005) was filmed on location in Nagasaki Bay in Japan, on the *Nisshin Maru*, the last whaling factory ship in operation in the world. Barney and his wife Björk appear as The Guests, occidental visitors to the ship decked out in mammal fur costumes based on traditional Shinto marriage costumes. During a lightning storm, a vast sculpture of molded petroleum jelly begins to melt, flooding the couple's cabin as they cut away at each other's feet and thighs to reveal traces of whale tails. *The Cremaster Cycle* (1994–2002), screened as part of a traveling exhibition of Barney's work, organized by the Solomon R. Guggenheim Museum in New York, contained five films that did not correspond to any chronological order but hewed to a general commentary on the male cremaster muscle controlling testicular contractions in response to external stimuli. Barney, a former athlete, puts himself, in the guise of a series of bizarre characters, through various ritualistic scenarios, including a memorable scene in *Cremaster 3* (2002) in which he overcomes obstacles on each level of the Guggenheim Museum's spiraling rotunda.

In den verrückten Installationen des bildenden Künstlers und Filmemachers Matthew Barney verschmelzen Elemente von Plastik, Performance, Architektur, Bühnenbild, Videokunst und Spezialeffekte zu einem faszinierenden Filmuniversum. Barneys wie Rituale angelegte, in ortstypischem Ambiente gedrehte Filme, in denen oft große Mengen flüssiger Vaseline Verwendung finden, sind herausragende, hochartifizielle und streng konzipierte Produktionen eines Meisters visueller und kinetischer Erfindungsgabe. *Drawing Restraint 9* (2005) wurde vor Ort in Japan auf dem Walfangschiff Nisshin Maru in der Bucht von Nagasaki gedreht. Barney und seine Frau Björk treten als „Die Gäste" auf, als westliche Besucher, die in traditionellen Shinto-Hochzeitstrachten nachempfundenen Kostüme aus Tierhäuten gehüllt sind. Während eines Unwetters beginnt eine riesige Vaseline-Skulptur zu schmelzen, das Material strömt in die Kabine des Paars, das sich nun gegenseitig die Beine zerhackt, die sich in Walschwänze verwandeln. *The Cremaster Cycle* (1994–2002), als Teil einer vom New Yorker Solomon R. Guggenheim Museum organisierten Wanderausstellung von Barneys Werken aufgeführt, setzt sich aus fünf Filmen zusammen, die keiner chronologischen Ordnung unterliegen, sondern um das Phänomen des Hodenhebermuskels (Cremaster) kreisen, der auf äußere Einflüsse reagiert. Barney, ehemals Athlet, tritt in verschiedenen ritualistischen Szenenfolgen selbst auf und verkörpert dabei die unterschiedlichsten bizarren Figuren. In einer denkwürdigen Szene in *Cremaster 3* (2002) überwindet er zum Beispiel Hindernisse, die sich ihm auf jeder Ebene der spiralförmigen Rotunde des New Yorker Guggenheim Museum in den Weg stellen.

Les installations stupéfiantes du plasticien et cinéaste Matthew Barney associent sculpture, performance, architecture, création de décors, art vidéo et effets spéciaux pour créer un univers filmique fascinant. Bâtis comme des rituels filmés dans des lieux bien précis, souvent à grand renfort de vaseline, les films de Barney sont généralement des œuvres impénétrables, mais remarquables par leur conception très achevée et très rigoureuse, de la part d'un maître de l'invention visuelle et cinétique. *Drawing Restraint 9* (2005) a été tourné sur une base de Nagasaki, au Japon, à bord du *Nisshin Maru*, dernier baleinier en activité au monde. Barney et son épouse, Björk, y sont les « invités », visiteurs occidentaux vêtus de fourrures de mammifères, inspirées des costumes de mariage traditionnels shintoïstes. Lors d'un orage, une immense sculpture en vaseline moulée se met à fondre et envahit la cabine du couple, que l'on voit découper la matière au niveau de ses pieds et de ses cuisses pour révéler des traces de queues de baleine. Projeté à l'occasion d'une exposition itinérante des œuvres de Barney, organisée par le musée Guggenheim de New York, *The Cremaster Cycle* comprend cinq films qui ignorent tout ordre chronologique, mais suivent un commentaire général expliquant comment le muscle crémastérien contrôle les contractions des testicules en réaction à des stimuli externes. Ancien athlète, Barney interprète divers personnages étranges selon des scénarios ritualistes ; une scène mémorable de *Cremaster 3* (2002) le montre en train de franchir des obstacles disposés sur chacun des niveaux de la rotonde en spirale du musée Guggenheim de New York.

FILMS →
1994 *Cremaster 4*
1995 *Cremaster 1*
1997 *Cremaster 5*
1999 *Cremaster 2*
2002 *Cremaster 3*
2005 *Drawing Restraint 9*

SELECTED AWARDS →
1991–1992 First solo exhibition, San Francisco Museum of Modern Art
1993 Europa 2000 Prize, 45th Venice Biennale
1996 Hugo Boss Prize, Guggenheim Museum

Cremaster 1

"A lot of my work has to do with not allowing my characters to have an ego in a way that the stomach doesn't have an ego when it's wanting to throw up. It just does it."

„In vieler Hinsicht hat meine Arbeit damit zu tun, dass ich meinen Figuren kein Ego zugestehe, ein Ego in jenem Sinne, wie auch der Magen keines hat, wenn er irgendetwas auskotzen will. Er tut es einfach."

«Une grande partie de mon travail consiste à priver mes personnages de tout amour-propre: l'estomac n'a pas d'amour-propre quand il veut vomir. Il vomit, c'est tout.»

From confined internal spaces to vast outdoor expanses, the astonishing, visionary installations on display in Matthew Barney's *Cremaster Cycle*, whether concrete, earthen, human or other, make for unforgettable cinematic visions.

Mit visionären Installationen schafft Matthew Barney in *Cremaster Cycle* (1994–2002) unvergessliche filmische Eindrücke. Dabei spielt es keine Rolle, ob die Szenerien aus Beton, Landschaften, menschlichen Körpern oder anderen Elementen gestaltet sind.

Des intérieurs confinés aux espaces en plein air, les installations visionnaires – concrètes, terriennes, humaines ou autres –, présentées dans le cycle des *Cremaster* de Matthew Barney, font de ces films des œuvres visuellement inoubliables.

Cremaster 5 / Cremaster 2

When Barney isn't casting unconventional stars like
Ursula Andress he appears himself as characters in
the *Cremaster Cycle*, including the satyr-like creature from the second installment.

Wenn Barney eine Figur nicht gerade mit unkonventionellen Stars wie Ursula Andress besetzt, taucht er
in seinem *Cremaster Cycle* selbst in verschiedenen
Rollen auf, zum Beispiel als die einem Satyr ähnliche
Kreatur in der zweiten Folge des Zyklus.

Lorsque Barney ne fait pas appel à des vedettes
inhabituelles comme Ursula Andress, il joue dans les
différents volets de ses *Cremaster*, notamment dans
le deuxième, sous les traits d'une espèce de satyre.

Cremaster 3

New York City landmarks including the Guggenheim Museum and the Chrysler Building lobby compete for screen space with wildly adorned human figures, including several played by Barney in *Cremaster 3*.

Wahrzeichen von New York City wie das Guggenheim-Museum und die Lobby des Chrysler Building müssen sich in *Cremaster 3* (2002) die Leinwand mit schrill aufgeputzten Figuren teilen, von denen Barney mehrere selbst verkörpert.

Des monuments new-yorkais, comme le musée Guggenheim et le Chrysler Building, deviennent des personnages à part entière, comme les figures humaines aux costumes étonnants, dont plusieurs sont interprétées par Barney dans *Cremaster 3*.

Drawing Restraint 9

For his epic meditation on Japanese whaling and the relationship between self-imposed resistance and creativity, Barney appeared onscreen alongside his wife, the pop star Björk, in traditional Japanese wedding costumes.

In seiner epischen Meditation über den japanischen Walfang und die Beziehung zwischen selbst auferlegtem Widerstand und Kreativität trat Barney an der Seite seiner Ehefrau, des Popstars Björk, in traditionellen japanischen Hochzeitskostümen auf.

Pour son épopée méditative consacrée à la chasse à la baleine au Japon, ainsi qu'au rapport entre la résistance que l'on s'impose à soi-même et à la créativité, Barney et Björk, son épouse, apparaissent en costumes nuptiaux traditionnels japonais.

BONG JOON-HO

Born 1969 in Daegu, South Korea

The popular hit of the 2006 Cannes Film Festival wasn't a Hollywood monstrosity with a nine-figure marketing budget – it was an old-fashioned monster movie that drew early comparisons to *Jaws* (1975), solidifying the reputation of its young director as a specialist in expertly crafted thrillers exuding a powerful socio-political resonance. *The Host* (*Gwoemul*, 2006), from South Korean genre specialist Bong Joon-ho wasn't just a movie about a giant catfish living in the Seoul sewer system that makes off with the daughter of a food kiosk owner after wreaking havoc on the city – it was also a scathing attack on global fearmongering and ecological abuse, with the muck-dwelling monster as much of a victim as the simple shopkeeper. Bong is no stranger to movies that leave bite marks and blood stains – his grisly police procedural *Memories of Murder* (*Salinui chueok*, 2003), the based-on-fact story of Korea's first serial killer on the loose in the provinces, was a trenchant social indictment of backwater politics that made its point without compromising the film's capacity to entertain. Bong studied sociology before attending film school at the Korean Academy of Film Arts, where his short films were playing international festivals before he graduated. His first feature was the jet-black romantic comedy *Barking Dogs Never Bite* (*Flandersui gae*, 1999/2000), a mordant gem about an unemployed university professor who takes action against his neighbor's yapping dog. In Bong's capable hands, a deceptively simple story of people who love dogs butting heads with those who don't becomes a sage critique of the human condition. Expect Bong's career to be massive.

Publikumsliebling des Filmfestivals von Cannes 2006 war keine mit üppigem Marketingbudget ausgestattete Hollywood-Monstrosität, sondern ein altmodischer Monsterfilm, der prompt mit *Der weiße Hai* (*Jaws*, 1975) verglichen wurde und den Ruf des jungen Regisseurs als Fachmann für handwerklich solide Thriller mit kraftvoller sozialpolitischer Ausstrahlung festigte. *The Host* (*Gwoemul*, 2006) des südkoreanischen Genrespezialisten Bong Joon-ho war nicht einfach nur ein Film über einen zu einem Riesenmonster mutierten, im Abwassersystem Seouls lebenden Wesser, nachdem er die Stadt völlig auf den Kopf gestellt hatte, die Tochter eines Imbissbudenbetreibers entführt, sondern auch eine ätzende Kritik an globaler Panikmache und ökologischen Sünden. Das im Dreck hausende Monster ist dabei ebenso Opfer wie der schlichte Ladeninhaber. Bongs Filme hinterlassen Bisswunden und Blutflecken – sein grausiger Ermittlungskrimi *Memories of Murder* (*Salinui chueok*, 2003), die auf wahren Begebenheiten basierende Geschichte des ersten koreanischen Serienkillers, der in den Provinzen sein Unwesen trieb, war eine scharfe soziale Anklage gegen rückständige Politik –, was den Unterhaltungswert des Films keineswegs minderte. Bong studierte zunächst Soziologie, und noch bevor er die koreanische Filmakademie absolviert hatte, waren seine Kurzfilme schon auf internationalen Festivals zu sehen. Sein erster Spielfilm war die tiefschwarze romantische Komödie *Barking Dogs Never Bite* (*Flandersui gae*, 1999/2000), ein sarkastisches Juwel, das von einem arbeitslosen Universitätsprofessor handelt, der sich gegen den kläffenden Hund seines Nachbarn zur Wehr setzt. In Bongs geschickten Händen verwandelt sich eine trügerisch einfache Geschichte über Hundeliebhaber und Hundegegner, die einander die Köpfe einschlagen, in eine weise Kritik am menschlichen Dasein. Von Bong ist mit Sicherheit noch einiges zu erwarten.

Le succès populaire du Festival de Cannes 2006 n'est pas venu d'une superproduction hollywoodienne au budget publicitaire énorme, mais d'un film d'horreur à l'ancienne qui, en faisant penser aux *Dents de la mer*, a consolidé la réputation de son jeune réalisateur sud-coréen, expert en thrillers bien menés aux résonances sociopolitiques. *The Host* (*Gwoemol*, 2006) ne se réduit pas à l'histoire d'un poisson-chat géant vivant dans les égouts de Séoul et qui enlève la fille d'un petit vendeur de rue, après avoir semé la panique dans toute la ville. C'est aussi une attaque en règle de la propagande sécuritaire et de la destruction de l'environnement, le monstre nauséeux étant tout aussi victime que le petit commerçant. Bong est un spécialiste du film saignant. *Memories of Murder* (*Salinui chueok*, 2003), film policier macabre, s'inspire du premier tueur en série qui a terrorisé la province coréenne. C'est une mise en accusation cinglante de la politique provinciale, qui fait mouche sans que le spectacle en pâtisse. Après des études de sociologie, Bong a suivi les cours de l'École de cinéma de Corée ; ses courts métrages étaient projetés dans les festivals internationaux avant même qu'il n'ait terminé ses études. Son premier film, *Chien qui aboie ne mord jamais* (*Flandersui gae*, 1999/2000), est un petit chef-d'œuvre de comédie romantique sombre, dans lequel un professeur d'université poursuit son voisin en justice à cause d'un chien qui aboie constamment. Cette histoire faussement simple, opposant les amoureux des chiens à leurs adversaires, se transforme en une sage critique de la condition humaine. À coup sûr, on reparlera de ce Bong Joon-ho.

FILMS →
1999/2000 *Flandersui gae*
(Barking Dogs Never Bite)
2003 *Salinui chueok (Memories of Murder)*
2006 *Gwoemul (The Host)*

SELECTED AWARDS →
2001 *Flandersui gae:* FIPRESCI Prize,
Hong Kong International Film Festival
2003 *Salinui chueok:* Best New Director, FIPRESCI Prize,
Silver Seashell, San Sebastián International Film Festival;
Asian Film Award, Tokyo International Film Festival

Salinui chueok
Memories of Murder

The brutal handiwork of a rural serial killer upsets the bucolic idyll of a provincial hamlet circa 1986, when South Korea was still under the control of a military dictatorship.

Die brutalen Verbrechen eines Serienmörders, der um 1986 im ländlichen, damals noch von einem Militärregime beherrschten Südkorea sein Unwesen treibt, bringen die bukolische Idylle eines Weilers tief in der Provinz aus dem Gleichgewicht.

Les actes brutaux d'un tueur en série en province bouleversent le bonheur bucolique d'un hameau vers 1986, lorsque la Corée du Sud était sous la botte d'une dictature militaire.

Gwoemul

The Host

A mutant creature emerging from Seoul's Han River wreaks havoc on the local populace in Bong's expertly crafted anti-globalization parable deriding Western cultural imperialism.

In Bongs handwerklich perfekt umgesetzter Anti-globalisierungsparabel, in der er sich auch über den Kulturimperialismus des Westens lustig macht, versetzt eine aus dem Han-Fluss auftauchende Mutantenkreatur die Bevölkerung von Seoul in Angst und Schrecken.

À Séoul, une créature mutante émerge de la rivière Han et terrorise la population. Dans cette parabole anti-mondialisation parfaitement maîtrisée, Bong raille l'impérialisme culturel occidental.

"*(The Host)* is a monster movie, but I wanted to break the rules. I would have hated it if it took half an hour just to see the monster's tail in dark sewage. The monster shows itself early on – it's what happens next that is important."

„*[The Host]* ist zwar ein Monsterfilm, doch ich wollte die Regeln brechen. Es hätte mir überhaupt nicht gepasst, wenn man eine halbe Stunde hätte warten müssen, bis man wenigstens den Schwanz des Monsters im Dunkel der Abwasserkanäle zu sehen bekommt. Das Monster zeigt sich schon sehr früh – wichtig ist, was als Nächstes geschieht."

«*[The Host]* est un film d'horreur, mais je voulais en détourner les règles. Je ne tenais vraiment pas à attendre une demi-heure pour montrer la queue du monstre dans les égouts obscurs. Le monstre se montre très tôt. Ce qui est important, c'est ce qui se passe ensuite.»

Born 13 July 1948 in Bressuire, France

The French writer-director Catherine Breillat published her first sexually explicit novel at 17 before appearing as an actress in *Last Tango in Paris* (*Ultimo tango a Parigi / Le Dernier Tango à Paris*, 1972); both proved inspirational on her feature films, notorious for their frank depiction of sexuality from a female perspective and for their propensity to shock and provoke. Her first feature, *A Real Young Girl* (*Une vraie jeune fille*, 1976), examined the sexual awakening of a teenage girl during a summer holiday. The semi-autobiographical *36 fillette* (1987/88), named for a French brassiere size, tracked another young woman on holiday determined to lose her virginity. In *Romance* (1998), a frustrated schoolteacher in a tepid relationship enters into risky situations to achieve orgasm. Co-starring the Italian porn actor Rocco Siffredi, *Romance* sparked a trend in French cinema for lurid sexual content in film, culminating in the notorious garden-tool penetration scene in *Anatomy of Hell* (*Anatomie de l'enfer*, 2003), whose female protagonist (Amira Casar) submerges a used tampon in a glass of hot water and serves it to Siffredi as tea. Her psychological drama *Fat Girl* (*À ma sœur!* 2000) was Breillat's most critically acclaimed work, an account of sibling rivalry between a 15-year-old coquette and her obese 12-year-old sister. Featuring a superb debut performance by Anaïs Reboux as the titular *Fat Girl*, the film concludes with a scene of abrupt violence that is, even by Breillat's standards, unnerving. Her latest film, *An Old Mistress* (*Une vieille maîtresse*, 2007), a period drama starring Asia Argento, examines a love triangle between a man, his older mistress and his younger bride.

Bereits mit 17, noch vor ihrem Auftritt als Schauspielerin in *Der letzte Tango in Paris* (*Ultimo tango a Parigi / Le Dernier Tango à Paris*, 1972), veröffentlichte die französische Autorin und Regisseurin Catherine Breillat ihren ersten sexuell expliziten Roman. Beides erwies sich als inspirierend für ihre Spielfilme, die berüchtigt sind für ihre aus weiblicher Sicht freizügigen sexuellen Darstellungen und ihre Tendenz, zu schockieren und zu provozieren. Ihr erster Spielfilm *Ein Mädchen* (*Une vraie jeune fille*, 1976) befasste sich mit dem sexuellen Erwachen eines weinlichen Teenagers während der Sommerferien. Der halb autobiografische Film *Lolita '90* (*36 fillette*, 1987/88), dessen französischer Originaltitel eine Büstenhaltergröße bezeichnet, erzählt die Geschichte der jungen Lili, die fest entschlossen ist, im Laufe eines Urlaubs ihre Jungfräulichkeit zu verlieren. In *Romance* (1998) lässt sich eine frustrierte Lehrerin, die in einer öden Beziehung lebt, auf gewagte Abenteuer ein, um sexuelle Erfüllung zu finden. *Romance*, bei dem auch der italienische Pornodarsteller Rocco Siffredi mitwirkte, initiierte im französischen Film einen Trend zu drastischen sexuellen Inhalten, der in der berüchtigten Gartenwerkzeug-Penetration in Breillats *Anatomie de l'enfer* (2003) gipfelte. Im selben Film taucht die weibliche Hauptdarstellerin (Amira Casar) einen benutzten Tampon in ein Glas heißes Wasser und serviert es Siffredi als Tee. Von der Kritik am besten aufgenommen wurde Breillats psychologisches Drama *Meine Schwester – À ma sœur!* (*À ma sœur!*, 2000), das die Rivalität zwischen einer koketten 15-Jährigen und ihrer fettleibigen 12-jährigen Schwester schildert. Der Film, in dem Anaïs Reboux als Dickerchen ein grandioses Debüt feiert, endet jäh in einer höchst gewalttätigen Szene, die selbst für Breillats Maßstäbe schwer verdaulich ist. Der bislang letzte Film der Regisseurin, das historische Drama *Une vieille maîtresse* (2007) mit Asia Argento, behandelt das Dreiecksverhältnis zwischen einem Mann, seiner älteren Geliebten und seiner jüngeren Braut.

Scénariste et réalisatrice, Catherine Breillat a publié son premier roman au contenu explicitement sexuel à l'âge de 17 ans, avant de jouer dans *Le Dernier Tango à Paris* (1972), deux événements qui l'ont inspirée dans ses films ultérieurs, connus pour leur représentation implacable et provocatrice de la sexualité vue par une femme. *Une vraie jeune fille* (1976), son premier film, évoque l'éveil à la sexualité d'une adolescente de 13 ans pendant les vacances d'été. En partie autobiographique, *36 fillette* (1987/88) – référence à la taille de ses vêtements – suit une autre jeune fille en vacances, bien décidée à perdre sa virginité. Dans *Romance* (1998), notamment interprété par l'acteur italien de films porno Rocco Siffredi, une institutrice insatisfaite dans son couple se met dans des situations risquées pour connaître l'orgasme. *Romance* a été le point de départ d'une série de films au contenu sexuel très explicite, dont le plus marquant est *Anatomie de l'enfer* (2003) avec sa célèbre scène de pénétration avec un outil de jardin et dans lequel l'héroïne (Amira Casar) plonge un tampon usagé dans un verre d'eau bouillante et le sert à Siffredi en guise d'infusion. De tous les films de Breillat, *À ma sœur!* (2000) a été le mieux accueilli par la critique. Ce drame psychologique oppose une fille coquette de 15 ans à sa sœur obèse de 12 ans. Anaïs Reboux y donne une interprétation magistrale dans le rôle-titre. Le film se termine par une scène d'une violence brutale et, même pour le cinéma de Breillat, très dérangeante. Son dernier film en date, *Une Vieille Maîtresse* (2007), avec Asia Argento, est un triangle amoureux en costumes, entre un homme, sa vieille maîtresse et sa jeune fiancée.

SELECTED FILMS →
1976 *Une vraie jeune fille (A Real Young Girl)*
1987/88 *36 fillette* **1991** *Sale comme un ange
(Dirty Like an Angel)* **1996** *Parfait amour
(Perfect Love)* **1998** *Romance* **2000** *À ma sœur!
(Fat Girl)* **2001** *Brève traversée
(Brief Crossing)* **2002** *Sex Is Comedy*
2003 *Anatomie de l'enfer (Anatomy of Hell)*

SELECTED AWARDS →
2001 *À ma sœur!*: Gold Hugo, Chicago International Film Festival;
France Culture Award, Cannes Film Festival; Manfred Salzberger Award,
Berlin International Film Festival **2002** *À ma sœur!*: MovieZone Award,
Rotterdam International Film Festival **2004** *Anatomie de l'enfer*: Jury
Prize (Best Feature Film), Philadelphia Film Festival

Romance

Sexual odysseys form the crux of Breillat's daring works, including her international hit *Romance*, in which a restless schoolteacher pushes the boundaries of her sexuality through increasingly audacious means.

Sexuelle Odysseen stehen im Mittelpunkt der kühnen Arbeiten Breillats, so auch in ihrem internationalen Erfolgsfilm *Romance*. Eine ruhelose Lehrerin erweitert die Grenzen ihrer eigenen Sexualität auf immer gewagtere Weise.

L'odyssée sexuelle est au cœur des œuvres audacieuses de Breillat, en particulier *Romance* qui a connu un succès international, dans lequel une institutrice insatisfaite repousse les limites de sa sexualité par des moyens de plus en plus hardis.

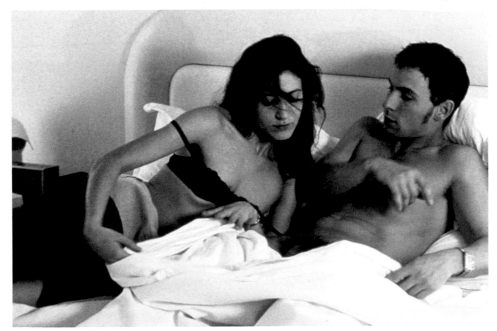

À ma sœur!

Fat Girl / Meine Schwester – À ma sœur!

Two sisters, one plump and homely, the other lis-
some and promiscuous, engage in sibling rivalry in
the unsettling psychodrama that is one of the director's most devastating works.

In diesem aufrüttelnden Psychodrama, einem der
bedrückendsten Filme der Regisseurin, geht es
um die Rivalität zweier Schwestern. Die eine ist ein
rundliches, unansehnliches Mädchen, die andere
ein graziöses, promiskes Wesen.

Deux sœurs, l'une obèse et sans charme, l'autre
agile et portée sur le sexe, se déchirent dans un
psychodrame qui constitue l'une des œuvres les
plus dérangeantes de la cinéaste.

Sex Is Comedy

In a meta-twist on Breillat's own *Fat Girl*, a director played by Anne Parrillaud attempts to film a sex scene between actors who don't get along.

In Anspielung auf Breillats Film *Meine Schwester – A ma sœur!* verkörpert Anne Parrillaud in diesem Werk eine Regisseurin, die versucht, eine Sexszene zu drehen. Doch die Akteure haben damit ein Problem.

Dans cette mise en abyme dont le point de départ est *À ma sœur!*, Anne Parrillaud interprète une cinéaste s'efforçant de filmer une scène de sexe entre deux acteurs qui ne s'entendent pas.

Sex is comedy, according to the title of Breillat's eighth feature, but it's also fraught with unexpected emotional turmoil, as characters played by Grégoire Colin and Roxane Mesquida discover.

Sex ist, nimmt man den Titel von Breillats neuntem Spielfilm wörtlich, eine Komödie. Manchmal jedoch ist er von einem unerwarteten Gefühlschaos geprägt. Diese Erfahrung müssen zumindest die beiden von Grégoire Colin und Roxane Mesquida dargestellten Figuren machen.

Comme l'indique le titre du huitième film de Breillat, le sexe est une comédie, débordant néanmoins de tourments émotionnels, comme le découvrent les personnages joués par Grégoire Colin et Roxane Mesquida.

"To be able to reach the heights of purity you have to suffer through deprivation and humiliations. What could have been a descent into hell becomes liberation."

„Um ein Maximum an Reinheit erlangen zu können, muss man zuvor Entbehrungen und Erniedrigungen durchleben. Was ein Abstieg in die Hölle zu sein schien, erweist sich als eine Befreiung."

«Pour atteindre les sommets de la pureté, il faut subir la privation et les humiliations. Ce qui aurait pu être une descente aux enfers devient une libération.»

Anatomie de l'enfer

Anatomy of Hell

Recurring Breillat cast member Rocco Siffredi, the famed Italian porn star, heats up the filmmaker's daring ninth feature.

Der berühmte italienische Pornostar Rocco Siffredi, den Breillat des Öfteren engagiert, sorgt im gewagten zehnten Spielfilm der Regisseurin für die entsprechende Stimmung.

Habitué du cinéma de Breillat, Rocco Siffredi, célèbre star du porno italien, apporte son piment à cette audacieuse neuvième œuvre.

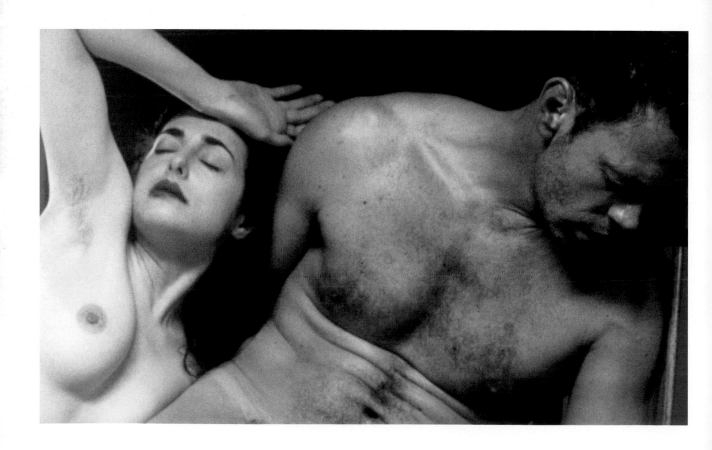

Une vieille maîtresse

An Old Mistress

Asia Argento stars in this period drama.

Asia Argento spielt in diesem historischen Drama eine Hauptrolle.

Asia Argento est la vedette de ce film en costumes.

CRAIG BREWER

Born 6 December 1971 in Virginia, USA

The Memphis-based Craig Brewer reignited a spark for American regional filmmaking – a rich tradition in independent film before it got co-opted by New York and Hollywood money – after his second feature, *Hustle & Flow* (2004/05), sold for $9 million at the Sundance Film Festival, making a star out of the character actor Terrence Howard, an Oscar nominee for his performance. Brewer cites Flannery O'Connor and Tennessee Williams as inspirations, peppering his hothouse melodramas with outcasts and underdogs, among them the *Hustle & Flow* protagonist DJay, a hardscrabble pimp who dreams of becoming a star rapper, and the two principal characters in Brewer's third feature, *Black Snake Moan* (2006), a backwoods bluesman (Samuel L. Jackson) who believes he can chase the devil out of an abused white woman (Christina Ricci) suffering from a sexual compulsion, whom he chains to the radiator in his Mississippi Delta shack. Brewer's films teem with evocative images of rough-and-tumble Memphis and its outlying areas, favoring parking lots, crumbling row houses and pawnshops over the familiar tourist traps of rock & roll's birthplace. The Memphis urban landscape is as much a character in Brewer's work as his deeply nuanced characters. *Hustle & Flow* centered on the musical phenomenon known as crunk, a subdivision of Southern hip-hop that drew a worldwide audience after Three 6 Mafia's 'It's Hard Out Here For A Pimp,' from the film's soundtrack, won the Academy Award for Best Original Song.

Mit dem Erfolg seines zweiten Spielfilms *Hustle & Flow* (2004/05), der beim Sundance Film Festival für neun Millionen Dollar verkauft wurde und dem Charakterdarsteller Terrence Howard Starruhm und eine Oscar-Nominierung einbrachte, sorgte der in Memphis lebende Craig Brewer für neue Bewegung im regionalen amerikanischen Kino, das – bevor es vom großen Geld aus New York und Hollywood vereinnahmt worden war – auf eine große Tradition unabhängiger Filmproduktion zurückblicken konnte. Brewer nennt Flannery O'Connor und Tennessee Williams als seine Inspirationsquellen und verleiht seinen Treibhaus-Melodramen mit Außenseitern und Underdogs entsprechende Würze. DJay, der Protagonist aus *Hustle & Flow*, ein beinharter Zuhälter, der davon träumt, Rap-Star zu werden, ist ein solcher Underdog, ebenso wie der hinterwäldlerische Bluesmusiker (Samuel L. Jackson) aus Brewers drittem Spielfilm *Black Snake Moan* (2006), der einer missbrauchten, krankhaft nymphomanen weißen Frau (Christina Ricci) den Teufel austreiben will. Brewers Filme wimmeln vor evokativen Bildern eines rauen und heruntergekommenen Memphis und seiner Außenbezirke, vom Geburtsort des Rock 'n' Roll zeigen sie Parkplätze, verfallende Häuserzeilen oder Pfandleihen statt der bekannten Touristenfallen. Die Stadtlandschaft von Memphis spielt in Brewers Werken eine ebenso wichtige Rolle wie die fein nuancierten Charaktere. *Hustle & Flow* dreht sich vor allem um das Musikphänomen „Crunk", eine Spielart des Südstaaten-Hip-Hops, die die Aufmerksamkeit eines größeren Publikums fand, nachdem Three 6 Mafia mit „It's Hard Out Here For A Pimp", der zum Soundtrack des Films gehört, den Oscar für den besten Originalsong gewonnen hatten.

C'est de Memphis que Brewer a ranimé la flamme du cinéma américain régional, riche veine du cinéma indépendant avant que la finance new-yorkaise et hollywoodienne ne se l'accapare. Son deuxième film *Hustle & Flow* (2004/05) a été acheté au Festival Sundance pour neuf millions de dollars et a fait de Terrence Howard une star, dans un rôle de composition qui lui a valu d'être sélectionné aux oscars. Inspiré par Flannery O'Connor et Tennessee Williams, Brewer truffe ses mélodrames survoltés de marginaux et d'opprimés, parmi lesquels le « héros » de *Hustle & Flow*, D. Jay, proxénète misérable qui rêve de devenir une vedette du rap. Les deux protagonistes de *Black Snake Moan* (2006), son troisième film, sont du même acabit : un joueur de blues dans un trou perdu (Samuel L. Jackson) est convaincu d'être en mesure de pouvoir extirper le diable d'une nymphomane blanche, victime d'un abus sexuel (Christina Ricci). Pour y parvenir il l'enchaîne à un radiateur dans son taudis du delta du Mississippi. Le cinéma de Brewer regorge d'images évocatrices d'un Memphis mouvementé et de ses environs, préférant les parkings, les rangées de maisons délabrées et les monts-de-piété aux pièges à touristes du berceau du rock'n'roll. La ville devient protagoniste au même titre que les personnages tout en nuances. La B. O. de *Hustle & Flow* a également révélé au monde entier le phénomène musical du *crunk*, version sudiste du hip-hop, après l'oscar remporté par la chanson *It's Hard Out Here for a Pimp*, du groupe Three 6 Mafia.

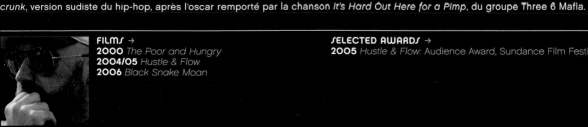

FILMS →
2000 *The Poor and Hungry*
2004/05 *Hustle & Flow*
2006 *Black Snake Moan*

SELECTED AWARDS →
2005 *Hustle & Flow:* Audience Award, Sundance Film Festival

Hustle & Flow

Played by Terrence Howard, the hard-luck Memphis pimp Djay dreams of hip-hop stardom as he struggles to make ends meet. Right: Director Craig Brewer (center) on set with Howard.

Terrence Howard spielt den vom Pech verfolgten Zuhälter DJay, der in Memphis versucht, über die Runden zu kommen, und von einer Zukunft als Hip-Hop-Star träumt. Rechts: Regisseur Craig Brewer (Mitte) mit Howard am Set.

Proxénète malchanceux de Memphis ayant bien du mal à joindre les deux bouts, D-Jay (Terrence Howard) rêve de devenir une star du hip-hop. À droite : le réalisateur Craig Brewer (au centre) sur le tournage, avec Howard.

Black Snake Moan

"I'm proud people consider me a regional filmmaker.
But it's about more than a region – it's the people who inspire me.
You could throw a stone in Memphis and chances are you'd hit
a songwriter or a storyteller."

„Ich bin stolz darauf, dass die Leute mich als einen regionalen Filmemacher sehen. Aber es geht um mehr als nur um die Region –
die Leute hier inspirieren mich. Wirft man in Memphis einen Stein, ist es gut möglich, dass man einen Songschreiber
oder einen Geschichtenerzähler trifft."

«Je suis fier que l'on me considère comme un cinéaste provincial. Mais cela dépasse cet aspect régional:
ce sont les gens qui m'inspirent. Lancez une pierre dans la foule de Memphis et vous toucherez sûrement un parolier
de chanson ou un conteur.»

Brewer directs Christina Ricci, Justin Timberlake and Samuel L. Jackson in another hothouse, Deep South drama, this one focusing on sexuality, redemption and the legacy of the blues.

In einem anderen Drama, das ebenfalls in der Treibhausatmosphäre des amerikanischen Südens spielt – Sexualität, Erlösung und das Erbe des Blues stehen diesmal im Mittelpunkt –, treten Christina Ricci, Justin Timberlake und Samuel L. Jackson unter der Regie Brewers auf.

Christina Ricci, Justin Timberlake et Samuel L. Jackson sont les interprètes d'un autre drame torride se déroulant dans le Sud profond de l'Amérique, sur fond de sexualité, de rédemption et de blues.

Above and right: Craig Brewer on the set of Black Snake Moan with Samuel L. Jackson and Justin Timberlake. Opposite: As the blues musician Lazarus, Jackson exorcizes personal demons through his music.

Oben und rechts: Craig Brewer mit Samuel L. Jackson und Justin Timberlake auf dem Set von *Black Snake Moan*. Gegenüber: Als Bluesmusiker Lazarus exorziert Jackson die eigenen Dämonen durch seine Musik.

Ci-dessus et à droite : Craig Brewer sur le tournage de *Black Snake Moan* avec Samuel L. Jackson et Justin Timberlake. À gauche : Le bluesman Lazarus (Jackson) exorcise les démons personnels grâce à la musique.

LAURENT CANTET

Born 15 June 1961 in Melle, France

The outstanding French director Laurent Cantet, in his three feature films to date, examines aspects of the world of work and leisure as viewed from the perspective of characters drawn mainly from the professional classes – whether it's a young managerial candidate at odds with some provincial factory workers, including his own father, in Cantet's riveting debut feature *Human Resources* (*Ressources humaines*, 1999), a downsized blue-collar professional fabricating a non-existent bureaucratic position in order to conceal the guilt and shame of redundancy from his wife and children in *Time Out* (*L'Emploi du temps*, 2001), or a trio of vacationing North American sophisticates in late 1970s Haiti dipping into the murky waters of sex tourism in *Heading South* (*Vers le sud*, 2005), Cantet's first production outside of his native France. What conjoins and permeates these works is a sense of mounting desperation on the part of its multifaceted protagonists – including women fleeing humdrum jobs and unsatisfying marriages for exotic, orgasmic pleasures with expendable Haitian hustlers, aging assembly-line workers addicted to their repetitive and menial tasks and a haughty, wounded soul who believes he can escape the workforce by retreating into a rich fantasy world. The suffocating, indifferent grasp of money looms large over these embattled souls, plummeting them into tragedy as it dawns on them that the economy is the ultimate invisible hand guiding one's destiny – as illustrated in the sad plight of the Haitian stud Legba in *Heading South*, whose flesh is a commodity to be bought and sold at the whim of wealthy white tourists.

In seinen bisherigen drei Spielfilmen untersucht der herausragende französische Regisseur Laurent Cantet die unterschiedlichen Facetten der Arbeitswelt und der Freizeit aus der Perspektive von Charakteren, die vor allem durch ihre Zugehörigkeit zu einer beruflichen Klasse gezeichnet sind – ob, wie in seinem fesselnden Spielfilmdebüt *Ressources humaines – Der Jobkiller* (*Ressources humaines*, 1999), aus Sicht eines jungen, angehenden Managers, der sich mit einer Gruppe provinzieller Fabrikarbeiter streitet, zu der auch sein Vater gehört. Oder eines entlassenen, wenig qualifizierten Berufstätigen, der in *Auszeit* (*L'Emploi du temps*, 2001) eine Neuanstellung erfindet, um Frau und Kindern gegenüber Schuldgefühle und Scham verbergen zu können. Oder auch, wie in seinem ersten außerhalb Frankreichs gedrehten Film *In den Süden* (*Vers le sud*, 2005), eines Trios kultivierter nordamerikanischer Damen, das im Haiti der späten 1970er-Jahre in den trüben Wassern des Sextourismus fischt. All diese Filme verbindet und prägt die wachsende Verzweiflung ihrer vielgestaltigen Protagonisten: Frauen, die vor öden Jobs und unbefriedigenden Ehen fliehen, um sich mit haitianischen Gigolos exotischen orgiastischen Vergnügungen hinzugeben; alternde Fließbandarbeiter, die an ihren immer gleichen, niederen Aufgaben hängen, und ein hochmütiger Mann mit lädierter Psyche, der meint, er könne dem beruflichen Druck entgehen, indem er sich in eine Fantasiewelt zurückzieht. Der bedrängende Zwang, ständig irgendwie an Geld kommen zu müssen, lastet schwer über diesen angeschlagenen Seelen und stürzt sie in tragische Verstrickungen, sobald ihnen aufgeht, dass letztendlich

L'Emploi du temps

Time Out / Auszeit

Vincent (Aurélien Recoing) tries to hide his redundancy from his family and friends, leading to acts of increasing desperation.

Vincent (Aurélien Recoing) versucht, seine Entlassung vor Familie und Freunden zu verbergen, gerät dadurch aber in eine immer verzweifeltere Lage.

Voulant cacher son licenciement à sa famille et à ses amis, Vincent (Aurélien Recoing) en arrive à commettre des actes de plus en plus désespérés.

"To my mind what makes a character exist is his own awareness, often very painful, of his exclusion and solitude."

„Was meiner Ansicht nach einer Figur Leben verleiht, ist ihre oft sehr schmerzvolle Erkenntnis, ausgeschlossen und einsam zu sein."

« À mon avis, ce qui fait qu'un personnage existe, c'est sa prise de conscience, souvent très douloureuse, de son exclusion et de sa solitude. »

Vers le sud

Heading South / In den Süden

Sex tourism in Haiti is the subject of Cantet's third feature, starring Charlotte Rampling and Karen Young as foreigners fighting to purchase the company of the black escort Legba (Ménothy Cesar).

Thema von Cantets viertem Spielfilm ist der Sextourismus auf Haiti. Zwei Urlauberinnen (Charlotte Rampling und Karen Young) streiten sich, welche von ihnen sich die Begleitung des Schwarzen Legba (Ménothy Cesar) erkaufen darf.

Le tourisme sexuel en Haïti est le thème du troisième film de Cantet. Charlotte Rampling et Karen Young interprètent deux étrangères qui se battent pour acheter la compagnie de Legba, un prostitué noir (Ménothy Cesar).

NURI BILGE CEYLAN

Born 1959 in Istanbul, Turkey

In the deliberately paced existential dramas of the Turkish maverick Nuri Bilge Ceylan, quiet moments of reflection take prominence over narrative exposition, resulting in a trio of elegantly composed and carefully observed works that have earned the director an international following for their measured simplicity and unadorned emotional honesty.

Clouds of May (Mayıs Sıkıntısı, 1999) honed in on a filmmaker returning to his home town to direct a film in which he casts locals and family members (including Ceylan's actual mother and father) – a technique Ceylan himself has used in most of his features to date, including his most recent feature Climates (Iklimler, 2006) in which he directs himself, playing a university lecturer, opposite real-life wife Ebru Ceylan, as a television art director, in this gorgeously photographed high-definition drama about marital discord that drew critical acclaim at Cannes in 2006. Ceylan's breakthrough feature Distant (Uzak, 2002) recounted the story of a redundant laborer from rural Turkey who travels to Istanbul in search of a better life, settling in with his successful, urbane and self-absorbed photographer cousin who grows increasingly dismayed with his backwater relative's casual style of living – an aimlessness that sums up the subdued rhythms, motionless camera and long-held shots that are the hallmark of Ceylan's work. Simmering underneath these quiet but transfixing character studies is Ceylan's modus operandi – capturing fragmented moments of existential beauty in which internalized emotions come to life against some of the most majestic backdrops in films today. Only the Russian director Aleksandr Sokurov can make roiling clouds appear more sumptuous.

Ruhige reflexive Momente bestimmen den Erzählfluss der existenziellen Dramen des türkischen Einzelgängers Nuri Bilge Ceylan, dessen Werk inzwischen ein Trio elegant komponierter Filme umfasst, die eine bemerkenswerte Beobachtungsgabe verraten und dem Regisseur aufgrund ihrer wohlbedachten Schlichtheit und ihrer ungekünstelten emotionalen Aufrichtigkeit eine internationale Anhängerschaft eingebracht haben.

Im Mittelpunkt von Mayıs Sıkıntısı – Bedrängnis im Mai (1999) steht ein Filmemacher, der in seine Heimatstadt zurückkehrt, um einen Film mit Familienmitgliedern (darunter auch Ceylans Eltern) und anderen Einwohnern des Ortes zu drehen. Ceylan selbst hat sich dieses Mittels in den meisten seiner Spielfilme bedient. In seinem jüngsten Werk Iklimler – Climates (2006) tritt er auch als Darsteller eines Universitätsdozenten in Erscheinung, während seine Ehefrau Ebru Ceylan den Gegenpart der TV-Produzentin verkörpert. Dieses mit einer High-Definition-Kamera gefilmte, wunderbar fotografierte Drama über ein Ehezerwürfnis fand bei der Kritik in Cannes 2006 viel Zustimmung. Seinen Durchbruch feierte Ceylan jedoch bereits mit dem Spielfilm Uzak – Weit (Uzak, 2002). Er erzählt die Geschichte eines Arbeitslosen aus der türkischen Provinz, der auf der Suche nach einem besseren Leben nach Istanbul reist. Dort kommt er bei seinem städtisch geprägten und mit sich selbst beschäftigten Cousin unter, der als Fotograf erfolgreich ist und dem gleichgültigen Lebensstil seines rückständigen Verwandten zunehmend entsetzt gegenübersteht – einer Ziellosigkeit, die Ceylan mit dem für ihn typischen ruhigen Rhythmus, mit bewegungsloser Kamera und langen Einstellungen, zum Ausdruck bringt. Dieses Brütende, das die stillen, aber faszinierenden Charakterstudien seiner Filme auszeichnet, ist Ceylans Modus Operandi. Dabei gelingt es ihm, flüchtige Momente von existenzieller Schönheit einzufangen, Situationen, in denen unterdrückte Gefühle vor Hintergründen zu Leben erwachen, die zum Majestätischsten gehören, was Kino heute zu bieten hat. Allein der russische Regisseur Aleksandr Sokurov vermag dräuende Wolken noch prachtvoller zur Geltung zu bringen.

Marqué par un parti pris rythmique, le cinéma existentiel du cinéaste turc indépendant Nuri Bilge Ceylan recèle des moments de réflexion qui prennent le pas sur la narration. Une composition élégante et des observations minutieuses, les trois œuvres de Ceylan lui ont valu une reconnaissance internationale, pour leur simplicité mesurée et leur franchise émotionnelle sans fioritures.

Dans Nuages de mai (Mayıs Sıkıntısı, 1999), un cinéaste revient dans sa ville natale pour y tourner un film avec les habitants et des membres de sa famille, dont les propres parents de Ceylan, procédé que ce dernier utilise dans la plupart de ses films. Dans Les Climats (Iklimler, 2006), son œuvre la plus récente, il interprète un universitaire, face à Ebru Ceylan, son épouse à la ville, décoratrice pour la télévision. Récit d'une discorde conjugale, magnifiquement photographié en haute définition, ce film a reçu un excellent accueil critique à Cannes en 2006. Dans Uzak (2002), qui a révélé Ceylan, un chômeur rural se rend à Istanbul pour y mener une vie meilleure et s'installe chez son cousin photographe, un homme raffiné et égocentrique, auquel tout réussit. Ce dernier est de plus en plus consterné par la désinvolture de son cousin de province, évoquée par la lenteur du rythme, l'immobilité de la caméra et les longs plans-séquences, caractéristiques du cinéma de Ceylan. Affleurant constamment à la surface de ces études de caractère, à la fois calmes et saisissantes, le modus operandi de cinéaste consiste à appréhender des fragments de beauté existentielle où des sentiments intériorisés prennent vie, dans les décors les plus majestueux du cinéma d'aujourd'hui. Seul le cinéaste russe Alexandre Sokourov sait rendre plus somptueux encore le bouillonnement des nuages.

FILMS →
1997/98 Kasaba (The Town)
1999 Mayıs Sıkıntısı (Clouds of May)
2002 Uzak (Distant)
2006 Iklimler (Climates)

SELECTED AWARDS →
1998 Kasaba: Caligari Film Award, Berlin International Film Festival; Silver Award, Tokyo International Film Festival
2000 Mayıs Sıkıntısı: FIPRESCI Prize, European Film Awards
2003 Uzak: Grand Jury Prize, Cannes Film Festival; Silver Hugo, Chicago International Film Festival
2004 Uzak: France Culture Award, Cannes Film Festival
2006 Iklimler: FIPRESCI Prize in Competition, Cannes Film Festival

Kasaba

The Town / Die Kleinstadt

Ceylan's penchant for stark, lyrical imagery was established in his debut feature, a story of a family living in a small town in rural Turkey told from the point of view of children.

Ceylans Vorliebe für karge, lyrische Bilder zeigte sich bereits in seinem ersten Spielfilm, der aus dem Blickwinkel von Kindern erzählten Geschichte einer Familie, die in einer ländlichen türkischen Kleinstadt lebt.

Ceylan fait preuve d'un penchant pour des images à la fois austères et lyriques, dès son premier film, l'histoire d'une famille habitant une petite ville turque, racontée du point de vue des enfants.

"My aim is to reach a certain reality, even if the reality is very ugly, or tragic, or the kind that most people would not like to face."

„Ich will eine bestimmte Wirklichkeit vergegenwärtigen, auch wenn sie sehr hässlich ist, tragisch oder eine Realität jener Art, mit der die meisten nichts zu tun haben wollen."

«Je veux atteindre une certaine réalité, même si cette réalité est très laide, ou tragique, ou de celles que la plupart des gens ne veulent pas voir.»

Mayıs Sıkıntısı

Clouds of May / Mayıs Sıkıntısı – Bedrängnis im Mai / Nuages de mai

Filmmaker Muzaffer (Muzaffer Özdemir) returns to his hometown to direct a film starring local townspeople. His romantic view of the past does not match the real people he encounters.

Der Filmemacher Muzaffer (Muzaffer Özdemir) kehrt in seine Heimatstadt zurück, um mit den Bewohnern des Ortes einen Film zu drehen. Seine romantische Sicht der Vergangenheit hat jedoch mit den Auffassungen der Menschen, mit denen er sich einlässt, nichts zu tun.

Le cinéaste Muzzaffer (Muzaffer Özdemir) revient dans sa ville natale pour réaliser un film avec les habitants. Mais sa vision romantique du passé ne cadre pas avec les gens du présent qu'il rencontre.

Uzak

Distant / Uzak – Weit

City life and country life collide in Ceylan's third feature, shot in Istanbul, about a photographer Mahmut (Muzaffer Özdemir, left) struggling to accommodate his rural cousin Yusuf (Emin Toprak, right).

In Ceylans drittem Spielfilm prallen städtisches Leben und ländliche Traditionen aufeinander. Der in Istanbul gedrehte Film erzählt von den Auseinandersetzungen des Fotografen Mahmut (Muzaffer Özdemir, links) mit Yusuf (Emin Toprak, rechts), seinem Cousin vom Lande, den er bei sich aufgenommen hat.

Dans le troisième film de Ceylan, vie urbaine et vie rurale se télescopent. À Istanbul, le photographe Mahmut (Muzaffer Özdemir, à gauche) cohabite difficilement avec son cousin de la campagne Yusuf (Emin Toprak, à droite).

Iklimler

Climates / Iklimler – Jahreszeiten / Les Climats

Ceylan directs himself as selfish university professor Isa grappling with a tempestuous marriage to wife Bahar, played by Ceylan's real-life spouse Ebru.

Unter eigener Regie spielt Ceylan den selbstsüchtigen Universitätsprofessor Isa, dem die stürmische Ehe mit Bahar zu schaffen macht. Bahar wird von Ebru Ceylan verkörpert, auch im wirklichen Leben die Frau des Regisseurs.

Ceylan interprète lui-même le rôle d'Isa, professeur d'université égoïste confronté à une relation houleuse avec son épouse Bahar, jouée par Ebru, l'épouse de Ceylan à la ville.

138

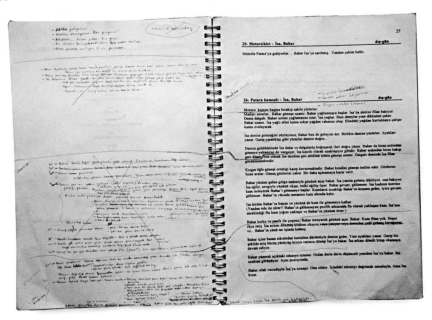

From script to filming to editing, Ceylan moulds ideas, characters, settings and time as only a master filmmaker can. For *Climates*, Ceylan employed high-definition technology to obtain his almost crystalline imagery.

Vom Abfassen des Skripts über die Dreharbeiten bis zum Schnitt – Ceylan weiß Ideen, Charaktere, Szenerien und zeitliche Abläufe so zu kombinieren, wie es nur ein Meisterregisseur kann. Um seine fast kristallinen Bilder schaffen zu können, arbeitete Ceylan für *Iklimler* mit hochauflösender Technik.

Du scénario au tournage, puis au montage, Ceylan façonne ses idées, ses personnages, ses décors et le temps avec l'assurance d'un maître. Pour *Les Climats*, il a recours à la haute définition pour obtenir des images presque cristallines.

STEPHEN CHOW

Born 22 June 1962 in Hong Kong, China

The biggest Hong Kong movie star of the 1990s honed his performing chops at the Shaw Brothers' acting school before hosting the popular children's show *430 Space Shuttle* with Tony Leung Chiu-wai, later a recurring player in Wong Kar-wai's opulent romances. Chow became a comic superstar in the wake of the gambling farce *All for the Winner* (*Du sheng*, 1990), a parody of Chow Yun-Fat movies featuring the comedian's trademark non sequitur Cantonese humor and introducing his signature character Sing. He began directing his own features in 1994, leading to the international breakthrough *Shaolin Soccer* (*Siu lam juk kau*, 2001), an action comedy heavy on digital effects that paid homage to Chow's childhood idol Bruce Lee. Playing a street cleaner who's also a martial arts master, Chow's wildly popular presence helped *Shaolin Soccer* sweep the Hong Kong Film Awards – it went on to become the city's highest-grossing domestic movie. Miramax Films bought the film and placed it on a shelf for two years before making extensive cuts and burying its theatrical release, owing to its widespread popularity in North America as a bootleg DVD. Chow attained more international acclaim for his next film, *Kung Fu Hustle* (*Kung fu*, 2004), a 1930s gang-warfare comedy that Chow wrote, directed and starred, with Yuen Woo-ping (*The Matrix*, 1999, *Crouching Tiger, Hidden Dragon*, 2000) providing choreography for its gravity-defying martial arts sequences, as hilarious as they were inventive. Chow's recent work has drawn comparisons in the West to everything from Buster Keaton and Charlie Chaplin comedies to Fred Astaire & Ginger Rogers musicals.

Seine Ausbildung zum Darsteller erwarb der größte Star des Hongkong-Kinos der 1990er-Jahre an der Schauspielschule der Shaw Brothers. Anschließend moderierte er zunächst, gemeinsam mit dem später durch Wong Kar-wais opulente Liebesfilme bekannt gewordenen Tony Leung Chiu-wai, die populäre Kindersendung *430 Space Shuttle*. Seinen Durchbruch zum Starkomiker erlebte Chow mit der Glücksspielfarce *All for the Winner* (*Du sheng*, 1990), einer Parodie auf Chow-Yun-Fat-Filme, in der er den irrwitzigen kantonesischen Humor Chows zur Geltung brachte und seine charakteristische Figur Sing erstmals vorstellte. 1994 begann Chow, eigene Filme zu drehen, internationale Berühmtheit erlangte er mit der Actionkomödie *Shaolin Kickers* (*Siu lam juk kau*, 2001) – einer Huldigung an sein Kindheitsidol Bruce Lee –, bei der ausgiebig digitale Effekte zum Einsatz kamen. Dank Chows unbändiger Präsenz in der Rolle eines Straßenkehrers (der gleichzeitig auch Kampfsportmeister ist) räumte *Shaolin Kickers* bei der Verleihung der Hong Kong Film Awards groß ab und erzielte Rekordeinspielergebnisse in der ehemaligen britischen Kronkolonie. Miramax Films kaufte daraufhin den Film, ließ ihn jedoch zwei Jahre lang liegen, kürzte ihn erheblich und verzichtete letztendlich sogar auf einen Kinostart, weil der Film als Bootleg-DVD in Nordamerika bereits sehr populär war. Noch mehr internationale Beachtung fand Chow mit seinem nächsten Film *Kung Fu Hustle* (*Kung fu*, 2004), einer Komödie über die Bandenkriege der 1930er-Jahre, bei der Chow sowohl als Drehbuchautor wie auch als Regisseur und Darsteller wirkte. Die urkomischen und erfindungsreichen, jeglicher Schwerkraft trotzenden Kampfkunstsequenzen choreografierte Yuen Woo-ping (*The Matrix*, 1999; *Tiger & Dragon*, 2000). Seit diesem Erfolg werden Chows Filme im Westen mit allen möglichen großen Vorbildern verglichen: mit den Komödien Buster Keatons oder Charlie Chaplins ebenso wie mit den Astaire-&-Rogers-Musicals.

Star incontestée du cinéma de Hong Kong des années 1990, Stephen Chow a fait ses armes à l'École d'art dramatique des Shaw Brothers, avant de présenter la célèbre émission pour enfants *430 Space Shuttle* avec Tony Leung Kar-fai, futur acteur fétiche des œuvres somptueuses de Wong Kar-wai. Il devient une vedette du cinéma comique grâce à *All for the Winner* (*Du Sheng*, 1990), parodie des films de Chow Yun-fat, où l'acteur joue pour la première fois le personnage de Sing, dans un climat absurde d'humour cantonais. Il se consacre à la mise en scène à partir de 1994 et connaît un succès international avec *Shaolin Soccer* (*Siu lam juk kau*, 2001), comédie d'action regorgeant d'effets spéciaux, hommage à Bruce Lee, idole de Chow enfant. Interprétant un balayeur maître en arts martiaux, Chow permet, par son énorme talent, à *Shaolin Soccer* de remporter la totalité des équivalents hong-kongais des oscars, ainsi que les meilleures recettes d'un film de Hong Kong sur le territoire de l'ancienne colonie britannique. Miramax Films l'achète, mais le met de côté pendant deux ans, renonçant à le distribuer malgré d'importantes coupes, en raison du succès en DVD, copie pirate qui circule en Amérique du Nord. Le succès international est encore au rendez-vous pour Chow avec *Crazy Kung-Fu* (*Kung fu*, 2004), comédie sur la guerre des gangs des années 1930, écrite, mise en scène et interprétée par l'acteur. Yuen Wo Ping (*Matrix*, *Tigre et Dragon*) en a assuré la chorégraphie des scènes de combat défiant les lois de la pesanteur, avec autant d'humour que d'inventivité. L'Occident compare le cinéma de Chow tant aux films comiques de Keaton et de Chaplin qu'aux comédies musicales avec Fred Astaire et Ginger Rogers.

SELECTED FILMS →
2001 *Siu lam juk kau* (*Shaolin Soccer*)
2004 *Kung fu* (*Kung Fu Hustle*)

SELECTED AWARDS →
2002 *Siu lam juk kau*: Best Picture, Best Director, Best Actor, Best Visual Effects, Best Sound Design, Hong Kong Film Awards
2005 *Kung fu*: Best Picture, Best Visual Effects, Best Action Choreography, Hong Kong Film Awards

Kung Fu

Kung Fu Hustle / Crazy Kung-Fu

"I used to cry when I watched Chaplin's films.
It was from him that I learned the role of the underdog.
Because I'm also from a poor family, this kind of thing moved me.
I found that it also worked for the audience because most
of them are like me – ordinary guys."

„Wenn ich mir Chaplins Filme ansah, musste ich immer weinen. Von ihm habe ich die Rolle des Underdogs gelernt.
Da ich auch aus einer armen Familie stamme, haben mich diese Figuren sehr bewegt. Ich stellte fest, dass sich auch das Publikum
mit ihnen identifizieren konnte, denn die meisten dieser Leute sind – wie ich – einfache Typen."

«Les films de Chaplin me faisaient pleurer. Il m'a fait découvrir le rôle de l'opprimé. Comme je viens aussi d'une famille pauvre,
j'en ai été touché. Et si cela marche auprès du public, c'est que la majorité des spectateurs sont comme moi,
des gens ordinaires.»

Chow directed and starred in his wildly popular feature, set in 1940s Canton, China, in which vicious gangsters take over a slum called Pig Sty Alley.

Im chinesischen Kanton der 1940er-Jahre bringen brutale Gangster einen Schweinekobengasse genannten Slum in ihre Gewalt. Regisseur Chow ist in dem außergewöhnlich populären Spielfilm auch als Darsteller zu sehen.

Chow a réalisé et interprété ce film très populaire, dont l'action se déroule à Canton dans les années 1940, où de redoutables gangsters tentent de prendre possession d'un bidonville appelé «la Porcherie».

The CGI-enhanced stunts also enhance the slapstick comedy, as old people with special kung fu powers battle with the hatchet-wielding gangsters.

Die Kampfszenen, in denen Kung-Fu-erprobte Alte sich mit skrupellosen Gangstern auseinandersetzen müssen, wurden digital überarbeitet. Dabei wurde auch der Slapstick-Effekt verstärkt.

Les images de synthèse renforcent les effets comiques et permettent à des vieillards versés dans l'art du kung-fu de combattre des gangsters armés de hachettes.

SOFIA COPPOLA

Born 14 May 1971 in New York City, USA

Privileged fashion plate or budding auteur? Such is the quandary surrounding the perceived reputation of the gifted writer-director who happens to be the daughter of Francis Ford Coppola – a child who grew up on film sets and went on to win the Best Original Screenplay Oscar for her second feature, *Lost in Translation* (2003), a drama about mondaine malaise that made the film world take Coppola *fille* seriously. She premiered her third feature, the audacious $40 million period romp *Marie Antoinette* (2006), starring Kirsten Dunst as the young spoiled French royal, to varied response at the Cannes Film Festival, though critics are not Coppola's chief cheerleaders – fashionable teenage girls adore her as an international style icon and art-house hipsters devour her pretty pictures set to hip tunes. But the glamour and glitz belies a cool, confident filmmaker whose awkward adolescence (don't forget her much-reviled performance in *The Godfather – Part III*, 1990) resulted in three exquisitely observed features about young women living in hermetic bubbles, including her feature debut, *The Virgin Suicides* (1999), the story of five precocious Michigan sisters who commit suicide. Aside from Coppola's refined taste in clothing – Milena Canonero was the costume designer for the ravishingly attired *Marie Antoinette* – it's the music that best accentuates Coppola's work. She anachronistically injected Gang of Four and Bow Wow Wow songs into *Marie Antoinette* to give the 18th-century contemporary punk resonance. She also placed the majestic slow burn of The Jesus & Mary Chain's 'Just Like Honey' in the coda to *Lost in Translation* to make the audience feel the dull ache of her characters' world-weary melancholy.

Ist sie nun eine privilegierte Modeerscheinung oder eine vielversprechende, eigenständige Filmemacherin? Diese Verlegenheit ist bezeichnend für die öffentliche Wahrnehmung dieser begabten Drehbuchautorin und Regisseurin, die zufällig die Tochter Francis Ford Coppolas ist. Als Kind an Filmsets aufgewachsen, wurde Sofia Coppola inzwischen für ihren zweiten Spielfilm *Lost in Translation* (2003) mit einem Oscar für das beste Originaldrehbuch ausgezeichnet. Mit der Geschichte um mondänen Lebensüberdruss begann die Filmwelt, das Coppola-„Mädchen" ernst zu nehmen. Ihr dritter Spielfilm, das gewagte 40-Millionen-Dollar-Spektakel *Marie Antoinette* (2006) mit Kirsten Dunst als zickiger junger Königin Frankreichs, stieß bei der Uraufführung in Cannes auf ein geteiltes Echo. Auch wenn die Kritiker nicht unbedingt zu Coppolas Herolden zählen: Modebewusste weibliche Teenager bewundern sie als internationale Stilikone, junge Kreative ergötzen sich an ihren schönen, mit coolen Klängen untermalten Bildern. Hinter all dem Glanz und Glamour steckt jedoch eine besonnene, selbstbewusste Filmemacherin, die nach einer durchaus schwierigen Jugend (es sei an ihre viel gescholtenen Auftritte als Darstellerin in *Der Pate – Teil III*, *The Godfather – Part III*, 1990, erinnert) mittlerweile drei Spielfilme vorgelegt hat – darunter ihr Erstling *The Virgin Suicides – Verlorene Jugend* (*The Virgin Suicides*, 1999), der von fünf frühreifen Schwestern aus Michigan erzählt, die Selbstmord begehen: ein Film, der sich durch die überzeugende Darstellung junger, in einer eigenen hermetischen Welt lebender Frauen auszeichnet. Abgesehen von Coppolas verfeinertem Geschmack für Kleidung – Milena Canonero zeichnete als Kostümbildnerin für die hinreißend herausgeputzte *Marie Antoinette* verantwortlich – setzt nicht zuletzt die Musik Akzente in ihren Filmen. Indem Coppola in *Marie Antoinette* Songs von Bow Wow Wow und der Gang of Four einsetzt, lässt sie den Geist des zeitgenössischen Punks im 18. Jahrhundert wieder lebendig werden. Auch das majestätisch dahintreibende „Just Like Honey" von The Jesus & Mary Chain, das den Abspann von *Lost in Translation* untermalt, dient dazu, dem Publikum ein Gefühl für den melancholischen Weltschmerz der Hauptfiguren zu vermitteln.

Gravure de mode ou auteur en devenir? Le débat fait rage quant à la réputation d'une scénariste et réalisatrice douée, qui se trouve être la fille de Francis Ford Coppola, et qui a grandi sur les plateaux de tournage et remporté l'oscar du meilleur scénario pour son deuxième film *Lost in Translation* (2003), lui valant d'être prise au sérieux. Sous le vernis chic se cache néanmoins une cinéaste sans complexe dont l'adolescence chaotique (on se souvient de ses débuts vilipendés dans *Le Parrain III*) a donné trois films très sensibles, consacrés à des portraits de jeunes femmes vivant dans leur bulle. Son premier opus, *The Virgin Suicides* (1999), raconte comment cinq sœurs précoces du Michigan se suicident. *Lost in Translation* est le récit d'une mélancolie mondaine où la musique joue un rôle capital. Son troisième film, une audacieuse comédie en costumes à 40 millions de dollars, *Marie-Antoinette* (2006), a connu à Cannes un succès mitigé, avec Kirsten Dunst en reine-enfant gâtée. Si les critiques laissent Sofia Coppola assez indifférente, les adolescentes à la mode ont fait d'elle l'emblème d'un style international, tandis que les jeunes gens branchés dévorent ses jolis films dont ils apprécient la musique. Outre le raffinement de ses costumes – on doit les tenues ravissantes de *Marie-Antoinette* à Milena Canonera –, la musique met particulièrement en valeur les films de la cinéaste. Elle ne recule pas devant l'anachronisme en recourant aux chansons de Gang of Four et de Bow Wow Wow, afin de souligner les échos punk qu'a aujourd'hui le XVIIIe siècle. La combustion lente de *Just Like Honey* du groupe The Jesus and Mary Chain, sert de coda à *Lost in Translation* et souligne la mélancolie sourde de ses personnages en mal de vivre.

FILMS →
1999 *The Virgin Suicides*
2003 *Lost in Translation*
2006 *Marie Antoinette*

SELECTED AWARDS →
2001 *The Virgin Suicides:* Best New Filmmaker, MTV Movie Awards
2003 *Lost in Translation:* Lina Mangiacapre Award, Venice Film Festival
2004 *Lost in Translation:* Best Original Screenplay, Academy Awards;
Best Screenplay, Golden Globes; Best Director, Best Screenplay,
Best Feature, Independent Spirit Awards
2005 *Lost in Translation:* Best Foreign Film, César Awards

Lost in Translation

"Melancholy is a topic I'm interested in more than something I deeply feel. There is indeed some form of melancholy in me, but I'm not the kind of girl who spends her afternoon looking out the window with a sad gaze."

„Melancholie ist mehr ein Motiv, für das ich mich interessiere, denn ein tief empfundenes Gefühl. Tatsächlich trage ich eine Art melancholischer Grundstimmung in mir, gehöre allerdings nicht zu jenen Frauen, die den ganzen Nachmittag damit verbringen, traurig aus dem Fenster zu schauen."

« La mélancolie est plus un sujet d'exploration qu'un sentiment que j'éprouve. Il y a de la mélancolie en moi, mais je ne passe pas des après-midi entiers à ma fenêtre, le regard triste. »

The jetlagged kindred spirits played by Bill Murray and Scarlett Johansson in Coppola's award-winning second feature navigate the frenzied, often surreal landscape of contemporary Tokyo.

Wie zwei verwandte Seelen leiden die beiden von Bill Murray und Scarlett Johansson verkörperten Figuren an einem ähnlichen Geisteszustand. Als könnten sie einen Jetlag nicht überwinden, irren sie durch die chaotische, oft surreal anmutende Stadtlandschaft des heutigen Tokio.

Perturbés par le décalage horaire, Bill Murray et Scarlett Johansson sont deux âmes sœurs qui naviguent dans le paysage frénétique et souvent surréaliste de Tokyo, dans le deuxième film, primé, de Coppola.

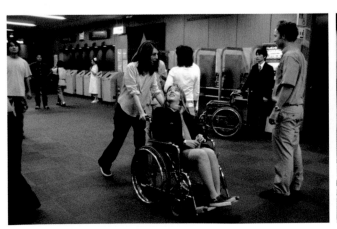

Marie Antoinette

Marie-Antoinette

For her opulent third feature, Coppola injected a punk rock spirit into the 18th-century Versailles court of Marie Antoinette, transforming a masked ball into a rebellious wonderland.

In ihrem opulenten dritten Spielfilm verpasste Coppola der im 18. Jahrhundert am Versailler Hof angesiedelten Geschichte eine Punk-Rock-Stimmung und verwandelte auf diese Weise einen Maskenball in ein rebellisches Wunderland.

Pour son troisième, et somptueux, film, Coppola a injecté une bonne dose d'esprit punk dans la cour versaillaise de Marie-Antoinette, en transformant un bal masqué en un pays des merveilles contestataire.

Much of Coppola's Marie Antoinette focuses on the quotidian ennui of the pampered Austrian queen, whose lavish court life was an impetus for the outbreak of the French Revolution.

In weiten Teilen von *Marie Antoinette* konzentriert sich Coppola auf den launischen Überdruss, den die aus Österreich stammende Königin von Frankreich, deren verschwenderische Lebensführung einer der Auslöser der Französischen Revolution war, an den Tag legte.

Le film de Coppola s'intéresse avant tout à l'ennui quotidien de la reine autrichienne dorlotée, dont la vie de luxe a contribué à déclencher la Révolution française.

Moviedom's most ambidextrous filmmaker jets back and forth between Hollywood blockbusters, like his widely admired *Harry Potter and the Prisoner of Azkaban* (2004), and smaller, character-driven works, including *And Your Mother Too* (*Y tu mamá también*, 2001), the art-house triumph starring Gael García Bernal and Diego Luna as horny teens road-tripping through rural Mexico with a sexy older woman. A student of filmmaking and philosophy who began his career in Mexican television, Cuarón's debut feature was the dark comedy *Love in the Time of Hysteria* (*Sólo con tu pareja*, 1991) about a businessman who contracts AIDS. His first foray into the English-language world, and Hollywood filmmaking, was an acclaimed adaptation of Frances Hodgson Burnett's childhood classic *A Little Princess* (1995), which helped Cuarón land his coveted Harry Potter assignment – though Cuarón's raucous depiction of racing hormones in *And Your Mother Too* was as much of an influence on the pubescent Hogwarts teens in *Harry Potter and The Prisoner of Azkaban*, a darker, more thought-provoking contribution to the successful franchise that received the best reviews of the series. Cuarón did another about-face with his subsequent feature, the circa 2027 futuristic drama *Children of Men* (2006), based on the dystopian P. D. James novel set in an infertile London where no woman has given birth in twenty years. Clive Owen starred as a revolutionary activist trying to smuggle a young pregnant woman who holds the key to the human race's survival out of a war-ravaged London. Shot vérité-style with hand-held cameras and employing long moving shots surveying harrowing scenes of violence, the visceral *Children of Men* showed an edgier side of Cuarón that earned him comparisons to Kubrick.

Im Reich des Kinos ist er der Meister des Spagats: Unentwegt düst er hin und her zwischen Hollywood-Blockbustern wie seinem weithin bewunderten Werk *Harry Potter und der Gefangene von Askaban* (*Harry Potter and the Prisoner of Azkaban*, 2004) und kleineren, von Charakterdarstellern getragenen Arbeiten wie *Y tu mamá también – Lust for Life!* (*Y tu mamá también*, 2001), einem Arthouse-Hit, in dem Gael García Bernal und Diego Luna als geile Teenager mit einer erwachsenen Traumfrau durch das ländliche Mexiko reisen. Cuarón, der Film und Philosophie studierte, begann seine Karriere beim mexikanischen Fernsehen und machte mit seinem ersten Spielfilm *Sólo con tu pareja* (1991), einer schwarzen Komödie über einen Geschäftsmann, der sich mit Aids ansteckt, auf sich aufmerksam. Sein erster Abstecher in die englischsprachige Welt und die Hollywood-Filmproduktion war *Little Princess* (*A Little Princess*, 1995), eine gefeierte Adaption von Frances Hodgson Burnetts Kinderbuchklassiker, was sich für den Mexikaner als hilfreich erwies, als er sich um den Auftrag zur Harry-Potter-Verfilmung bewarb – auch wenn die wüste Schilderung hormoneller Turbulenzen in *Y tu mamá también* die Zeichnung der pubertierenden Jugendlichen aus Hogwart in *Harry Potter und der Gefangene von Askaban* erkennbar beeinflusste. Cuaróns Harry-Potter-Version gehörte zu den dunkleren, nachdenklich stimmenden Teilen der Serie und erhielt von allen Verfilmungen der Potter-Romane die besten Kritiken. Eine neuerliche Kehrtwendung vollzog Cuarón mit seinem nächsten Spielfilm, der auf einem Roman von P. D. James basierenden Science-Fiction-Story *Children of Men* (2006), die im lebensfeindlichen London des Jahres 2027 angesiedelt ist, wo seit 20 Jahren keine Frau mehr ein Kind geboren hat. Clive Owen spielt einen revolutionären Aktivisten, der versucht, eine junge schwangere Frau, die den Schlüssel zum Überleben der menschlichen Spezies in sich trägt, aus der kriegszerstörten Stadt zu schmuggeln. Gedreht im Stil des Cinéma vérité, mit Handkameras und aufwühlend langen, die grausamen Szenerien durchwandernden Einstellungen, zeigt *Children of Men* einen extremeren Cuarón – was ihm Vergleiche mit Kubrick einbrachte.

Ce cinéaste versatile va et vient entre les superproductions hollywoodiennes, comme le très admiré *Harry Potter et le prisonnier d'Azkaban* (*Harry Potter and the Prisoner of Azkaban*, 2004), et des films plus modestes dont les personnages sont les moteurs, comme *Et ta mère aussi* (*Y tu mamá también*, 2001). Dans ce road movie qui a fait un triomphe dans les salles d'art et d'essai, des adolescents en rut (Gael García Bernal et Diego Luna) traversent le Mexique avec une séduisante femme d'âge mûr. Cuarón a étudié le cinéma et la philosophie, et débuté à la télévision mexicaine. *Uniquement avec ton partenaire* (*Sólo con tu pareja*, 1991) est une comédie noire dont le personnage principal est un homme d'affaires victime du sida. Ses débuts dans le cinéma anglophone et hollywoodien avec *La Petite Princesse* (*A Little Princess*, 1995), une adaptation réussie du roman pour enfants de Frances Hodgson Burnett, est son passeport pour la mission Harry Potter, tant convoitée. Les hormones en ébullition de *Et ta mère aussi* auront une influence importante sur les adolescents pubères de Poudlard dans *Harry Potter et le prisonnier d'Azkaban*, épisode le plus stimulant de la série à succès et le mieux accueilli par la critique. Nouvelle volte-face avec le film suivant. Situé vers 2027, *Les Fils de l'homme* (*Children of Men*, 2006), d'après le roman futuriste de P. D. James, se déroule dans une ville de Londres où aucune femme ne fait plus d'enfants depuis vingt ans. Clive Owen y incarne un militant révolutionnaire qui tente de faire sortir clandestinement de Londres une jeune femme enceinte détenant la clé de la survie de la race humaine. Filmé caméra à l'épaule dans un style documentaire, en longs plans-séquences décrivant des scènes de violence dérangeantes, cet opus révèle un aspect plus mordant de Cuarón, qui n'est pas sans rappeler Kubrick.

Children of Men

Les Fils de l'homme

"I wanted to make a film that when the final credits roll ... that's really the beginning of the film."

„Ich wollte einen Film drehen, der eigentlich erst dann beginnt, wenn der Abspann läuft."

«Je voulais tourner un film qui commence en fait quand défile le générique de fin.»

In Cuaron's dystopian vision of London circa 2027, starring Clive Owen and Julianne Moore, infertility, heightened security and armed terrorist cells combine to create a nervous police state not far removed from the present day.

In seiner dystopischen Vision Londons um das Jahr 2027 entwirft Cuarón die Atmosphäre eines nervösen Polizeistaats, in dem eine unfruchtbare Bevölkerung scharfen Sicherheitsvorkehrungen und bewaffneten Terroristenzellen ausgesetzt ist. Clive Owen und Julianne Moore gehören zu den Hauptdarstellern.

Dans le Londres futuriste de 2027 dessiné par Cuarón, avec Clive Owen et Julianne Moore, la stérilité, l'hypersécurité et les groupes terroristes armés produisent un État policier sur le qui-vive, guère éloigné de notre époque.

Clive Owen's everyman freedom fighter Theo Faron risks terrorist attacks in an effort to smuggle a lone pregnant woman to safety.

Clive Owen spielt Theo Faron, einen für Freiheit kämpfenden Durchschnittsbürger, der bei seinem Versuch, die einzige schwangere Frau in Sicherheit zu bringen, terroristischen Gefahren ausgesetzt ist.

Theo Faron (Clive Owen), résistant ordinaire, s'expose à des attaques terroristes pour mettre en sécurité une femme célibataire enceinte.

160

LUC & JEAN-PIERRE DARDENNE

Born 10 March 1954 in Awirs, Belgium and 21 April 1951 in Engis, Belgium

The Belgian social realists Luc and Jean-Pierre Dardenne fabricate simple but not simplistic human dramas examining the moral and ethical dilemmas of working-class characters scraping together a meager existence in the brothers' hometown of Liège. Critical darlings who have twice won the prestigious Palme d'Or at the Cannes Film Festival, the Dardennes started their filmmaking career in 1975 when they formed the production company Derives, which has produced more than 50 documentaries. They turned to narrative features with *La Promesse* in 1996. With each successive feature the Dardennes affirm, with the methodical grace of established professionals, why they are hailed among the most gifted filmmakers in the world. For *The Son* (*Le Fils*, 2002), the brothers employed a vérité-style camera for their story of a Belgian carpenter (Olivier Gourmet, winner of the acting prize at Cannes for his performance) who takes on an apprentice, knowing that the young man was the murderer of his own child. The furthest thing from the Dardennes' mind is retribution – by filming the proceedings over the shoulder of Gourmet's character, the technique lets the audience experience the world through the carpenter's eyes, feeling his impossible dilemma as though the spectator was in his shoes. Dispensing with the formalities of backstory, reaction shots or musical score, a typical Dardennes film often feels banal and grim – trapped in an intense present, as in their recent feature *The Child* (*L'Enfant*, 2005), about a desperate young thief (Jérémie Renier) who sells his newborn son to a smuggler for a handful of cash. What is miraculous about the brothers' body of work is how they manage with each feature to locate poetry and transcendence in otherwise miserable and pathetic lives.

Die sozialrealistischen Filme der Belgier Luc und Jean-Pierre Dardenne sind einfache, keineswegs aber simple menschliche Dramen. Sie untersuchen das moralische und ethische Dilemma von Angehörigen der Arbeiterklasse, die in Lüttich – der Stadt, in der die Brüder aufgewachsen sind – eine dürftige Existenz fristen. Von den Kritikern geliebt und bereits zweifach in Cannes mit der prestigeträchtigen Goldenen Palme ausgezeichnet, starteten die Dardennes ihre Karriere als Filmemacher 1975 mit der Gründung der Produktionsfirma Derives, die mehr als 50 Dokumentarfilme realisierte. 1996 erlangten sie mit dem Spielfilm *La Promesse – Das Versprechen* (*La Promesse*) internationale Anerkennung. Seither unterstrichen die Dardennes mit jedem weiteren Film – mit der methodischen Anmut langjähriger Profis –, warum sie zu den talentiertesten Filmemachern der Welt zählen. Für *Der Sohn* (*Le Fils*, 2002), die Geschichte eines belgischen Zimmermanns (Olivier Gourmet erhielt für seine Leistung den Darstellerpreis in Cannes), der einen Lehrling aufnimmt, obwohl er weiß, dass es sich bei diesem um den Mörder seines eigenen Kindes handelt, entschieden sich die Brüder für eine Kameraführung im Stil des Cinéma vérité. Wie sich auch an diesem Film zeigt, ist Vergeltung ein Begriff, der den Dardennes offenbar besonders fern liegt: Indem sie das Geschehen über die Schulter des Protagonisten filmen, versetzen sie den Zuschauer in die Lage, die Welt durch die Augen des Zimmermanns wahrzunehmen und dessen fürchterliches Dilemma nachzuempfinden, als wäre er an seiner Stelle. Ein typischer Dardenne-Film verzichtet weitgehend auf eine ausgearbeitete Hintergrundgeschichte, auf Gegenschnitte oder musikalische Untermalung und wirkt häufig zunächst banal und trostlos. Stattdessen fängt er intensiv dargestellte Gegenwart ein, so auch in ihrem jüngsten Film *L'Enfant* (2005), der von einem verzweifelten jungen Dieb (Jérémie Renier) erzählt, der seinen neugeborenen Sohn für eine Handvoll Bargeld an einen Schmuggler verkauft. Das Wunderbare am bislang vorliegenden Werk der Brüder ist, dass es ihnen in jedem Spielfilm gelingt, eigentlich miserablen und pathetischen Lebensverhältnissen Poesie und Transzendenz abzugewinnen.

Les drames humains des frères Dardenne, adeptes du réalisme social, sont simples, mais jamais simplistes. Ils explorent les dilemmes moraux de personnages de la classe ouvrière menant une vie de misère, dans leur ville de Liège. Chouchous de la critique, deux fois lauréats de la palme d'or, les Dardenne ont entamé leur carrière cinématographique en 1975, avec la création de leur maison de production, Dérives, où sont nés plus de cinquante documentaires. Ils se lancent dans la fiction en 1996, avec *La Promesse* (1996). Avec la grâce méthodique de professionnels chevronnés, ils confirment, dans chacun de leurs films, leur réputation de cinéastes très doués. Pour *Le Fils* (2002), les Dardenne racontent, dans le style du cinéma-vérité, l'histoire d'un menuisier belge (Olivier Gourmet, prix d'interprétation masculine à Cannes) qui embauche un apprenti, tout en sachant que le jeune homme est l'assassin de son fils. La récompense est le cadet des soucis des deux frères : en filmant cette histoire par-dessus l'épaule de Gourmet, ils cherchent à faire vivre l'impossible dilemme du menuisier comme si le spectateur était à sa place. En l'absence de tout arrière-plan narratif, de contrechamps ou de musique, un film des Dardenne peut paraître triste et banal, mais aux prises avec l'intensité du présent, c'est le cas de *L'Enfant* (2005), leur film le plus récent, dans lequel un jeune voleur aux abois (Jérémie Rénier) vend son propre enfant nouveau-né à un trafiquant contre quelques billets de banque. L'œuvre des frères Dardenne a ceci de miraculeux que dans chaque film, elle fait surgir la poésie et la transcendance d'existences par ailleurs misérables et pathétiques.

SELECTED FILMS →
1996 *La Promesse*
1999 *Rosetta*
2002 *Le Fils (The Son)*
2005 *L'Enfant (The Child)*

SELECTED AWARDS →
1999 *Rosetta:* Golden Palm, Cannes Film Festival
2005 *L'Enfant:* Golden Palm, Cannes Film Festival

L'Enfant

The Child / L'Enfant – Das Kind

"In order to film what you want to show on a face or a body, you first have to decide what you want to hide." *Jean-Pierre Dardenne*

„Wenn man mit filmischen Mitteln irgendetwas in einem Gesicht oder über einen Körper zu zeigen beabsichtigt, muss man sich zunächst einmal entscheiden, was man verbergen will." – *Jean-Pierre Dardenne*

«Pour filmer ce que l'on veut montrer sur un visage ou sur un corps, il faut d'abord savoir ce que l'on veut cacher.» – *Jean-Pierre Dardenne*

Economic desperation is a hallmark of the Dardennes' often devastating works, including their Palme d'Or-winning *The Child*, in which a young thief sells his baby to raise petty cash.

Das wirtschaftliche Elend der Protagonisten ist eine Art Markenzeichen der oft niederschmetternden Filme der Brüder Dardenne. In ihrem mit der Goldenen Palme ausgezeichneten Film *L'Enfant* verkauft ein junger Dieb sein Baby für einen lächerlichen Geldbetrag.

Le désespoir économique est le thème de prédilection des œuvres souvent implacables des frères Dardenne, notamment *L'Enfant*, dans lequel un jeune voleur vend son bébé pour quelques billets.

GUILLERMO DEL TORO

Born 9 October 1964 in Guadalajara, Mexico

In the world of the Mexican fabulist Guillermo del Toro, moody atmospherics share screen space with mournful child ghosts, killer cock-roaches, vampire-human hybrids and magical underground forest creatures sprung from the fecund imagination of this former make-up designer from Guadalajara whose first feature, the elegant chiller *Cronos* (1993), served up a gold scarab device containing an insect creature that bores into the human skin of its bearer, unleashing immortality. Del Toro's feverish concoctions, steeped in religious imagery and supernat-ural dread, are phantasmagorical entertainments that satisfy horror-fantasy purists and general moviegoers alike, most recently in del Toro's dream project *Hellboy* (2003/04), a studio-produced comic-book fantasy about a crime-fighting creature that emerges from a portal to hell, and the action-horror sequel *Blade II* (2001/02) about human vampires battling a ferocious new breed of undead predator. But it's del Toro's Span-ish-language material that makes for his most arresting work, including the melancholy ghost story *The Devil's Backbone* (*El espinazo del dia-blo*, 2001) and its more animated companion piece, *Pan's Labyrinth* (*El laberinto del fauno*, 2006), both set during the Spanish Civil War, and both featuring child protagonists confronted with the horrors of fascism under Franco. The hallucinatory animated creatures in *Pan's Labyrinth*, inhabiting a magical realm infiltrated by a lonely little girl, recall *Dark Crystal*-era Jim Henson by way of H. P. Lovecraft without resorting to an overabundance of creature effects. A real-world parallel narrative features the girl's treacherous stepfather, one of Franco's generals, hellbent on suppressing a guerrilla revolt.

In der Welt des mexikanischen Geschichtenerzählers Guillermo del Toro wimmelt es von traurigen Kindgeistern, Killerkakerlaken, vampi-risch-menschlichen Zwitterwesen und aus den Tiefen der Wälder auftauchenden Zauberwesen, die auf der Leinwand eine zumeist übellaunige Atmosphäre verbreiten. Eine blühende Fantasie bezeugte schon der erste Spielfilm des einstigen Maskenbildners aus Guadalajara, der elegan-te Thriller *Cronos* (1993), in dem ein in einem goldenen käferförmigen Apparat verborgenes Insektenwesen eine Rolle spielt, das die Haut desje-nigen anbohrt, der es in Händen hält und ihm dadurch Unsterblichkeit verleiht. Del Toros fiebrige, von religiösen Bilderwelten und übernatürlichen Bedrohungen durchdrungene Kreationen sind phantasmagorische Unterhaltung, die gleichermaßen Horror-Fantasy-Puristen wie normale Kino-besucher zufriedenstellt. Das gilt auch für seine jüngsten Werke, das Wunschprojekt *Hellboy* (2003/04), eine auf einem Fantasy-Comic basieren-de Studioproduktion um ein durch ein Höllentor gekommenes Wesen, das gegen das Verbrechen antritt, oder die Action-Horror-Fortsetzung *Blade II* (2001/02), in der menschliche Vampire eine grimmige Rasse untoter Raubtiere bekämpfen. Am eindrucksvollsten jedoch sind del Toros spanischsprachige Produktionen, darunter die melancholische Geistergeschichte *The Devil's Backbone – Das Rückgrat des Teufels* (*El espina-zo del diablo*, 2001) und ihr lebhafteres Gegenstück *Pans Labyrinth* (*El laberinto del fauno*, 2006). Beide sind in der Zeit des Spanischen Bürger-kriegs angesiedelt, und in beiden spielt ein Kind die Hauptrolle, das mit den Schrecken des Franco-Faschismus konfrontiert wird. Die halluzina-torisch belebten Wesen, die in *Pans Labyrinth* die Fantasiewelt eines einsamen Mädchens bevölkern, lassen – ohne dass sich del Toro einem Übermaß an Effekten hingeben würde – an einen H.-P.-Lovecraft-erprobten Jim Henson aus der Entstehungszeit von *Der dunkle Kristall* (*The Dark Crystal*, 1982) denken. In der parallel dargestellten wirklichen Welt ist das Mädchen ihrem tückischen Stiefvater ausgesetzt, einem General Francos, der die Aufständischen gnadenlos unterdrückt.

Dans le monde du fabuliste Guillermo del Toro, la météorologie changeante partage l'écran avec des fantômes d'enfants mélancoliques, des cafards tueurs, des hybrides d'humains et de vampires, des créatures magiques habitant des forêts souterraines. Cet ancien maquilleur a l'imagination féconde. Dans *Cronos* (1993), élégant film d'épouvante, un écrin d'or en forme de scarabée contient un insecte qui fore la peau de celui ou celle qui le porte et y injecte l'immortalité. Ancrées dans l'imagerie religieuse et la peur du surnaturel, les créations de del Toro sont des spectacles fantasmagoriques qui font le plaisir autant des puristes du film d'horreur que du grand public. Tourné en studio, *Hellboy* (2003/04) raconte, sur le mode de la BD, comment un justicier surgit d'un portail qui mène en enfer, tandis que dans le film d'horreur et d'action *Blade II* (2001/02), des vampires humains se battent contre une nouvelle race de prédateurs ayant échappé à la mort. Ses œuvres les plus captivantes sont celles tournées en espagnol, dont l'histoire de fantômes mélancoliques *L'Échine du diable* (*El espinazo del diablo*, 2001) et son pendant, plus animé, *Le Labyrinthe de Pan* (*El laberinto del fauno*, 2006) ; l'un et l'autre se déroulent pendant la guerre d'Espagne et mettent en scène des enfants face aux horreurs du fascisme franquiste. Les créatures hallucinatoires du *Labyrinthe de Pan*, qui habitent un univers magique où s'immisce une petite fille solitaire, rappellent le Jim Henson de *Dark Crystal*, mâtiné de H. P. Lovecraft, sans excès d'effets spéciaux. Dans une intrigue parallèle située dans le monde réel, le beau-père fourbe de la petite fille, et général franquiste, s'obstine à écraser une révolte.

FILMS →
1993 *Cronos* **1997** *Mimic* **2001** *El espinazo del diablo (The Devil's Backbone)* **2001/02** *Blade II* **2003/04** *Hellboy* **2006** *El laberinto del fauno (Pan's Labyrinth)*

SELECTED AWARDS →
1993 *Cronos:* Mercedes-Benz Award, Cannes Film Festival; Golden Ariel (Best Picture), Silver Ariel (Best Director, Best First Film, Best Original Story, Best Screenplay), Ariel Awards **2007** *El laberinto del fauno:* Silver Ariel (Best Director), Ariel Awards; BAFTA Film Award, Best Film not in the English Language, BAFTA Awards

Hellboy

"When you have the intuition that there is something which is there, but out of the reach of your physical world, art and religion are the only means to get to it."

„Wenn du das intuitive Gefühl hast, dass da irgendetwas ist, jedoch außerhalb der Reichweite deiner physischen Welt, dann sind Kunst und Religion die einzigen Mittel, sich diesem Etwas zu nähern."

«Quand on a l'intuition qu'il y a quelque chose quelque part, mais hors d'atteinte de votre monde physique, l'art et la religion sont les seuls moyens d'y parvenir.»

Featuring sumptuous production design and copious visual effects, del Toro's fifth feature doesn't neglect the human factor, as illustrated by Selma Blair's Liz Sherman and Ron Perelman's Hellboy.

In del Toros fünftem Spielfilm kommt der menschliche Aspekt, wie er von Selma Blair als Liz Sherman und Ron Perlman als Hellboy verkörpert wird, trotz üppiger Ausstattung und unzähligen visuellen Effekten nicht zu kurz.

Décors somptueux et abondance d'effets visuels caractérisent le cinquième film de del Toro qui ne néglige pas le facteur humain, comme le montrent les personnages de Liz Sherman (Selma Blair) et Hellboy (Ron Perlman).

Ron Perelman, under heavy makeup and prosthetics, is transformed into the benevolent demon known as Hellboy, rescued from the Nazis and raised to battle the forces of darkness.

Mit kräftigem Make-up und maskenbildnerischen Elementen wird Ron Perlman in den gutartigen Dämon Hellboy verwandelt. Hellboy war vor den Nazis gerettet worden und ist geschult, die Mächte der Finsternis zu bekämpfen.

Arborant un impressionnant maquillage, Ron Perlman devient Hellboy, démon bienveillant sauvé des nazis et éduqué pour combattre les forces des ténèbres.

El laberinto del fauno

Pan's Labyrinth / Pans Labyrinth / Le Labyrinthe de Pan

Del Toro's most acclaimed feature to date stars Ivana Baquero as Ofelia, a young girl enduring life under Franco who escapes into a vivid imaginary world rife with fantastic creatures.

In del Toros bislang erfolgreichstem Film spielt Ivana Baquero das Mädchen Ofelia, das die Schrecken des Franco-Regimes erleben muss und sich in eine Fantasiewelt voller wundersamer Geschöpfe flüchtet.

Dans le film le plus apprécié de del Toro à ce jour, la jeune Ofélia (Ivana Baquero) quitte le quotidien du franquisme en s'échappant dans un monde imaginaire, riche de créatures fantastiques.

MARK DORNFORD-MAY

Born 29 May 1955 in Swinefleet, UK

The Christ parable has resulted in many different cinematic permutations of the man or myth that preached a gospel of compassion and forgiveness more than 2,000 years ago. *Son of Man* (2006), the rousing new film from the theater director Mark Dornford-May and his South African-based Dimpho Di Kopane performance troupe, recreates familiar biblical tropes in a teeming modern-day shantytown ruled by an oppressive military regime gunning down piles of children inside classrooms and executing dissenters in an effort to keep democracy out of the townships. Amid this horrific violence, a young woman receives a visit by the angel Gabriel, delivering a prophecy that she will give birth to the Son of God. Her child is raised amid township bloodshed, amassing adherents for his benevolent message of non-violence and forgiveness. But military goons catch wind of his peaceful admonitions and the young messiah is slain and buried in an unmarked grave. His mother exhumes the corpse, crucifying her son. Dimpho Di Kopane roughly translates to "combined talents" and *Son of Man* is a group effort unlike anything in the film world today. It was formed several years ago, after Dornford-May and his musical director, Charles Hazlewood, mounted successful theater productions at the Queen's Theatre in London, starring South African performers reinterpreting classic European stories through regional dance and song. The troupe went on to play theater festivals the world over before achieving cinematic success at the 2005 Berlin Film Festival, where *U-Carmen e-Khayelitsha* (2004), a vibrant retelling of Bizet's *Carmen*, set in the same South African shantytown where *Son of Man* was filmed, became the surprise winner of the Golden Bear for best feature film.

Das Gleichnis über Christus hat die unterschiedlichsten filmischen Wandlungen jenes Mannes oder Mythos hervorgebracht, der vor mehr als 2000 Jahren ein Evangelium des Mitgefühls und der Vergebung predigte. *Son of Man* (2006), der mitreißende neue Film des Theaterregisseurs Mark Dornford-May und seiner in Südafrika beheimateten Schauspieltruppe Dimpho Di Kopane, lässt vertraute biblische Tropen in einer dicht bevölkerten Elendssiedlung unserer Tage wiederauferstehen. Hier herrscht ein brutales Militärregime, das ganze Kindergruppen in Klassenräumen niederschießt und Andersdenkende exekutiert, um jede Bestrebung nach Demokratie zunichte zu machen. In dieser von grausamer Gewalt geprägten Welt erscheint einer jungen Frau der Engel Gabriel und verkündet ihr, sie werde Gottes Sohn gebären. Das Kind wächst mitten im Blutvergießen der Townships auf und versammelt Anhänger um sich, die seine Botschaft von Gewaltverzicht und Vergebung teilen. Als die Häscher des Regimes davon Wind bekommen, ermorden sie den jungen Messias und verscharren ihn in einem nicht gekennzeichneten Grab. Die Mutter jedoch exhumiert den Leib ihres Sohnes und kreuzigt ihn. Dimpho Di Kopane lässt sich mit „Vereinte Talente" übersetzen, und tatsächlich ist *Son of Man*, wie kaum Vergleichbares im zeitgenössischen Kino, das Werk eines Kollektivs. Es wurde vor einigen Jahren gegründet, nachdem Dornford-May und sein musikalischer Direktor, Charles Hazlewood, am Londoner Queens Theater mit Theaterproduktionen Erfolg hatten, in denen südafrikanische Darsteller klassische europäische Geschichten mit ihren landestypischen Tänzen und Gesängen neu interpretierten. In der Folge trat die Truppe auf Theaterfestivals in der ganzen Welt auf, bevor sie mit einem Filmprojekt erfolgreich war: Bei den Berliner Filmfestspielen 2005 erhielt *U-Carmen* (*U-Carmen e-Khayelitsha*, 2004), eine pulsierende Version von Bizets *Carmen*, die im gleichen südafrikanischen Elendsviertel angesiedelt ist wie *Son of Man*, als Überraschungssieger den Goldenen Bären für den besten Spielfilm.

Nombreuses sont les adaptations cinématographiques de l'homme, ou du mythe, qui prêche un évangile de compassion et de pardon depuis plus de 2000 ans. Film passionnant du metteur en scène Mark Dornford-May et de sa troupe sud-africaine Dimpho Di Kopane, *Son of Man* (2006) transpose les tropes bibliques dans un bidonville contemporain surpeuplé, dominé par un régime militaire répressif qui abat les enfants dans leurs écoles et exécute les opposants, afin d'empêcher la démocratie de gagner les ghettos. Dans cet univers de violence, l'ange Gabriel visite une jeune femme et lui annonce qu'elle va mettre au monde le fils de Dieu. L'enfant grandit pris dans les carnages du ghetto bientôt suivi par des disciples qui adhèrent à son message de non-violence et de pardon. La soldatesque a vent de ses paroles de paix assassiné, le jeune messie est enterré dans une tombe anonyme. Sa mère exhume son corps et crucifie son fils. L'entreprise de Dimpho Di Kopane («talents associés») est sans équivalent dans le cinéma d'aujourd'hui. La troupe est née il y a quelques années, à la suite de la mise en scène, par Dornford-May et son directeur musical Charles Hazlewood, de pièces classiques européennes, revisitées avec succès au Queen's Theater de Londres par des comédiens sud-africains s'inspirant de leurs danses et de leur chants régionaux. Après une tournée mondiale, la troupe connaît le succès au Festival de Berlin avec *Carmen* (*U-Carmen e-Khayelitsha*, 2004), adaptation vivante de l'œuvre de Bizet tournée dans le bidonville qui avait servi de décor à *Son of Man*. En 2005, contre toute attente, l'ours d'or lui a été attribué.

FILMS →
2004 *U-Carmen e-Khayelitsha*
2006 *Son of Man*

SELECTED AWARDS →
2005 *U-Carmen e-Khayelitsha*: Golden Bear,
Berlin International Film Festival

U-Carmen e-Khayelitsha

U-Carmen / Carmen

Employing the local denizens of a South African township, Dornford-May and his Dimpho Di Kopane theatre company revitalize Georges Bizet's *Carmen*; cigarette factory worker Pauline Malefane stars as the titular Carmen.

Dornford-May haucht Georges Bizets „Carmen" (1873/74) mit seinem Ensemble Dimpho Di Kopane, einer Theatertruppe aus Bewohnern eines südafrikanischen Township, neues Leben ein. Pauline Malefane, Arbeiterin in einer Zigarettenfabrik, verkörpert die Titelheldin.

Avec le concours des habitants d'un ghetto sud-africain, Dornford-May et sa troupe théâtrale Dimpho Di Kopane remettent la Carmen de Bizet au goût du jour. Ouvrière d'une manufacture de tabac, Pauline Malefane joue le rôle-titre.

Son of Man

Dornford-May and Dimpho Di Kopane turn to the
Christ parable, conjoining biblical imagery and
contemporary South African politics.

Mit diesem Projekt wandten sich Dornford-May
und Dimpho Di Kopane der Geschichte von Jesus
Christus zu. Dabei verknüpften sie biblische Bilderwelten mit politischen Ereignissen aus der jüngsten
Vergangenheit Südafrikas.

Dornford-May et Dimpho Di Kopane associent
imagerie biblique et politique sud-africaine
contemporaine pour faire le récit de la parabole
du Christ.

"Filmmaking is like playmaking only you get more fresh air."

„Filmemachen ist wie Theaterinszenieren, nur dass man öfter an der frischen Luft ist."

« Le cinéma, c'est comme le théâtre, avec plus d'air frais. »

Featuring a cast of hundreds, many culled from local townships, *Son of Man* also makes use of the natural beauty of South Africa to add atmosphere to its potent blend.

Neben Hunderten von Mitwirkenden – darunter viele Darsteller, die unter den Bewohnern der örtlichen Townships ausgewählt wurden – nutzt der Regisseur für *Son of Man* auch die Schönheit der südafrikanischen Natur, um seinem aussagekräftigen Werk die entsprechende Atmosphäre zu verschaffen.

Des centaines de figurants, recrutés dans les quartiers noirs, et les splendides décors naturels de l'Afrique du Sud créent une ambiance convaincante dans *Son of Man*.

BRUNO DUMONT

Born 14 March 1958 in Bailleul, France

The philosopher-turned-filmmaker Bruno Dumont specializes in a despairing view of humanity in which simple country people – typically played by stone-faced, non-professional actors plucked from rural anonymity à la Bresson – disrupt the boredom of their lives with casual sexual couplings that verge on the animalistic. But rather than exploit these unsophisticated souls, as Dumont was accused of doing after the two leads of his miraculous second feature Humanité (L'Humanité, 1999) won the acting prize at Cannes Film Festival in 1999, he infuses his characters with unexpected grace and compassion, even when they are confronted with the grimmer aspects of the human condition. Humanité – his masterpiece – was a metaphysical detective yarn about the seemingly autistic provincial detective Pharaon de Winter (Emmanuel Schotté) who pines for his 23-year-old neighbor (Séverine Caneele) while investigating the brutal murder of a young girl. Shot in widescreen and featuring painterly long shots and close-ups, it was one of the finest French films of recent years. His third feature, the English-language road movie and self-described experimental horror film Twentynine Palms (2003) was widely loathed for its sadistic dénouement filmed in widescreen in the unforgiving desert surrounding Joshua Tree National Park. For Flandres (2006), Dumont won the Grand Jury Prize at Cannes for the second time, drawing raves for his naturalistic portrait of a randy farm girl in love with two men from her village who get drafted and sent off to fight in an unnamed war in the Middle East. Like his debut feature The Life of Jesus (La Vie de Jésus, 1997), Flandres addressed boredom and anomie in rural France with minimal dialogue, broadening Dumont's palette to include the senselessness of the modern war machine.

Der zum Filmemacher avancierte Philosoph Bruno Dumont blickt mit einer gewissen Hoffnungslosigkeit auf die Menschheit. Die Charaktere seiner Filme – einfache Leute vom Land, in der Regel mit versteinerten Mienen von Laien verkörpert, die sich der Regisseur im Stil Bressons aus anonymen Gesichtern der Provinz herausgepickt hat – brechen die Ödnis ihres Daseins mit sexuellen Zufallsbegegnungen auf, die das Tierische des Triebs andeuten. Dumont jedoch beutet jene schlichten Gemüter nicht aus – das wurde ihm vorgeworfen, nachdem die beiden Hauptakteure seines wundervollen zweiten Spielfilms Humanität (L'Humanité, 1999) auf dem Filmfestival von Cannes 1999 den Darstellerpreis gewonnen hatten –, vielmehr stattet er seine Figuren, selbst wenn er sie mit düsteren Aspekten menschlichen Daseins konfrontiert, mit überraschender Anmut und Mitgefühl aus. Dumonts Meisterwerk L'Humanité ist eine metaphysische Kriminalgeschichte über den scheinbar autistischen Provinzpolizisten Pharaon de Winter (Emmanuel Schotté), der sich, während er in einem brutalen Mordfall an einem Mädchen ermittelt, nach seiner 23-jährigen Nachbarin (Séverine Caneele) verzehrt. Der im Breitwandformat inszenierte Film mit seinen malerischen Totalen und Nahaufnahmen zählt zum Besten, was das französische Kino in den vergangenen Jahren hervorgebracht hat. Dumonts dritter Spielfilm, das englischsprachige, in der erbarmungslosen Wüstenlandschaft des Joshua Tree National Parks in Cinemascope gedrehte Roadmovie Twentynine Palms (2003), vom Regisseur selbst als experimenteller Horrorfilm bezeichnet, stieß wegen seines sadistischen Ausgangs auf weitgehende Ablehnung. Für Flandres (2006) wurde Dumont in Cannes zum zweiten Mal mit dem Großen Preis der Jury ausgezeichnet. In diesem naturalistischen Porträt eines lüsternen Mädchens vom Lande, das zwei Männer aus ihrem Dorf liebt, die eingezogen werden, um im Nahen Osten in einem nicht näher bezeichneten Krieg zu kämpfen, zeigt die Protagonistin Anzeichen beginnenden Wahnsinns. Wie in seinem Erstling Das Leben Jesu (La Vie de Jésus, 1997) lässt Dumont auch hier mit minimalen Dialogen Langeweile und Anomie im ländlichen Frankreich anklingen, bezieht nun aber darüber hinaus das sinnlose Wüten der modernen Kriegsmaschinerie mit ein.

Philosophe devenu cinéaste, Bruno Dumont propose dans ses films une vision désespérée de l'humanité, où des ruraux simples – interprétés par des acteurs amateurs au visage inexpressif, extrait de l'anonymat à la manière de Bresson – rompent l'ennui de leur existence par des copulations quasi animales. Mais, au lieu d'exploiter ces âmes simples – reproche qui lui a été adressé après le prix d'interprétation remporté à Cannes par les deux acteurs du miraculeux L'Humanité (1999) –, Dumont insuffle à ses personnages une grâce et une compassion inattendues, même lorsqu'ils sont confrontés aux aspects les plus sombres de la condition humaine. Dans le film policier métaphysique qu'est L'Humanité, son chef-d'œuvre, Pharaon de Winter (Emmanuel Schotté), détective de province vaguement autiste, tombe amoureux de sa voisine de 23 ans (Séverine Caneele) en enquêtant sur le meurtre brutal d'une jeune femme. Les plans d'ensemble et les gros plans très composés, en format large, font de ce film l'un des plus réussis de ces dernières années. Son troisième film, Twentynine Palms (2003), est un road movie en anglais et, selon son auteur, un film d'horreur expérimental. La critique l'a honni en raison de son dénouement sadique filmé en cinémascope dans le désert inhospitalier californien, voisin du parc national de Joshua Tree. Dumont remporte le prix du jury cannois pour la deuxième fois avec Flandres en 2006, grâce à son portrait naturaliste, très apprécié, d'une fille de ferme portée sur le sexe, amoureuse de deux hommes de son village enrôlés pour se battre dans une guerre non identifiée au Moyen-Orient. Comme dans son premier film La Vie de Jésus (1997), Flandres dépeint, avec des dialogues minimalistes, l'ennui et l'anomie de la France rurale, évoquant aussi l'absurdité de la machine de guerre moderne.

FILMS →
1997 La Vie de Jésus (The Life of Jesus)
1999 L'Humanité (Humanité)
2003 Twentynine Palms
2006 Flandres

SELECTED AWARDS →
1997 La Vie de Jésus: Golden Camera – Special Mention, Cannes Film Festival; FIPRESCI Prize, Chicago International Film Festival; European Discovery of the Year Award, European Film Awards; Prix Jean Vigo **1999** L'Humanité: Grand Prize of the Jury, Cannes Film Festival **2006** Flandres: Grand Prize of the Jury, Cannes Film Festival

La Vie de Jésus

The Life of Jesus / Das Leben Jesu

"In film, you don't see the mise-en-scène; it is what constitutes
the story itself. As long as something remains visible, the story has not
yet come to an end and continues to develop until it evaporates.
All that counts are the story and its characters, without any commentary.
The complexity of the means used to achieve this must melt into this
unity. It takes hard work to create this degree of simplicity …
film is therefore not a means of expression."

„Im Film sieht man die Inszenierung nicht, sie ist konstitutiv für die Geschichte selbst. Solange etwas sichtbar bleibt,
ist die Geschichte noch nicht an ihrem Ende angelangt und entwickelt sich bis zu ihrer Verflüchtigung weiter. Einzig die Geschichte
und ihre Figuren zählen, ohne jegliche Kommentierung. Alle aufgewandten Mittel müssen in ihrer ganzen Komplexität in dieser Einheit
verschmelzen. Eine solche Einfachheit herzustellen ist harte Arbeit … Film ist also kein Ausdrucksmittel."

«La mise en scène au cinéma ne se voit pas, elle est constitutive de l'histoire elle-même. Visible, c'est qu'elle n'est pas
arrivée jusqu'au bout et elle se travaille tant qu'elle n'a pas disparu. Seule l'histoire et ses personnages valent, sans autres commentaires.
Toute la complexité des moyens mis en œuvre doit se fondre dans cette unité : il faut beaucoup travailler pour atteindre cette simplicité…
Le cinéma n'est donc pas un moyen d'expression.»

Bruno Dumont's debut feature examines the boredom and lethargy of youth in a small northern French village, where the epileptic protagonist Freddy (David Douche) grapples with sex, young love, racism and mopeds.

In seinem ersten Spielfilm thematisiert Bruno Dumont Langeweile und Lethargie von Jugendlichen, die in einem kleinen nordfranzösischen Ort aufwachsen. Der epileptische Protagonist Freddy (David Douche) muss sich dabei mit einer Welt auseinandersetzen, die um Sex, Jugendlieben, Rassismus und Mopeds kreist.

Le premier film de Bruno Dumont s'intéresse à l'ennui et à la léthargie des jeunes d'un petit village du Nord de la France. Freddy (David Douche), épileptique, y est confronté au sexe, à l'amour naissant, au racisme et aux mobylettes.

L'Humanité

Humanité / Humanität

Filmed in CinemaScope, Dumont's controversial, award-winning *Humanity* starred non-professional actor Emmanuel Schotté as a police detective investigating the rape and murder of a young girl.

In Dumonts in Cinemascope gedrehtem, preisgekröntem, aber kontrovers diskutiertem Film *Humanität* spielt der Laiendarsteller Emmanuel Schotté einen Polizeiermittler, der den Mord an einem vergewaltigten Mädchen aufklären soll.

Tourné en cinémascope, *L'Humanité* a suscité la controverse et récolté des récompenses. Comédien amateur, Emmanuel Schotte y joue un inspecteur de police enquêtant sur le viol et le meurtre d'une jeune fille.

Twentynine Palms

This minimalist horror film starred David Wissack and Katia Golubeva as a combative, sexually charged young couple traveling by Hummer through Joshua Tree National Park, where they encounter sadistic mayhem.

In diesem minimalistischen Horrorfilm spielen David Wissak und Katia Golubeva ein streitlustiges junges Paar. Die beiden, zwischen denen sich immer wieder auch sexuelle Spannung aufbaut, kurven in einem Hummer-Geländewagen durch den JoshuaTree-Nationalpark, eine Fahrt, die in einem sadistischen Chaos endet.

Dans ce film d'horreur minimaliste, David Wissack et Katia Golubeva interprètent un jeune couple combatif et sexuellement très actif. À bord d'un 4 x 4, ils traversent le parc national de Joshua Tree où ils seront confrontés à la violence sadique.

Flandres

The visceral horrors of an unnamed distant war share screen space with the idyllic sexual couplings of rural French countryfolk in Dumont's animalistic fourth feature *Flandres*, a winner at Cannes.

In Dumonts animalistischem vierten Spielfilm *Flandres*, in Cannes mit dem Großen Preis der Jury ausgezeichnet, wechseln sich Bilder von Grausamkeiten aus einem fernen, nie bezeichneten Krieg mit idyllischen Szenerien ab, in denen sich Pärchen in einem ländlichen Frankreich sexuellen Vergnügungen hingeben.

Dans *Flandres*, quatrième film très « animal » de Dumont, récompensé à Cannes, l'horreur absolue d'une guerre lointaine et anonyme se superpose aux accouplements idylliques d'habitants de la France profonde.

ATOM EGOYAN

Born 19 July 1960 in Cairo, Egypt

Cairo-born of Armenian descent, Canada's Atom Egoyan graduated from arcane, homegrown independent films about distorted reality to a trio of densely woven, exquisitely crafted literary adaptations, pausing along the way to write, direct and produce an epic drama about the Armenian genocide in Turkey prior to World War I that was a distillation of all Egoyan's themes as well as his most personal film to date. *Ararat* (2002), starring his wife, Arsinée Khanjian, and a slew of Armenian actors, including Charles Aznavour and Eric Bogosian, functioned best as a historical memory piece framed by three intersecting stories, one of which involved the making of an epic film about the Armenian genocide in which the director (like Egoyan himself) is confronted with how best to represent a historical fact that has been repeatedly denied by the Turk establishment. Egoyan's finest and most lauded film was *The Sweet Hereafter* (1997), an adaptation of Russell Banks' novel about a small Canadian town coping with unimaginable grief in the wake of a bus accident that leaves fourteen children dead and the guilt-ridden lawyer (Ian Holm, in an astounding performance) who tries to rally the close-knit community around a class-action lawsuit. Following the psychodrama *Felicia's Journey* (1999), Egoyan's third literary adaptation and most recent feature was *Where the Truth Lies* (2005), an intricately twisted noir based on the Rupert Holmes novel that starred Kevin Bacon and Colin Firth as 1950s Hollywood entertainers embroiled in the murder of a young journalist.

Nach seinen Anfängen mit obskuren, selbst produzierten Independent-Filmen über gefälschte Wirklichkeit tat sich Atom Egoyan, in Kairo geborener kanadischer Regisseur armenischer Herkunft, mit drei dicht erzählten, handwerklich vorzüglich umgesetzten literarischen Adaptionen hervor. Dazwischen inszenierte und produzierte er ein episches Drama über den Genozid der Türken an den Armeniern während des Ersten Weltkriegs, das sämtliche seiner Themen zusammenfasst und zugleich als Egoyans bislang persönlichster Film betrachtet werden kann: *Ararat* (2002), in dem seine Frau Arsinée Khanjian und andere Schauspieler armenischer Abstammung – darunter Charles Aznavour und Eric Bogosian – mitwirkten, gliedert den Stoff sinnvollerweise als ein historisches Erinnerungsstück, das von drei sich kreuzenden Geschichten zusammengehalten wird. In einer der Episoden wird ein Regisseur, der (wie Egoyan selbst) einen epischen Film über den Völkermord drehen soll, mit dem Problem konfrontiert, wie man historische Fakten, die von türkischer Seite bis heute immer wieder geleugnet werden, darstellen soll. Egoyans schönster und meistgepriesener Film *Das süße Jenseits* (*The Sweet Hereafter*, 1997) – die Adaption eines Romans von Russell Banks – spielt in einer kanadischen Kleinstadt, deren Bewohner mit ihrer Trauer um 14 Schulkinder fertig werden müssen, die bei einem Busunglück ums Leben gekommen sind. Ein von Schuldgefühlen geplagter Anwalt (Ian Holm bietet eine erstaunliche Performance) versucht, die eng miteinander verbundenen Betroffenen zu einer Sammelklage zu bewegen. Nach dem Psychodrama *Felicia, mein Engel* (*Felicia's Journey*, 1999) folgte mit seinem jüngsten Spielfilm *Wahre Lügen* (*Where the Truth Lies,* 2005) Egoyans dritte literarische Adaption: ein verwickelter, auf dem Roman von Rupert Holmes basierender Film noir, in dem Kevin Bacon und Colin Firth als Hollywood-Entertainer der 1950er-Jahre in den ungeklärten Mord an einer jungen Frau verwickelt sind.

D'origine arménienne, le Canadien Atom Egoyan est passé d'un cinéma indépendant, très personnel et obscur, à une trilogie d'adaptations littéraires, denses et raffinées. Entre ces deux pôles, il a écrit, réalisé et produit une épopée consacrée au génocide arménien en Turquie, à la veille de la Première Guerre mondiale : Egoyan réunit ses thèmes favoris dans *Ararat* (2002), son film le plus personnel, interprété par son épouse, Arsinée Khanjian, et une pléiade d'acteurs arméniens, dont Charles Aznavour et Éric Bogosian. Cette œuvre sur la mémoire historique est composée de trois histoires qui s'enchevêtrent, l'une d'elles étant la réalisation d'un film épique sur le génocide arménien, dans laquelle le metteur en scène (à l'instar d'Egoyan) se demande comment représenter un fait historique constamment nié par les Turcs qui l'ont perpétré. Le film le plus réussi et le mieux accueilli est *De beaux lendemains* (*The Sweet Hereafter*, 1997), d'après le roman de Russell Banks : une petite ville canadienne tente de surmonter le chagrin incommensurable provoqué par la mort de 14 enfants dans un accident de car. Un avocat rongé par la culpabilité (le stupéfiant Ian Holm) veut rallier la population, très unie, en vue d'une action collective en justice. Après le psychodrame du *Voyage d'Alicia* (*Felicia's Journey*, 1999), la troisième adaptation d'Egoyan est *La Vérité nue* (*Where the Truth Lies*, 2005), son film le plus récent. Dans ce film noir très complexe, d'après le roman de Rupert Holmes, Kevin Bacon et Colin Firth sont des acteurs hollywoodiens mêlés au meurtre d'une jeune journaliste.

FILMS →
1984 *Next of Kin* **1987** *Family Viewing*
1989 *Speaking Parts* **1991** *The Adjuster*
1993 *Calendar* **1994** *Exotica* **1997** *The Sweet Hereafter* **1999** *Felicia's Journey* **2002** *Ararat*
2005 *Where the Truth Lies*

SELECTED AWARDS →
1988 *Family Viewing:* Prize of the Ecumenical Jury, Locarno International Film Festival; Interfilm Award – Honorable Mention, Forum of New Cinema, Berlin International Film Festival **1994** *Exotica:* FIPRESCI Prize, Cannes Film Festival **1997** *The Sweet Hereafter:* Grand Prize of the Jury, FIPRESCI Prize, Prize of the Ecumenical Jury, Cannes Film Festival; Best Motion Picture, Best Achievement in Direction, Genie Awards **1998** *The Sweet Hereafter:* Best Foreign Film, Independent Spirit Awards, **2000** *Felicia's Journey:* Best Screenplay, Genie Awards **2003** *Ararat:* Best Motion Picture, Genie Awards

The Sweet Hereafter

Das süße Jenseits / De beaux lendemains

A small Canadian community grapples with the loss of fourteen children in a school bus accident in Egoyan's breakthrough feature, starring Ian Holm as a lawyer fleeing his personal demons.

In diesem Film, mit dem Egoyan seinen Durchbruch feierte, müssen die Bewohner einer kanadischen Kleinstadt mit dem Tod von 14 Kindern fertig werden, die mit einem Schulbus verunglückt sind. Ian Holm spielt einen Anwalt, der vor seinen ganz persönlichen Dämonen davonläuft.

Une petite ville canadienne est frappée par la perte de 14 enfants dans l'accident d'un car scolaire. Tel est le sujet du film qui a révélé Egoyan, avec Ian Holm dans le rôle d'un avocat fuyant ses propres démons.

Ararat

Egoyan mines the personal and the political in this movie-within-a-movie, which documents the making of a historical epic about the Armenian genocide.

In diesem selbstreflexiven Film – er handelt von den Arbeiten an einer Dokumentation über den Völkermord an den Armeniern – setzt sich Egoyan sowohl mit persönlichen Erfahrungen als auch mit politischen Aspekten auseinander.

Egoyan sonde les univers individuels et politiques dans ce film construit en abyme, consacré au tournage d'une épopée historique autour du génocide arménien.

Where the Truth Lies

Wahre Lügen / La Vérité nue

"I think with all directors there are ideas that recur, at least for the ones that have creative control of their films."

„Ich glaube, alle Regisseure haben gewisse Ideen, die in ihren Filmen wiederkehren. Zumindest diejenigen, die die kreative Kontrolle über ihre Filme ausüben."

«Je crois que tous les réalisateurs ont des idées récurrentes, au moins ceux qui peuvent maîtriser leurs films de bout en bout.»

Kevin Bacon and Colin Firth are showbiz legends investigated by journalist Alison Lohman in this film noir, which alternates between the present day and 1950s Hollywood.

In diesem Film noir, der abwechselnd im Hollywood von heute und dem der 1950er-Jahre spielt, verkörpern Kevin Bacon und Colin Firth zwei Legenden des Showbusiness. Die Journalistin Karen (Alison Lohman) stellt Nachforschungen über einen dunklen Fleck in der Vergangenheit der beiden an.

Une journaliste (Alison Lohman) enquête sur deux légendes du show-business (Kevin Bacon et Colin Firth) dans ce film noir situé tantôt dans le Hollywood des années 1950 tantôt aujourd'hui.

ALEJANDRO GONZÁLEZ IÑÁRRITU

Born 15 August 1963 in Mexico City, Mexico

The Mexican director of a trilogy of films whose separate installments employ interwoven narrative strands as a social equalizer began his career as a radio DJ, entertaining listeners of all social castes for several hours a day in the wildly stratified Mexico City of his birth. A second career in commercials and music videos resulted in his debut feature, *Love's a Bitch* (*Amores perros*, 2000), a triptych of distinct yet loosely related stories, based on a screenplay by Guillermo Arriaga that featured characters from different social strata united by a single car accident – not to mention the presence of dogs in every story. Employing the same strategy for his second feature, *21 Grams* (2003), a story of tragedy and redemption set in an unnamed American city starring Sean Penn, Naomi Watts and Benicio Del Toro, González Iñárritu twisted narrative conventions even further by telling his story out of chronology. His latest feature *Babel* (2006), starring Brad Pitt, Cate Blanchett and Gael García Bernal, relocates the triptych structure to the world stage, in a conjoined saga played out on three continents in several languages, united by a shooting incident involving American tourists in Morocco that gets misperceived as a terrorist act. Reverberations course through parallel stories set at the US/Mexico border and in Tokyo. Featuring the gritty, washed-out cinematography of Rodrigo Prieto that made González Iñárritu's first two features so visually arresting, *Babel* examines fearmongering and how miscommunication and misunderstanding persist across geographical borders and cloud levels of perception.

Der mexikanische Regisseur einer Trilogie von Filmen, in deren einzelnen Teilen die miteinander verwobenen Erzählstränge ein breites gesellschaftliches Spektrum abdecken, begann seine Karriere als DJ beim Radio. Im Verlauf der Sendungen unterhielt er täglich stundenlang Hörer aller sozialen Schichten seiner spannungsreich zusammengesetzten Heimat Mexiko-Stadt. Über die Produktion von Werbespots und Musikvideos kam er zu seinem ersten Spielfilm *Amores perros* (2000), einem Triptychon getrennt spielender, jedoch locker miteinander verbundener Episoden. Der auf einem Drehbuch von Guillermo Arriaga basierende Film schildert die Schicksale von Vertretern verschiedener sozialer Schichten, die alle auf irgendeine Weise mit demselben Autounfall zu tun haben – abgesehen davon, dass in jeder der Geschichten auch Hunde eine Rolle spielen. González Iñárritus zweiter Spielfilm *21 Gramm* (*21 Grams*, 2003) folgt dem gleichen Muster. In dieser – in den Hauptrollen mit Sean Penn, Naomi Watts und Benicio del Toro besetzten und in einer ungenannten amerikanischen Stadt angesiedelten – Story von Tragik und Wiedergutmachung trieb González Iñárritu sein komplexes Spiel mit Handlungsfäden insofern noch weiter, als er sich an keine zeitliche Abfolge hielt. Sein jüngster Spielfilm *Babel* (2006) – mit Brad Pitt, Cate Blanchett und Gael García Bernal ebenfalls starbesetzt – unterlegt die Triptychon-Struktur mit einem globalen Szenario: Die auf drei Kontinenten angesiedelte und in verschiedenen Sprachen gespielte Saga verknüpft Handlungsstränge miteinander, die alle durch dasselbe Ereignis verbunden sind – den Beschuss eines Busses mit amerikanischen Touristen in Marokko, der irrtümlich als terroristischer Akt eingeschätzt wird und Widerhall in parallel verlaufenden Geschichten an der amerikanisch-mexikanischen Grenze und in Japan findet. *Babel* – mit den grobkörnigen, verwaschenen Bildern von Kameramann Rodrigo Prieto, der schon die ersten beiden Spielfilme González Iñárritus zu einem visuellen Erlebnis machte – prangert Panikmache an und führt vor Augen, wie hartnäckig sich Missverständnisse und Fehlinterpretationen über Grenzen hinweg fortsetzen und alle Ebenen der Wahrnehmung eintrüben.

Auteur d'une trilogie dont les épisodes entremêlent les intrigues à des fins d'égalité sociale, ce cinéaste mexicain a d'abord été animateur de radio, pour le plaisir de ses auditeurs de toutes conditions dans son Mexico natal, ville aux multiples couches sociales. Sa deuxième carrière, dans le film publicitaire et le vidéoclip, le conduit à ses débuts au cinéma avec *Amours chiennes* (*Amores perros*, 2000). Écrit par Guillermo Arriaga, le premier volet du triptyque est composé d'histoires indépendantes, pourtant vaguement liées, dans lesquelles des personnages de différents milieux sociaux sont réunis par un accident de voiture, sans oublier la présence de chiens dans chaque histoire. *21 grammes* (*21 grams*, 2003), son deuxième film, fonctionne de la même façon. Sean Penn, Naomi Watts et Benicio del Toro interprètent ce récit tragique mais rédempteur, dans une ville américaine non identifiée. González Iñárritu tord un peu plus le cou aux conventions en ne respectant pas la chronologie. Brad Pitt, Cate Blanchett et Gael García Bernal sont les vedettes de *Babel* (2006), le dernier film en date. Ce nouveau triptyque, tourné en plusieurs langues, se déroule sur trois continents : des touristes américains sont victimes d'un prétendu acte terroriste au Maroc. Les répercussions se font sentir dans des intrigues parallèles, à la frontière américano-mexicaine et à Tokyo. *Babel* partage avec les films précédents du cinéaste les images brutes et stupéfiantes que l'on doit au chef opérateur Rodrigo Prieto. C'est une étude sur la manière d'entretenir la peur et sur les malentendus persistants d'un pays à l'autre qui brouillent la perception.

FILMS →
2000 *Amores perros (Love's a Bitch)*
2003 *21 Grams*
2006 *Babel*

SELECTED AWARDS →
2000 *Amores perros:* Critics Week Grand Prize, Cannes Film Festival; New Director's Award, Edinburgh International Film Festival; Gold Hugo, Audience Choice Award, Chicago International Film Festival **2001** *Amores perros:* Silver Ariel (Best Direction, Best First Work, Best Editing), Ariel Awards **2002** *Amores perros:* Best Film not in the English Language, BAFTA Awards **2004** *21 Grams:* Special Distinction Award, Independent Spirit Awards **2006** *Babel:* Best Director, Cannes Film Festival

Amores perros

Love's a Bitch / Amours chiennes

The savage underbelly of Mexico City dogfights forms the backdrop for one of three intertwined narratives in González Iñárritu's feature debut, showcasing the gritty cinematography of Rodrigo Prieto.

Hundewettkämpfe in den Elendsvierteln von Mexico City sind der Hintergrund einer der drei miteinander verwobenen Erzählungen in González Iñárritus Spielfilmdebüt, dem der Kameramann Rodrigo Prieto mit seinen grobkörnigen Bildern einen besonderen Charakter verleiht.

Le monde sordide des combats de chiens à Mexico est le décor de l'un des trois récits enchevêtrés du premier film d'Iñárritu, dont les images brutes sont signées Rodrigo Prieto.

Amores perros was a breakout vehicle for Gael García Bernal, playing a struggling young man whose fate becomes entwined with other characters in the film following a car accident.

Amores perros gehört zu den Filmen, mit denen Gael García Bernal der Durchbruch gelang. Er spielt einen jungen Mann, der sich durchs Leben schlägt und dessen Schicksal sich im Verlauf des Films nach einem Autounfall mit dem Leben anderer Figuren verbindet.

Ce film a révélé l'acteur Gael García Bernal, dans le rôle d'un jeune homme pauvre dont le destin se trouve lié aux autres personnages du film à la suite d'un accident de voiture.

21 Grams

21 Gramm / 21 grammes

Iñárritu coaxed an anguished performance out of Sean Penn, playing an ailing mathematician trapped in a loveless marriage whose fate becomes entwined with several seemingly disparate characters. Benicio del Toro (opposite) is an emotionally scarred ex-convict and family man whose Christian faith becomes tested in the wake of a devastating tragedy.

González Iñárritu betraute Sean Penn mit der Rolle eines leidgeprüften, kranken Mathematikers, der eine perspektivlose Ehe führt und dessen Schicksal sich mit den Lebenswegen verschiedener, auf den ersten Blick gegensätzlicher Charaktere kreuzt. Benicio Del Toro (gegenüber) spielt einen emotional verunsicherten Exsträfling und Familienvater, dessen christlicher Glaube durch eine verheerende Tragödie einer Prüfung unterzogen wird.

Iñárritu a su faire de Sean Penn un mathématicien malade et angoissé, piégé dans un mariage dépourvu d'amour, et dont le destin s'entremêle à ceux d'autres personnages disparates. Benicio del Toro (ci-contre) incarne un ancien détenu, père de famille psychologiquement brisé, dont la foi chrétienne est mise à l'épreuve à la suite d'une tragédie.

Naomi Watts plays an upper-middle class suburban housewife whose picture-perfect life gradually unravels as the multiple storylines converge out of chronology.

Naomi Watts verkörpert eine Vorstadthausfrau aus der oberen Mittelklasse, deren mustergültiges Leben umso mehr aus dem Ruder gerät, je dichter sich die unterschiedlichen Erzählstränge unabhängig von einer Chronologie einander nähern.

Naomi Watts interprète une femme aisée d'une banlieue résidentielle, dont la vie trop parfaite est peu à peu révélée à mesure que convergent les intrigues multiples, sans respect de la chronologie.

Babel

"I don't care about the chronological order of the facts but rather the emotional impact of the events, because after all is said and done, cinema is just a fragmented emotional experience. Having a profound ADD, my films are not just an extension of myself but a testimony of my virtues, my miseries and limitations too."

„Die chronologische Ordnung von Fakten interessiert mich weniger als die emotionalen Auswirkungen von Ereignissen, denn nachdem alles gesagt und getan ist, bleibt dem Kino eigentlich nur, fragmentierte emotionale Erfahrungen einzufangen. Da ich an einem ausgeprägten Aufmerksamkeitsdefizitsyndrom leide, sind meine Filme nicht nur Erweiterungen meines Ichs, sondern auch Zeugnisse meiner Tugenden, meines Elends und meiner Grenzen."

«Ce n'est pas la chronologie des faits qui m'intéressent, mais leur impact émotionnel. Car, après tout, le cinéma est une expérience émotionnelle fragmentée. Comme je souffre de troubles déficitaires de l'attention, mes films ne sont pas un prolongement de ce que je suis, mais un témoignage de mes qualités, de mes malheurs et de mes limites.»

The Mexican desert, stunningly filmed by Rodrigo Prieto, is one of several international locations used in Iñárritu's third feature; its four interlocking stories include the immigration woes of an undocumented Mexican nanny.

Die mexikanische Wüste, von Rodrigo Prieto in atemberaubenden Bildern eingefangen, ist einer der über die Welt verstreuten Schauplätze, die González Iñárritu für seinen dritten Spielfilm nutzt. Die Probleme einer mexikanischen Kinderfrau, die ohne Papiere in den USA arbeitet, spielen in einer der drei miteinander verknüpften Geschichten eine wichtige Rolle.

Magnifiquement filmé par Rodrigo Prieto, le désert du Mexique est l'un des nombreux endroits du monde qui servent de décors au troisième film du cinéaste. L'un des quatre récits entrecroisés met en scène les difficultés d'une nounou mexicaine sans papiers.

A stray bullet hits an American tourist vacationing in the Moroccan desert, sparking international jitters and creating a bureaucratic nightmare for an American couple played by Brad Pitt and Cate Blanchett.

Eine amerikanische Touristin, die in der marokkanischen Wüste Urlaub macht, wird von einer verirrten Kugel getroffen. Der Vorfall sorgt international für Aufregung und setzt eine bürokratische Maschinerie in Gang, die das von Brad Pitt und Cate Blanchett gespielte amerikanische Ehepaar als wahren Albtraum erleben.

Une balle perdue frappe une touriste américaine dans le désert marocain, déclenchant une crise diplomatique et tournant au cauchemar bureaucratique pour le couple américain interprété par Brad Pitt et Cate Blanchett.

In a stunning debut performance, Rinko Kikuchi stars as the deaf-mute schoolgirl Chieko, who longs for affection in the wake of her mother's death.

Rinko Kikuchi glänzt als gehörloses Schulmädchen, das den Tod der Mutter verkraften muss und sich nach Zuwendung sehnt.

Faisant de remarquables débuts à l'écran, Rinko Kikuchi incarne Chieko, collégienne sourde et muette, en mal d'affection après la mort de sa mère.

PAUL GREENGRASS

Born 13 August 1955 in Cheam, UK

Nervous anticipation in the film world accompanied the arrival of Universal Pictures' *United 93* (2006), the first major motion picture to address the terror attacks of September 11, 2001, specifically the doomed flight that crash-landed into a Pennsylvania field after passengers overcame their Islamic fundamentalist hijackers. Was it too soon to relive this horrifying scenario through the medium of filmed entertainment? Would audiences show up? They did, thanks in no small part to the stellar craftsmanship of Greengrass, a veteran of British film, television and theater whose riveting *Bloody Sunday* (2001), about the massacre of Northern Irish civil rights activists by British army paratroopers on 30 January 1972 only hinted at the filmmaker's gift for eliciting plausible truth out of historical incident. Transforming his visceral docudramas, cinema vérité-style, through the use of handheld cameras and quick-cut editing techniques, Greengrass manages as credible an approximation of the truth as fiction will allow. His *United 93* was a technical marvel filmed in real time, featuring a cast of unknown actors and aviation professionals playing themselves. Greengrass and crew reconditioned a disused Boeing 757 into a live set at Pinewood Studios inside which the cast re-enacted the 91-minute flight based on interviews culled from flight controllers, black-box recordings and family members of the deceased, resulting in unnerving verisimilitude. Greengrass, who reinvented the Hollywood action thriller with *The Bourne Supremacy* (2004), incorporating his familiar quick-cut editing and dispensing with extraneous narrative strands, returns to the paranoid thriller with *The Bourne Ultimatum* in summer 2007, confirming his status as one of Hollywood's most innovative talents.

In der Filmwelt herrschte angespannte Nervosität, als Universal Pictures mit *Flug 93* (*United 93*, 2006) den ersten großen Kinofilm über die Terrorangriffe vom 11. September 2001 herausbrachte – genauer gesagt: über jenen unglückseligen Flug, der, nachdem Passagiere die islamistischen Entführer überwältigt hatten, mit dem Absturz der Maschine auf einem Feld in Pennsylvania endete. War es zu früh, diese grausame Geschichte als Kinounterhaltung aufzubereiten? Würde der Film ein Publikum finden? Die Zuschauer kamen, und das hatte viel mit der brillanten Inszenierung von Paul Greengrass zu tun, einem Veteranen der britischen Film-, Fernseh- und Theaterproduktion. *Bloody Sunday* (2001), ein fesselnder Spielfilm über das Massaker, das britische Fallschirmjäger am 30. Januar 1972 unter nordirischen Bürgerrechtlern anrichteten, hatte die Fähigkeit des Filmemachers, aus historischen Ereignissen schlüssige Wahrheiten herauszufiltern, nur angedeutet. In seinen mit Handkameras im Cinéma-vérité-Stil gedrehten und in schnellen Schnittfolgen komponierten emotionalen Dokudramen gelingt es Greengrass, der Wahrheit auf glaubwürdige Art so nahe zu kommen, wie es einer Fiktion überhaupt möglich ist. Sein *Flug 93* ist ein in Echtzeit gefilmtes, mit unbekannten Schauspielern und professionellem Flugpersonal besetztes technisches Wunderwerk. Für den Film hatten sich Greengrass und seine Crew in den Pinewood Studios eine ausgemusterte Boeing 757 als Set herrichten lassen, in dem die Darsteller den 91-Minuten-Flug – wie er sich nach Interviews mit Fluglotsen, Blackbox-Aufzeichnungen und Zeugnissen von Familienangehörigen der Opfer darstellte – packend authentisch nachvollziehen konnten. Mit seinem jüngsten Film *Das Bourne Ultimatum* (*The Bourne Ultimatum*, 2007) kehrt Greengrass, der den Hollywood-Actionthriller bereits mit dem rasant geschnittenen und gradlinig erzählten *Die Bourne Verschwörung* (*The Bourne Supremacy*, 2004) wiederbelebt hatte, zum Paranoia-Thriller zurück – und unterstreicht damit seine Stellung als eines der innovativsten Regietalente Hollywoods.

L'arrivée de *Vol 93* (*United 93*, 2006), production Universal, dans le ciel du cinéma mondial a suscité l'inquiétude : un cinéaste portrait pour la première fois à l'écran les attaques du 11 septembre 2001, notamment celle visant l'avion qui s'est écrasé en Pennsylvanie, après que les passagers ont tenté de supplanter les pirates de l'air fondamentalistes. Était-il trop tôt pour revivre l'horrible scénario au cinéma ? Le public serait-il au rendez-vous ? Oui, grâce au savoir-faire brillant de Greengrass, vieux routier du cinéma, de la télévision et du théâtre en Grande-Bretagne. Son captivant *Bloody Sunday* (2001), consacré au massacre de militants nord-irlandais pour les droits civiques par les parachutistes britanniques le 30 janvier 1972, donne un aperçu de son talent à faire jaillir une vérité plausible d'un événement historique. Greengrass modifie le docu-fiction brut, grâce à la caméra portée et au montage vif, et parvient à approcher la vérité de manière aussi crédible que le permet la fiction. *Vol 93* est un chef-d'œuvre filmé en temps réel, avec des acteurs inconnus et des professionnels de l'aviation dans leur propre rôle. Greengrass et son équipe ont transformé un Boeing 757 désaffecté en plateau de tournage, dans les studios anglais de Pinewood, pour reconstituer les 91 minutes du vol, à partir des enregistrements de la boîte noire et d'entretiens avec les aiguilleurs du ciel et les familles des victimes. La vraisemblance est troublante. En 2004, le cinéaste réinventait le film d'action à suspense avec *La Mort dans la peau* (*The Bourne Supremacy*), grâce à un montage intense et sans intrigues secondaires. En 2007, il doit tourner un thriller, *The Bourne Ultimatum*, qui devrait confirmer que Greengrass est l'un des cinéastes hollywoodiens les plus innovateurs.

FILMS →
1988 *Resurrected* **1998** *The Theory of Flight*
2001 *Bloody Sunday* **2004** *The Bourne Supremacy* **2004** *Omagh* [writer / producer, TV]
2006 *United 93* **2007** *The Bourne Ultimatum*

SELECTED AWARDS →
2002 *Bloody Sunday:* Audience Award, Sundance Film Festival;
Golden Bear, Berlin International Film Festival

United 93

Flug 93 / Vol 93

The minute-by-minute events resulting in the crash-landing of United flight 93 on 11 September 2001 in a Pennsylvania field are recreated with chilling verisimilitude.

Mit packender Wahrhaftigkeit rekonstruiert der Film Minute für Minute die Ereignisse, die am 11. September 2001 zum Absturz der Maschine mit der Flugnummer United 93 auf einem Feld in Pennsylvania führten.

Avec une vraisemblance qui fait froid dans le dos, *Vol 93* relate minute par minute les événements qui ont conduit l'un des avions du 11 septembre 2001 à s'écraser dans un champ de Pennsylvanie.

"Sometimes, if you look clearly and unflinchingly at a single event, you can find in its shape something much larger than the event itself – the DNA of our times."

„Betrachtet man ein einzelnes Ereignis unbeirrbar und mit klarem Kopf, kann man in dem, wie es sich darbietet, manchmal etwas entdecken, das gewichtiger ist als das Ereignis selbst – die DNA unserer Zeit."

«Parfois, lorsqu'on observe un événement froidement et clairement, on peut trouver dans sa forme quelque chose qui le dépasse: l'ADN de notre temps.»

For her beguiling feature debut, the dreamlike coming-of-age fable *Innocence* (2004), set in an isolated all-girls boarding school in the middle of a sinister European forest, Lucile Hadzihalilovic adapted Frank Wedekind's symbolist text "Mine-Haha: The Corporal Education of Young Girls" (1903) – the same source material on which Dario Argento's baroque horror classic *Suspiria* (1976/77) was inspired. Shot on Super 16mm stock and blown up to look like CinemaScope, *Innocence* is a masterful, Magritte-like banquet of colors and shadowplay courtesy of cinematographer Benoît Debie, who shot Argento's *The Card Player* (*Il cartaio*, 2003) and Gaspar Noé's *Irreversible* (*Irréversible*, 2002) – Hazdihalilovic, Noé's spouse, worked as editor and producer on his debut feature *I Stand Alone* (*Seul contre tous*, 1998). Described by Hadzihalilovic as "a child's-eye vision of real life," *Innocence* follows Iris, Alice and Bianca – three girls at various stages of early womanhood who are unwittingly being groomed for reproduction – as they undergo training in natural science and physical exercise in the all-female environment of a remote boarding school separated from the outside world by a massive stone wall with no entry or exit. Students are delivered and ferried away via railway tunnels beneath the school – the film's sparse soundtrack is comprised exclusively of natural sounds, including animal cries, running water, ticking clocks, creaking floorboards and the ominous rumblings of arriving and departing trains. Demonstrating a keen flair for generating creepy atmospherics out of young girls aged six to twelve performing dance moves in a verdant utopia-like setting, *Innocence* is a premenstrual existential horror film laden with anxiety, mystery and beauty – an intoxicating debut film from a name to remember.

Für ihr betörendes Spielfilmdebüt *Innocence* (2004), eine märchenhafte Fabel über das Erwachsenwerden, die in einem durch einen finsteren Wald von der Außenwelt abgeschnittenen Mädcheninternat spielt, adaptierte Lucile Hadzihalilovic Frank Wedekinds symbolistischen Text „Mine-Haha oder Über die körperliche Erziehung der jungen Mädchen" (1901) – die gleiche Quelle, aus der auch Dario Argentos barocker Horrorklassiker *Suspiria* (1976/77) schöpft. Auf 16-mm-Material gedreht, das anschließend so „aufgeblasen" wurde, dass es wie Cinemascope wirkt, begeistern die Farben- und Schattenspiele in *Innocence* als ein meisterhafter, an Magritte erinnernder Augenschmaus. Ein Verdienst des Kameramannes Benoît Debie, der bereits Argentos *Il cartaio* (2003) fotografiert hatte – und auch *Irreversibel* (*Irréversible*, 2002) von Hadzihalilovics Ehemann Gaspar Noé (an dessen ersten Spielfilm *Seul contre tous* (1998) Hadzihalilovic übrigens als Cutterin und Produzentin beteiligt war). *Innocence*, laut der Regisseurin „eine Vorstellung vom wirklichen Leben, gesehen durch die Augen eines Kindes", zeichnet die unterschiedlichen Entwicklungsstadien dreier Mädchen nach. Sie werden in einem einzig von weiblichen Lehrkräften und Schülerinnen bevölkerten, von einer mächtigen, torlosen Steinmauer umgebenen und durch unterirdische Eisenbahntunnels versorgten Internat in Biologie und Ballett unterrichtet, ohne zu ahnen, dass man sie zu Fortpflanzungszwecken heranzieht. Der sehr reduzierte Soundtrack des Films beschränkt sich auf Laute der Umgebung – Schreie von Tieren, plätscherndes Wasser, tickende Uhren, knarrende Dielen oder die Erschütterungen der rätselhaften Züge, die immer neue Schülerinnen ins Internat bringen und abtransportieren. *Innocence* gelingt es, selbst dann Grusel zu erzeugen, wenn 6- bis 12-jährige Mädchen in dem von üppiger Natur umgebenen, Utopia-ähnlichen Schauplatz Tanzschritte üben: Der berauschende Erstling einer Regisseurin, deren Namen man sich merken sollte, ist ein mit Angst, Geheimnis und Schönheit aufgeladener Horrorfilm über Heranwachsende vor der Geschlechtsreife.

D'abord connue pour ses contributions à des films de Dario Argento et de Gaspar Noé (elle est la monteuse et productrice du premier film de son mari, *Seul contre tous* de 1998), Lucile Hadzihalilovic a présenté son premier film intitulé *Innocence* en 2004. C'est une fable onirique et saisissante sur le passage à l'âge adulte dans un pensionnat de jeunes filles, isolé en pleine forêt. La cinéaste a adapté la nouvelle du symboliste allemand Frank Wedekind, *Mine-Haha ou l'éducation corporelle des jeunes filles*, dont est également tiré *Suspiria*, un film d'horreur baroque de Dario Argento. Filmé en super 16 mm et gonflé pour ressembler à du cinémascope, *Innocence* est un feu d'artifice de couleurs et de jeux d'ombres, grâce au talent du chef opérateur Benoît Debie, auquel on doit aussi la photo de *The Card Player* (*Il Cartaio*) d'Argento et d'*Irréversible* de Gaspar Noé. *Innocence* est, selon Hadzihalilovic, « la vie réelle vue par les yeux d'un enfant ». Iris, Alice et Bianca sont trois filles à différents stades prépubères que l'on prépare, à leur insu, à la reproduction. Elles étudient la biologie et l'éducation physique dans le cadre exclusivement féminin d'un pensionnat isolé du monde extérieur par un énorme mur d'enceinte de pierres, infranchissable. Les élèves arrivent et repartent par des tunnels ferroviaires souterrains. La bande-son très minimaliste est uniquement composée de sons naturels : cris d'animaux, eau qui coule, tic-tac de l'horloge, planchers qui craquent, grondement menaçant des trains. Le film dénote une grande maîtrise dans la suggestion d'ambiances inquiétantes, où des petites filles âgées de six à douze ans dansent dans des décors utopiques verdoyants. *Innocence* est un film d'horreur existentiel qui regorge d'angoisse, de mystère et de beauté. Un film enivrant, un nom à retenir.

Innocence

"As a spectator, I like films that take you into a particular physical world by playing on sound and sensorial perception."

„Als Zuschauerin mag ich Filme, die mich durch Klänge und sinnliche Wahrnehmung in eine völlig andere Welt entführen."

«Comme spectatrice, j'aime les films qui vous emmène dans un monde physique particulier en jouant sur la perception auditive et sensorielle.»

Young girls come of age inside an ominous boarding school, where they arrive via coffin and remain contained within its walled confines, subject to enforced rituals. Right: A teacher pins butterflies, while the girls dance with butterfly wings.

In einem Sarg gelangen die Neuankömmlinge in das mysteriöse, von einer torlosen Mauer umgebene Mädcheninternat, wo sie sich strengen Vorschriften unterwerfen müssen. Rechts: Während die Mädchen mit Schmetterlingsflügeln tanzen, spießt eine Lehrerin Schmetterlinge auf.

Les jeunes élèves d'un sinistre pensionnat de jeunes filles atteignent l'âge adulte, après y avoir été acheminées en cercueil, confinées dans son enceinte et soumises à des rituels obligatoires. À droite : Une enseignante épingle des papillons, tandis que les jeunes filles dansent avec des ailes de papillon.

The girls experience pain and suffering as they grow. Right: Water is a recurring motif symbolizing feminine purity and adding to the dreamlike nature of Benoît Debie's sumptuous – and foreboding – cinematography.

Die heranwachsenden Mädchen müssen Qualen und Leid ertragen. Rechts: Wasser, ein immer wiederkehrendes Motiv, symbolisiert weibliche Reinheit. Als Element einer berauschenden Natur bringt es der Kameramann Benoît Debie in üppigen Bildern voller düsterer Vorahnungen zur Geltung.

Douleur et souffrance sont le lot de l'éducation des jeunes filles. À droite : Motif récurrent, l'eau symbolise la pureté féminine et contribue à l'ambiance onirique créée par la photo somptueuse et inquiétante de Benoît Debie.

MICHAEL HANEKE

Born 23 March 1942 in Munich, Germany

The German-born, Austrian director Michael Haneke studied psychology, philosophy and theatrical sciences at the University of Vienna before embarking on a career as a playwright. He found his voice as a filmmaker of intellectual, rigidly composed psychological suspense thrillers, including the Emotional Glaciation trilogy comprising his first three features: *The Seventh Continent* (*Der siebente Kontinent*, 1989), *Benny's Video* (1992), and *71 Fragments of a Chronology of Chance* (*71 Fragmente einer Chronologie des Zufalls*, 1994), unsettling glimpses of urban bourgeois disaffection set at the intersection between media alienation and violence. Haneke honed his sadistic streak in the elegant, twisted *The Piano Teacher* (*Die Klavierspielerin / La Pianiste*, 2001), starring Isabelle Huppert as a sadomasochistic music instructor who embarks on a torrid affair with a younger student, played by Benoît Magimel. Huppert – in one of her greatest (and iciest) performances – won the best actress prize at Cannes in 2001 for the role. But it was *Hidden* (*Caché*, 2005), that confirmed Haneke as a world-class director, winning him the directing prize at Cannes and drawing comparisons to Fritz Lang for his ability to casually manipulate, provoke and even tease his audience into recognizing the horrors of the modern self. A suspense thriller about a bourgeois Parisian couple (Daniel Auteuil and Juliette Binoche) terrorized by an unseen stalker, possibly from Auteuil's past, *Hidden* was another of Haneke's superbly crafted psychological endurance tests, with scathing allegorical overtones hinting at Western contempt for the Muslim world. Haneke next brings his cinematic terror to America for an English-language remake of his own *Funny Games* (1997), the story of a bourgeois family attacked by a pair of urbane serial killers.

Bevor er eine Karriere als Dramaturg begann, studierte der in Deutschland geborene und in Österreich beheimatete Michael Haneke Psychologie, Philosophie und Theaterwissenschaften an der Universität Wien. Einen Namen als Filmregisseur machte er sich mit intellektuell anspruchsvollen, streng komponierten, psychologischen Thrillern, zu denen auch seine ersten Spielfilme gehören, die eine Trilogie über emotionale Kälte bilden: *Der siebente Kontinent* (1989), *Benny's Video* (1992) und *71 Fragmente einer Chronologie des Zufalls* (1994) – irritierende Beobachtungen der Entfremdung innerhalb des städtischen Bürgertums, die an der Grenze zwischen Kommunikationsstörungen und dem Ausbruch von Gewalt angesiedelt sind. In seinem ebenso eleganten wie verwickelten Film *Die Klavierspielerin – La Pianiste* (2001), in dem Isabelle Huppert eine sadomasochistisch veranlagte Klavierlehrerin spielt, die sich auf eine gefühlsgeladene Affäre mit einem ihrer Schüler (Benoît Magimel) einlässt, verfeinerte Haneke seine Vorliebe für sadistisch geprägte Konstellationen. Für ihre Leistung – eine ihrer grandiosesten und zugleich eisigsten Darbietungen – wurde Huppert in Cannes 2001 als beste Schauspielerin geehrt. Mit *Caché* (2005), der ihm den Regiepreis in Cannes einbrachte, unterstrich Haneke seinen Nimbus als Regisseur von Weltrang. Sein in diesem Film abermals offenbartes Talent, das Publikum beiläufig so weit zu manipulieren, zu provozieren und sogar zu ärgern, bis es die Ängste moderner Menschen zu erkennen vermag, veranlasste die Kritik zu Vergleichen mit Fritz Lang. Der spannungsreiche Thriller erzählt von einem bürgerlichen Pariser Ehepaar (Daniel Auteuil und Juliette Binoche), das von einem nie in Erscheinung tretenden Fremden terrorisiert wird, der möglicherweise mit der Vergangenheit des Ehemannes in Verbindung steht. Auch *Caché* erwies sich als ein handwerklich vorzüglich umgesetzter Film, der den Zuschauer auf die Folter spannt und zudem mit bissigem allegorischen Unterton auf die westliche Geringschätzung der muslimischen Welt anspielt. Mit dem englischsprachigen Remake seines Films *Funny Games* (1997), der Geschichte einer bürgerlichen Familie, die von einem Duo höflicher, psychopathischer Killer gequält wird, trägt Haneke seine filmischen Albträume bald auch nach Amerika.

Haneke fait des études de psychologie, de philosophie et de théâtre à l'université de Vienne, avant de se lancer dans la mise en scène théâtrale. Il se tourne ensuite vers le cinéma, en réalisant des films psychologiques à suspense, d'une composition très rigoureuse. Ses trois premiers films forment la trilogie de la «glaciation émotionnelle»: *Le Septième Continent* (*Der siebente Kontinent*, 1989), *Benny's Video* (1992), *71 fragments d'une chronologie du hasard* (*71 Fragmente einer Chronologie des Zufalls*, 1994), autant d'aperçus dérangeants sur la bourgeoisie urbaine désabusée, au croisement de l'aliénation médiatique et de la violence. Haneke laisse libre cours à son sadisme dans *La Pianiste* (*Die Klavierspielerin*, 2001), film élégant et retors, avec Isabelle Huppert en professeur de musique sadomasochiste, happée par une liaison ardente avec un jeune élève (Benoît Magimel). Ce rôle, l'un des plus beaux (et les plus froids) de sa carrière, vaut à Huppert le prix d'interprétation féminine à Cannes en 2001. *Caché* (2005) fait de Haneke un cinéaste de classe internationale, lauréat du prix de la mise en scène à Cannes. On le compare à Fritz Lang pour sa capacité à manipuler et à provoquer le spectateur et, même, à l'amener à admettre les horreurs du moi moderne. Dans *Caché*, un couple de bobos parisiens (Daniel Auteuil et Juliette Binoche) est terrorisé par un observateur invisible, sans doute surgi du passé du personnage joué par Auteuil. Épreuve psychologique parfaitement maîtrisée, *Caché* recèle quelques allégories mettant vertement en accusation le mépris occidental pour le monde musulman. Pour son prochain film, Haneke transporte sa terreur cinématographique en Amérique, avec un remake en anglais de son *Funny Games* (1997), l'agression d'une famille bourgeoise par deux tueurs en série courtois.

FILMS →
1989 *Der siebente Kontinent (The Seventh Continent)* **1992** *Benny's Video* **1994** *71 Fragmente einer Chronologie des Zufalls (71 Fragments of a Chronology of Chance)* **1997** *Funny Games* **2000** *Code inconnu (Code Unknown)* **2001** *Die Klavierspielerin / La Pianiste (The Piano Teacher)* **2003** *Le Temps du loup / Wolfzeit (Time of the Wolf)* **2005** *Caché (Hidden)* **2007** *Funny Games*

SELECTED AWARDS →
1993 *Benny's Video:* FIPRESCI Prize, European Film Awards
1997 *Funny Games:* Silver Hugo, Chicago International Film Festival
2000 *Code inconnu:* Prize of the Ecumenical Jury, Cannes Film Festival
2001 *Die Klavierspielerin:* Grand Jury Prize, Cannes Film Festival **2005** *Caché:* Best Director, FIPRESCI Prize, Prize of the Ecumenical Jury, Cannes Film Festival; Best Director, European Film Awards

Caché

Hidden

"What we know of the world is little more than the mediated world, the image. We have no reality, but a derivative of reality, which is extremely dangerous, most certainly from a political standpoint but in a larger sense to our ability to have a palpable sense of the truth of everyday experience."

„Was wir von der Welt wissen, ist wenig mehr als das Bild, das uns von ihr vermittelt wird. Wir haben es nicht mit der Realität als solcher, sondern mit einem Derivat der Realität zu tun. Und das ist sehr gefährlich, sicherlich gerade von einem politischen Standpunkt aus betrachtet, in weiterem Sinne aber auch für unsere Fähigkeit, die Wahrheit in unserem Alltagsleben erspüren zu können."

«Ce que nous savons du monde ne va guère au-delà du monde médiatisé, de l'image. Nous ne vivons pas la réalité, mais un dérivé de la réalité, ce qui est extrêmement dangereux, assurément du point de vue politique, mais dans un sens plus large, pour notre capacité à appréhender la vérité tangible de la vie quotidienne.»

Voyeurism and surveillance become mechanisms for suspense in Haneke's eighth feature, starring Daniel Auteuil and Juliette Binoche as a bourgeois couple under attack by an unseen menace.

Voyeurismus und Überwachung sind die Elemente, die in Hanekes achtem Spielfilm für Spannung sorgen. Daniel Auteuil und Juliette Binoche spielen ein bürgerliches Ehepaar, das sich von einem unsichtbaren Fremden bedroht fühlt.

Voyeurisme et surveillance constituent la mécanique du suspense dans le huitième film de Haneke. Un couple de bobos parisiens (Daniel Auteuil et Juliette Binoche) y subit les attaques d'un danger invisible.

MARY HARRON

Born 12 January 1953 in Gravenhurst, Canada

This Canadian-born, Oxford-educated, American-based filmmaker delves deeper into popular culture than most directors working today, unearthing glossy, nuanced and rebellious productions centering on iconic or infamous zeitgeist protagonists, each one encapsulating the immediate era in which a Mary Harron film is set. A former rock journalist, Harron was the first North American scribe to interview the Sex Pistols, covering the nascent punk scene in New York for the *New Musical Express*, and co-founded *Punk magazine* with Legs McNeil. She began her filmmaking career making documentaries for British television. Her first feature was *I Shot Andy Warhol* (1995), about the renegade feminist and *S. C. U. M. Manifesto* author Valerie Solanas' attack on Warhol in protest against art-world patriarchy, though Harron was shrewd to depict Solanas' ulterior motive as a struggling playwright denied the limelight of the Factory crowd. She followed that with a brilliant, masterful adaptation of Bret Easton Ellis's definitive novel of 1980s greed and excess, *American Psycho* (1999), featuring a ferocious central performance by Christian Bale as Patrick Bateman, the Wall Street stock trader whose sadistic lust for power and material consumption translated into vain preening and sadistic chainsaw attacks on prostitutes. Harron contextualized *American Psycho* with satirical horror flourishes, employing gory black humor to summarize its era's corruptive sheen. She examined the paradoxical roots of feminism in *The Notorious Bettie Page* (2005), about the 1950s pin-up model and fetish icon (played by Gretchen Mol) who unwittingly helped commodify pornography in conservative America – at the same time planting the seed for women's liberation.

Die in Kanada geborene, in Oxford ausgebildete und in den USA lebende Filmemacherin forscht tiefer in den Abgründen der Populärkultur als die meisten Regisseure unserer Tage. So gelingen ihr schillernde, nuancierte und zugleich widerspenstige Produktionen über ikonenhafte oder berüchtigte Zeitgeist-Protagonisten, die stets auch mustergültig die Epoche verkörpern, in der Harrons Filme angesiedelt sind. Die einstige Rockjournalistin Harron war die erste nordamerikanische Autorin, die die Sex Pistols interviewte. Für den *New Musical Express* berichtete sie über die entstehende New Yorker Punkszene, und gemeinsam mit Legs McNeil gründete sie das *Punk Magazine*. Ihre Karriere als Filmemacherin begann sie mit Dokumentationen für das britische Fernsehen. Im Mittelpunkt ihres ersten Spielfilms *I Shot Andy Warhol* (1995) stand Valerie Solanas – jene Radikalfeministin und Verfasserin des *SCUM (Society for Cutting Up Men)-Manifests*, die aus Protest gegen die Männerherrschaft im Kunstbetrieb einen Anschlag auf Andy Warhol verübt hatte. Harron war allerdings klug genug, Solanas eigentliches Motiv in der Zurückweisung als Theaterautorin zu sehen, der man das Rampenlicht der Factory verwehrte. Danach ließ Harron *American Psycho* (1999) folgen – eine brillante Adaption von Bret Easton Ellis' definitivem Roman über die Gier und die Exzesse der 1980er-Jahre, die nicht zuletzt durch Christian Bales intensive Darstellung eines Wall-Street-Investmentbankers begeistert, dessen sadistische Lust auf Macht und Konsum in eitle Selbstdarstellung und in mörderische Kettensägenattacken auf Prostituierte umschlägt. Harron schmückte *American Psycho* mit satirischem Horror aus, der dem verderbten Glanz jener Ära mit blutrünstigem schwarzen Humor zu Leibe rückte. In *Die legendäre Bettie Page* (*The Notorious Bettie Page*, 2005) ergründet die Regisseurin die widersprüchlichen Wurzeln des Feminismus. Der Film erzählt von dem zur Fetischikone avancierten Pin-up-Model der 1950er-Jahre (Gretchen Mol), das der Pornografie im konservativen Amerika unabsichtlich eine Bresche schlug – und gleichzeitig den Keim für die Frauenbefreiung legte.

Canadienne, scolarisée à Oxford et résidant aux États-Unis, Mary Harron s'intéresse à la culture populaire en créant des films bien léchés, tout en nuances, mais rebelles, autour de personnages emblématiques de leur temps. Ancienne critique de rock, Harron est la première journaliste américaine à avoir interviewé les Sex Pistols. Elle a couvert les débuts de la scène punk new-yorkaise pour le *New Musical Express* et cofondé *Punk Magazine* avec Legs McNeil. Après plusieurs documentaires pour la télévision britannique, elle signe son premier film de fiction, *I Shot Andy Warhol* (1995). Elle y dépeint l'attaque commise sur l'artiste par Valerie Solanas, féministe renégate et auteur de *S. C. U. M. Manifesto*, pour dénoncer le monde de l'art machiste. Cependant, Harron justifie cet acte par le fait que Solanas n'arrivait pas à s'imposer comme dramaturge dans le milieu artistique de la Factory. Vient ensuite une adaptation brillante du roman de Bret Easton Ellis, emblématique des années 1980, les années fric, *American Psycho* (1999). Christian Bale y incarne le féroce Patrick Bateman, agent boursier new-yorkais dont le désir sadique de pouvoir et de consommation se traduit par une débauche vestimentaire et des attaques à la tronçonneuse contre des prostituées. Images d'horreur et humour noir sanglant illustrent bien une époque au vernis corrompu. Avec *The Notorious Bettie Page* (2005), elle examine les racines paradoxales du féminisme. Pin-up des années 1950, devenue une icône fétichiste, Bettie Page (interprétée par Gretchen Mol) a, sans le vouloir, contribué à la fois à la marchandisation de la pornographie dans l'Amérique conservatrice et à la naissance future du mouvement de libération des femmes.

FILMS →
1995 *I Shot Andy Warhol*
1999 *American Psycho*
2005 *The Notorious Bettie Page*

SELECTED AWARDS →
2001 *American Psycho*: Best Film, IHG Awards
2005 Filmmaker on the Edge, Provincetown International Film Festival
2006 *The Notorious Bettie Page*: CineKink Tribute, CineKink Awards

American Psycho

Christian Bale delivers a ferocious performance as the narcissistic, sadistic Wall Street trader Patrick Bateman in Harron's adaptation of the Bret Easton Ellis novel about vanity and greed in 1980s Manhattan.

In Harrons Adaption von Bret Easton Ellis' Roman über Eitelkeit und Gier im Manhattan der 1980er-Jahre liefert Christian Bales eine eindrucksvolle schauspielerische Darbietung als ebenso narzisstischer wie sadistischer Wall-Street-Händler Patrick Bateman.

Christian Bale incarne avec férocité Patrick Bateman, agent boursier narcissique et sadique, dans cette adaptation du roman de Bret Easton Ellis, portrait de la vanité et de la cupidité des années 1980 à Manhattan.

The Notorious Bettie Page

Die legendäre Bettie Page

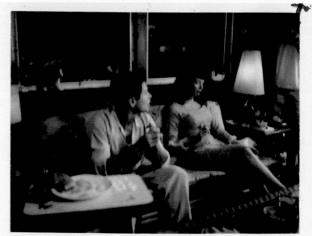

Polaroids from the set depict Gretchen Mol as Bettie Page, torn between domesticity and the urge to break out of the constricting femininity of the 1950s.

Polaroids vom Set zeigen Gretchen Mol als Bettie Page, eine Frau, die hin- und hergerissen ist zwischen biederer Häuslichkeit und der Notwendigkeit, aus der einengenden Frauenrolle der 1950er-Jahre auszubrechen.

Sur ces photos de plateau, Bettie Page a les traits de Gretchen Mol, qui incarne son déchirement entre la vie de famille et le désir de se libérer des contraintes de la féminité des années 1950.

"The most important ideas I have for a film just pop into my head. Only later, when I'm filming the movie, or editing it, do I finally begin to understand why I did what I did."

„Die wichtigsten Ideen für einen Film schießen mir einfach so durch den Kopf.
Erst später, bei den Dreharbeiten oder beim Schnitt des Films, wird mir langsam bewusst,
warum ich dies oder das gemacht habe."

«Mes idées de film les plus fortes me viennent comme ça. Ce n'est que plus tard,
au tournage ou au montage, que je commence à comprendre pourquoi je m'y suis prise comme ça.»

Bunny Yaeger transforms Bettie Page into a pin-up icon whose sadomasochistic poses would result in obscenity charges.

Bunny Yaeger verwandelt Bettie Page in eine Pin-up-Ikone, deren sadomasochistische Posen zu Anklagen wegen Obszönität führten.

Bunny Yaeger fait de Bettie Page une pin-up dont les poses sadomasochistes allaient la conduire au tribunal pour obscénité.

TODD HAYNES

Born 2 January 1961 in Encino, USA

Todd Haynes has made a fascinating career out of examining the artificial through a variety of prisms, including Barbie dolls, glitter rock and the 1950s suburban housewife. One of the pioneers of the New Queer Cinema that evolved out of American independent film's breakout phase in the 1980s, Haynes abandoned overtly gay themes beginning with his masterpiece, *Safe* (1995) – an existential horror movie about a Los Angeles woman allergic to her own environment – opting to subtextualize his queer sensibility in the guise of a protagonist heroine (played by Julianne Moore in a breakout performance) who discovers her true nature at a New Age retreat on the fringes of society. *Velvet Goldmine* (1998), with its ode to glam rock artifice and Oscar Wildean camp flourishes coursing virally through the ages, brought an intellectual luster to its weighty analysis of a Bowie-like performance icon and his fandom, including a sexually conflicted rock journalist played by Christian Bale. Subtext became text in the revisionist Douglas Sirk-style weepie *Far from Heaven* (2002), in which Haynes examined 1950s surface tension in his story of a Connecticut housewife whose closeted gay husband propels her into a secret affair with a black gardener – resulting in a stunning simulacrum that was also a classic women's picture. His penchant for capturing on film via unconventional methods the interior states of characters at odds with their environment was inventively addressed in his biggest production to date, the $25 million *I'm Not There* (2007), a self-proclaimed "ferocious musical romp" starring Heath Ledger and Cate Blanchett as incarnations of Bob Dylan during different stages of his five decades as a performer.

Todd Haynes' faszinierendes Werk widmet sich dem Phänomen der Künstlichkeit, das der Regisseur in seinen Filmen wie durch verschiedenste Prismen betrachtet – sei es in Gestalt von Barbiepuppen, Glamrock oder Vorstadthausfrauen der 1950er-Jahre. In den 1980er-Jahren gehörte Haynes zu den Pionieren des aus dem amerikanischen Independent-Film hervorgegangenen New Queer Cinema. Mit seinem Meisterwerk *Safe* (1995), einem existenziellen Horrorfilm über eine Frau in Los Angeles, die allergisch auf ihre Umwelt reagiert, entfernte er sich von den unverhohlen schwulen Themen seiner früheren Arbeiten – doch vermittelte Haynes seine schwule Sensibilität zugleich über die Heldin (Julianne Moore liefert in der Hauptrolle eine Glanzleistung), die ihre wahre Natur in einem New-Age-Therapiezentrum fern vom normalen gesellschaftlichen Alltag entdeckt. *Velvet Goldmine* (1998), eine Ode an die Glitzerwelt des Glamrock und die Exzentrik eines Oscar Wilde, verlieh der ernsthaften Analyse eines nach dem Vorbild Bowies angelegten, ikonenhaften Bühnenstars und seiner Fangemeinde – darunter auch ein von Christian Bale verkörperter Rockjournalist, der mit sexuellen Konflikten kämpft – intellektuellen Glanz. In *Dem Himmel so fern* (*Far from Heaven*, 2002), einer Schnulze à la Douglas Sirk, in der Haynes die Spannungen hinter der sauberen Fassade der 1950er-Jahre zum Vorschein kommen ließ, wird der Subtext zum Text. Der Film erzählt die Geschichte einer Hausfrau in Connecticut, die von ihrem heimlich schwulen Ehemann in eine prekäre Affäre mit einem schwarzen Gärtner getrieben wird – ein fantastisch dargebotenes Verwirrspiel, das sich auch als ein klassischer Frauenfilm entpuppt. Seine Neigung, das Innenleben von Charakteren, die mit ihrer Umwelt auf Kriegsfuß stehen, durch unkonventionelle Methoden einzufangen, setzt Haynes in seiner bislang größten Produktion, dem 25-Millionen-Dollar-Projekt *I'm Not There* (2007), besonders kreativ um: Dieses „wilde musikalische Spektakel" (Haynes) zeigt Bob Dylan in den verschiedenen Phasen seiner jahrzehntelangen Karriere – dargestellt wird er unter anderem von Heath Ledger und Cate Blanchett.

Le cinéma de Todd Haynes est fascinant pour son étude de l'artificiel par toutes sortes de prismes : les poupées Barbie, le rock clinquant et la ménagère des classes moyennes dans les années 1950. Pionnier du nouveau cinéma *queer*, né de la phase de rupture du cinéma américain indépendant dans les années 1980, Haynes a renoncé aux thèmes ouvertement gays avec son chef-d'œuvre *Safe* (1995), film d'horreur existentiel autour d'une femme de Los Angeles allergique à son environnement. Il atténue sa sensibilité *queer* grâce à l'héroïne (Julianne Moore, dans une interprétation étonnante) qui découvre sa véritable nature lors d'une retraite New Age en marge de la société. Marquée par le virus intemporel du maniérisme gay, l'ode à l'artifice du glam rock qu'est *Velvet Goldmine* (1998) donne au film un vernis intellectuel, sans lequel cet opus ne serait qu'une analyse lourde d'un artiste façon Bowie et de ses fans, parmi lesquels un critique de rock incertain de sa sexualité (Christian Bale). Le sous-texte revient au premier plan dans *Loin du paradis* (*Far From Heaven*, 2002), mélo révisionniste à la Douglas Sirk. Une ménagère du Connecticut est secrètement jetée dans les bras d'un jardinier noir par son propre mari, homosexuel refoulé. La tension superficielle des années 1950 aboutit à un étonnant simulacre qui plaît au public féminin. Haynes aime saisir par des moyens inhabituels les états intérieurs de personnages en conflit avec leur environnement. Il s'y prend très habilement dans sa plus grosse production à ce jour (25 millions de dollars), *I'm Not There* (2007), « féroce débauche musicale », selon Haynes, avec Heath Ledger, incarnant Bob Dylan à diverses périodes de ses cinquante années de scène, et Cate Blanchett.

FILMS →
1990 *Poison* **1995** *Safe* **1998** *Velvet Goldmine*
2002 *Far from Heaven* **2007** *I'm Not There*

Velvet Goldmine

Haynes examines the sexuality, androgyny and artifice of the 1970s glam rock scene in London. Jonathan Rhys Meyers (left) plays a Bowie-esque pop icon in bodysuit and feathers.

Haynes widmet sich der Sexualität, Androgynität und den Extravaganzen der Glam-Rock-Szene im London der 1970er-Jahre. Jonathan Rhys Meyers (links) spielt, im hautengen Body und mit Federn geschmückt, eine Popikone, die an David Bowie erinnert.

La sexualité, l'androgynie et l'artifice du *glam rock* londonien des années 1970 sont les thèmes de *Velvet Goldmine*, avec Jonathan Rhys Meyers (à gauche) en star arborant justaucorps et plumes à la David Bowie.

Far from Heaven

Dem Himmel *so* fern / *Loin du paradis*

This homage to the melodramatic 1950s Technicolor weepies of Douglas Sirk stars Julianne Moore as Connecticut housewife Cathy Whitaker, who has an affair with her black gardener.

In dieser Hommage an Douglas Sirks Technicolor-Melodramen der 1950er-Jahre spielt Julianne Moore eine Hausfrau aus Connecticut, die sich auf eine Affäre mit ihrem schwarzen Gärtner einlässt.

Dans cet hommage aux mélos en Technicolor réalisés par Douglas Sirk dans les années 1950, Julianne Moore interprète Cathy Whitaker, ménagère du Connecticut qui a une liaison avec son jardinier noir.

"The best films don't offer redemption. They understand their own artificiality and are truthful as a result."

„Die besten Filme gaukeln keine Erlösung vor. Sie gehen mit ihrer eigenen Künstlichkeit offen um, und deshalb sind sie wahrhaftig."

«Les meilleurs films n'offrent aucune rédemption.
Ils connaissent leur propre artificialité et en sont d'autant plus sincères.»

Dennis Quaid gives an achingly convincing perform-ance as a sexually repressed company man who frequents back-alley gay bars and lives in fear of being discovered as gay.

Dennis Quaid gibt eine überzeugende Vorstellung als sexuell unterdrückter Firmenangestellter, der sich in geheimen Schwulenbars herumtreibt und dessen Leben von der Furcht geprägt ist, dass seine Homo-sexualität bekannt wird.

Dans une interprétation poignante, Dennis Quaid est un cadre à la sexualité refoulée, qui fréquente les bars gays clandestins et vit dans la peur d'être démasqué.

Haynes' subtle palette of deep colors helped to accentuate Julianne Moore's fragile portrayal of prim, restless 1950s middle-class American femininity that made her performance one of the year's most acclaimed.

Haynes subtile Palette intensiver Farben unterstrich noch die Zerbrechlichkeit des von Julianne Moore verkörperten Typs der mustergültigen, rastlosen amerikanischen Mittelklassehausfrau der 1950er-Jahre. Die Leistung der Schauspielerin gehörte zu den am meisten bewunderten Darbietungen des Kinojahres.

Avec une palette subtile de teintes vives, Haynes souligne le portrait délicat que Julianne Moore fait de la bourgeoise américaine, guindée mais tourmentée, des années 1950, dans l'un des rôles les plus appréciés cette année-là.

I'm Not There

SHOT BREAKDOWN — UNDERWATER SEQUENCE (WOODY)

(65) Woody tumbles into water

CU Woody (turning thru foam)

(66) UNDERWATER MONTAGE :
(Studio shots super-ed over water)

Woody with train / Gorgeous George
(CROSS-DISSOLVE)

Woody with the Arvins
(CROSS DISSOLVE)

Woody with Thief, Beggar, Moonshiner
(CROSS DISSOLVE)

Haynes drew these shot breakdowns for an underwater sequence in his fictional Bob Dylan biography.

Haynes skizzierte diese Abfolge von Aufnahmen für eine Unterwassersequenz in seiner fiktionalen Bob-Dylan-Biografie.

Haynes a dessiné ce story-board d'une séquence sous l'eau, pour sa biographie fictive de Bob Dylan.

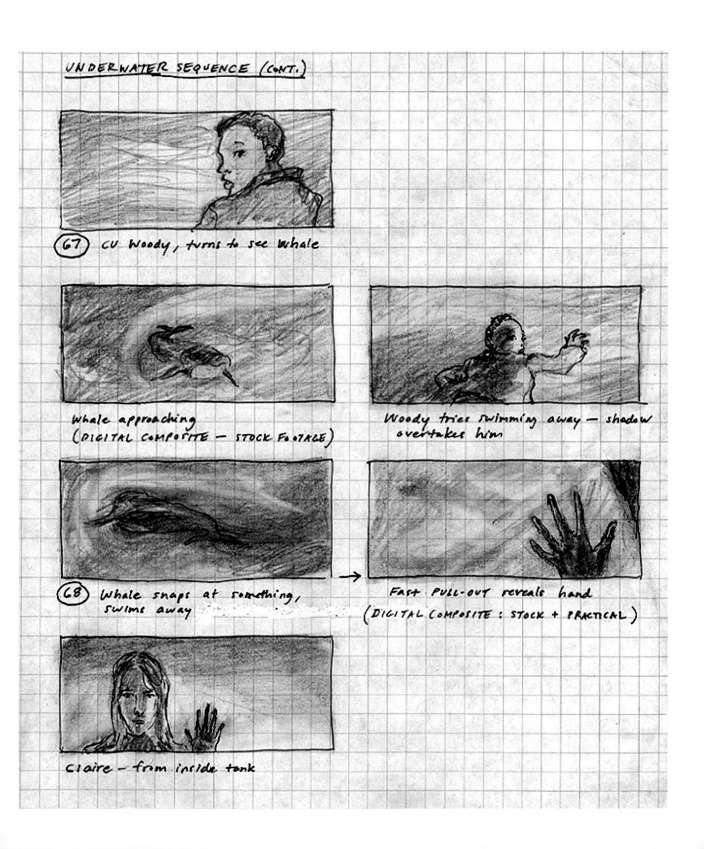

UNDERWATER SEQUENCE (CONT.)

(67) CU Woody, turns to see whale

Whale approaching
(DIGITAL COMPOSITE — STOCK FOOTAGE)

Woody tries swimming away — shadow overtakes him

(68) Whale snaps at something, swims away

Fast PULL-OUT reveals hand
(DIGITAL COMPOSITE: STOCK + PRACTICAL)

Claire — from inside tank

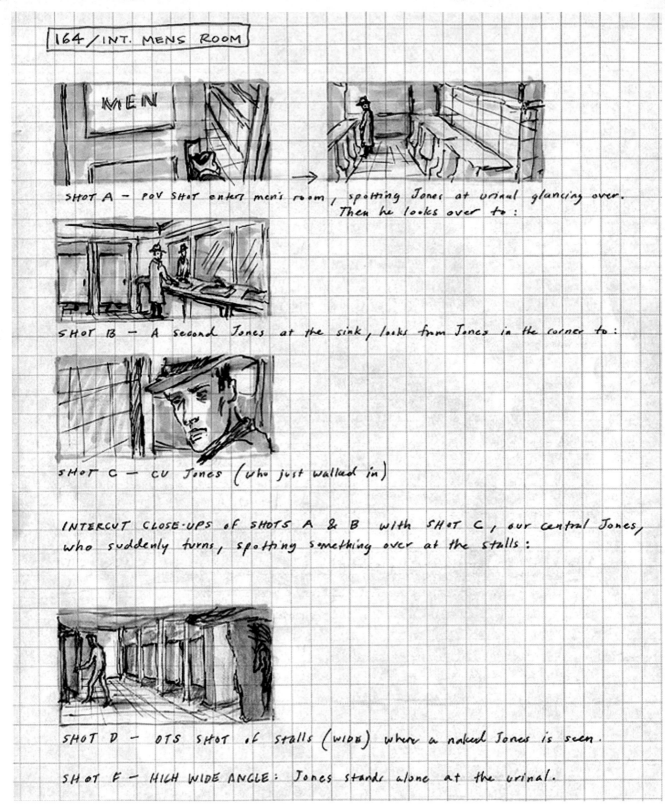

164 / INT. MENS ROOM

SHOT A — POV SHOT enters men's room, spotting Jones at urinal glancing over. Then he looks over to:

SHOT B — A second Jones at the sink, looks from Jones in the corner to:

SHOT C — CU Jones (who just walked in)

INTERCUT CLOSE-UPS of SHOTS A & B with SHOT C, our central Jones, who suddenly turns, spotting something over at the stalls:

SHOT D — OTS SHOT of stalls (WIDE) where a naked Jones is seen.

SHOT F — HIGH WIDE ANGLE: Jones stands alone at the urinal.

Actors as diverse as Richard Gere, Heath Ledger, Christian Bale and Cate Blanchett portray Bob Dylan during various phases of his decades-spanning career.

So unterschiedliche Schauspieler wie Richard Gere, Heath Ledger, Christian Bale und Cate Blanchett verkörpern Bob Dylan in den verschiedenen Phasen seiner jahrzehntelangen Karriere.

Bob Dylan est incarné par des acteurs aussi divers que Richard Gere, Heath Ledger, Christian Bale et Cate Blanchett, au fil de sa longue carrière.

HOU HSIAO-HSIEN

Born 8 April 1947 in Meixian, China

The Taiwanese filmmaker Hou Hsiao-hsien has been a festival staple for 20 years, though his 2001 feature *Millennium Mambo (Qianxi manbo)* was the first to receive accolades outside of his core base of devotees, earning him comparisons to his idol Yasujiro Ozu. In collaboration with his long-time cinematographer Lee Pin-bing, Hou creates languid, rigorous dramas emphasizing long shots and extended takes awash in feverish colors or exquisite lighting displays, as in the 1998 period drama *Flowers of Shanghai (Hai shang hua)*, set in a 19th-century Shanghai brothel. *Millennium Mambo* was a departure for Hou in that it was not a period piece, though it is narrated through the eyes of a young heroine, played by the Hong Kong superstar Shu Qi, looking back from the year 2010 on her errant youth as a bar hostess and club fixture as the century turned. These fragmentary, fleeting memories of lost moments suspended in time constitute Hou's stock in trade. For the 2005 romantic triptych *Three Times (Zui hao de shi guang)* Hou concocted three separate love stories set in different time periods examining how people's behaviors are circumscribed by the times and places they live in – another recurring motif in Hou's work. In the 2003 feature *Café Lumière (Kôhî jikô)*, made in celebration of the centenary of Ozu's birth, Hou incorporated imagery from Ozu's masterwork *Tokyo Story (Tokyo monogatari*, 1953), in homage to the singular influence on his work. With the exception of Wong Kar-wai, no living filmmaker more thoroughly examines the exacting pull of time than Hou, a master of transforming generational shift into celluloid dreams.

20 Jahre lang war der taiwanesische Filmemacher Hou Hsiao-hsien bei vielen Festivals zu Gast, doch erst sein 2001 entstandener Spielfilm *Millennium Mambo (Qianxi manbo)* brachte ihm Anerkennung über den Kreis seiner Anhänger hinaus: Fortan verglich man ihn mit seinem Idol Yasujiro Ozu. Gemeinsam mit seinem Stammkameramann Lee Pin-bing entwickelt Hou seine träge dahinfließenden und zugleich unerbittlichen Dramen in ausgedehnten Totalen, die in fiebrigen Farben glühen oder in betörendes Licht getaucht sind – wie etwa in dem 1998 gedrehten Historienfilm *Flowers of Shanghai (Hai shang hua)*, der in einem Schanghaier Bordell des 19. Jahrhunderts spielt. *Millennium Mambo* war für Hou insofern ein Neuanfang, als dass es sich bei diesem Film um kein historisches Stück handelt, auch wenn die Geschichte aus der Sicht einer jungen Heldin (gespielt von der Hongkonger Starschauspielerin Shu Qi) erzählt wird, die auf ihre orientierungslose Jugend um die Jahrhundertwende zurückblickt, als sie sich als Barhostess und Clubanimateurin verdingte. Fragmentarischen, flüchtigen Erinnerungen an verlorene Momente vergangener Zeiten widmet sich Hou in besonderem Maße. In dem 2005 entstandenen romantischen Triptychon *Three Times (Zui hao de shi guang)* zeigt er drei in unterschiedlichen Epochen angesiedelte Liebesgeschichten und zeigt, wie das Verhalten der Menschen je nach Zeit und Ort ihres Daseins Beschränkungen unterworfen ist – auch das ein immer wiederkehrendes Motiv in Hous Werk. Für seinen 2003 anlässlich von Ozus hundertstem Geburtstag realisierten Spielfilm *Café Lumière (Kôhî jikô)* greift Hou in einer Huldigung an sein Vorbild die Bildwelten aus Ozus Meisterwerk *Die Reise nach Tokio (Tokyo monogatari*, 1953) auf. Kein anderer lebender Filmemacher – mit Ausnahme von Wong Kar-wai – stellt sich den harten Proben der Vergänglichkeit mit so gründlicher Besessenheit wie Hou, der den Wechsel der Generationen in Träume aus Zelluloid zu verwandeln weiß.

Le Taïwanais Hou Hsiao-hsien est un habitué des festivals depuis vingt ans. Mais c'est *Millennium Mambo (Qianxi manbo*, 2001) qui a su le sortir d'un cercle restreint d'admirateurs et qui lui a valu la comparaison avec son idole Yasujiro Ozu. Avec Lee Pin-bing, son chef opérateur de toujours, Hou crée des films languissants et rigoureux, faits de plans larges et de plans-séquences très colorés ou aux lumières exquises, comme dans le film en costumes *Fleurs de Shanghaï (Hai shang hua*, 1998), qui se déroule dans un bordel de Shanghaï au XIXe siècle. *Millenium Mambo* est une rupture dans le cinéma de Hou : ce n'est pas une reconstitution historique, bien que le récit soit vu à travers les yeux de la jeune héroïne, interprétée par Shu Qi (vedette du cinéma de Hong Kong), qui jette un regard, en 2010, sur sa jeunesse dévoyée d'hôtesse de bar et de boîte, au tournant du siècle. Ces fragments de souvenirs fugaces, suspendus dans le temps, sont le matériau du cinéma de Hou. Triptyque romantique, composé d'histoires d'amour individuelles se déroulant à diverses périodes, *Three Times (Zui hao de shi guang*, 2005) se penche sur la manière dont le temps et l'espace circonscrivent les comportements humains, autre motif récurrent de l'œuvre de Hou. Pour fêter le centenaire de la naissance d'Ozu, *Café Lumière (Kôhî jikô*, 2003) incorpore des images de *Voyage à Tokyo*, le chef-d'œuvre d'Ozu, en hommage au maître japonais qui exerce une influence singulière sur son œuvre. Maître dans l'art de transposer à l'écran le passage d'une génération à l'autre, Hou est, avec Wong Kar-wai, le seul cinéaste vivant qui explore aussi profondément le poids du temps.

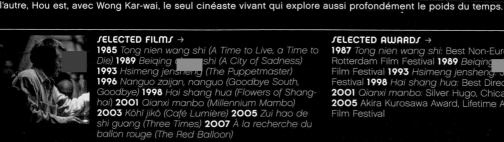

SELECTED FILMS →
1985 *Tong nien wang shi (A Time to Live, a Time to Die)* **1989** *Beiqing c___shi (A City of Sadness)* **1993** *Hsimeng jensheng (The Puppetmaster)* **1996** *Nanguo zaijan, nanguo (Goodbye South, Goodbye)* **1998** *Hai shang hua (Flowers of Shanghai)* **2001** *Qianxi manbo (Millennium Mambo)* **2003** *Kôhî jikô (Café Lumière)* **2005** *Zui hao de shi guang (Three Times)* **2007** *À la recherche du ballon rouge (The Red Balloon)*

SELECTED AWARDS →
1987 *Tong nien wang shi*: Best Non-European, Non-American Film, Rotterdam Film Festival **1989** *Beiqing ___gshi*: Golden Lion, Venice Film Festival **1993** *Hsimeng jensheng*: Jury Prize, Cannes Film Festival **1998** *Hai shang hua*: Best Director, Asia-Pacific Film Festival **2001** *Qianxi manbo*: Silver Hugo, Chicago International Film Festival **2005** Akira Kurosawa Award, Lifetime Achievement, Tokyo International Film Festival

Qianxi manbo
Millennium Mambo

Shu Qi stars as the alienated club hostess Vicky, torn between alternating lovers and the inevitable passage of time. The slicing, manipulation and passing of time is a recurrent theme in Hou's films.

Shu Qi spielt die entfremdete Barhostess Vicky. Sie gibt sich mit wechselnden Liebhabern ab, verspürt jedoch auch das gnadenlose Verrinnen der Zeit. Dieses Vergehen der Zeit, ihr Auseinanderbrechen in Phasen und der Umgang mit ihr, ist ein immer wiederkehrendes Thema in Hous Filmen.

Hôtesse de bar isolée du monde, Vicky (Shu Qi) est tiraillée entre le défilement des amants et l'inévitable fuite du temps. Le découpage, la manipulation et le temps qui passe constituent l'un des thèmes récurrents du cinéma de Hou.

Zui hao de shi guang

Three Times

Hou muse Shu Qi returns in this elegant cinematic triptych, the story of three women living in different historical periods (1911, 1966 and 2005), each grappling with a lover played by Chang Chen.

Auch in diesem eleganten filmischen Triptychon – den Geschichten dreier Frauen, die während unterschiedlicher Epochen leben (1911, 1966 und 2005) und sich mit einem von Chang Chen gespielten Liebhaber auseinandersetzen müssen – steht Hous Muse Shu Qi wieder im Mittelpunkt.

Muse de Hou, Shu Qi est aussi la vedette de cet élégant triptyque, portrait de trois femmes vivant à trois époques différentes (1911, 1966 et 2005), chacune étant aux prises avec un amant interprété par Chang Chen.

"Our lives are full of fragmentary memories. We can't give them names, we can't classify them and they have no great significance. But they lodge in the mind, somehow unshakeable."

„Unser Leben ist gesättigt mit fragmentarischen Erinnerungen. Wir können sie weder bezeichnen noch einordnen, und sie haben auch keine große Bedeutung. Doch in unserem Kopf lagern sie sich ab und bleiben auf irgendeine Art unauslöschlich."

«Nos existences sont remplies de souvenirs fragmentaires. Nous ne savons pas les nommer, nous ne savons pas les classer et ils n'ont pas grande importance. Pourtant, ils restent dans notre esprit, immuables en quelque sorte.»

SPIKE JONZE

Born 22 October 1969 in Rockville, USA

This merry prankster, whose influence has coursed through extreme sports, alternative rock and independent film, directed gonzo skateboard videos in Southern California, which led Spike Jonze to the music video world. His 1994 clip for the Beastie Boys' 'Sabotage' is a classic of the medium, with its zany salute to undercover cop shows of the 1970s. Even better was his clip for Fatboy Slim's 'Praise You' (1998) featuring the director's goofy alter ego, Richard Koufey, and his Torrance Community Dance Group performing spontaneous break dancing moves in public. Jonze's rambunctious spirit was evident in his feature debut, *Being John Malkovich* (1999), a surreal comedy about a puppeteer who discovers a portal into the mind of actor John Malkovich, playing himself. The indie hit also marked the screenwriting debut of Charlie Kaufman, whose neurotic life became the stuff of Hollywood legend in Jonze's second feature, *Adaptation* (2002), a comedy about screenwriting. The *ne plus ultra* of meta movies, with its gleefully cavalier blurring of reality and fiction, featured Nicolas Cage playing both Charlie Kaufman and his nonexistent twin brother, a runaway plot involving stolen orchids and a story structure that Jonze controlled with aplomb. Jonze appeared as an actor in David O. Russell's *Three Kings* (1999) and co-created and produced MTV's puerile prank show *Jackass* (2000–2002) and its movie spin-offs, making Jonze a street culture icon. His third feature, an adaptation of the 1963 children's book *Where the Wild Things Are*, began filming in Australia in the summer of 2006. Its story of a child's wild rumpus into an imaginary jungle filled with playful monsters is vintage Jonze.

Dieser fröhliche Scherzbold, dessen Einfluss sowohl in die Sphären des Extremsports und der alternativen Rockmusik als auch in die Szene des Independent-Films hineinreicht, drehte in Südkalifornien exzentrische Skateboard-Videos und produzierte schließlich Musikvideos. Sein 1994 entstandener Clip für „Sabotage", einen Song der Beastie Boys, ist mit seinen skurrilen Anspielungen auf die Undercoveragenten der TV-Serien aus den 1970er-Jahren ein Klassiker dieses Mediums. Noch besser war sein Video für „Praise You" (1998) von Fatboy Slim, in dem Richard Koufey – das tumbe Alter Ego des Regisseurs – auftritt und die Torrance Community Dance Group in der Öffentlichkeit spontane Breakdance-Einlagen vollführt. Jonze' aufrührerischer Geist prägte seinen ersten Spielfilm *Being John Malkovich* (1999), eine surreale Komödie über einen Puppenspieler, der einen Eingang in den Kopf von John Malkovich (der sich selbst spielt) entdeckt. Der Erfolg dieser unabhängigen Produktion war auch dem Drehbuchdebütanten Charlie Kaufman zu verdanken, dessen neurotisches Leben als typisches Hollywoodthema Grundlage für Jonzes zweiten Spielfilm *Adaption* (*Adaptation*, 2002) war. In dieser Komödie über das Drehbuchschreiben – die ausgelassen und unbekümmert gemeisterten Übergänge zwischen Wirklichkeit und Fiktion machen sie zum Nonplusultra des Metafilms – spielt Nicholas Cage sowohl Charlie Kaufman als auch dessen nicht existierenden Zwillingsbruder. Dabei behielt Jonze die Fäden der turbulenten Handlung, die sich um einen Orchideendiebstahl dreht, sicher im Griff. Als Schauspieler trat Jonze in David O. Russels *Three Kings – Es ist schön, König zu sein* (*Three Kings*, 1999) auf. Als Miterfinder und Produzent der durchgeknallten MTV-Ulkserie *Jackass* (2000–2002) sowie des Films zur Serie avancierte Jonze zu einer Ikone der Off-Kultur. Die Dreharbeiten für seinen dritten Spielfilm *Where the Wild Things Are* (2007), eine Adaption des 1963 erschienenen Kinderbuchklassikers „Wo die wilden Kerle wohnen" von Maurice Sendak, begannen im Sommer 2006 in Australien. Die Geschichte um den frechen Auftritt eines Kindes in einem imaginären Dschungel voller verspielter Monster passt zu diesem Regisseur.

L'influence de ce joyeux blagueur touche les sports extrêmes, le rock alternatif et le cinéma indépendant. Après des vidéos déjantées consacrées aux skaters californiens, Jonze se lance dans le vidéoclip. *Sabotage*, tourné en 1994 pour les Beastie Boys, est devenu un classique du genre, grâce à l'hommage loufoque qu'il rend aux séries policières des années 1970. *Praise You* (1998), pour Fatboy Slim, est encore meilleur, interprété par Richard Koufey, alter ego dingo du cinéaste, et par sa troupe du Torrance Community Dance Group, qui se livre à une *break dance* spontanée. Le premier film de Jonze baigne dans l'exubérance, il s'agit d'une comédie surréaliste intitulée *Dans la peau de John Malkovich* (*Being John Malkovich*,1999), dans laquelle un marionnettiste découvre une porte d'accès à l'esprit de l'acteur John Malkovich, dans son propre rôle. Ce film marque aussi les débuts du scénariste Charlie Kaufman, dont la névrose est devenue légende hollywoodienne avec *Adaptation* (2002). Dans ce *nec plus ultra* du métacinéma, qui brouille allègrement la limite entre réalité et fiction, Nicolas Cage joue le rôle de Kaufman et de son jumeau imaginaire. Jonze maîtrise de bout en bout la structure de ce scénario brillant, où l'on vole des orchidées. Il a également été acteur dans *Les Rois du désert* de David O. Russell. Cocréateur et producteur de la série *Jackass* pour MTV, ainsi que de ses adaptations au cinéma, Jonze est emblématique de la culture populaire. En 2006, il a commencé en Australie le tournage de l'adaptation du livre pour enfants *Max et les maximonstres* (1963), ces aventures animées d'un enfant dans une jungle imaginaire qui grouille de monstres taquins sont dans le plus pur style de Jonze (*Where the Wild Things Are*).

FILMS →
1999 *Being John Malkovich*
2002 *Adaptation*
2008 *Where the Wild Things Are*

SELECTED AWARDS →
1999 *Being John Malkovich*: Critics Award, Grand Special Prize, Deauville Film Festival; FIPRESCI Prize, Venice Film Festival
2000 *Being John Malkovich*: Best First Feature – Over $500,000, Independent Spirit Awards; Best New Filmmaker, MTV Movie Awards
2003 *Adaptation*: Silver Bear, Grand Jury Prize, Berlin International Film Festival

Being John Malkovich

Dans la peau de John Malkovich

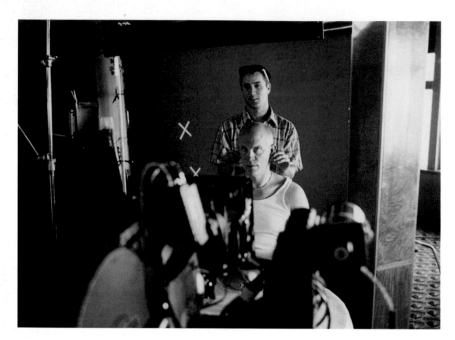

These Spike Jonze set photos show Catherine Keener and John Malkovich having fun while the special effects team try to interpret screenwriter Charlie Kaufman's meta movie hijinks.

Diese Set-Fotos von Spike Jonze zeigen Catherine Keener und John Malkovich, die sich amüsieren, während sich das für die Spezialeffekte verantwortliche Team bemüht, Anweisungen des Drehbuchautors Charlie Kaufman zu interpretieren.

Sur ces photos de plateau prises par Spike Jonze, Catherine Keener et John Malkovich s'amusent, tandis que les techniciens des effets spéciaux tentent d'interpréter les mises en abyme pleines d'humour du scénariste Charlie Kaufman.

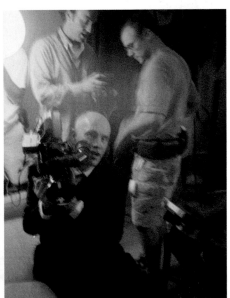

Above: Malkovich and John Cusack on the surrealis-tic set. Below: Spike Jonze (second left) confers with cast members Keener and Cusack.

Oben: Malkovich und John Cusack am surrealistisch anmutenden Set. Unten: Spike Jonze (Zweiter von links) bespricht sich mit den Darstellern Keener und Cusack.

Ci-dessus: Malkovich et John Cusack sur un plateau surréaliste. Ci-dessous: Spike Jonze (deuxième à partir de la gauche) s'entretient avec Keener et Cusack.

Adaptation
Adaption

Overleaf: Chris Cooper takes a break.

Folgende Doppelseite: Chris Cooper gönnt sich eine Pause.

Pages suivantes : Chris Cooper en pause.

On location in the Florida Everglades. Meryl Streep and Chris Cooper play true-life characters from Susan Orlean's book 'The Orchid Thief', whilst Nicolas Cage plays screenwriter Charlie Kaufman, who tries to adapt the book into a Hollywood blockbuster.

Am Drehort in den Everglades von Florida. Meryl Streep und Chris Cooper spielen lebensechte Charaktere aus Susan Orleans Buch *Der Orchideendieb*. Nicolas Cage indes verkörpert den Drehbuchautor Charlie Kaufman, der versucht, die Buchvorlage zu einem Hollywood-Blockbuster umzuarbeiten.

En tournage dans les Everglades, en Floride. Meryl Streep et Chris Cooper interprètent les personnages réels du roman de Susan Orlean *Le Voleur d'orchidées*, tandis que Nicolas Cage joue le rôle du scénariste Charlie Kaufman qui tente de faire de ce livre un succès hollywoodien.

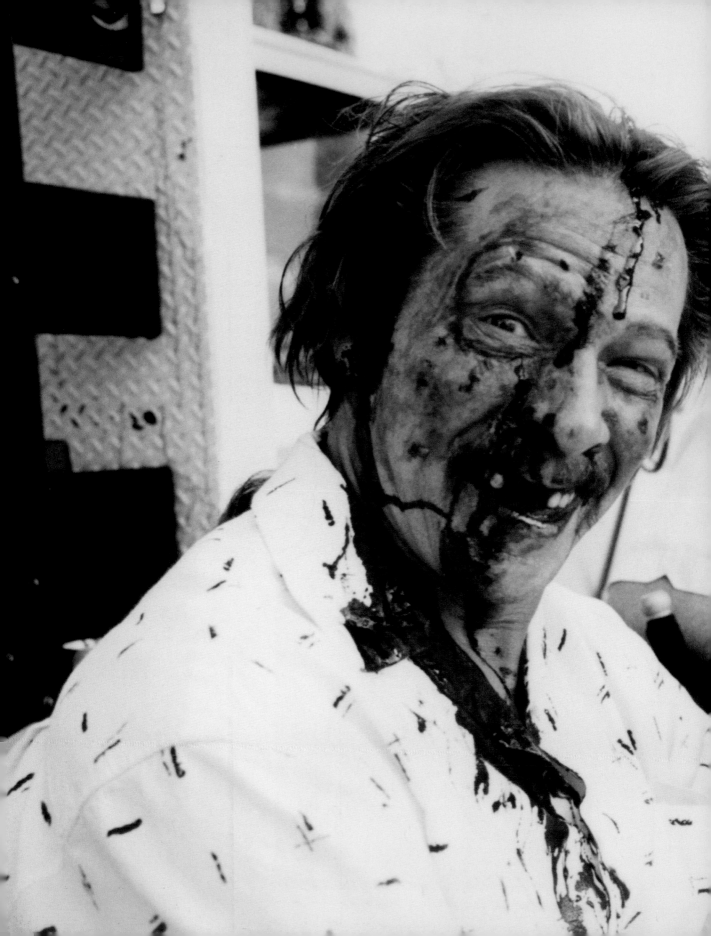

MIRANDA JULY

Born 1 February 1974 in Barre, USA

A breakout hit of the 2005 Sundance Film Festival, *Me and You and Everyone We Know* (2004) was the debut feature written, directed by and starring multimedia darling Miranda July, a quirky romantic comedy-drama that also won two prizes at the Cannes Film Festival before charming audiences around the world in general release. This small, personal film follows senior-citizen caretaker and struggling artist Christine Jesperson (played by July) searching for love and acceptance in a disconnected present-day Los Angeles of shoebox apartments and dour suburban streets far removed from romantic Hollywood fantasy. Christine connects with Richard (John Hawkes), a newly single shoe salesman and father of two boys – including 7-year-old Robby (Brandon Ratcliff), a scene-stealing scatological charmer engaged in a torrid Internet affair with a much-older woman, and his 14-year-old brother Peter (Miles Thompson) who finds himself the target of some rampaging pubescent neighborhood girls. Exuding a droll, unpretentious sweetness with its lonely souls struggling to connect in an isolated world, *Me and You and Everyone We Know* was an impressive debut from the multifaceted July, a performance and video artist who has also produced radio plays, published short stories in *The Paris Review* and directed music videos for the likes of Sleater-Kinney and The Gossip. July's short films and sound installations have screened in major venues, including the Guggenheim Museum and The Museum of Modern Art in New York and the Institute of Contemporary Arts in London.

Ich und du und alle, die wir kennen (*Me and You and Everyone We Know*, 2004) war der erste Spielfilm der Multimedia-Künstlerin Miranda July, die dabei außer als Regisseurin auch noch als ihre eigene Hauptdarstellerin in Erscheinung trat. Auf dem Sundance Film Festival 2005 mit großem Erfolg uraufgeführt und in Cannes mit zwei Preisen geehrt, bezauberte die schrullige romantische Komödie weltweit das Publikum. Der bescheidene, sehr persönliche Film erzählt die Geschichte der Seniorentaxi-Betreiberin und angehenden Künstlerin Christine Jesperson (Miranda July), die im Chaos des heutigen Los Angeles (der Film zeigt die Stadt mit ihren engen Wohnungen und öden Vorortstraßen fernab von beschönigenden Hollywoodfantasien) nach Liebe und Anerkennung sucht. Christine begegnet Richard (John Hawkes), einem seit kurzem alleinstehenden Schuhverkäufer und Vater zweier Jungen. Der siebenjährige Robby (Brandon Ratcliff) verdreht mit seinem skatologischen Charme einer deutlich älteren Internetbekanntschaft den Kopf, während die pubertierenden Mädchen aus der Nachbarschaft hinter seinem 14 Jahre alten Bruder Peter (Miles Thompson) her sind. *Ich und du und alle, die wir kennen* – das beeindruckende Debüt des Multitalents July, einer Performance- und Videokünstlerin, die auch Hörspiele produziert, Kurzgeschichten in *The Paris Review* veröffentlicht und Musikvideos für Sleater-Kinney, The Gossip und andere gedreht hat – bezaubert durch die drollige, unprätentiöse Art, in der einsame Seelen auf ihrer Suche nach Nähe in einer Welt der Vereinzelung gezeigt werden. Julys Kurzfilme und Klanginstallationen wurden bereits in wichtigen Ausstellungshäusern wie dem Guggenheim Museum, dem New Yorker Museum of Modern Art und dem Londoner Institute of Contemporary Arts aufgeführt.

Succès inattendu du Festival Sundance 2005, Moi, toi et tous les autres (Me and You and Everyone We Know) est un premier film, écrit, réalisé et interprété par Miranda July. Cette comédie romantique décalée a remporté deux prix à Cannes, avant de séduire le public du monde entier. Dans ce petit film très personnel, Christine Jesperson (jouée par la cinéaste) est une artiste qui galère et qui s'occupe de personnes âgées. Elle est en quête d'amour et de reconnaissance dans le Los Angeles fragmenté d'aujourd'hui, faits d'appartements minuscules et d'austères rues de banlieue, bien loin des paillettes hollywoodiennes. Christine se lie d'amitié avec Richard (John Hawkes), vendeur de chaussures et nouvellement père célibataire de deux garçons : Robby (Brandon Ratcliff), 7 ans, étonnant séducteur scatologique, entretient une liaison torride sur Internet avec une femme beaucoup plus âgée ; Peter (Miles Thompson), son frère de 14 ans, est la cible d'adolescentes du quartier en pleine puberté. Ces personnages esseulés font tout pour renouer les liens sociaux d'un monde solitaire, dans un film sans prétention, empreint d'une tendresse drôle. Artiste polymorphe, July se consacre aussi à la performance, à la vidéo et aux pièces radiophoniques. Elle a publié des nouvelles dans *The Paris Review* et a réalisé des clips pour Sleater-Kinney et The Gossip. Ses courts métrages et ses installations sonores ont été présentés dans de grands musées comme le musée Guggenheim, le Museum of Modern Art de New York et l'Institute of Contemporary Arts de Londres.

FILMS →
2004 *Me and You and Everyone We Know*

SELECTED AWARDS →
2004 *Me and You and Everyone We Know*: NHK Award, Sundance Film Festival **2005** *Me and You and Everyone We Know*: Special Jury Prize (Dramatic), Sundance Film Festival; Critics Week Grand Prize, Golden Camera, Cannes Film Festival; Jury Award (Best Director), Audience Award, Newport International Film Festival; Audience Award, SKYY Prize, San Francisco International Film Festival

Me and You and Everyone We Know

Ich und du und alle, die wir kennen / Moi, toi et tous les autres

"Every day I am compelled to make things, in whatever medium. I do it because I'm totally captivated by other people and their lives."

„Ich habe täglich das Bedürfnis, irgendetwas zu produzieren, in welchem Medium auch immer. Ich tue das, weil mich andere Menschen und das Leben dieser Leute völlig in ihren Bann ziehen."

«Chaque jour, j'éprouve l'envie de créer des choses, quel que soit le support. Si je fais ça, c'est parce que je suis fascinée par les autres et par leur vie.»

In this romantic comedy about lost souls aching to connect, performance artist and writer-director Miranda July concocts a cuddly, melancholic universe where adults and children are equally adrift.

Mit dieser romantischen Komödie über verlorene Seelen, die sich nach einem Partner sehnen, hat die Performancekünstlerin, Autorin und Regisseurin Miranda July ein kuscheliges, melancholisches Universum geschaffen, in dem Erwachsene und Kinder gleichermaßen auf der Suche sind.

Pour cette comédie romantique dans laquelle des individus perdus rêvent de lien social, Miranda July, scénariste, réalisatrice et artiste de performance, a concocté un univers tendre et mélancolique où adultes et enfants sont pareillement à la dérive.

LODGE KERRIGAN

Born 23 March 1964 in New York City, USA

The underrated American auteur Lodge Kerrigan specializes in existential dramas exuding a distinctly European veneer with their emotional rigidity, outsider protagonists and subjective visual strategies, placing him in the company of Claire Denis, Carlos Reygadas and the brothers Dardenne in the way that Kerrigan's camera serves as a tool for limning the rich inner lives of his psychologically conflicted screen characters. He studied philosophy and filmmaking in his native New York City, spending more than a decade in Europe before achieving his breakthrough with the Steven Soderbergh-produced *Keane* (2004), the story of a schizophrenic man (Damian Lewis) searching New York City for his abducted daughter. Kerrigan's first two features earned the filmmaker a cult following in Europe for their disparate portraits of outcasts living on the margins of society. *Clean, Shaven* (1993) featured another schizophrenic – who may or may not be a serial killer – re-entering life after spending time in an institution; *Claire Dolan* (1998) tracked an immigrant prostitute (played by the late actress Katrin Cartlidge) working in New York City who longs to quit the profession despite owing money to her pimp. From the hallucinatory sound design in *Clean, Shaven* to the impersonal cityscape of New York City in *Claire Dolan* to the subjective camera work in *Keane* that places the viewer in the shoes of the desperate, possibly disturbed title character, Kerrigan is a master at eliciting cinematic poetry from the harrowing quandaries of his protagonists. His three features to date share an uncompromising penchant for minimal dialogue, challenging subject matter and emotional truthfulness that rank Kerrigan among a handful of visionary renegades.

Der unterschätzte amerikanische Filmemacher Lodge Kerrigan ist auf existenzielle Dramen spezialisiert, die in ihrer emotionalen Rigidität, subjektiven Sichtweise und mit ihren Außenseitern als Hauptfiguren ausgesprochen europäisch wirken. Man könnte Kerrigan in einem Atemzug mit Claire Denis, Carlos Reygadas und den Brüdern Dardenne nennen, denn der Regisseur nutzt die Kamera, um das unerschöpfliche Innenleben seiner Leinwandcharaktere zu schildern, die allesamt psychologische Konflikte austragen. Bevor ihm mit dem von Steven Soderbergh produzierten Film *Keane* (2004) – der Geschichte eines schizophrenen Mannes (Damian Lewis), der in New York City nach seiner verschwundenen Tochter sucht – der Durchbruch gelang, hatte Kerrigan in seiner Heimatstadt Philosophie und Film studiert und mehr als zehn Jahre in Europa verbracht. Mit seinen ersten beiden Spielfilmen, die grundverschiedene, am Rande der Gesellschaft lebende Menschen porträtierten, eroberte sich der Filmemacher in Europa eine Fangemeinde. Schon *Clean, Shaven* (1993) kreiste um einen Schizophrenen, der nach einem Aufenthalt in einer Anstalt wieder ins normale Leben tritt und von dem keiner weiß, ob er ein Serienmörder ist oder nicht. *Claire Dolan* (1998) zeichnet das Porträt einer in New York lebenden irischen Prostituierten (gespielt von der inzwischen verstorbenen Katrin Cartlidge), die ihren Beruf aufgeben will, ihrem Zuhälter jedoch Geld schuldet. Ob über das halluzinatorische Klangdesign von *Clean, Shaven*, die Inszenierung der unpersönlichen Stadtlandschaft New York Citys in *Claire Dolan* oder die subjektive Kameraführung in *Keane*, die den Betrachter in die Haut des verzweifelten, vielleicht auch geistig verwirrten Titelhelden versetzt – Kerrigan versteht es meisterhaft, die qualvolle, ausweglos scheinende Situation seiner Protagonisten in filmische Poesie umzumünzen. Die drei bisherigen Spielfilme Kerrigans, den man zur kleinen Gruppe visionärer Eigenbrötler zählen muss, offenbaren die Vorliebe des Regisseurs für minimalistische Dialoge, herausfordernde Thematiken und emotionale Wahrhaftigkeit.

Auteur américain sous-estimé, Lodge Kerrigan met en scène des récits existentiels au parfum nettement européen, marqués par une rigueur émotionnelle, des personnages en marge et la subjectivité de la caméra. En cela, il est l'égal de Claire Denis, de Carlos Reygadas et des frères Dardenne, par sa manière de peindre à petites touches la richesse de la vie intérieure de personnages en proie à des conflits psychologiques. Après avoir étudié la philosophie et le cinéma à New York, il a passé plus de dix ans en Europe. Produit par Steven Soderbergh, *Keane* (2004) est le film qui l'a révélé. C'est le récit de la recherche, par un père schizophrène (Damien Lewis), de sa jeune fille qui a été enlevée. Ses deux premiers films lui valent de devenir culte en Europe pour ses portraits disparates de marginaux. Le personnage principal de *Clean, Shaven* (1993) est un autre schizophrène, et possible tueur en série, qui retrouve la vie en société après un séjour en milieu fermé. *Claire Dolan* (1998) suit une prostituée immigrée (incarnée par la regrettée Katrin Cartlidge) qui ne rêve que de quitter le trottoir new-yorkais, malgré l'argent qu'elle doit à son maquereau. La création sonore hallucinatoire de *Clean, Shaven*, le paysage new-yorkais impersonnel de *Claire Dolan*, la caméra subjective de *Keane* qui met le spectateur à la place du personnage désespéré et, peut-être, dérangé – autant d'aspects qui démontrent la parfaite maîtrise de Kerrigan dans sa création d'un cinéma poétique à partir des situations poignantes de ses protagonistes. Ses trois films ont en commun une tendance au dialogue minimaliste, des thèmes exigeants et une sincérité émotionnelle. Kerrigan fait ainsi partie des rares rebelles du cinéma.

FILMS →
1993 *Clean, Shaven*
1998 *Claire Dolan*
2004 *Keane*

SELECTED AWARDS →
1994 *Clean, Shaven:* Silver Hugo Award (Best First Feature), Chicago International Film Festival **1995** *Clean, Shaven:* Someone to Watch Award, Independent Spirit Awards; Special Jury Prize, Best Director Award, Oporto International Film Festival; Best Director Award, Durban International Film Festival **1998** George Delerue Prize, Flanders International Film Festival **2005** *Keane:* Jury Special Prize, International Critics Award, Deauville Film Festival; Prix de l'AQCC

Clean, Shaven

Peter Greene is the schizophrenic protagonist – a deranged man in search of his missing daughter – who may or may not be a killer.

Peter Greene spielt einen Schizophrenen, der nach seiner verschwundenen Tochter sucht und von dem man nicht weiß, ob er ein Mörder ist oder nicht.

Peter Greene interprète un schizophrène à la recherche de sa fille disparue. Est-il aussi un assassin?

Claire Dolan

The late Katrin Cartlidge stars as Claire Dolan, a Manhattan prostitute determined to abandon the call-girl trade in favor of motherhood.

Die inzwischen verstorbene Katrin Cartlidge in der Rolle der Claire Dolan – einer Prostituierten in Manhattan, die ihr Callgirl-Dasein aufgeben und Mutter werden will.

Claire Dolan (la regrettée Katrin Cartlidge) est une prostituée de Manhattan, bien décidée à quitter le métier de call-girl pour devenir mère de famille.

Keane

"It is a thin line between mental health and mental illness. In our day-to-day (lives) many people don't feel that far removed from crossing that line."

„Geistige Gesundheit und Geisteskrankheit trennt nur ein schmaler Grat. Viele Menschen haben in unserem Alltagsleben das Gefühl, kurz davor zu sein, diesen Grat zu überschreiten."

« La limite est ténue entre bonne santé mentale et folie.
Dans notre quotidien, bien des gens sont trés près de franchir cette limite. »

Damian Lewis is Keane, a tormented man who combs Manhattan for a missing daughter who may or may not be a figment of his addled imagination.

Damian Lewis verkörpert Keane, einen Verwirrten, der Manhattan nach seiner vermissten Tochter durchkämmt, einem Mädchen, das möglicherweise aber nur in der Einbildung seines kranken Kopfes existiert.

Homme tourmenté, Keane (Damian Lewis) ratisse Manhattan à la recherche de sa fille disparue. À moins qu'elle ne soit que le fruit de son imagination perturbée...

KIM KI-DUK

Born 20 December 1960 in Bonghwa, South Korea

The South Korea-born Kim Ki-duk moved to Paris in his twenties and worked as a sidewalk artist after a peripatetic youth, in which he attended agricultural training school, worked in factories, and enlisted in the Marines. After returning to Seoul in the early 1990s, Kim wrote several screenplays that won local prizes, resulting in financing for his violent and misogynist first feature *Crocodile* (*Ag-o*, 1996). His international breakthrough was *The Isle* (*Seom*, 2000), another gruesome drama featuring minimal dialogue that became notorious after an Italian critic fainted during a screening at the Venice Film Festival. During his nascent years, Kim became known for turning out one or two low-budget productions each year, notable for their quick shoots and extreme violence – including orally and vaginally inserted fishhooks in *The Isle*. His themes began softening in the wake of the widely heralded *Spring, Summer, Fall, Winter ... and Spring* (*Bom, yeoreum, gaeul, gyeowool, geurigo bom*, 2003), a spare Buddhist fable set in a floating monastery on a placid lake featuring Kim in a supporting performance. His predilection for scant dialogue and clever visual puns resurfaced in *3-Iron* (*Bin-jip*, 2004), a drama about a loner who breaks into the homes of people on vacation. Arguably Kim's most popular film, *3-Iron* earned him the directing prize at the Venice Film Festival but drew critical animosity for its resemblance to Tsai Ming-liang's *Vive l'Amour* (*Aiqing wansui*, 1994). A self-taught director whose work is mostly embraced in Europe, Kim's most recent features are *Time* (*Shi gan*, 2006), a drama featuring a young girl who pushes the limits of the relationship with her boyfriend when she goes under the plastic surgeon's knife, and *Breath* (*Soom*, 2007).

Nach einer unsteten Jugend, während er eine Landwirtschaftsschule besucht, in Fabriken gearbeitet und bei der Marine gedient hatte, ließ sich Kim Ki-duk mit Mitte zwanzig in Paris nieder und schlug sich als Straßenkünstler durch. In den frühen 1990er-Jahren kehrte er nach Seoul zurück und gewann als Drehbuchschreiber mehrere Preise, die es ihm ermöglichten, seinen brutalen und frauenfeindlichen ersten Spielfilm *Crocodile* (*Ag-o*, 1996) zu finanzieren. Seinen internationalen Durchbruch hatte er mit *The Isle* (*Seom*, 2000), einem ebenfalls grausigen Drama, bei dessen Vorführung während des Filmfestivals von Venedig ein italienischer Kritiker in Ohnmacht fiel. Während seiner frühen Jahre war Kim dafür bekannt, jedes Jahr ein oder zwei Low-Budget-Filme zu drehen, die durch schnelle Aufnahmen und extreme Gewaltdarstellungen hervorstachen: In *Die Insel* sind zum Beispiel Szenen zu sehen, bei denen Angelhaken oral und vaginal versenkt werden. Mit seinem allgemein gelobten Film *Frühling, Sommer, Herbst, Winter ... und Frühling* (*Bom, yeoreum, gaeul, gyeowool, geurigo bom*, 2003), einer kargen buddhistischen Fabel, die in einem auf einem einsam gelegenen See als Floß schwimmenden Kloster spielt und in der Kim in einer Nebenrolle auftritt, wurden seine Themen etwas verträglicher. In *Bin-jip* (2004), einem Drama um einen Einzelgänger, der in Wohnungen einbricht, deren Eigentümer im Urlaub sind, zeigt sich wieder die Vorliebe des Regisseurs für knappe Dialoge und clevere optische Tricks. Für *Bin-jip*, seinen populärsten Film, wurde Kim zwar beim Filmfestival von Venedig mit dem Regiepreis ausgezeichnet, Kritiker bemängelten jedoch eine allzu große Ähnlichkeit mit Tsai Ming-liangs *Vive l'amour – Es lebe die Liebe* (*Aiqing wansui*, 1994). Kims Werk wird vor allem in Europa geschätzt. Die jüngsten Filme des autodidaktischen Regisseurs sind *Time* (*Shi gan*, 2006) und *Breath* (*Soom*, 2007). *Time* handelt von einem jungen Paar: Die Frau unterzieht sich einer Schönheitsoperation, um die Liebe ihres Partners zu prüfen.

Vers l'âge de vingt ans, Kim Ki-duk quitte sa Corée natale pour Paris, où il travaille comme artiste de rue. Durant sa jeunesse, il a fait des études d'agriculture, travaillé en usine et s'est engagé dans la marine. Après son retour en Corée du Sud dans les années 1990, il écrit plusieurs scénarios qui seront primés. Il peut ainsi tourner *Crocodile* (*Yasaeng dongmul bohoguyeog*, 1996), son premier film, violent et misogyne. L'histoire de *L'Île* (*Seom*, 2000), qui le propulse sur la scène internationale, est également atroce et comporte peu de dialogues. Il a été la cause de l'évanouissement d'un critique au Festival de Venise. À ses débuts, Kim enchaîne d'année en année des films à petit budget, connus pour un temps de tournage réduit et d'une violence extrême (avec prise à l'hameçon d'un être humain dans *L'Île*). Il s'adoucit un peu après *Printemps, été, automne, hiver ... et printemps* (*Bom yeoreum gaeul gyeowool geurigo bom*, 2003), fable bouddhiste dépouillée se déroulant dans un monastère flottant sur un lac paisible, avec Kim dans un rôle secondaire. Sa prédilection pour les dialogues succincts et les astuces visuelles réapparaît dans *Locataires* (*Bin-jip*, 2004), où un personnage solitaire entre par effraction chez des personnes parties en vacances. Le plus populaire de ses films, *Locataires*, a remporté le prix de la mise en scène à Venise, tout en se voyant vivement reproché de trop ressembler à *Vive l'amour* de Tsaï Ming-liang. Cinéaste autodidacte surtout apprécié en Europe, Kim a réalisé, en 2006, *Time* (*Shigan*), dans lequel une femme jalouse recourt à la chirurgie esthétique pour attiser le désir de son partenaire, et, en 2007, le film *Breath* (*Soom*).

SELECTED FILMS →
1998 *Palan taemun (The Birdcage Inn)*
2000 *Shilje sanghwang (Real Fiction)*
2000 *Seom (The Isle)* **2001** *Soochwieen boolmyung (Address Unknown)* **2001** *Nabbeun namja (Bad Guy)* **2002** *Haeanseon (The Coast Guard)* **2003** *Bom, yeoreum, gaeul, gyeowool, geurigo bom (Spring, Summer, Fall, Winter... and Spring)* **2003/04** *Samaria (Samaritan Girl)* **2004** *Bin-jip (3-Iron)* **2005** *Hwal (The Bow)* **2006** *Shi gan (Time)* **2007** *Soom (Breath)*

SELECTED AWARDS →
2003 *Haeanseon:* FIPRESCI Prize, Netpac Award, Karlovy Vary International Film Festival **2003** *Bom, yeoreum, gaeul, gyeowool, geurigo bom:* Don Quixote Award, Netpac Award, Youth Jury Award, Locarno International Film Festival **2004** *Samaria:* Silver Bear (Best Director), Berlin International Film Festival **2004** *Bin-jip:* Special Director's Award, FIPRESCI Prize, Little Golden Lion, Venice Film Festival **2005** *Bin-jip:* FIPRESCI Film of the Year, San Sebastián International Film Festival

Bom, yeoreum, gaeul, gyeowool, geurigo bom

Spring, Summer, Fall, Winter ... and Spring / Frühling, Sommer, Herbst, Winter ... und Frühling / Printemps, été, automne, hiver ... et printemps

"I don't make films to serve the audience. I don't try to entice viewers to watch, understand, or even like my films – that's not my job."

„Ich mache keine Filme, um mich dem Publikum anzudienen. Ich unternehme nichts, um Leute in meine Filme zu locken, ihnen das Verständnis zu erleichtern, und erwarte auch nicht, dass sie meine Filme mögen – das ist nicht meine Aufgabe."

« Je ne fais pas des films pour plaire au public. Je n'essaie pas d'inciter les spectateurs à regarder, à comprendre ou même à aimer mes films. Ce n'est pas mon boulot. »

Kim's quiet and contemplative coming-of-age drama examines, over the course of five vignettes, the natural ebb and flow of life.

Kims ruhiges und kontemplatives Drama über das Erwachsenwerden thematisiert in einer Folge von fünf Vignetten das natürliche Auf und Ab des Lebens.

En cinq tableaux, Kim évoque, avec une tranquillité contemplative, le passage à l'âge adulte et le cycle naturel de la vie.

Samaria
Samaritan Girl

In Kim's bittersweet and tragic film Kwak Ji-min and Seo Min-jeong play childhood friends who take up prostitution to fund a trip to Europe.

In Kims bittersüßem und tragischem Film spielen Kwak Ji-min und Seo Min-jeong Jugendfreundinnen, die sich als Prostituierte verdingen, um eine Reise nach Europa finanzieren zu können.

Dans cette tragédie douce-amère, Kwak Ji-min et Seo Min-jeong interprètent deux amies d'enfance qui se livrent à la prostitution pour financer un voyage en Europe.

Bin-jip
3-Iron / Locataires

Jae Hee is a motorcycle deliveryman in this almost-silent comedy-drama about a winsome home invader who falls in love with the wife of an abusive businessman.

In diesem fast wortlosen komödiantischen Drama spielt Hee Jae einen Motorradkurier, der auf charmante Weise in fremde Wohnungen einbricht und sich eines Tages in die Frau eines gewalttätigen Geschäftsmanns verliebt.

Livreur à moto, le séduisant Jae Hee s'introduit dans les maisons et tombe amoureux de l'épouse d'un homme d'affaires odieux, dans une comédie dramatique presque entièrement sans dialogues.

Hwal

The Bow / Hwal – Der Bogen / L'Arc

The bow, which can be used as a weapon or
musical instrument, is a metaphor for the love that
wizened old seafarer Jeon Sung-hwan feels for
16-year-old Han Yeo-reum.

Der Bogen, der sowohl als Waffe wie auch als
Musikinstrument benutzt werden kann, ist eine
Metapher für die Liebe, die der knorrige alte
Seemann Jeon Sung-hwan für die 16-jährige
Han Yeo-rum empfindet.

À la fois arme et instrument de musique, l'arc est
la métaphore de l'amour qu'éprouve le vieux loup
de mer Jeon Sung-hwan pour Han Yeo-reum, une
adolescente de 16 ans.

Shi gan

Time

Kim Ki-duk's treatise investigates the social phenomenon of plastic surgery in South Korea, by showing how jealous Se-heui (Park Ji-yeon) changes her face to test her boyfriend's love.

Am Beispiel der eifersüchtigen Se-heui (Park Ji-yeon), die sich ihr Gesicht verändern lässt, um die Liebe ihres Freundes auf die Probe zu stellen, untersucht Kim Ki-duk das soziale Phänomen der Schönheitsoperationen in Südkorea.

Ce film à thèse examine le phénomène de la chirurgie plastique en Corée du Sud, en montrant comment, par jalousie, Se-heui (Park Ji-yeon) modifie son visage pour mettre son amant à l'épreuve.

By treating her face and body like a malleable sculpture, Se-heui recklessly endangers her relationship and her mind.

Indem sie ihr Gesicht und ihren Körper wie eine formbare Skulptur behandelt, setzt Se-heui unbesonnen ihre Beziehung und ihr geistiges Wohlbefinden aufs Spiel.

En traitant son visage et son corps comme une sculpture malléable, Se-heui met inconsidérément en danger sa relation et son bien-être mental.

Born 28 February 1956 in Winnipeg, Canada

Existing in his own unique crackpot universe is the Canadian fabulist Guy Maddin, whose rousing 2000 short *The Heart of the World*, about a woman who travels to the earth's core to jump-start its wavering heart, channeled the frenzied rush of early filmmaking and catapulted the cult hero from Winnipeg, Manitoba to a new level of adulation – reminding cinephiles, with his familiar expressionistic stylings, of the visceral rush that the best movies provide, even in brevity. An invigorating run of wondrous gems followed, including: *Dracula: Pages from a Virgin's Diary* (2002), Maddin's silent, monochromatic dance film collaboration with the Royal Winnipeg Ballet; *Cowards Bend the Knee* (2002/03), his voyeuristic ode to vintage peephole movies, Greek tragedy and film noir that was in its original incarnation a museum installation; and *The Saddest Music in the World* (2003), a mock musical and social satire set during the Great Depression that starred Isabella Rossellini as a beer baroness (sporting glass legs filled with beer!) offering a $25,000 cash prize to the most sorrowful international musical act. Maddin's key themes – as embodied in his most recent film, *My Winnipeg* (2006/07), a meta docu-memoir starring noir icon Ann Savage – include love, amnesia, paternal betrayal, tortured emotions, hockey and, of course, Winnipeg. Enamored with the silent film era, Maddin typically shoots on grainy Super 8 or 16 mm film stock, applying various filtering and tinting effects in post-production to create era-approximate screwball comedies that defy comparison but never cease to delight. His latest narrative feature is the marketing spoof *Brand upon the Brain!* (2006).

Der kanadische Fabulierer Guy Maddin lebt in einem eigenen versponnenen Universum. Sein mitreißender Kurzfilm *The Heart of the World* (2000), der von einer Frau handelt, die zum Mittelpunkt der Erde reist, um das aus dem Takt geratene Herz unserer Welt wieder in Gang zu bringen, greift das hektisch-turbulente Tempo früher Filme auf und verschaffte dem Kultregisseur aus Winnipeg Aufmerksamkeit über den Kreis seiner Bewunderer hinaus – und machte Kinoliebhabern mit dem gekonnten Einsatz expressionistischer Stilmittel wieder einmal deutlich, dass auch Kurzfilme emotional berühren können. Dann folgte ein wundersames Juwel nach dem anderen, darunter *Dracula: Pages from a Virgin's Diary* (2002), Maddins monochromatischer Tanzstummfilm, den er zusammen mit dem Royal Winnipeg Ballet produzierte; *Cowards Bend the Knee* (2002/03), seine ursprünglich als Installation in einem Museum angelegte voyeuristische Huldigung an klassische Guckkastenfilme, griechische Tragödien und den Film noir; schließlich *The Saddest Music in the World* (2003), zugleich Pseudomusical und Sozialsatire, ein Film, der zu Zeiten der Weltwirtschaftskrise spielt und in dem Isabella Rossellini eine Bierbaronin (mit zwei biergefüllten Beinprothesen!) verkörpert, die einen Preis von 25.000 Dollar für die traurigste internationale Musikdarbietung auslobt. Zu Maddins auch in seinem Film *My Winnipeg* (2006/07) – einer autobiografischen Meta-Doku mit der Film-noir-Ikone Ann Savage – wiederkehrenden Themen gehören Liebe, Gedächtnisverlust, väterlicher Verrat, Gefühlsnöte, Hockey und natürlich Winnipeg. Typisch für den in die Stummfilmära vernarrten Maddin ist, dass er auf körnigem Super-8- oder 16-mm-Material dreht und die Filme in der Postproduktion mit unterschiedlichen Filtern und durch Einfärbungen in alt erscheinende Screwball-Komödien verwandelt, die mit nichts zu vergleichen, stets aber vergnüglich sind. Sein jüngster Spielfilm ist die Marketingparodie *Brand upon the Brain!* (2006).

Le fabuliste canadien Guy Maddin vit dans un monde de douce folie. Il crée l'enthousiasme en 2000 avec *The Heart of the World* (2000), voyage au centre de la Terre d'une femme qui doit en relancer le cœur faiblissant. Riche de la frénésie digne des premiers temps du cinéma, ce film fait soudain du réalisateur de Winnipeg un héros adulé des cinéphiles, grâce à son style expressionniste et à l'urgence caractéristique des meilleurs films, même brefs. Suit une série roborative de petites merveilles : *Dracula, pages tirées du journal d'une vierge* (*Dracula : Pages from a Virgin's Diary*, 2002), film chorégraphique, muet et monochrome, avec le Royal Winnipeg Ballet ; *Et les lâches s'agenouillent* (*Cowards Bend the Knee*, 2002/03), initialement une installation présentée dans un musée, devenue une ode aux vieux films voyeuristes, à la tragédie grecque et au film noir ; et *The Saddest Music in the World* (2003), parodie des comédies musicales et satire sociale sur la grande Crise, avec Isabella Rossellini en baronne de la bière (portant jambes de verre remplies de bière !), prête à offrir 25 000 dollars au numéro musical le plus triste au monde. *Winnipeg* (*My Winnipeg*, 2006) est un métadocumentaire sur la mémoire, avec la star du film noir Ann Savage. Les thèmes sont ceux de toute son œuvre : l'amour, l'amnésie, la trahison paternelle, les tourments émotionnels, le hockey et Winnipeg. Amoureux du cinéma muet, Maddin aime le grain du super 8 ou du 16 mm, y ajoute des filtres, teint les images pour créer des comédies débridées, guère comparables à leurs aînées, mais toujours séduisantes. Son dernier film en date est une satire du marketing, intitulée *Des Trous dans la tête !* (*Brand upon the Brain!*, 2006).

FILMS →
1988 *Tales from the Gimli Hospital* 1990 *Archangel*
1992 *Careful* 1997 *Twilight of the Ice Nymphs*
2000 *The Heart of the World* 2002 *Dracula: Pages from a Virgin's Diary* 2002/03 *Cowards Bend the Knee* 2003 *The Saddest Music in the World* 2006 *Brand upon the Brain!* 2006/07 *My Winnipeg*

SELECTED AWARDS →
2003 *Cowards Bend the Knee*: FIPRESCI Prize – Special Mention, Rotterdam International Film Festival 2004 *The Saddest Music in the World*: Film Discovery Jury Award (Best Director), U.S. Comedy Arts Festival

The Heart of the World

"Whenever someone asks me to describe the highlights of my own life, I describe them with a mythic quality and they were usually the family tragedies, the most miserable things. I find the best way of showing these things is to play them for comedy."

„Wann immer mich jemand bittet, ihm die Höhepunkte meines Lebens zu benennen, verleihe ich ihnen eine mythische Qualität. Gewöhnlich handelt es sich dabei um Familientragödien, um die elendigsten Dinge. Ich finde, die beste Art, solche Themen darzustellen, ist, sie als Komödie aufzubereiten."

«Quand on me demande de parler des plus beaux moments de ma vie, je les décris avec un côté mythique, alors qu'il s'agit en général de tragédies familiales, des moments les plus tristes. La meilleure façon de les montrer, c'est sur le mode de la comédie.»

Opposite: Guy Maddin's rollicking six-minute short film, in which the intrepid Russian scientist Anna travels to the earth's core to save the world from heart failure, is a homage to the early silent cinema of Sergei Eisenstein and Georges Méliès.

Below: Maddin directs, and then degrades and processes the film to achieve the desired retro effect.

Rechts: Guy Maddins witziger sechsminütiger Kurzfilm, in dem die unerschrockene russische Wissenschaftlerin Anna (Leslie Bais) zum Erdkern vordringt, um das aus dem Takt geratene Herz der Welt zu retten, ist eine Hommage an Stummfilme von Sergej M. Eisenstein und Georges Méliès.

Unten: Nachdem er einen Film gedreht hat, bearbeitet und entwickelt Maddin das Material auf spezielle Weise, um den gewünschten Retro-Effekt zu erzielen.

Ci-contre : Dans les six minutes exubérantes de ce court métrage de Guy Maddin, Anna, intrépide scientifique russe, voyage au centre de la Terre pour sauver la planète d'un arrêt du cœur. Maddin rend hommage au cinéma muet de Sergueï Eisenstein et de Georges Méliès.

Ci-dessous : Maddin filme, puis détériore et traite la pellicule pour obtenir l'effet rétro désiré.

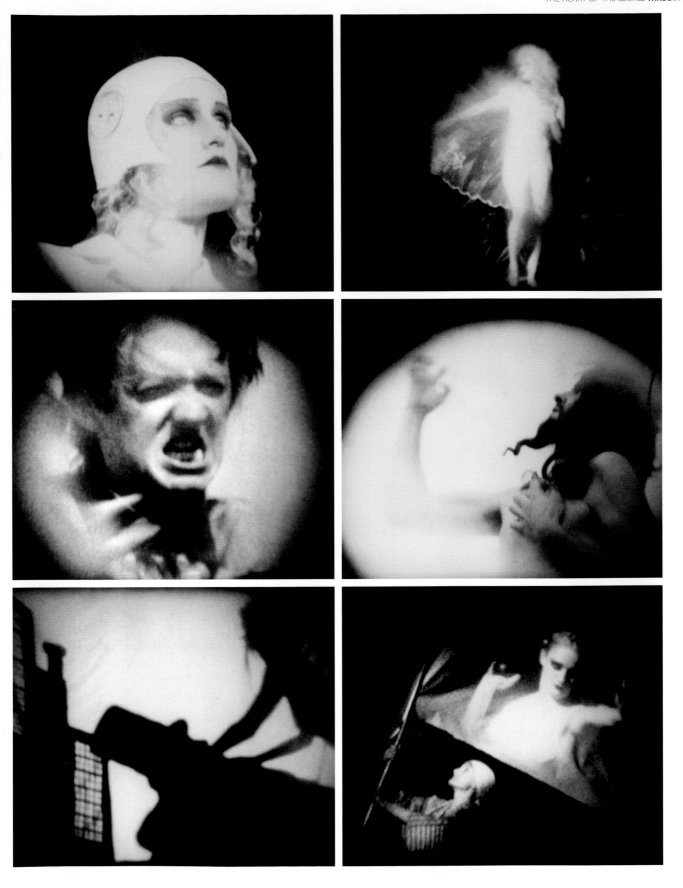

Dracula: Pages from a Virgin's Diary

Dracula, pages tirées du journal d'une vierge

By filming the Royal Winnipeg Ballet in a mostly silent and expressionistic style, Canadian Guy Maddin reinvents the Dracula myth.

Mit seinem in expressionistischem Stil gehaltenen Stummfilm, den er zusammen mit dem Royal Winnipeg Ballet produzierte, erfand Guy Maddin den Dracula-Mythos neu.

En filmant la Compagnie chorégraphique royale de Winnipeg selon un style expressionniste et presque muet, le Canadien Guy Maddin réinvente le mythe de Dracula.

Maddin on the set with principal cast members Zhang Wei-qiang as Dracula, CindyMarie Small as Mina and David Moroni as Dr. Van Helsing.

Maddin am Set mit den Hauptdarstellern Zhang Wei-qiang (als Dracula), CindyMarie Small (als Mina) und David Moroni (als Dr. Van Helsing).

Maddin en tournage avec les principaux acteurs : Zhang Wei-qiang (Dracula), CindyMarie Small (Mina) et David Moroni (docteur Van Helsing).

Cowards Bend the Knee

Et les lâches s'agenouillent

Guy believes his hands to be transplants belonging to his girlfriend's dead father – the hands exact a grisly revenge on all they meet. This mad horror film conjoins peep shows, incest and ice hockey.

Guy (Darcy Fehr) glaubt, seine Hände seien die transplantierten Hände des toten Vaters seiner Freundin – jeder, der von ihnen berührt wird, wird zum Opfer einer grausamen Rache. Dieser verrückte Horrorfilm bringt Peepshows, Inzest und Eishockey zusammen.

Guy croit que ses mains lui ont été greffées et qu'elles appartenaient au défunt père de sa fiancée. Elles se vengent atrocement de tous ceux qu'elles rencontrent. Un film d'horreur délirant qui mêle voyeurisme, inceste et hockey sur glace.

The Saddest Music in the World

Maddin's breakthrough feature is a raucous performance spectacle centering on a one-legged beer baroness (Isabella Rosselini) who sponsors a competition for the world's most melancholy song.

Mit seinem schrillen Pseudomusical um eine einbeinige Bierbaronin (Isabella Rossellini), die einen Wettbewerb um das traurigste Lied sponsert, feierte Maddin seinen Durchbruch.

Maddin a été révélé au grand public par ce spectacle osé dans lequel une patronne de brasserie unijambiste (Isabella Rosselini) parraine le concours de la chanson la plus mélancolique du monde.

Brand upon the Brain!

Des trous dans la tête!

Combining live performance and Lumière-era silent film, Maddin's most ambitious work is this Freudian comic melodrama, in which a live orchestra and sound effects technicians provided sonic accompaniment to a dizzy family saga set on a remote island.

Maddins ambitioniertestes Werk, für das er Liveelemente mit einem Stummfilm im Stil der Lumière-Ära kombiniert, ist ein komisches freudsches Melodrama, dessen auf einer einsamen Insel angesiedelte verwirrende Familiensaga mit der Musik eines Liveorchesters und ausgefeilten Soundeffekten klanglich untermalt wird.

Pour ce mélodrame comique et freudien – son œuvre la plus ambitieuse –, Maddin associe prises de vues conventionnelles et cinéma muet façon Lumière. Un orchestre jouant en direct a créé, avec les ingénieurs du son, la bande-son d'une étourdissante saga familiale sur une île déserte.

TERRENCE MALICK

Born 30 November 1943 in Waco, USA

The reclusive, enigmatic Terrence Malick, whose four features span four decades and share a common naturalistic beauty that renders him a transcendental poet of the moving image, came of age as a farmhand and oil-field worker in Texas and Oklahoma before studying philosophy at Harvard and Oxford. He was a philosophy professor and freelance journalist before he pursued a Master's degree in filmmaking at the American Film Institute, resulting in his first feature, *Badlands* (1973), a serial-killer romance set in the Midwest that was lauded for its striking cinematography reminiscent of still portraiture. In the two decades between his second and third features – the agrarian turn-of-the-century love triangle *Days of Heaven* (1978) and the combat epic *The Thin Red Line* (1998), both of which expanded Malick's dual fascination with human nature and the natural world – the director took an extended teaching sojourn in France. Malick's latest is perhaps his most maligned and misunderstood work to date, the historical drama *The New World* (2005). A romantic interpretation of the Pocahontas myth, the film examines the clash of cultures between Native Americans and British settlers who landed at Jamestown in 1607. Centering on the Powhatan princess (played by 14-year-old newcomer Q'orianka Kilcher) and her doomed love affair with the British Captain John Smith (Colin Farrell), *The New World* featured sumptuous camerawork by Emmanuel Lubezki and the same rapturous reverence for the natural world that defined the maverick's previous works. Malick released his fourth feature in three different versions, confusing casual moviegoers while enchanting select critics and his coterie of admirers, for whom roiling fields of tall grass or a ground-level glimpse up fir trees is akin to cinematic ecstasy.

Der publikumsscheue, geheimnisumwitterte Terrence Malick, der in vier Jahrzehnten vier Spielfilme drehte, die allesamt eine solche natürliche Schönheit ausstrahlen, dass der Regisseur seither als transzendentaler Poet des bewegten Bildes gilt, war in jungen Jahren als Hilfsarbeiter auf einer Farm und auf Ölfeldern in Texas und Oklahoma tätig, bevor er schließlich Philosophie in Harvard und Oxford studierte. Nach einiger Zeit als Philosophiedozent und freier Journalist schloss er ein Filmstudium am American Film Institute mit dem Master-Grad ab. Sein erster Film *Badlands – Zerschossene Träume* (*Badlands*, 1973), eine im Mittleren Westen angesiedelte Romanze um zwei Serienkiller, wurde für die herausragende Kameraarbeit, bei der jedes Bild wie ein Gemälde wirkte, hochgelobt. In den beiden Jahrzehnten zwischen seinem zweiten und seinem dritten Spielfilm – der im ländlichen Texas zu Beginn des 20. Jahrhunderts spielenden Dreiecksgeschichte *In der Glut des Südens / Tage des Himmels – Days of Heaven* (*Days of Heaven*, 1978) und dem Kriegsepos *Der schmale Grat* (*The Thin Red Line*, 1998), beides Filme, in denen Malick sich intensiv seiner besonderen Leidenschaft für das menschliche Wesen und die Natur widmete – zog sich der Regisseur für längere Zeit aus dem Filmgeschäft zurück und lehrte in Frankreich. Malicks jüngster Film, das auf einem in den späten 1970er-Jahren vollendeten Drehbuch basierende historische Drama *The New World* (2005), ist sein bislang wohl am meisten geschmähtes und missverstandenes Werk. Der Film setzt sich in einer romantischen Interpretation mit dem Pocahontas-Mythos und dem Zusammenprall europäischer und indianischer Kultur auseinander, der sich abspielte, nachdem britische Siedler 1607 in der Nähe des heutigen Jamestown in Amerika gelandet waren. Im Mittelpunkt steht die Liebesgeschichte zwischen der (von der 14-jährigen Debütantin Q'orianka Kilcher verkörperten) Powhatan-Prinzessin und dem britischen Kapitän John Smith (Colin Farrell). Wie schon die früheren Werke des Einzelgängers zelebrierte auch *The New World* schwelgerische Bilder (Kameramann: Emmanuel Lubezki) und hinreißende Naturaufnahmen. Malick brachte seinen vierten Spielfilm in drei verschiedenen Versionen heraus, was manchen Gelegenheitskinogänger verwirrte, bestimmte Kritiker und die Schar seiner Anhänger, die beim Anblick von wogenden Feldern oder Kamerafahrten vom Waldboden empor zu den Tannenspitzen in Verzückung geraten, jedoch begeisterte.

Énigmatique et reclus, Terrence Malick est l'auteur de quatre films en quarante ans, dont la beauté naturaliste fait de lui un poète transcendantal du cinéma. Après avoir été ouvrier agricole et manœuvre sur les puits de pétrole au Texas et en Oklahoma, il étudie la philosophie à Harvard et à Oxford. Puis il enseigne la philosophie, devient journaliste et fait des études de cinéma à l'American Film Institute. En 1973, il réalise son premier film, *La Balade sauvage* (*Badlands*, 1973), histoire d'amour sur fond d'assassinats en série dans le Middle West, saluée pour ses images magnifiques, dans le style de la nature morte. Vingt ans séparent ses deuxième et troisième films, *Les Moissons du ciel* (*Days of Heaven*, 1978), triangle amoureux en milieu agricole au tournant du siècle, et *La Ligne rouge* (*The Thin Red Line*, 1998), épopée sur la bataille de Guadalcanal. L'un et l'autre amplifient la fascination de Malick pour la nature humaine et le monde naturel. Il abandonne ensuite le cinéma, pour un séjour d'enseignement prolongé en France. Sa dernière œuvre en date a été la plus malmenée et la plus mal comprise. Inspiré d'un scénario achevé à la fin des années 1970, *Le Nouveau Monde* (*The New World*, 2005) est une reconstitution historique. Interprétation romantique du mythe de Pocahontas, le film évoque le choc des cultures entre Amérindiens et colons britanniques débarqués à Jamestown en 1607, en s'intéressant particulièrement à l'idylle contrariée entre la princesse powhatan (incarnée par Q'orianka Kilcher, âgée de 14 ans) et le capitaine John Smith (Colin Farrell). Emmanuel Lubezki a signé une photo somptueuse pour ce film qui dénote le même ravissement pour le monde naturel que les films précédents. Trois versions différentes du film ont été distribuées, suscitant la confusion chez le spectateur commun, mais c'est pour le plaisir de ses admirateurs et critiques qui s'extasient devant des prés de hautes herbes ou des sapins vus en contre-plongée.

FILMS →
1973 *Badlands*
1978 *Days of Heaven*
1998 *The Thin Red Line*
2005 *The New World*

SELECTED AWARDS →
1974 *Badlands:* Golden Seashell, Best Film, San Sebastián International Film Festival
1979 *Days of Heaven:* Best Director, Cannes Film Festival; Best Screenplay – Foreign Language, David di Donatello Awards
1999 *The Thin Red Line:* Golden Bear (Best Film), Berlin International Film Festival

The New World

Le Nouveau Monde

Native Americans clash with English settlers over land that would become the Jamestown Colony; explorer John Smith (Colin Farrell) falls in love with the princess Pocahontas (Q'Orianka Kilcher).

Amerikanische Ureinwohner werden in einem Gebiet, das sich zur Jamestown-Kolonie entwickeln sollte, mit englischen Siedlern konfrontiert. Der Entdecker John Smith (Colin Farrell) verliebt sich in die Indianerprinzessin Pocahontas (Q'orianka Kilcher).

Amérindiens et colons anglais s'affrontent pour une terre qui allait devenir la colonie de Jamestown. John Smith, l'explorateur (Colin Farrell), s'éprend de la princesse Pocahontas (Q'orianka Kilcher).

The difference in culture and values lies at the heart of Malick's historical drama, in which Pocahontas is uprooted from her homeland and visits a world new to her: the 17th-century English court.

Kulturelle Differenzen und unterschiedliche Wertvorstellungen sind die zentralen Themen, um die Malicks historisches Drama kreist. Pocahontas wird aus ihrer gewohnten Umgebung herausgerissen und bereist eine für sie völlig neue Welt, die des englischen Hofes im 17. Jahrhundert.

Les différences culturelles et morales sont au cœur de la reconstitution historique de Malick, dans laquelle Pocahontas, arrachée à sa terre, découvre un monde entièrement nouveau : la cour anglaise du XVIIe siècle.

"I will find joy in all I see." – Pocahontas, *The New World*

„An allem, was ich sehe, will ich mich erfreuen." – Pocahontas, *The New World*

« Je trouverai le bonheur dans tout ce que je vois. » – Pocahontas dans *Le Nouveau Monde*

MICHAEL MANN

Born 5 February 1943 in Chicago, USA

The master visualist and sensualist who became enamored of movies after seeing Kubrick's *Dr. Strangelove or: How I Learned to Stop Worrying and Love the Bomb* (1963) studied film in London during the 1960s. Mann returned to the US in 1971 and began writing and directing crime dramas for television. His debut feature, *Thief* (1981), the story of a safecracker yearning to go straight retained by the Mafia to pull off a series of daring jewel heists, illuminated Mann's recurring theme of men at work under pressure – a theme that coursed through his thieves-versus-cops epic *Heat* (1995), tobacco industry exposé *The Insider* (1999), prizefighter biopic *Ali* (2001) and Los Angeles crime thriller *Collateral* (2004), whose grainy nocturnal exteriors (shot on a Viper FilmStream high-definition digital camera by Dion Beebe) reflected Mann's consummate knack for transforming urban spaces and cityscapes into screen characters in their own right. Mann repeated this formula in *Miami Vice* (2006), a big-screen re-imagining of the influential television crime drama he executive produced in the 1980s, replacing that show's era-defining pastels with a darker, more somber palette. The story of undercover drug operatives Ricardo Tubbs (Jamie Foxx) and Sonny Crockett (Colin Farrell) in South Florida, *Miami Vice* was unrelenting in its depiction of danger and violence in the narcotrafficking underworld – yet, like *Collateral*, it was also seductively beautiful, with stunning overhead shots of speedboats racing in tandem across the Florida Keys, cool, minimalist interiors that put most boutique hotels to shame and a ravishing, refreshingly rapacious Gong Li as a Chinese-Cuban cartel leader.

Dieser meisterhafte und sinnliche Bilderzähler, der seine Leidenschaft für das Kino entdeckte, nachdem er Kubricks *Dr. Seltsam oder Wie ich lernte, die Bombe zu lieben* (*Dr. Strangelove or: How I Learned to Stop Worrying and Love the Bomb*, 1963) gesehen hatte, studierte in den 1960er-Jahren Film in London. 1971 kehrte Mann in die USA zurück und begann, Krimiserien für das Fernsehen zu schreiben und zu drehen. Sein erster Spielfilm *Der Einzelgänger* (*Thief*, 1981), die Geschichte eines aussteigewilligen Tresorknackers, der von der Mafia gezwungen wird, eine Reihe riskanter Juwelendiebstähle zu begehen, ließ bereits Manns Grundthema – das Verhalten von Männern, die unter Druck gesetzt werden – aufscheinen, das sich auch durch viele seiner späteren Filme zieht: durch das Gangster-gegen-Polizisten-Epos *Heat* (1995), *Insider* (*The Insider*, 1999), einen Thriller um Machenschaften der Tabakindustrie; die Boxer-Biografie *Ali* (2001) und den Los-Angeles-Krimi *Collateral* (2004), dessen (von Dion Beebe mit einer hochauflösenden Viper-FilmStream-Digitalkamera eingefangene) körnige Nachtaufnahmen Manns unübertroffenes Geschick verdeutlichten, urbanen Räumen und Stadtlandschaften eine ganz eigene Rolle auf der Leinwand zuzuweisen. Dieses Rezept wandte Mann auch auf *Miami Vice* (2006) an, eine Kinofassung der einflussreichen Fernsehkrimiserie, an der er in den 1980er-Jahren als ausführender Produzent beteiligt war. Allerdings ersetzte er nun die Pastelltöne jener Serienära durch eine dunklere, düsterere Palette. *Miami Vice*, die Geschichte der in Südflorida operierenden verdeckten Drogenermittler Ricardo Tubbs (Jamie Foxx) und Sonny Crockett (Colin Farrell), beschreibt unerbittlich Gefahren und Gewalttätigkeit in der Unterwelt des Drogenhandels. Doch ähnlich wie *Collateral* war der Film auch von verführerischer Schönheit – es gibt Luftaufnahmen von Rennbooten, die nebeneinander über die Florida Keys preschen, coole, minimalistische Interieurs, hinter denen sich die meisten Designerhotels verstecken müssen, und eine hinreißende, erfrischend unersättlich auftrumpfende Gong Li, die den chinesisch-kubanischen Kopf eines Drogenkartells spielt.

Cinéaste de la sensualité, tombé amoureux du cinéma après avoir vu *Docteur Folamour* de Kubrick, Mann étudie le cinéma à Londres dans les années 1960. Après son retour aux États-Unis en 1971, il écrit et réalise des séries policières télévisées. *Le Solitaire* (*Thief*, 1981), marque ses débuts au cinéma : un perceur de coffre-fort veut se retirer du métier, mais la Mafia le contraint à effectuer une série de vols de bijoux audacieux. Le thème des hommes au travail y est déjà présent, comme dans *Heat* (1995), histoire de gendarmes et de voleurs, *Révélations* (*The Insider*, 1999), consacré à l'industrie du tabac, *Ali* (2001), biographie du champion de boxe, et *Collateral* (2004), thriller qui se déroule à Los Angeles. Les extérieurs nocturnes granuleux de *Collateral* (filmés par Dion Beebe avec une caméra numérique haute définition Viper FilmStream) témoigne de son art de transformer un paysage urbain en un personnage. Mann reprend la formule pour *Deux Flics à Miami* (*Miami Vice*, 2006), adaptation de la célèbre série dont il était le producteur exécutif dans les années 1980. Les tons pastels de la série télévisée cèdent la place à une palette plus sombre. Ricardo Tubbs (Jamie Foxx) et Sonny Crockett (Colin Farrell) sont deux agents de la brigade des stupéfiants en mission en Floride. Mann dépeint sans concession le danger et la violence du trafic de narcotiques. Mais les images sont à couper le souffle : deux hors-bord en pleine course vus en plongées verticales dans l'archipel des Keys ; intérieurs minimalistes à faire pâlir les chaînes hôtelières ; et Gong Li en chef de cartel, Sino-cubaine ravissante, mais vénéneuse.

SELECTED FILMS →
1992 *The Last of the Mohicans*
1995 *Heat*
1999 *The Insider*
2001 *Ali*
2004 *Collateral*
2006 *Miami Vice*

SELECTED AWARDS →
1999 *The Insider:* Freedom of Expression Award,
National Board of Review, USA
2004 *Collateral:* Future Film Festival Digital Award,
Venice Film Festival; Best Director, National Board of Review, USA

Miami Vice
Miami Vice – Deux Flics à Miami

"This work is for people who are artistically ambitious. This is for people who like challenges. If you want to kick back and take life easy, this is not for you."

„Das ist was für Leute mit künstlerischem Anspruch, für Leute, die Herausforderungen mögen. Nichts für die, die sich nur zurücklehnen und das Leben leichtnehmen wollen."

«Ce métier est fait pour ceux qui ont une ambition artistique, pour ceux qui aiment les défis. Si vous voulez vous la couler douce, vous n'êtes pas fait pour ce métier.»

In Michael Mann's location photos his co-producer Gusmano Cesaretti and assistant director Michael Waxman are often used as models to test how light and color will fall on the actors.

Für Location-Fotos nutzte Michael Mann oft seinen Koproduzenten Gusmano Cesaretti und den Regie-assistenten Michael Waxman als Double, um zu testen, mit welchem Lichteinfall und welchen Farbwirkungen er bei den Schauspielern zu rechnen hat.

Pour les photos de repérage de Michael Mann, son coproducteur Gusmano Cesaretti et son assistant-réalisateur Michael Waxman jouent les doublures afin de faire des essais de lumière et de couleur.

Digital cameras see the night differently, and Mann tests the technology to the limit during his research. He even visited the Ferrari factory to see how light was reflected on the glistening bodywork.

Digitalkameras nehmen ganz andere Bilder der Nacht auf, und so stellte Mann mit dieser Technologie bei seinen Vorbereitungen gründliche Experimente an. Er suchte sogar die Ferrari-Werke auf, um zu überprüfen, wie die schimmernden Karosserien der Sportwagen das Licht reflektieren.

La caméra numérique perçoit la nuit différemment. Mann met cette technologie à l'épreuve durant la préparation. Il a même visité l'usine Ferrari pour voir comment la lumière est réfléchie sur les carrosseries rutilantes.

Mann photographed Gong Li and Colin Farrell during rehearsals (below) to see their body language together, and later took them on location (above) to rehearse for his sensual, seductive big-screen re-imagining of *Miami Vice*.

Während der Proben fotografierte Mann Gong Li und Colin Farrell (unten), um zu sehen, mit welcher Körpersprache die beiden kommunizieren. Später hat er sie dann noch einmal bei Proben an den Drehorten aufgenommen (oben) – bis schließlich die sinnlichen, verführerischen Leinwandbilder von *Miami Vice* entstanden.

Pendant les répétitions, Mann a photographié Gong Li et Colin Farrell (ci-dessous) pour voir comment s'associaient leurs gestuelles respectives, puis en extérieur (ci-dessus), pour une nouvelle approche, sensuelle et séduisante, de la série télévisée.

Naomie Harris and Jamie Foxx play undercover vice detectives Trudy Joplin and Ricardo 'Rico' Tubbs.

Naomie Harris und Jamie Foxx spielen die verdeckten Ermittler Trudy Joplin und Ricardo „Rico" Tubbs.

Naomie Harris et Jamie Foxx sont Trudy Joplin et Ricardo « Rico » Tubbs, agents secrets de la brigade des mœurs.

Latin American street culture figures prominently in *Miami Vice*, which was filmed in Florida, Paraguay, the Dominican Republic, Uruguay and Brazil. These 'visual notes' helped Mann to develop his layered visual language.

Die lateinamerikanische Straßenkultur spielt eine wesentliche Rolle in *Miami Vice*, der in Florida, Paraguay, der Dominikanischen Republik, Uruguay und Brasilien gedreht wurde. Solche visuellen Verweise sind typisch für Manns vielschichtige Bildsprache.

La culture populaire latino-américaine baigne le film, tourné en Floride, au Paraguay, en République dominicaine, en Uruguay et au Brésil. Mann s'est servi de ces «notes visuelles» pour élaborer la multiplicité de ses images.

NEIL MARSHALL

Born 25 May 1970 in Newcastle upon Tyne, UK

The British creature-feature maestro Neil Marshall earned praise for his 2001/02 comedy-horror-suspense hybrid *Dog Soldiers*, about a squadron of British army officers on a training mission in the Scottish Highlands who stumble upon the savaged human remains of their intended rivals, spurring them into battle with a voracious breed of giant wolf-like creatures starved for human flesh. *Dog Soldiers* served up effective creature effects on a budget and drew comparisons to both *The Howling* (1980) and *An American Werewolf in London* (1981) for its innovative update on familiar werewolf conceits. Not even the most seasoned horror and suspense devotee was prepared for Marshall's second feature, *The Descent* (2005), one of the most terrifying movies ever made. A spelunking movie savaging the sort of Girl Power camaraderie introduced by the Spice Girls, *The Descent* tracks six buxom female extreme-sports aficionados through a cave in the American wilderness where they quickly discover they are not alone. After an underground earthquake, there is no exit. When they aren't getting stuck in narrow passages (for claustrophobics, *The Descent* is truly the stuff of nightmares) the scantily clad women battle a vicious breed of amphibious creatures (modeled after, of all people, Iggy Pop) that made for some frighteningly convincing effects work, considering the film's relatively low budget. Adept at breakneck pacing and shocking reversals, Marshall injects black comedy into his mix, making him an heir to Sam Raimi and Peter Jackson, meaning he won't stay a secret for long. His next feature is the big-budget science-fiction thriller *Doomsday* (2007).

Der Brite Neil Marshall, ein Meister der Inszenierung von Monsterfilmen, erntete für seinen spannenden Comedy-Horror-Zwitter *Dog Soldiers* (2001/02) großes Lob. Der Film erzählt die Geschichte eines Trupps britischer Armeeangehöriger, die zu einer Kampfübung in den schottischen Highlands abgesetzt werden. Statt auf ihre Gegenspieler treffen sie nur noch auf deren übel zugerichtete Leichen und werden in einen verzweifelten Kampf gegen eine Horde wolfsähnlicher Kreaturen, die nach Menschenfleisch gieren, verwickelt. *Dog Soldiers* bot mit bescheidenen Mitteln umgesetzte, doch wirkungsvolle Monstereffekte und wurde für seine innovative Interpretation der überlieferten Werwolfmythen sowohl mit *Das Tier* (*The Howling*, 1980) als auch mit *American Werewolf* (*An American Werewolf in London*, 1981) verglichen. Auf Marshalls zweiten Spielfilm *The Descent – Abgrund des Grauens* (*The Descent,* 2005), einen der schreckenerregendsten Filme, die je gedreht wurden, waren nicht einmal die ausgebufftesten Horror- und Thrillerfreunde vorbereitet. Dieser Höhlenforscherfilm nimmt jene Art von Kameraderie unter Frauen aufs Korn, die von den Spice Girls vorexerziert worden war. *The Descent* folgt sechs vollbusigen Extremsportlerinnen, die in ein Höhlensystem in der amerikanischen Wildnis eindringen und bald merken, dass sie nicht alleine sind. Nach einem unterirdischen Erdbeben ist auch der Ausgang verschüttet. Und so müssen sich die spärlich bekleideten Damen – wenn sie nicht gerade in engen Gängen stecken bleiben (für Klaustrophobe ist *The Descent* ein wahrer Albtraum) – gegen heimtückische, amphibische Wesen zur Wehr setzen (die offenbar vor allem dem Äußeren von Iggy Pop nachempfunden sind). Berücksichtigt man das bescheidene Budget, mit dem der Film produziert wurde, gelingen dem Regisseur so manche überzeugende Horroreffekte. Marshall, der geschickt mit halsbrecherischem Tempo und schockierenden Kehrtwenden arbeitet, bezieht auch Elemente schwarzen Humors mit ein und steht so in der Tradition von Sam Raimi und Peter Jackson – soll heißen: Geheimnisse haben bei ihm eine kurze Halbwertszeit. Sein nächster Spielfilm ist der mit einem großzügigen Budget geplante Science-Fiction-Thriller *Doomsday* (2007).

Neil Marshall a été couvert de louanges avec *Dog Soldiers* (2001/02), film d'horreur comique à suspense, dans lequel un escadron britannique en manœuvre dans les Highlands écossais découvre les restes de ses « adversaires » et se retrouve à combattre des loups-garous géants et voraces, en manque de chair humaine. Malgré le petit budget de ce film, les créatures n'ont rien à envier à *Hurlements* ni au *Loup-garou de Londres*, tant il renouvelle le genre. Même les amateurs les plus endurcis de films d'horreur ne s'attendaient pas au deuxième film de Marshall, *The Descent* (2005), l'un des films les plus terrifiants jamais réalisés. Dans cette aventure spéléologique, qui anéantit l'esprit de camaraderie féminine façon Spice Girls, six femmes plantureuses, adeptes des sports extrêmes, explorent une grotte du désert américain, mais découvrent vite qu'elles ne sont pas seules. Un tremblement de terre les prend au piège. Quand elles ne se retrouvent pas coincées dans un passage étroit (claustrophobes, attention aux cauchemars !), nos héroïnes court vêtues se débattent contre des amphibiens agressifs (inspirés d'Iggy Pop !). Les effets spéciaux sont effroyablement convaincants, surtout pour un film à petit budget. Adepte du montage vif et du coup de théâtre, Marshall aime aussi l'humour noir et se pose ainsi en héritier de Sam Raimi et de Peter Jackson. Son œuvre devrait bientôt connaître la célébrité. Son nouveau film sera un thriller de science-fiction à gros budget, intitulé *Doomsday* (2007).

FILMS →
2001/02 *Dog Soldiers*
2005 *The Descent* **2007** *Doomsday*

SELECTED AWARDS →
2002 *Dog Soldiers:* Golden Raven, Brussels International Festival of Fantasy Film **2005** *The Descent:* Best Director, British Independent Film Awards

The Descent

The Descent – Abgrund des Grauens

The cavernous interiors of Neil Marshall's claustro-phobic second feature were meticulously planned (above), constructed (opposite top, with director Marshall at center) and filmed (below) at Pinewood Studios in the UK, despite being set in the US Appalachian Mountains.

Die Höhlenräume für Neil Marshalls klaustrophobi-schen zweiten Spielfilm wurden in den britischen Pinewood-Studios bis ins kleinste Detail geplant (oben), konstruiert (oben gegenüber, Regisseur Marshall ist in der Mitte zu sehen) und gefilmt – obwohl die Handlung im Gebirgszug der amerika-nischen Appalachen spielt.

Les intérieurs souterrains du deuxième film de Neil Marshall ont été méticuleusement préparés (ci-dessus), construits (ci-contre, en haut ; Marshall est au centre) et filmés (ci-dessous) pour créer une atmosphère oppressante aux studios anglais de Pinewood, bien que l'action se déroule dans les Appalaches aux États-Unis.

"My belief is that if you start a film all the way up at level 10 you've got nowhere to go."

„Ich meine, wenn man einen Film schon auf einem allzu forcierten Level beginnen lässt, bleiben kaum noch Möglichkeiten, ihn weiterzutreiben."

« À mon avis, quand on fait démarrer son film au niveau le plus élevé, on ne sait plus où aller. »

When the group of adventurous girls are trapped in an unmapped cave system, Saskia Mulder (opposite) emerges as the fittest to survive after they encounter cannibalistic cave dwellers (above). Left: The girls bid a fond farewell to director Neil Marshall.

Als die Gruppe abenteuerlustiger junger Frauen in einem unerforschten Höhlensystem verschüttet wird, erweist sich Rebecca (Saskia Mulder, gegenüber) als die Geschickteste im Überlebenskampf gegen kannibalische Höhlenwesen (oben). Links: Liebevoll verabschieden sich die Damen von Regisseur Neil Marshall.

Les jeunes aventurières se retrouvent piégées dans une grotte ne figurant sur aucune carte. Saskia Mulder (ci-contre) s'avère la plus apte à survivre à la rencontre avec des créatures cannibales (ci-dessus). À gauche : Le tendre au revoir des jeunes femmes au cinéaste Neil Marshall.

LUCRECIA MARTEL

Born 14 December 1966 in Salta, Argentina

A standout name in New Argentine Cinema, Lucrecia Martel directed documentaries, children's programs and short films, including the award-winning *Dead King* (*Rey muerto*, 1995). Her debut feature was *The Swamp* (*La Ciénaga*, 2000/01), a sweltering domestic drama with dark comic undercurrents about an extended middle-class family's summer vacation on a mouldering country estate in northern Argentina. Featuring an opening sequence that was among the most vivid in memory – a family cocktail hour next to a fetid swimming pool turns raucous and bloody after the matriarch steps on broken glass – it demonstrated Martel's unique talent for capturing small, aggravated moments through circumspection as opposed to brute force. *The Swamp*'s remarkable sound design was stunning in its own right, with patio chairs dragged across concrete, wine glasses clinking and shattering, children shouting into electric fans, adults bickering, dogs barking, mud-stuck cows moaning, the television blaring – the film may have been about a torpid swamp but Martel's restless debut couldn't sit still or shut up. You couldn't ignore it if you tried. Her second feature, the more restrained *The Holy Girl* (*La niña santa*, 2004), returned to the town of *La Ciénaga* for a solemn coming-of-age drama about the sexually curious Catholic schoolgirl Amalia (María Alche) who tries to save a married doctor from a life of sin after he sexually molests her in a crowd. Executive produced by Pedro and Agustín Almodóvar, *The Holy Girl* advanced Martel's predilection for nuanced characters stuck in miasmas both literal and figurative – in Amalia's case, the awkward middle ground between good and evil and innocence and experience, where temptation makes it difficult to distinguish one from the other. Her latest feature is the psychological thriller *Headless Woman* (*La mujer sin cabeza*, 2007).

Lucrecia Martel, eine der profiliertesten Vertreterinnen des neuen argentinischen Films, produzierte zu Beginn ihrer Karriere Dokumentationen, Kindersendungen und Kurzfilme, darunter der preisgekrönte *Rey muerto* (1995). Ihr erster Spielfilm *La Ciénaga – Morast* (*La Ciénaga*, 2000/01) ist ein mit düster-schrägen Untertönen versetztes, brütendes häusliches Drama über eine weitverzweigte Mittelklassefamilie, die auf einem verfallenen Landsitz in Nordargentinien Ferien macht. Die höchst lebhafte Eröffnungssequenz gehört zu den denkwürdigsten, die je zu sehen waren: Die harmlose Cocktailstunde der Familie am Rande eines stinkenden Swimmingpools verwandelt sich, nachdem die Matriarchin in Glasscherben getreten ist, in ein wüstes und blutiges Spektakel – und demonstriert Martels einzigartige Begabung, kurze, aggressionsgeladene Momente genau und bedacht einzufangen, statt sich roher Gewalt zu bedienen. Die bemerkenswerte Geräuschkulisse, mit der die Regisseurin *La ciénaga – Morast* unterlegt hat, ist für sich schon etwas Besonderes. Da werden die Stühle des Patios über Beton gezogen, Weingläser klirren und scheppern, Kinder schreien Ventilatoren an, Erwachsene zetern zänkisch, Hunde kläffen, im Schlamm versinkende Kühe muhen erbärmlich, ein Fernseher dröhnt vor sich hin – der Film hätte ja auch wie träger Morast dahingleiten können, doch in Martels ruhelosem Debüt hält nichts inne, verstummt nichts. Und man kann sich dem auch kaum entziehen. Ihr zweiter Spielfilm, der zurückhaltendere *La niña santa* (2004), spielt in der gleichen Stadt wie *La Ciénaga – Morast* und ist ein ernstes Drama über das Heranreifen des sexuell neugierigen katholischen Schulmädchens Amalia (María Alche), das versucht, einen verheirateten Arzt von seinem sündigen Leben abzubringen, nachdem dieser sie zuvor sexuell belästigt hat. Der von Pedro und Agustín Almodóvar produzierte Film unterstrich einmal mehr Martels Vorliebe für nuancierte Charaktere, die sowohl im wörtlichen als auch im übertragenen Sinne in einem Sumpf stecken – in Amalias Fall ist es die prekäre Lage zwischen Gut und Böse oder Unschuld und Erfahrung –, und immer wieder erschwert es ihnen die Versuchung, zwischen beidem zu unterscheiden. Martels neuer Spielfilm ist der psychologische Thriller *La mujer sin cabeza* (2007).

Auteur de documentaires, d'émissions pour enfants et de courts métrages, parfois récompensés comme *Le Roi est mort* (*Rey muerto*, 1995), Lucrecia Martel s'est fait un nom dans le nouveau cinéma argentin. Dans son premier long métrage, *La Ciénaga* (2001), une famille bourgeoise passe ses vacances d'été dans une propriété décatie du Nord de l'Argentine. Dans une atmosphère suffocante, ce drame familial n'est pas exempt d'humour noir. Au cours de la mémorable scène d'ouverture, la famille est réunie à l'heure de l'apéritif, près d'une piscine nauséabonde. La matrone marche sur du verre brisé et la tension monte instantanément. C'est par la circonspection, plutôt que par la brutalité, que Martel sait rendre la tension des petits instants. Le film est aussi remarquable par son brillant traitement du son : chaises traînées sur le ciment, verres qui s'entrechoquent et se brisent, enfants qui hurlent dans des ventilateurs, adultes qui se querellent, chiens qui aboient, vaches embourbées qui meuglent, télévision à tue-tête. Les débuts de Martel n'ont rien de la torpeur du marais où se déroule *La Ciénaga*. Située dans la même ville que ce dernier, mais avec plus de retenue, *La Niña Santa* (*La niña santa*, 2004) raconte, avec solennité, le passage à l'âge adulte d'Amalia (Maria Alché), lycéenne catholique, obnubilée par les questions sexuelles, qui tente d'arracher à sa vie de débauche un médecin marié, après qu'il a tenté de caresser une jeune femme en pleine rue. *La niña santa*, dont Pedro et Agustín Almodóvar sont les producteurs exécutifs, témoigne du goût de Martel pour des personnages nuancés, pris dans un bourbier aussi concret que métaphorique : Amalia se débat entre le bien et le mal, entre innocence et expérience là où la tentation brouille les distinctions. Film psychologique à suspense, *La Mujer sin cabeza* (2007) est le dernier film en date de Martel

FILMS →
2000/01 *La Ciénaga (The Swamp)*
2004 *La niña santa (The Holy Girl)*
2007 *La mujer sin cabeza (Headless Woman)*

SELECTED AWARDS →
1999 *La Ciénaga:* NHK Award, Sundance Film Festival
2001 *La Ciénaga:* Alfred Bauer Award, Berlin International Film Festival; Best Director, Grand Coral – First Prize, Havana Film Festival

La Ciénaga

The Swamp / La Ciénaga – Morast

An extended family endures the sultry summer heat in provincial Salta, Argentina. An atmosphere of sexual repression and jealousy is mixed with forebodings of death by director Lucrecia Martel (right).

Eine Großfamilie verbringt die Zeit der schwülen Sommerhitze in der argentinischen Provinzstadt Salta. Regisseurin Lucrecia Martel (rechts) kreiert eine Atmosphäre, die von sexueller Unterdrückung, Eifersucht und Todesahnung geprägt ist.

À Salta, une famille souffre de la chaleur étouffante de la province argentine. La cinéaste Lucrecia Martel (à droite) met en scène des présages de mort, sur fond de refoulement sexuel et de jalousie.

La niña santa

The Holy Girl / La Niña Santa

A doctor (left) at a convention tries to seduce the hotel manager (right), unaware that her daughter (above) is the girl he fondled in the street.

Nicht ahnend, dass sie die Mutter des Mädchens ist (oben), das er zuvor auf der Straße belästigt hat, versucht der an einem Kongress teilnehmende Arzt (Carlos Belloso, links), die Hotelmanagerin (Mercedes Morán, rechts) zu verführen.

Lors d'un congrès, un médecin (à gauche) tente de séduire la directrice de l'hôtel (à droite), sans se douter qu'elle est la mère de la jeune fille (ci-dessus) qu'il a tenté de caresser en pleine rue.

"I'm not trying to make stories about Argentina. That is something that doesn't interest me in the slightest."

„Ich versuche nicht, Geschichten über Argentinien zu erzählen. Das interessiert mich nicht im Geringsten."

« Je ne cherche pas à raconter des histoires sur l'Argentine. Cela ne m'intéresse absolument pas. »

An astute director of youths as well as adults, Martel (right) specializes in the restlessness of human nature, embodied in the erotic interplay between the 14-year-old protagonist Amalia and an older doctor.

Martel (rechts), die als Regisseurin sowohl mit Jugendlichen wie auch mit Erwachsenen umzugehen weiß, hat sich auf die Rastlosigkeit der menschlichen Natur spezialisiert. Im erotischen Wechselspiel zwischen der 14-jährigen Amalia (María Alche) und einem deutlich älteren Arzt kommt dies beispielhaft zum Ausdruck.

Excellente directrice de comédiens, aussi bien jeunes qu'adultes, Martel (à droite) scrute l'insatisfaction de la nature humaine, symbolisée par le jeu érotique qui s'instaure entre Amalia, l'adolescente de 14 ans, et le médecin.

FERNANDO MEIRELLES

Born 9 November 1955 in São Paulo, Brazil

Bursting onto the international film scene with the decades-spanning favela gangster epic *City of God* (*Cidade de Deus*, 2002) – which earned Meirelles and his co-director Katia Lund comparisons to Scorsese – this art-house sensation, set in a sprawling Rio de Janeiro slum, grew in popularity thanks to a shrewd platform distribution strategy conceived by its distributor Miramax, which kept *City of God* in theaters for over a year, followed by a healthy afterlife on DVD where its unflinching violence, endlessly quotable dialogue and vibrant visual style made it destined for repeat viewings among crime movie buffs. For his first English-language feature, the quietly devastasting romantic conspiracy thriller *The Constant Gardener* (2005), Meirelles – sans Lund – exercized measurable restraint in an adaptation of John le Carré's subdued bestseller about a British diplomat (Ralph Fiennes) searching for clues in the slaying of his activist wife (Rachel Weisz, winner of the Best Supporting Actor Oscar for her work). Less hyperkinetic than *City of God* but still employing the dense narrative, rapid-fire editing and skittish camera work – courtesy of returning cinematographer César Charlone – of its predecessor, *The Constant Gardener* was sophisticated entertainment boasting a meaty supporting cast, including Danny Huston, Bill Nighy and Pete Postlethwaite. Working with another panoramic backdrop – this time modern-day Kenya, rife with scheming diplomats, idealistic whistle blowers and insidious pharmaceutical hawks swooping in to exploit impoverished, AIDS-plagued refugees as drug-trial guinea pigs, Meirelles proved himself a deft hand at high-class, awards-caliber material that studio specialty divisions were created to release.

Die in einem wuchernden Slum von Rio de Janeiro spielende Arthouse-Sensation *City of God* (*Cidade de Deus*, 2002), ein Gangsterepos aus der Welt der Favelas, dessen Geschichte sich über mehrere Jahrzehnte erstreckt, brachte Meirelles und seiner Co-Regisseurin Katia Lund nicht nur Vergleiche mit Scorsese ein. Der Film mit seinen schonungslosen Schilderungen von Gewalt, zitierwürdigen Dialogen und lebhaften Bildern bot nicht nur Krimifreunden den richtigen Stoff zum wiederholten Genuss: Dank einer klugen Marketingstrategie des Verleihers Miramax erlangte *City of God* große Popularität, lief mehr als ein Jahr in den Kinos und fand anschließend auch als DVD ein breites Publikum. Für seinen ersten englischsprachigen Spielfilm, den schleichend einem unheilvollen Ende zustrebenden romantischen Konspirationsthriller *Der ewige Gärtner* (*The Constant Gardener*, 2005), adaptierte Meirelles – diesmal ohne Lund – sehr behutsam John le Carrés düsteren Bestseller über einen britischen Diplomaten (Ralph Fiennes), der nach Hinweisen zum Mord an seiner politisch aktiven Ehefrau (Rachel Weisz erhielt für ihre Leistung den Oscar als beste Nebendarstellerin) sucht. Der Film war zwar nicht ganz so actiongeladen wie *City of God*, aber dennoch dicht erzählt und rasant geschnitten. Er schwelgt – dank der Kameraarbeit von César Charlone, der nach *City of God* abermals dabei war – ausgelassen in Bildern und bietet, gerade auch durch ausdrucksstarke Nebendarsteller wie Danny Huston, Bill Nighy und Pete Postlethwaite, spannende Unterhaltung. Wieder vor einem weit gesteckten Hintergrund – in diesem Fall das heutige Kenia, in dem sich intrigante Diplomaten, idealistische Informanten und heimtückische Pharmavertreter tummeln, die Aids-geplagte Flüchtlinge als Versuchskaninchen für Medikamente ausnutzen – beweist Meirelles sein Geschick zur Umsetzung eines ebenso hochkarätigen wie preiswürdigen Stoffs, für dessen Filmfassung sich mehrere Produktionsfirmen zusammengeschlossen hatten.

La Cité de Dieu (*Cidade de Deus*, 2002), épopée historique autour de gangsters d'une favela, a propulsé Meirelles, et sa coréalisatrice Katia Lund, sur le devant de la scène internationale, au point qu'on les a comparés à Scorsese. Se déroulant dans un bidonville grandissant de Rio, ce film d'art et d'essai a bénéficié d'une habile stratégie de distribution, mise au point par Miramax. Resté à l'affiche pendant plus d'un an, le film connaît une belle carrière en DVD. Les amateurs de films de gangsters apprécient la violence brute, les répliques mémorables et les images dynamiques. Implacable thriller romantique, *The Constant Gardener* (2005) est le premier film en anglais tourné par Meirelles, sans Lund. Le cinéaste fait preuve d'une certaine retenue pour l'adaptation du best-seller de John Le Carré, dans lequel un diplomate britannique (Ralph Fiennes) enquête sur l'assassinat de son épouse militante (Rachel Weisz, oscar du meilleur second rôle). Si les images sont moins agitées que dans *La Cité de Dieu*, le récit n'en est pas moins dense, le montage rapide et la caméra nerveuse (grâce au même chef opérateur César Charlone). *The Constant Gardener* est une œuvre raffinée, au casting solide, avec Danny Huston, Bill Nighy et Pete Postlethwaite. L'action se situe dans un Kenya contemporain, où pullulent diplomates intriguants, militants idéalistes et faucons insidieux de l'industrie pharmaceutique, prêts à utiliser comme cobayes des réfugiés appauvris, porteurs du virus du sida. Meirelles s'avère capable de réaliser des films de très haute tenue, produits par les départements des studios hollywoodiens créés à cet effet.

SELECTED FILMS →
2000 *Domésticas (Maids)*
2002 *Cidade de Deus (City of God)*
2005 *The Constant Gardener*

SELECTED AWARDS →
2002 *Cidade de Deus:* Grand Coral –
First Prize, FIPRESCI Prize, Havana Film Festival;
Visions Award – Special Citation, Toronto International Film Festival
2003 International Filmmaker of the Year, ShoWest, USA

Cidade de Deus

City of God / La Cité de Dieu

Meirelles (above, in sunglasses) and his crew shot on location in Rio de Janeiro's Ciudade de Deus, the labyrinthine, crime-riddled housing project that lies at the core of the Brazilian director's breakthrough feature.

Meirelles (oben, mit Sonnenbrille) und seine Crew drehten in der Cidade de Deus von Rio de Janeiro – einer labyrinthischen, von Kriminalität geplagten Elendssiedlung, die im Mittelpunkt des Spielfilms steht, mit dem der brasilianische Regisseur bekannt wurde.

C'est à la Cité de Dieu, quartier labyrinthique de Rio de Janeiro où règne la violence, que le Brésilien Meirelles (ci-dessus, avec les lunettes) et son équipe ont tourné le film qui l'a révélé.

The Constant Gardener

Der ewige Gärtner

"I've always been very independent, I've always produced my own things; I don't know how to share. A big studio invests a lot of money, and they want control. I'm not prepared for that yet."

„Ich habe immer sehr unabhängig gearbeitet, stets meine eigenen Sachen produziert. Ich wüsste nicht, wie ich die Verantwortung teilen sollte. Große Studios investieren einen Haufen Geld, und dann wollen sie auch die Kontrolle. Damit kann ich noch nicht umgehen."

« J'ai toujours été très indépendant, je me suis toujours autoproduit ; je ne sais pas partager. Un grand studio qui investit beaucoup d'argent veut tout contrôler. Je ne suis pas prêt à ça. »

Adapting John le Carré's novel, Meirelles showed how the pharmaceutical industry has used Africans as human guinea pigs for new drugs. Rachel Weisz (above), Ralph Fiennes and Pete Postlethwaite give the story a human dimension.

Als Vorlage für Meirelles Film, der die Machenschaften der Pharmaindustrie anprangert, die Afrikaner als Versuchskaninchen für Medikamente ausnutzt, diente John le Carrés gleichnamiger Roman. Rachel Weisz (oben), Ralph Fiennes und Pete Postlethwaite verleihen der Geschichte eine menschliche Dimension.

Dans cette adaptation du roman de John Le Carré, Meirelles démontre comment l'industrie pharmaceutique s'est servi d'Africains comme cobayes pour de nouveaux médicaments. Rachel Weisz (ci-dessus), Ralph Fiennes et Pete Postlethwaite donnent une dimension humaine à ce récit.

JOHN CAMERON MITCHELL

Born 21 April 1963 in El Paso, USA

The writer, actor and director John Cameron Mitchell began attending art- and sex-fueled underground salons in post-9/11 New York City, inspiring him to organize his own monthly nocturnal gathering, Shortbus, modeled after Gertrude Stein's legendary literary mixers from 1920s bohemian Paris. Shortbus – a slang name for a school bus reserved for disabled, emotionally disturbed and/or gifted students – evolved into Mitchell's long-awaited feature film follow-up to *Hedwig and the Angry Inch* (2000), the exhilarating transsexual rock opera that itself debuted in a New York City nightclub before evolving into an off-Broadway play and musical film sensation. After placing an open casting call in alternative newspapers, Mitchell began a two-year improvisational experiment in a Lower Manhattan loft in which his non-professional *Shortbus* actors developed character biographies à la Mike Leigh and explored sexual compatibility among themselves and their characters, as the script called for warts-and-all sex scenes that pushed the envelope of screen sex even further than Michael Winterbottom's *9 Songs* (2004). The resulting film (2006) examines an intersection of emotionally challenged characters of every possible sexual persuasion who meet in a weekly underground salon and wind up in a polysexual carnality that's refreshing in the wake of the overwhelming conservatism that has softened New York City nightlife – and that of much of the rest of the United States – in recent years. There's no ignoring the political message of a gay three-way choreographed to the tune of the American patriotic anthem 'The Star-Spangled Banner'.

Der Autor, Schauspieler und Regisseur John Cameron Mitchell trieb sich im New York nach dem 11. September 2001 in Underground-Salons herum, in denen sich alles um Kunst und Sex drehte. Diese Erfahrungen inspirierten ihn, nach dem Vorbild von Gertrude Steins legendären Bohème-Treffen im Paris der 1920er-Jahre seine eigene monatliche nächtliche Zusammenkunft „Shortbus" zu organisieren. Aus „Shortbus" (ein Slangausdruck für Schulbusse, die behinderten, emotional verunsicherten und/oder besonders begabten Schülern vorbehalten sind) ging Mitchells lange erwarteter erster Spielfilm hervor. Zuvor hatte er *Hedwig and the Angry Inch* (2000) inszeniert, eine in einem New Yorker Nachtclub uraufgeführte hinreißende Rockoper um Transsexuelle, die anschließend zu einer Off-Broadway-Theater- und Musicalfilm-Sensation wurde. Für *Shortbus* castete Mitchell seine Darsteller über Anzeigen in Zeitschriften der alternativen Szene und startete dann mit den Auserwählten ein improvisiertes, zweijähriges Experiment in einem Loft in Lower Manhattan. Die Amateurdarsteller entwickelten dabei – im Stil von Mike Leigh – die Geschichte der dargestellten Figuren und erprobten, inwiefern sie selbst und die von ihnen verkörperten Charaktere sexuell miteinander umgehen konnten, denn im Drehbuch waren Sexszenen mit allen Fehlern und Schwächen vorgesehen – womit der Film in seiner Darstellung von Sex auf der Leinwand noch deutlich weiter ging als Michael Winterbottoms *9 Songs* (2004). Herausgekommen ist ein Film (2006), in dem emotional herausgeforderte Charaktere jeglicher sexueller Orientierung sich einmal in der Woche in einem Underground-Salon einer polysexuellen Fleischeslust hingeben, die im Gefolge eines überhandnehmenden Konservativismus, der das Nachtleben von New York City wie auch sonst in den Vereinigten Staaten während der letzten Jahre in Harmlosigkeiten hat abgleiten lassen, ausgesprochen erfrischend wirkt. Die politische Botschaft eines zum Klang der amerikanischen Nationalhymne „Star-Spangled Banner" choreografierten schwulen Vergnügens zu dritt lässt an Deutlichkeit nichts zu wünschen übrig.

Dans le New York de l'après-11 septembre, le scénariste, acteur et réalisateur John Cameron Mitchell fréquente les salons artistiques et érotiques de l'*underground*, ce qui l'incite à organiser ses propres réunions nocturnes mensuelles, baptisées «shortbus». Il s'inspire des réunions littéraires organisées par Gertrude Stein dans le Paris des années 1920. *Shortbus* est un terme argotique désignant un bus scolaire réservé aux étudiants handicapés, psychologiquement perturbés et/ou doués. En 2006, l'expérience devient un film très attendu, après *Hedwig and the Angry Inch* (2000), exaltant opéra-rock transsexuel, lui-même adaptation d'un spectacle de boîte de nuit, transformé en pièce de théâtre off-Broadway, puis en un surprenant film musical. Après avoir recherché ses acteurs par le biais d'annonces dans des journaux alternatifs, Mitchell entame une expérience d'improvisation qui durera deux ans, dans un loft de Manhattan où ses acteurs amateurs conçoivent les biographies de personnages à la Mike Leigh et étudient la compatibilité sexuelle entre ces personnages et eux-mêmes. Les scènes de sexe sont, en effet, plus que réalistes et repoussent encore plus loin les limites atteintes par *Nine Songs* de Michael Winterbottom. *Shortbus* fait se croiser des personnages émotionnellement instables et de toutes obédiences sexuelles, lors de réunions hebdomadaires. S'ensuivent des ébats polysexuels rafraîchissants, étant donné la vague de conservatisme qui deferle sur la vie nocturne new-yorkaise, et américaine, depuis quelques années. On ne peut ignorer le message politique d'une partie gay à trois, chorégraphiée au son de l'hymne américain.

FILMS →
2000 *Hedwig and the Angry Inch*
2006 *Shortbus*

SELECTED AWARDS →
2001 *Hedwig and the Angry Inch:* Audience Award, Directing Award, Sundance Film Festival; Teddy Award (Best Feature Film), Berlin International Film Festival; Grand Special Prize, Critics Award, Deauville Film Festival; Audience Award, Best Narrative Feature, San Francisco International Film Festival; Golden Space Needle Award (Best Actor), Seattle International Film Festival

Hedwig and the Angry Inch

John Cameron Mitchell wrote, directed and starred in his debut feature, a rock opera adapted from the off-Broadway hit musical about a transsexual rock singer on tour across the US.

In seinem ersten Spielfilm, für den er auch das Drehbuch schrieb, übernahm Regisseur John Cameron Mitchell sogar eine Rolle als Darsteller. Der Film ist die Adaption eines erfolgreichen Broadway-Musicals über die US-Tournee eines transsexuellen Rocksängers.

John Cameron Mitchell a écrit, réalisé et interprété ce premier film, opéra-rock inspiré d'un spectacle musical d'avant-garde, sur la tournée américaine d'un chanteur de rock transsexuel.

Shortbus

"I have seen so few films in which the sex felt really respected by the filmmaker. Hollywood too often shies away from it or makes adolescent jokes about it. Sex is only connected to the negative because people are scared of it."

„Ich kenne nur wenige Filme, bei denen ich das Gefühl habe, dass der Filmemacher den Sex wirklich respektiert. Hollywood drückt sich viel zu oft davor oder behandelt das Thema nur in Form von Witzen für Erwachsene. Sex wird nur mit Negativem in Verbindung gebracht, weil die Leute Angst davor haben."

« J'ai vu tellement peu de films dans lesquels le réalisateur respecte vraiment le sexe. À Hollywood, soit on l'évite en rougissant, soit on fait des blagues d'ados. Le sexe a une connotation négative parce que les gens en ont peur. »

Examining post-9/11 sexual mores in a gentrifying Manhattan, *Shortbus* examines a series of erotic couplings and dysfunctions in and around an exclusive nocturnal salon.

In Manhattan, das sich seit den Ereignissen vom 11.9.2001 in ein immer schickeres Quartier verwandelt hat, gibt es eine Szene von Leuten, die sich gelegentlich in einem nächtlichen Privatsalon treffen. *Shortbus* untersucht ihre erotischen Beziehungen und sexuellen Probleme genauer.

Shortbus s'intéresse aux mœurs sexuelles du Manhattan embourgeoisé de l'après-11 septembre, autour d'un salon privé pour noctambules, avec accouplements et dysfonctionnements érotiques à la clé.

LUKAS MOODYSSON

Born 17 January 1969 in Malmö, Sweden

The most popular Swedish filmmaker since Ingmar Bergman cites The Cure and Morrissey as major influences, having ignited his career with the adolescent romance *Show Me Love* (*Fucking Åmål*, 1998) and the hippie commune comedy *Together* (*Tillsammans*, 2000), before detouring into the morose nihilism of *Lilya 4-ever* (*Lilja 4-ever*, 2002), a harrowing account of a charming Russian teenage girl unwittingly sold into sexual slavery in western Europe. That was nothing compared to *A Hole in My Heart* (*Ett hål i mitt hjärta*, 2004), a transgressive digital video production about an amateur pornographer holed up in a squalid suburban apartment with an aspiring actress and a cameraman. Over the course of an orgiastic weekend, all three become increasingly drunk and uninhibited while the camera documents their degrading antics. Featuring scenes of almost unimaginable degradation, Moodysson described *A Hole in My Heart* as a personal exorcism resulting from the pornification of the mass media. The breath of fresh air his fans hoped would materialize in the wake of his incendiary fourth feature did no such thing; instead Moodysson followed with the experimental curio *Container* (2005/06), featuring grainy black-and-white images of a lumpen schizophrenic protagonist romping with an Asian female dancer through the ruins of Chernobyl while the American actress Jena Malone pontificates in voiceover about the Spice Girls. Shot on 16 mm reversal stock and blown up to 35 mm, Moodysson described *Container* as an "autistic" film about the "little darling that lives inside of us – like Jesus lived inside Mary, or Mary lived inside Jesus," aiming to capture on film the unique perspective of those whose mental capabilities differentiate from what is considered normal.

Der populärste schwedische Filmemacher seit Ingmar Bergman nennt The Cure und Morrissey als prägende Einflüsse auf seine Karriere, in deren Verlauf er Filme wie die Jugendromanze *Raus aus Åmål* (*Fucking Åmål*, 1998) und *Zusammen!* (*Tillsammans*, 2000), eine Komödie über eine Hippiekommune vorlegte, bevor er sich dem verbitterten Nihilismus von *Lilja 4-ever* (2002) zuwandte, der grausamen Geschichte eines reizenden russischen Mädchens, das arglos als Zwangsprostituierte in Westeuropa landet. Das war noch harmlos verglichen mit *Ett hål i mitt hjärta* (2004), einer alle Normen sprengenden digitalen Videoproduktion über einen Amateurpornofilmer, der sich zusammen mit einer ehrgeizigen Darstellerin und seinem Kameramann in einer verwahrlosten Vorstadtwohnung verkriecht. Im Laufe eines orgiastischen Wochenendes werden alle drei immer besoffener und hemmungsloser, während die Kamera ihre zunehmend entwürdigenden Bizarrerien dokumentiert. Moodysson erklärte die Szenen fast unbeschreiblicher Erniedrigung als persönlichen Exorzismus gegen die Durchdringung der Massenmedien mit Pornografie. Die Frischluft, die sich die Fans des Regisseurs von einem vierten aufrüttelnden Spielfilm erhofften, kam nicht auf. Stattdessen ließ Moodysson eine Kuriosität folgen, den grobkörnigen, schwarz-weißen Experimentalfilm *Container* (2005/06), in dem ein plumper, schizophrener Protagonist mit einer asiatischen Tänzerin durch die Ruinen von Tschernobyl tollt, während sich die amerikanische Schauspielerin Jena Malone mit ihrer der Handlung unterlegten Stimme über die Spice Girls auslässt. Moodysson beschreibt den auf 16 mm gedrehten und auf 35 mm vergrößerten Film als ein „autistisches" Werk über „den kleinen Liebling, der in uns allen lebt – wie Jesus in Maria lebte oder Maria in Jesus". Seine Intention war es, den einzigartigen Blick jener, deren geistige Fähigkeiten sich von dem unterscheiden, was gemeinhin als normal betrachtet wird, auf das Medium Film einzufangen.

Le plus populaire des cinéastes suédois depuis Ingmar Bergman revendique l'influence capitale du groupe The Cure et de Morrissey, déclencheurs de sa carrière, entamée avec *Fucking Åmål* (1998) et *Together* (*Tillsammans*, 2000), comédie située dans une communauté hippie. Il se tourne ensuite vers le nihilisme morose avec *Lilja 4-ever* (2002), récit poignant de la vente, à son insu, d'une jolie adolescente russe à un réseau de prostitution en Europe occidentale. Mais *A Hole in My Heart* (*Ett hål i mitt hjärta*, 2004) va beaucoup plus loin. Tourné en vidéo, ce film transgresse les tabous. Un pornographe amateur se cloître dans un appartement sordide, avec une actrice en herbe et un cameraman. Durant un week-end orgiaque, le trio s'enivre et se désinhibe devant la caméra qui enregistre leurs acrobaties dégradantes. Contenant des scènes inimaginables d'avilissement, le film est, pour son réalisateur, une façon d'exorciser la pornification des médias. Le quatrième film incendiaire de Moodysson n'apporte pas l'air frais attendu par ses admirateurs. *Container* (2005/06) est une curiosité expérimentale, tourné en noir et blanc granuleux. Un sous-prolétaire schizophrène se livre à des ébats avec une danseuse asiatique dans les ruines de Tchernobyl, tandis qu'en voix off, l'actrice américaine Jena Malone enchaîne les poncifs à propos des Spice Girls. Filmé en 16 mm réversible et gonflé à 35 mm, *Container* est, selon Moodysson, un film «autiste», consacré au «petit chéri qui vit en nous, comme Jésus en Marie, ou Marie en Jésus». Le cinéaste tente de montrer à l'écran le point de vue particulier de ceux dont les capacités mentales diffèrent de la normale.

FILMS →
1998 *Fucking Åmål (Show Me Love)* **2000** *Tillsammans (Together)* **2002** *Lilja 4-ever (Lilya 4-ever)* **2004** *Ett hål i mitt hjärta (A Hole in My Heart)* **2005/06** *Container*

SELECTED AWARDS →
1999 *Fucking Åmål:* Teddy Award (Best Feature Film), Berlin International Film Festival; Audience Award, Special Prize of the Jury, Karlovy Vary International Film Festival; Sutherland Trophy – Special Mention, London Film Festival **2001** *Tillsammans:* Special Jury Award, Newport International Film Festival; New Director's Showcase Award, Seattle International Film Festival **2002** *Lilja 4-ever:* FIPRESCI Prize – Honorable Mention, Stockholm Film Festival

Fucking Åmål
Show Me Love / Raus aus Åmål

"Sometimes I feel that Swedish films should get less money. Because we don't make very good films, so why should we make more films?"

„Manchmal meine ich, schwedische Filme sollten nicht so einfach finanziert werden. Warum sollten wir, da wir keine besonders guten Filme machen, noch mehr Filme produzieren?

«Parfois, je me dis que le cinéma suédois ne mérite pas autant d'argent. Nous ne faisons pas de très bons films, alors pourquoi en faire d'autres?»

Rebecca Liljeberg and Alexandra Dahlstrom star as aspiring lesbian and beauty queen, respectively, in Lukas Moodysson's achingly sweet and youthful debut feature set in the Swedish suburb of Åmål.

In Lukas Moodyssons bittersüßem Debütfilm, der unter Jugendlichen in der schwedischen Kleinstadt Åmål spielt, verkörpert Rebecca Liljeberg ein Mädchen, das seine lesbischen Neigungen entdeckt, während Alexandra Dahlström das schönste Mädchen an der Schule spielt.

Rebecca Liljeberg et Alexandra Dahlstrom incarnent respectivement une lesbienne potentielle et une reine de beauté, dans le film, d'une tendresse et d'une jeunesse poignantes, de Lukas Moodysson, dont le quartier suédois d'Åmål est le décor.

Tillsammans

Together / Zusammen!

In a suburban Swedish commune circa 1975, various sexual permutations and competing political ideologies result in divisive tension among its eclectic members.

Sexuelle Verwicklungen und konkurrierende politische Ideologien entzweien eine bunt zusammengewürfelte Kommune in einem schwedischen Vorort der 1970er-Jahre.

Vers 1975, permutations sexuelles et idéologies conflictuelles suscitent la zizanie chez les membres hétérogènes d'une communauté hippie suédoise.

Lilja 4-ever

Lilya 4-ever

Oksana Akinshina and Artyom Bogucharsky are childhood friends living in a Russian housing project before Oksana (as Lilja) is kidnapped and made a sex slave.

Oksana Akinshina und Artyom Bogucharsky spielen zwei befreundete Jugendliche, die in einer russischen Sozialwohnungssiedlung leben. Dann aber wird das Mädchen – Lilja – entführt und einem Schicksal als Sexsklavin ausgeliefert.

L'adolescente Lilya (Oksana Akinshina) vit dans une cité russe avec son jeune ami Volodya (Artyom Bogucharsky). Mais Lilya est enlevée et contrainte de se prostituer.

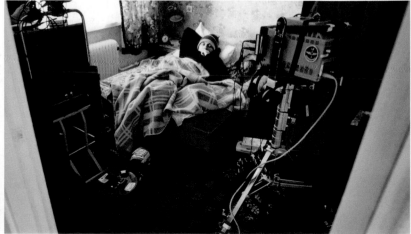

Left: Moodysson on set, filming a scene with his young protagonist (Oksana Akinshina), living with her mother in a cramped Russian housing project. Below: Akinshina with her co-star, Artyom Bogucharsky.

Links: Moodysson am Set. Er filmt gerade eine Szene mit seiner jungen Darstellerin (Oksana Akinshina), die mit ihrer Mutter in einer beengten russischen Sozialwohnung lebt. Unten: Akinshina mit Artyom Bogucharsky, ihrem Filmkumpanen.

À gauche : Moodysson en tournage avec sa jeune actrice (Oksana Akinshina), qui vit avec sa mère dans une cité russe surpeuplée. Ci-dessous : Akinshina et son partenaire, Artyom Bogucharsky.

Ett hål i mitt hjärta

A Hole in My Heart

Two amateur pornographers videotape acts of
extreme human degradation with Sanna Bråding
(left). The morally outraged son of one of the pornographers (above) refuses to participate. Moodysson
(right) sees all.

Zwei Amateurpornofilmer nehmen mit Sanna Bråding
(links) Szenen auf, die extreme menschliche Erniedrigungen zeigen. Der Sohn eines der beiden Filmer
(oben) ist darüber entrüstet und lehnt es ab, sich zu
beteiligen. Moodysson (rechts) hat alles im Blick.

Deux pornographes amateurs filment des scènes
d'avilissement extrême, avec Sanna Bråding
(à gauche). Scandalisé, le fils de l'un d'eux (ci-dessus)
refuse d'y participer. Rien n'échappe à l'œil de
Moodysson (à droite).

Container

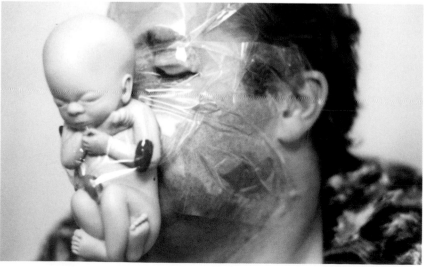

Peter Lorentzon (above) believes he is a woman (right) trapped in a man's body, which is reinforced by the female voiceover speaking his thoughts. Moodysson filmed this avant-garde rumination on 16mm black-and-white film with cinematographer Jesper Kurlandsky.

Peter Lorentzon (oben) glaubt, er sei eine Frau (rechts), die in einem Männerkörper gefangen ist. Die unterlegte weibliche Stimme, die seinen Gedanken Ausdruck verleiht, verstärkt das Gefühl für diese Vorstellung. Moodysson drehte diesen grüblerischen Avantgardefilm mit dem Kameramann Jesper Kurlandsky auf 16-mm-Schwarz-Weiß-Material.

Peter Lorentzon (ci-dessus) incarne un homme convaincu d'être une femme (à droite) enfermée dans un corps masculin, ce que souligne la voix off féminine exprimant ses pensées. Moodysson a tourné cette méditation avant-gardiste en 16 mm noir et blanc, avec le chef opérateur Jesper Kurlandsky.

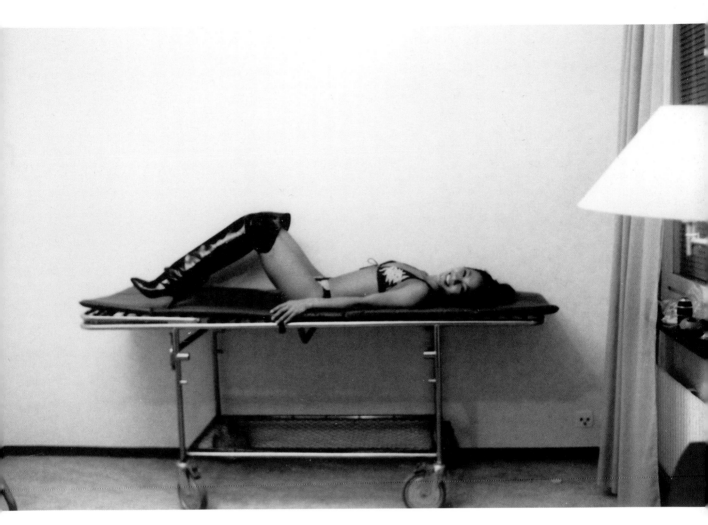

ANDERS MORGENTHALER

Born 5 December 1972 in Copenhagen, Denmark

Inspired by the *anime* films popular in Japan – films in which graphic violence and sexuality make them a far cry from mere cartoons – the Danish filmmaker Anders Morgenthaler set out to make one of the first feature-length European *animes* in the form of *Princess* (2006), an innovative revenge drama featuring 80 percent animation and 20 percent live action, the same formula Morgenthaler employed in his award-winning student graduation film *Araki: The Killing of a Japanese Photographer* (2002), which premiered at the Berlin International Film Festival in 2003. *Princess*, a selection of the Director's Fortnight program at the 2006 Cannes Film Festival, follows the Dutch clergyman August as he descends into the pornographic film underworld intent on killing the gangster film producers responsible for the drug-overdose death of his sister Christina – also known as the porn superstar "The Princess." Morgenthaler's commentary on the pornification of society and the porno-graphic film industry's merciless consumption of human lives, *Princess* is rife with animated sex and violence – though Morgenthaler shrewdly includes live-action footage of Christina as depicted in flashbacks by the real-life actress Stine Fischer Christensen. Morgenthaler began his career in animation as the director of children's television, having studied animation at the Danish Film School. He also contributed a daily comic strip to the Danish national newspaper, which later became a popular television series. Morgenthaler is also the author of several children's books. *Princess*, co-written by Mette Heeno, was a production of Lars von Trier's Zentropa Productions. His next feature is the crime thriller *Echo* (2007), from the new Perestroika division of Zentropa dedicated to producing seven genre films for less than 10 million euros.

Der dänische Filmemacher Anders Morgenthaler wagte sich, inspiriert von den in Japan populären Anime-Filmen – Werken, die mit ihren grafischen Darstellungen von Gewalt und Sexualität kaum noch etwas mit herkömmlichen Cartoons zu tun haben – an eine der ersten europäi-schen Anime-Produktionen in Spielfilmlänge. Dabei nutzte er für *Princess* (2006) – ein innovatives Rachedrama – mit 80 Prozent Animation und 20 Prozent echter Handlung und auf Videomaterial gefilmt die gleiche Mischung wie für seinen mit einem Preis bedachten Studienabschluss-film *Araki: The Killing of a Japanese Photographer* (2002), der 2003 auf der Berlinale uraufgeführt worden war. *Princess*, der in Cannes 2006 im Director's-Fortnight-Programm lief, erzählt, wie sich der Geistliche August in die Niederungen der Pornoszene begibt, weil er die verbrecheri-schen Produzenten umbringen will, die am Tod seiner Schwester Christina schuldig sind. Christina, die als Porno-Superstar unter dem Namen „The Princess" bekannt war, starb an einer Überdosis Drogen. Der Film ist Morgenthalers Stellungnahme zur zunehmenden Präsenz von Porno-grafie in der Gesellschaft und zur gnadenlosen Ausnutzung von Menschen durch die Pornoindustrie. In die Fülle von Trickfilmszenen mit Sex und Gewalt fügt der Regisseur klugerweise auch echtes Filmmaterial ein, das Christina, dargestellt von der Schauspielerin Stine Fischer Chris-tensen, in Rückblenden zeigt. Morgenthaler, der Animation an der dänischen Filmakademie studiert hatte, startete seine Karriere als Trickfilmer mit Fernsehsendungen für Kinder. Eine Zeit lang lieferte er einer dänischen Zeitung auch einen täglichen Comicstrip, der sich später zu einer populären TV-Serie entwickelte. Morgenthaler tat sich auch als Autor mehrerer Kinderbücher hervor. Das Drehbuch zu *Princess*, von Lars von Triers Zentropa Productions produziert, verfasste er gemeinsam mit Mette Heeno. Sein nächster Spielfilm ist der Kriminalthriller *Echo* (2007), den die neue Perestrojka-Abteilung von Zentropa betreut, die sieben Genrefilme für weniger als insgesamt zehn Millionen Euro drehen will.

Inspiré par le genre *animé*, populaire au Japon – dont la violence et les thèmes sexuels le distinguent nettement des films d'animation courants – le cinéaste danois Anders Morgenthaler a signé l'un des premiers *animés* européens avec *Princess* (2006), histoire très originale d'une vengeance, composée à 80 % d'images animées et à 20 % de prises de vues réelles. C'est ainsi que Morgenthaler avait tourné son film de fin d'études, récompensé, *Araki : the Killing of a Japanese Photographer*, présenté à Cannes en 2003. Sélectionné à la Quinzaine des Réa-lisateurs en 2006, *Princess* raconte la descente, dans les enfers du porno, d'August, ecclésiastique hollandais, bien décidé à supprimer les ban-dits producteurs de cinéma, responsables de la mort par overdose de sa sœur Christina, connue sous son nom de vedette du porno, « Prin-cesse ». Avec ce film, Morgenthaler dénonce la pornification de la société et la consommation impitoyable de chair humaine par l'industrie du cinéma pornographique. *Princess* regorge de séquences animées de violence et de sexe, auxquelles le cinéaste ajoute avec ruse des prises de vues réelles de Christina, flash-backs interprétés par l'actrice Stine Fischer Christensen. Après avoir étudié le cinéma d'animation à l'École danoise du cinéma, Morgenthaler a réalisé des émissions télévisées pour enfants. Il est aussi l'auteur d'une BD parue dans le quotidien natio-nal danois, devenue ensuite une célèbre série télévisée, et de plusieurs livres pour enfants. Coécrit par Mette Heeno, *Princess* a été produit par Zentropa Films, la société de Lars von Trier. Cette dernière produit actuellement une série de sept films de genre pour moins de 10 millions d'euros, dans le cadre de sa nouvelle entité Perestroïka. L'un d'eux, le film à suspense *Echo* (2007), est réalisé par Morgenthaler.

FILMS →
2006 *Princess*
2007 *Echo*

SELECTED AWARDS →
2006 The Nordisk Film Award
2006 *Princess:* Silver Méliès (Best European Motion Picture), Sitges International Film Festival of Catalonia; Mine Xplore Award, Flanders International Film Festival-Ghent

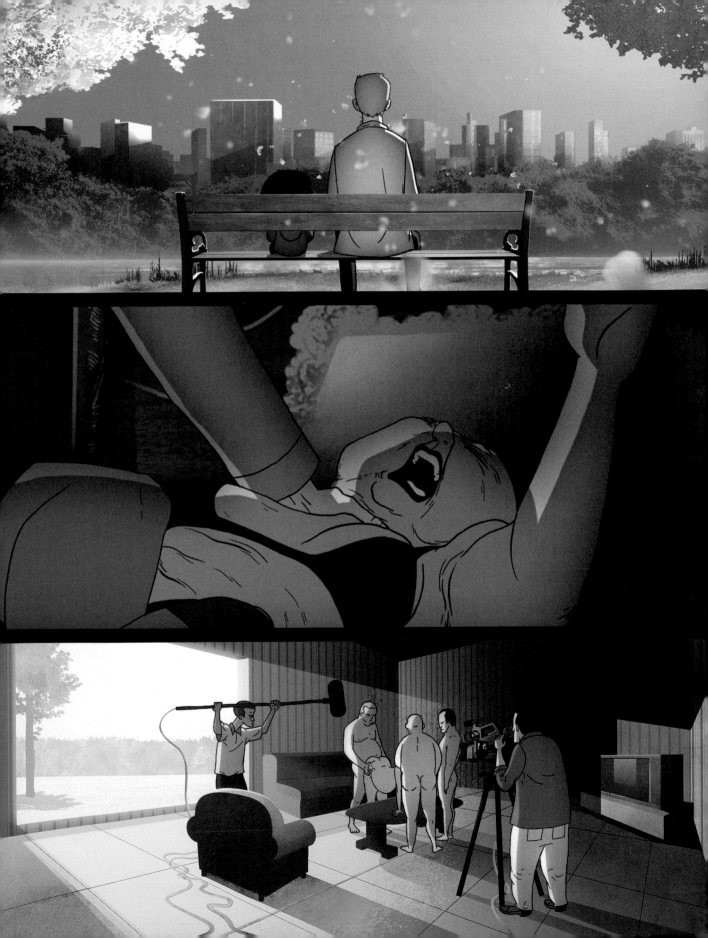

Princess

Anders Morgenthaler's hardboiled, hand-drawn feature debut is awash in pouring rain and bloodshed, centering on an avenger who takes on the porn industry. The sketches above were transformed into finished animation cels (left).

In Anders Morgenthalers knallhartem, handgezeichnetem Spielfilmdebüt strömt unaufhörlich Regen oder auch Blut. Im Mittelpunkt steht ein Rächer, der sich die Pornoindustrie vorgenommen hat. Die oben abgebildeten Zeichnungen wurden zu Bildelementen der Animation ausgearbeitet (links).

Dans son premier long métrage, dessiné à la main, baigné de pluie torrentielle et de sang, Anders Morgenthaler raconte l'aventure d'un justicier affrontant l'industrie du porno. Les dessins ci-dessus sont devenus les cellulos des images finales (à gauche).

"*Princess* is not for kids. It's not nice. It's tough and incredibly depressing. I'm enormously proud of it."

„*Princess* ist nichts für Kinder. Das ist kein schöner Film, er ist brutal und unglaublich deprimierend. Ich bin sehr stolz auf ihn."

«*Princess* n'est pas un film pour enfants. Il n'a rien de mignon. Il est dur et incroyablement déprimant. J'en suis extrêmement fier.»

CHRISTOPHER NOLAN

Born 30 July 1970 in London, UK

The savior of the Batman franchise directed Super 8 movies at age seven starring miniature action figures before segueing into English literature during his university studies in London. His debut feature *Following* (1998) demonstrated an early predilection for the film noir sensibility in the story of a young man's obsession with following strangers that leads him into the criminal underworld. Shot vérité-style with a handheld 16mm on black-and-white stock, *Following* incorporated noir conceits like chiaroscuro lighting and flashbacks that would serve Nolan well in his second feature, the cerebral indie smash *Memento* (2000), about an insurance investigator (Guy Pearce) suffering from amnesia who tries to solve his wife's murder *sans* short-term memory. *Memento*'s convoluted story unraveled in reverse, with the hapless protagonist – bedecked in hand-scrawled tattoos and bearing Polaroids to keep him abreast of his own antics – uttering memorable lines such as "I can't remember to forget you." After his underrated studio calling card *Insomnia* (2002), a moody detective thriller set in Alaska's perpetual daylight that was remade from Erik Skjoldbjærg's 1997 Norwegian hit of the same name, Nolan brought his witty, hardboiled flourishes to *Batman Begins* (2005), re-energizing that dormant war horse and eliciting a terrific central performance from Christian Bale as a less campy Caped Crusader. Nolan reunited with Bale for *The Prestige* (2006), a lavish period fantasy set in turn-of-the-century London co-starring Hugh Jackman in a story of rival magicians battling each other for trade secrets. Next up is his Batman sequel, *The Dark Knight*, scheduled for summer 2008 and co-starring Heath Ledger as The Joker.

Der Retter des „Batman"-Franchise drehte schon im Alter von sieben Jahren Super-8-Filme, in denen seine Spielzeug-Actionfiguren auftraten. In London studierte Nolan dann englische Literatur. Seinem ersten Spielfilm *Following* (1998) – der Geschichte eines jungen Mannes, der obsessiv Fremde verfolgt und so in die Welt des Verbrechens gerät – merkte man bereits die Vorliebe des Regisseurs für eine vom Film noir geprägte Sicht der Dinge an. Der mit einer 16-mm-Handkamera in Schwarz-Weiß im Cinéma-vérité-Stil gedrehte Film nutzt typische Film-noir-Effekte wie starke Helldunkelkontraste und Rückblenden, Techniken, die Nolan auch in seinem zweiten Spielfilm einsetzte. *Memento* (2000) erzählt von einem Versicherungsagenten, der nach einem Überfall an Amnesie leidet und versucht, den Mord an seiner Frau aufzuklären. Die verwickelte Story von *Memento* wird vom Ende zum Anfang erzählt, wobei der unglückselige Protagonist – der sich als Erinnerungsstütze Tattoos auf die Haut kritzelt und gerade Erlebtes auf Polaroids festhält – denkwürdige Sätze wie „Ich kann mich nicht daran erinnern, dich zu vergessen" von sich gibt. Nach dem unterschätzten *Insomnia* (2002), seiner ersten Produktion für ein großes Studio, einem im Alaska der Mitternachtssonne angesiedelten Thriller um einen verdrossenen Polizeiermittler (ein Remake des gleichnamigen norwegischen Erfolgsfilms (1997) von Erik Skoldbjærg), brachte Nolan seine Cleverness und seinen Sinn für Hartgesottenes in die Verfilmung von *Batman Begins* (2005) ein. Es gelang ihm nicht nur, dem schlafenden Schlachtross neues Leben einzuhauchen, sondern auch Hauptdarsteller Christian Bale, der dem schwarzen Ritter weniger sentimentale Züge verleiht, eine herausragende schauspielerische Leistung zu entlocken. Auch bei *Prestige – Die Meister der Magie* (*The Prestige*, 2006), einem im London der Wende vom 19. zum 20. Jahrhundert angesiedelten, üppig ausgestatteten Film über zwei konkurrierende Zauberer, die sich gegenseitig ihre Berufsgeheimnisse klauen, arbeitete Nolan wieder mit Bale zusammen. Auch Hugh Jackman war wieder dabei. Nolans nächstes Projekt ist die für den Sommer 2008 angekündigte neue Folge einer Batman-Geschichte, *The Dark Knight*, in der Heath Ledger den „Joker" spielen soll.

À sept ans, le sauveur de Batman tourne des films en super 8 avec des figurines. Puis il étudie la littérature à Londres. *Following* (1998), son premier long métrage, témoigne d'un penchant pour le film noir : un jeune homme obsédé à suivre des inconnus se retrouve au cœur du monde de la pègre. Tourné en noir et blanc, caméra à l'épaule, *Following* a recours aux caractéristiques du film noir (clair-obscur et flash-back), que Nolan réutilise dans son film suivant, *Memento* (2000), succès du cinéma indépendant intellectuel. Amnésique, ralenti par son handicap, un enquêteur d'une société d'assurances (Guy Pearce) tente de résoudre l'énigme du meurtre de sa femme. L'histoire se déroule à rebours. L'infortuné héros se barde de tatouages manuscrits et porte sur lui des polaroïds lui permettant de se rappeler ses propres actes. Il prononce des phrases mémorables comme « Je n'arrive pas à me souvenir de vous oublier ». Remake du succès norvégien d'Erik Skjoldbjaerg, l'*Insomnia* de Nolan (2002) est une commande hollywoodienne sous-estimée, un film policier taciturne qui se déroule dans la lumière permanente de l'été en Alaska. Le cinéaste appose ensuite sa griffe à la fois rude et pleine d'esprit sur *Batman Begins* (2005), et revigore le héros endormi, grâce à l'interprétation magnifique de Christian Bale qui fait du justicier encapé un personnage moins cabotin. Nolan retrouve Bale pour *Le Prestige* (*The Prestige*, 2006), somptueux film en costumes se déroulant au tournant du siècle dernier à Londres. Deux magiciens rivaux (Bale et Hugh Jackman) se déchirent pour obtenir des secrets de métier. Nolan doit tourner un nouveau Batman, *The Dark Knight*, dont la sortie est prévue pour l'été 2008, avec Heath Ledger dans le rôle du Joker.

FILMS →
1998 *Following* **2000** *Memento*
2002 *Insomnia* **2005** *Batman Begins*
2006 *The Prestige* **2008** *The Dark Knight*

SELECTED AWARDS →
1998 *Following*: Tiger Award, Rotterdam International Film Festival; Best Director Award, Newport International Film Festival
2000 *Memento*: Jury Special Prize, Critics Award, Deauville Film Festival
2001 *Memento*: Waldo Salt Screenwriting Award, Sundance Film Festival
2002 *Memento*: Best Director, Best Screenplay, Independent Spirit Awards; Best New Filmmaker, MTV Movie Awards **2003** Visionary Award, Palm Springs International Film Festival

Following

"I think there's a vague sense out there
that movies are becoming more and more unreal.
I know I've felt it."

„Ich glaube, so langsam macht sich eine Vorahnung breit, dass Filme immer unwirklicher werden.
Ich weiß, dass ich das schon lange im Gefühl habe."

«J'ai l'impression que les gens trouvent les films de plus en plus irréels.
C'est ce que je ressens aussi.»

Nolan's distinct noir sensibility made its auspicious debut in the stark, low-budget thriller *Following*, an observation of one man's dangerous curiosity in following strangers around London.

Nolans ausgeprägter Sinn für den Film noir kam bereits in seinem Debüt vielversprechend zum Ausdruck: Die karge Low-Budget-Produktion *Following* erzählt von einem Mann, der in London und Umgebung Fremde verfolgt und durch seine Neugierde in Gefahr gerät.

Avec un goût marqué pour le film noir, Nolan fait des débuts prometteurs grâce à ce thriller sombre à petit budget et observe la curiosité dangereuse d'un homme pour ses contemporains qu'il suit dans Londres.

Memento

DODD

TEDDY
-555 0134

The tortured anti-hero played by Guy Pearce finds himself bereft of short-term memories, so he leaves messages for himself using Polaroids (above) and tattoos (right) to help find his wife's murderer.

Der von Guy Pearce verkörperte Antiheld leidet am Verlust seines Kurzzeitgedächtnisses. So hält er Bemerkenswertes, das ihm bei der Aufklärung des Mordes an seiner Frau weiterhelfen könnte, mit Polaroids (oben) und Tattoos (rechts) fest.

Guy Pearce interprète un antihéros torturé, privé de mémoire immédiate, qui se barde de tatouages manuscrits (ci-contre) et porte sur lui des polaroïds (ci-dessus) pour se rappeler ses propres actes et retrouver l'assassin de sa femme.

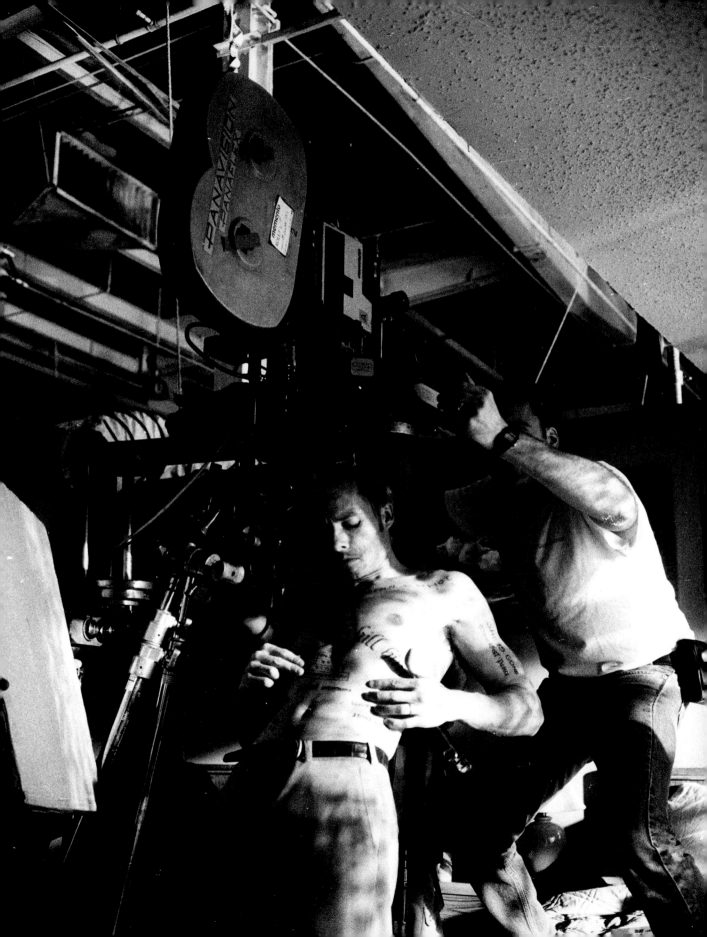

Insomnia

Nolan directs Al Pacino as a grizzled detective who can't sleep in Alaska's endless sunlight. But is it the sunlight or his conscience keeping him awake?

Nolan lässt Al Pacino einen mürrischen Polizeiermittler spielen, der unter der Mitternachtssonne Alaskas keinen Schlaf findet. Ist es tatsächlich das Licht, das ihn wach hält, oder sind es seine Gedanken, die ihm keine Ruhe lassen?

Nolan dirige Al Pacino en inspecteur de police grisonnant, que le soleil de minuit en Alaska empêche de trouver le sommeil. Mais n'est-ce pas sa conscience qui l'empêche de dormir?

Pacino plays cat and mouse with serial killer Robin Williams, whilst policewoman Hilary Swank investigates Pacino.

Detective Dormer (Pacino) spielt mit dem Serienmörder Finch (Robin Williams) Katz und Maus. Gleichzeitig sucht die Polizistin Burr (Hilary Swank) nach dunklen Flecken auf Dormers Weste.

Pacino joue au chat et à la souris avec un tueur en série (Robin Williams), tandis qu'une policière (Hilary Swank) enquête sur son collègue.

Batman Begins

Nolan reinvented the Batman franchise, casting Christian Bale as the Caped Crusader and filling his palette with the noir undercurrents of his previous features.

Dank Christian Bale in der Rolle des berühmten Kämpfers mit dem Fledermauskostüm und durch den geschickten Einsatz der in seinen anderen Spielfilmen bereits erprobten Noir-Elemente gelang es Nolan, die Batman-Geschichten wiederzubeleben.

Nolan a renouvelé la série des *Batman* en confiant à Christian Bale le rôle du justicier et en donnant au film la teinte « film noir » de ses œuvres précédentes.

The Prestige

Prestige – Die Meister der Magie / Le Prestige

Hugh Jackman and Christian Bale are rival magicians in turn-of-the-century London. Are they tricksters, playing with mirrors, or is real magic involved?

Hugh Jackman und Christian Bale spielen rivalisierende Zauberer im London der Wende vom 19. zum 20. Jahrhundert. Betrügen sie mit Spiegeln, oder ist es wirklich Zauberei?

Hugh Jackman et Christian Bale incarnent deux magiciens rivaux dans un Londres fin de siècle. Simple illusionnisme ou véritable magie?

Above: Christopher Nolan directs Hugh Jackman in a scene from *The Prestige*. Right: a drawing of a magician's coat of tricks.

Oben: Christopher Nolan gibt Hugh Jackman Regie-anweisungen bei den Dreharbeiten zu *The Prestige – Die Meister der Magie.* Rechts: Zeichnung eines der präparierten Umhänge eines Zauberers.

Ci-dessus : Christopher Nolan dirige Hugh Jackman dans une scène du *Prestige.* À droite : Dessin des armes secrètes de l'un des magiciens.

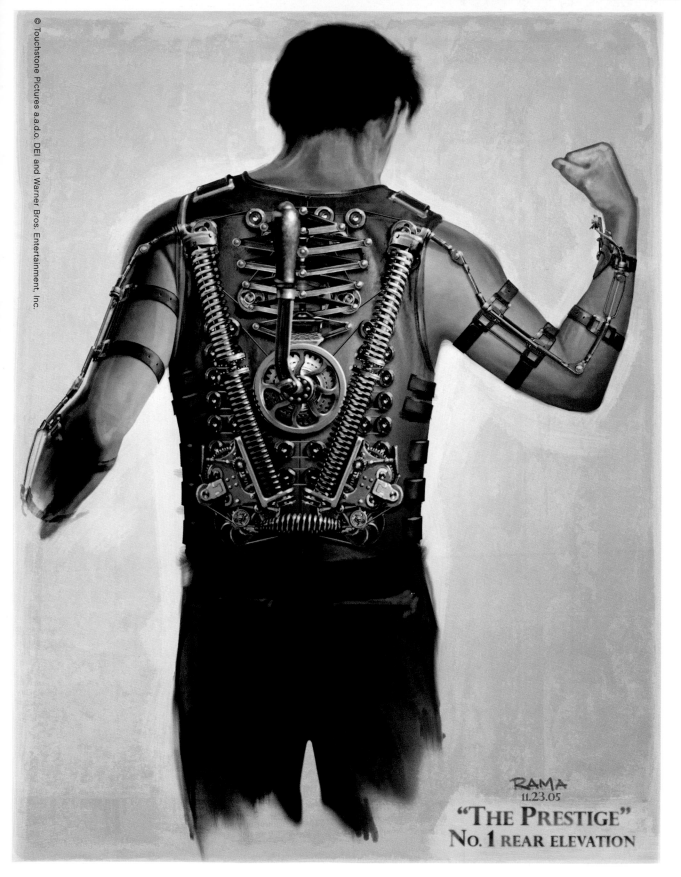

RAMA
11.23.05
"THE PRESTIGE"
NO. 1 REAR ELEVATION

GYÖRGY PÁLFI

Born 11 April 1974 in Budapest, Hungary

The Hungarian surrealist György Pálfi's first feature was the astonishing *Hukkle* (2002), containing no dialogue and all manner of naturalistic sound effects, including an old man's recurring hiccups from which the film takes its enigmatic title. Set in a rural Hungarian village, *Hukkle* is both nature documentary and murder mystery, with Pálfi's camera stopping to investigate anyone and everything, from swarming insects to barnyard animals to farming machinery, using sound effects to advance the film's mysterious plot. Pálfi's second feature was the outrageous generational drama *Taxidermia* (2005), which premiered at the 2006 Hungarian Film Festival. Continuing his obsession with machinery and processes, Pálfi divides *Taxidermia* into three segments: one featuring a World War Two-era grandfather with a bizarre sexual fantasy life, another featuring his morbidly obese competitive-eater son in post-Soviet Russia and yet another featuring the obese man's emaciated son, a modern-day taxidermist whose ambition is to stuff his own body before he dies (*Taxidermia*'s jaw-dropping final scene is one for the ages). Based on two stories by the Hungarian magical realist writer Lajos Parti Nagy – the taxidermy segment is Pálfi's own – *Taxidermia* is an explosive triptych of bodily functions and freakish desires from one of the most imaginative filmmakers working in the world today.

Das erstaunliche Werk *Hukkle – Das Dorf* (*Hukkle*, 2002), der erste Spielfilm des ungarischen Surrealisten György Pálfi, kommt gänzlich ohne Dialoge aus. Stattdessen ist er erfüllt von allerlei Geräuschen des Handlungsorts, wie etwa vom immer wiederkehrenden Schluckauf eines alten Mannes, einem Phänomen, von dem auch der rätselhafte Titel des Films herrührt. *Hukkle* spielt in einem ungarischen Dorf und ist sowohl eine naturalistische Dokumentation als auch ein Kriminalfilm. Dabei untersucht Pálfis Kamera alles und jeden: Insektenschwärme, die Tiere eines Bauernhofs oder Landmaschinen. Die Klangeffekte nutzt er, um den geheimnisvollen Plot des Films voranzubringen. Pálfis zweiter Spielfilm ist das außergewöhnliche Generationendrama *Taxidermia* (2005), das seine internationale Premiere 2006 auf dem ungarischen Filmfestival erlebte. Um seine Obsession für Maschinen und Prozesse ausleben zu können, hat Pálfi *Taxidermia* in drei Teilen angelegt. Teil eins porträtiert den Großvater, der in den 1930er- und 1940er-Jahren aufwuchs, und dessen bizarre, sexuelle Fantasien, Teil zwei dessen krankhaft fettleibigen Sohn, der sich im postsowjetischen Russland als Wettkampfesser zu profilieren sucht, während der dritte Teil den abgemagerten Sohn des fetten Kerls porträtiert, einen in unserer heutigen Zeit lebenden Präparator, der unbedingt noch vor seinem Tod den eigenen Körper ausgestopft haben will (der verblüffenden Schlussszene von *Taxidermia* gebührt ein Platz in der Filmhistorie). Zwei der Geschichten hat der ungarische Schriftsteller Lajos Parti Nagy, ein Vertreter des magischen Realismus, verfasst, die Story um den Präparator stammt von Pálfi selbst. *Taxidermia*, ein explosives Triptychon über Körperfunktionen und seltsame Bedürfnisse, ist der Film eines der weltweit einfallsreichsten Filmemacher unserer Tage.

Le premier film du surréaliste hongrois Györgi Pálfi est l'étonnant *Hic (de crimes en crimes)* (*Hukkle*, 2002), qui ne contient aucun dialogue mais toutes sortes de bruits naturalistes, parmi lesquels le hoquet d'un homme qui donne au film son titre énigmatique. *Hic (de crimes en crimes)* est à la fois un documentaire animalier et un film policier. Dans un village hongrois, la caméra de Pálfi interroge tout et tout le monde, insectes pullulants, animaux de la ferme, engins agricoles, l'intrigue mystérieuse se développant au rythme des effets sonores. Son deuxième film, *Taxidermie* (*Taxidermia*, 2005), est une histoire intergénérationnelle présentée à la Quinzaine des Réalisateurs cannoise en 2006. Toujours obsédé par les engins et les processus, Pálfi divise son film en trois segments : pendant la Seconde Guerre mondiale, un grand-père mène une curieuse vie sexuelle fantasmée ; son fils, atteint d'obésité morbide, participe à des concours du plus gros mangeur dans la Russie postsoviétique ; le fils squelettique de ce dernier, taxidermiste, rêve d'empailler son propre corps avant de mourir (à voir la scène d'anthologie qui clôt le film). Inspiré de deux récits de l'écrivain Lajos Parti Nagy, adepte du réalisme magique – Pálfi étant l'auteur de l'épisode taxidermiste –, *Taxidermie* est un triptyque où explosent les fonctions corporelles et les désirs bizarres. On doit cette œuvre à l'un des cinéastes contemporains les plus imaginatifs.

FILMS →
2002 *Hukkle*
2005 *Taxidermia*

SELECTED AWARDS →
2002 *Hukkle*: European Discovery of the Year, European Film Awards; Best New Director – Special Mention, San Sebastián International Film Festival **2003** *Hukkle*: Golden Firebird Award, Hong Kong International Film Festival **2004** *Taxidermia*: NHK Award, Sundance Film Festival

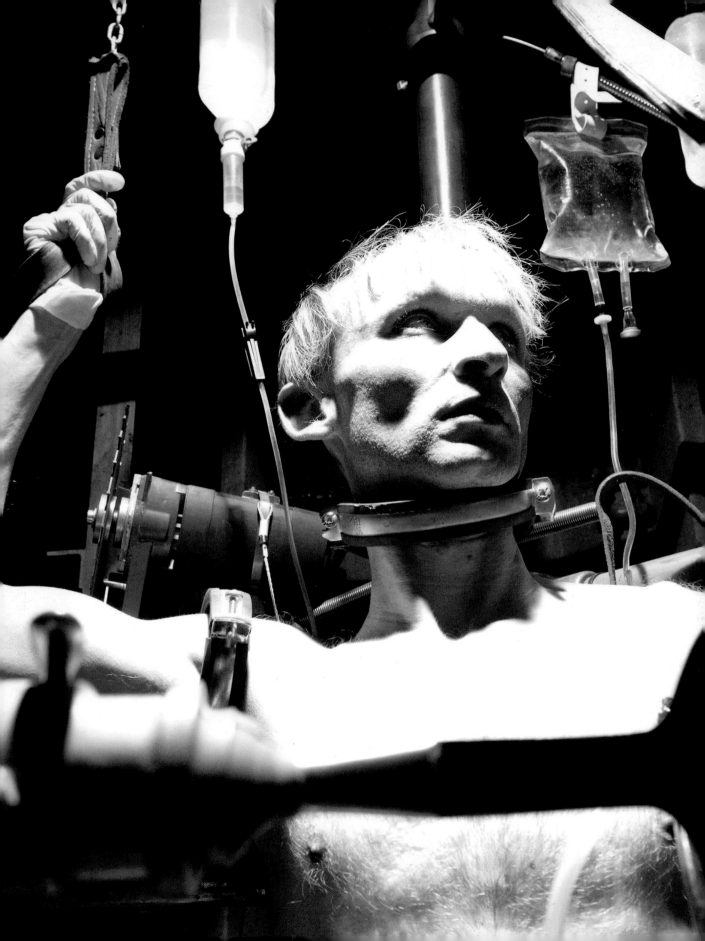

Hukkle

Hukkle – Das Dorf / Hic (de crimes en crimes)

"Just as the body is overcome with desire, so naturalism is overcome by surrealism, which organizes the variation of physicality into a single aesthetic system."

„So, wie der Körper von Begierden überwältigt wird, bezwingt der Surrealismus den Naturalismus und fasst alles Körperliche in einem einzigen ästhetischen System zusammen."

«De même que le corps est submergé par le désir, le naturalisme est submergé par le surréalisme qui organise les divers aspects du physique en un système esthétique unique.»

Humans and animals compete for eccentricity in the wordless, but not silent, Hungarian curiosity that made for Palfi's memorable and innovative feature debut.

Menschen und Tiere wetteifern in dieser ungarischen Kuriosität um ein Höchstmaß an Exzentrik. Pálfis denkwürdiger und innovativer erster Spielfilm kommt ohne Worte aus, ist aber kein Stummfilm.

Humains et animaux rivalisent d'excentricité dans cette curiosité hongroise, sans paroles, mais non sans bruits, qui constitue le premier film, innovateur et mémorable, de Pálfi.

Taxidermia

Taxidermie

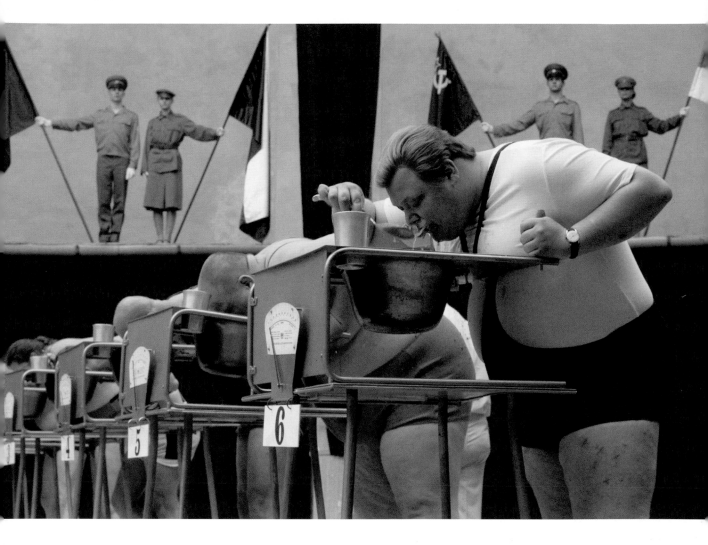

Three stories feature three generations of men: an obese speed eater (also see overleaf), an embalmer of giant cats, and a man who shoots fire out of his penis.

In drei Geschichten werden Männer porträtiert, die drei unterschiedlichen Generationen angehören: ein fettleibiger Wettkampfesser (siehe auch folgende Seite), ein Tierpräparator und ein Mann, aus dessen Penis Feuer schießt.

Trois récits pour trois générations d'hommes : un obèse, lauréat du prix du «plus gros mangeur» (voir aussi pages suivantes), un empailleur de chats géants, un cracheur de feu par le pénis.

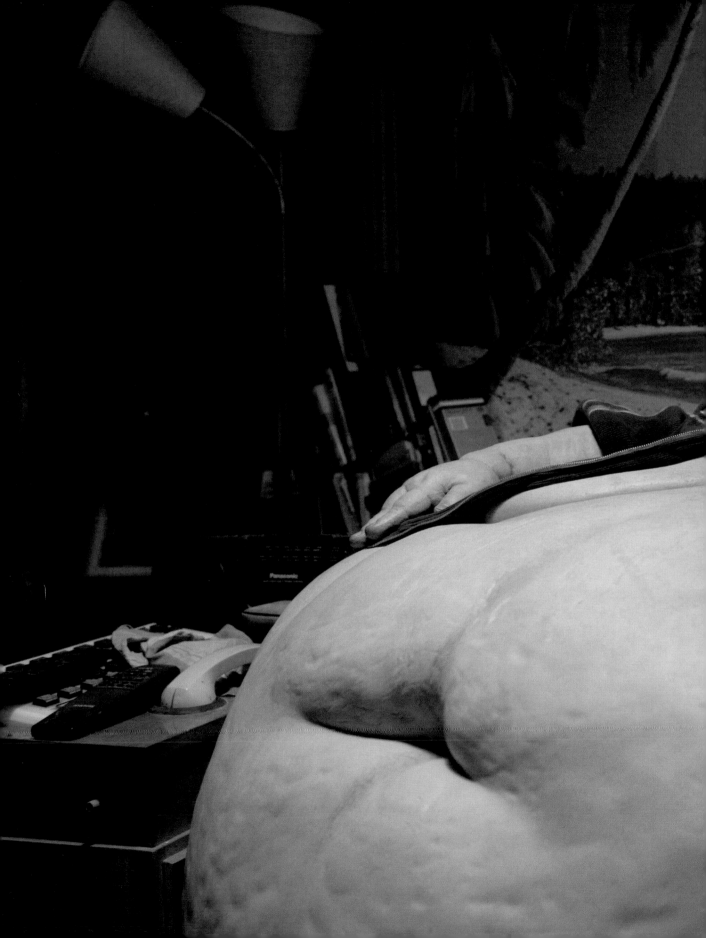

The reigning godfather of extreme cinema studied philosophy and toiled as a film critic. Having seen *Vertigo* (1958) one too many times, he decided on a career as a director. After his breakthrough feature *Joint Security Area* (*Gongdong gyeongbi guyeok JSA*, 2000) became a blockbuster in South Korea, Park Chan-wook turned to a trilogy of independently produced revenge thrillers that would win him international recognition as a baroque craftsman of artful violence – a Hitchcock for the Asia extreme set. Beginning with *Sympathy for Mr. Vengeance* (*Boksuneun naui geot*, 2001/02), in which a deaf factory worker kidnaps his boss's daughter so he can use the ransom money to pay for his sister's kidney transplant, Park showed an affinity for fluid camerawork and elaborate overhead shots that made his films as gorgeous as they were garish. *Oldboy* (2003), second in the trilogy, served up the embattled protagonist Oh Dae-su (Choi Min-sik), imprisoned and tortured for fifteen years, then set free, prompting him to take extravagant revenge on his captors. *Oldboy* culminated in a memorable overhead hallway shot in which Oh Dae-su single-handedly takes on dozens of captors in one of the most brazenly executed action sequences in years. *Lady Vengeance* (*Chin-jeol-han Geum-ja-ssi*, 2005) – equal parts prison drama and revenge thriller – exhibited a less violent touch, even delving into light comedy in a story about a female convict imprisoned for murder who avenges herself on the man who locked her away. Park's latest feature, *I'm a Cyborg, but That's OK* (*Saibogeujiman gwaenchanha*, 2006), is a light romantic comedy set in a mental institution centering on a female protagonist who is convinced she's a robot.

Der amtierende Gottvater des Extremfilms studierte Philosophie und mühte sich als Filmkritiker ab. Nachdem er *Vertigo – Aus dem Reich der Toten* (*Vertigo*, 1958) einmal zu oft gesehen hatte, beschloss er, Regisseur zu werden. Seinen Durchbruch hatte er mit dem Spielfilm *Joint Security Area* (*Gongdong gyeongbi guyeok JSA*, 2000), in Korea ein Blockbuster. Anschließend wandte er sich einer Trilogie von unabhängig produzierten Rachethrillern zu, die ihm internationale Anerkennung als barocker Meister kunstvoller Gewaltszenen eintrug – als Hitchcock asiatischer Extremszenen. Schon mit dem ersten Film *Sympathy for Mr. Vengeance* (*Boksuneun naui geot*, 2001/02), in dem ein tauber Fabrikarbeiter die Tochter seines Chefs kidnappt, um mit dem Lösegeld eine Nierentransplantation für seine Schwester bezahlen zu können, bewies Park seine Vorliebe für fließende Kameraführung und raffinierte Aufnahmen von oben, die seinen Filmen ihre großartige, aber auch grelle Eigentümlichkeit verleihen. *Oldboy* (2003), der zweite Film der Trilogie, macht das Publikum mit dem bedrängten Protagonisten Oh Dae-su (Choi Min-sik) bekannt, der 15 Jahre lang eingekerkert und gefoltert, schließlich freigelassen und aufgefordert wird, einen ungewöhnlichen Rachefeldzug gegen seine Entführer zu unternehmen. *Oldboy* kulminierte in von oben aufgenommenen Kampfszenen in einem Korridor, in dem Oh Dae-su ganz auf sich gestellt mit Dutzenden von Gegnern fertig werden muss – eine der dreistesten Actionsequenzen der letzten Jahre. In *Lady Vengeance* (*Chin-jeol-han Geum-ja-ssi*, 2005), Gefängnisdrama und Rachethriller in einem, geht es nicht ganz so gewalttätig zu. Die Story über eine Frau, die wegen angeblichen Mordes im Gefängnis saß und sich nun an jenem Mann rächt, der sie hinter Gitter gebracht hatte, weist gelegentlich gar Züge einer Komödie auf. Parks jüngster Spielfilm, *Ich bin ein Cyborg, aber das macht nichts* (*Saibogeujiman gwaenchanha*, 2006), eine romantische Komödie, die in einer Nervenklinik spielt, handelt von einer Frau, die davon überzeugt ist, sie sei ein Roboter.

Le parrain du cinéma extrême a d'abord étudié la philosophie et travaillé comme critique. Après avoir vu *Sueurs froides* une fois de trop, il se lance dans la réalisation. *Joint Security Area* (*Gongdong gyeongbi guyeok JSA*, 2000) le révèle et fait un tabac en Corée du Sud. Park Chan-wook signe ensuite une trilogie de films indépendants (des histoires de vengeance) qui lui vaut une reconnaissance internationale comme maître de la violence baroque, un Hitchcock du cinéma extrême asiatique. Dans *Sympathy for Mr. Vengeance* (*Boksuneun naui geot*, 2002), un ouvrier d'usine sourd enlève la fille de son patron afin de pouvoir payer, avec la rançon, la greffe du rein qu'attend sa sœur. Dès ce film, il montre son goût pour des mouvements de caméra fluides et des plongées très élaborées qui donnent à ses œuvres une beauté éclatante. Deuxième épisode de la trilogie, *Old Boy* (*Oldboy*, 2003) met en scène Oh Dae-su (Choi Min-sik), emprisonné et torturé pendant quinze ans, puis libéré. Il décide aussitôt de se venger de ses geôliers. *Old Boy* est marqué par une mémorable plongée au-dessus d'un couloir où Oh Dae-su affronte des dizaines d'attaquants dans l'une des scènes d'action les plus ambitieuses de ces dernières années. À la fois récit carcéral et histoire de vengeance, *Lady Vengeance* (*Chin-jeol-han Geum-ja-ssi*, 2005) est moins violent et lorgne même du côté de la comédie : une meurtrière condamnée à la prison se venge de celui qui l'y a envoyée (interprété par Park). Son dernier film en date, *Je suis un cyborg ...* (*Saibogeujiman gwaenchanha*, 2007) est une comédie qui se déroule dans un asile de fous, où une femme est convaincue d'être un robot.

Boksuneun naui geot

Sympathy for Mr. Vengeance

**"In my films, I focus on pain and fear –
the fear just before an act of violence and the pain after.
This applies to the perpetrators as well as the victims."**

„In meinen Filmen geht es vor allem um Schmerz und Furcht – die Furcht kurz vor einem Gewaltakt und den Schmerz,
den er verursacht. Das betrifft sowohl die Täter als auch die Opfer."

«Dans mes films, je m'intéresse à la peur et à la douleur, la peur qui précède la violence et la douleur qui s'ensuit.
Tant pour les auteurs des violences que pour les victimes.»

A deaf man (above) hatches a kidnapping scheme to finance his sister's kidney transplant, but this sympathetic cause leads to tragedy.

Ein tauber Mann heckt ein Kidnapping aus, um eine Nierentransplantation für seine kranke Schwester bezahlen zu können. Doch die gut gemeinte Sache entwickelt sich zu einer Tragödie.

Un sourd (ci-dessus) prépare un enlèvement pour financer la greffe de rein de sa sœur, mais sa cause honorable le mène à la tragédie.

Oldboy
Old Boy

Park's breakthrough feature was the second installment of his vengeance trilogy, this time focusing
on the unjustly imprisoned Oh Dae-su (Choi Min-sik),
who extracts elaborate revenge on his captors.

Mit dem zweiten Teil seiner Rachetrilogie feierte Park
seinen Durchbruch. In dem Film geht es um den
zu Unrecht eingekerkerten Oh Dae-su (Choi Min-sik),
der einen ungewöhnlichen Rachefeldzug gegen
seine Häscher unternimmt.

Park s'est révélé au grand public grâce au deuxième
volet de sa trilogie de la vengeance. Injustement
emprisonné, Oh Dae-su (Choi Min-sik) se venge avec
sophistication de ses geôliers.

Park's images in *Oldboy* run the gamut from beautiful and horrific to violent and tender, giving the film a wildly unpredictable and ultimately tragic tone.

Schönheit und Entsetzliches, Gewalttätigkeit und Zärtlichkeit – in *Oldboy* präsentiert Park eine ganze Skala von Bildern, die dem Film etwas völlig Unvorhersehbares und schließlich auch Tragisches verleihen.

Splendides, horribles, violentes, tendres : toute la gamme des images est mise à contribution pour donner à *Old Boy* un ton totalement imprévisible et, finalement, tragique.

Chin-jeol-han Geum-ja-ssi

Lady Vengeance

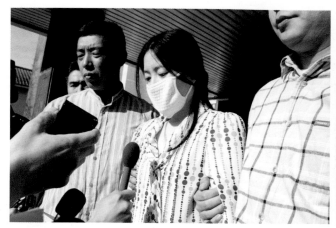

For the final part of Park's vengeance trilogy, glamorous female parolee Lee Geum-ja (Lee Yeong-ae) seeks retribution for a murder she did not commit. Below: Lee Yeong-ae and Park Chan-wook.

Im letzten Film von Parks Rachetrilogie sinnt die glamouröse Lee Geum-ja (Lee Yeong-ae) nach ihrer Haftentlassung auf Vergeltung für einen Mord, den sie nicht begangen hat. Unten: Lee Yeong-ae und Park Chan-wook.

Dans le dernier volet de la trilogie, Lee Geum-ja (Lee Yeong-ae), séduisante détenue en liberté conditionnelle, veut se laver d'un meurtre qu'elle n'a pas commis. Ci-dessous : Lee Yeong-ae et Park Chan-wook.

Although rife with mayhem and violence, *Lady Vengeance* is a more contemplative piece, exploring the gray moral areas of his characters.

Auch wenn in *Lady Vengeance* Gewalt und Chaos durchaus präsent sind, so ist es doch eher ein nachdenkliches Werk, in dem die moralischen Grauzonen der Charaktere erkundet werden.

Malgré son bruit et sa fureur, *Lady Vengeance* est une œuvre contemplative qui explore la part d'ombre de ses personnages.

Saibogeujiman gwaenchanha

I'm a Cyborg, but That's OK / Ich bin ein Cyborg, aber das macht nichts / Je suis un cyborg ...

Park's latest film is a radical departure for him – a romantic comedy set in a mental hospital.

Parks jüngster Film ist für diesen Regisseur ein radikaler Neuanfang – eine romantische Komödie, die in einer Nervenklinik spielt.

Pour son tout dernier film, une comédie romantique se déroulant dans un hôpital psychiatrique, Park change radicalement de genre.

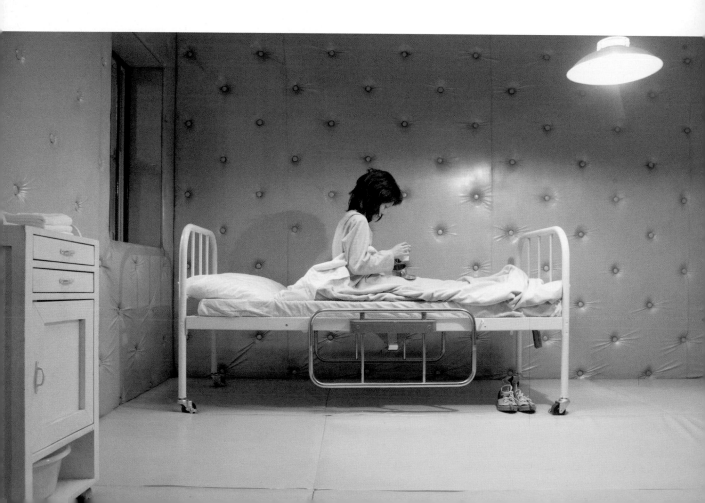

Young-goon (Lim Soo-jung) is a mental patient who thinks she's a robot; her unlikely paramour Il-soon (played by the pop star Rain) believes he can steal people's souls.

Young-goon (Lim Soo-jung) ist eine Geistesgestörte, die glaubt, ein Roboter zu sein. Ihr seltsamer Geliebter Il-soon (der von dem Popstar Rain verkörpert wird) meint, er könne anderen die Seele rauben.

Young-goon (Lim Su-jeong) se prend pour un robot. Il-soon, son amant improbable (incarné par Rain, rocker célèbre), croit pouvoir voler les âmes des gens.

ALEXANDER PAYNE

Born 10 February 1961 in Omaha, USA

After honing his craft as a story editor for Universal Pictures, Alexander Payne wrote and directed the indie hit *Citizen Ruth* (1995), a social satire starring Laura Dern as a pregnant glue sniffer who becomes enmeshed in right-to-life politics. His next feature was *Election* (1999), satirizing student politics and high school life and helping turn Reese Witherspoon into a star, followed by *About Schmidt* (2002), a road movie starring Jack Nicholson as a retired Omaha insurance salesman searching for meaning after his wife's death. A memorable hot-tub scene earned Kathy Bates a Best Supporting Actress Oscar nomination. The award-winning *Sideways* (2004) introduced a failed novelist and his lothario best friend wreaking havoc in California wine country and confirming Payne as the unofficial leader of a loose-knit band of bleak comic mavericks including his friends David O. Russell and Spike Jonze. With his writing partner Jim Taylor, Payne specializes in a breed of hapless everyman loser whose comical failures in life make him (or her, as Payne and Taylor write equally rich female characters) accessible to indie purists and general audiences alike. Payne is the heir to Billy Wilder and *The Apartment* (1960) in his ability to generate bittersweet comedy out of otherwise dark material. A heartwrenching scene in *Sideways*, in which Virginia Madsen's endearing beauty Maya compared growing old with the Pinot Noir grape, capturing the heart of the luckless writer Miles (Paul Giamatti), was one of those memorable scenes that guaranteed a best screenplay Oscar. Payne's latest work is the short film *14th arrondissement*, one of twenty short works in the omnibus feature *Paris, je t'aime* (2006), in which twenty directors offer varying glimpses of Parisian districts.

Nachdem er sein Talent zunächst mit dem Überarbeiten von Drehbüchern für United Pictures erprobt hatte, schrieb und verfilmte Alexander Payne den Independent-Hit *Baby Business* (*Citizen Ruth*, 1995), eine Sozialsatire mit Laura Dern als schwangerer Klebstoff-Schnüfflerin, die plötzlich in die politischen Auseinandersetzungen um Abtreibung verwickelt wird. Sein nächster Spielfilm *Election* (1999) befasste sich satirisch mit dem Hochschulleben und Studentenpolitik und machte Reese Witherspoon zum Star. Dann folgte *About Schmidt* (2002), ein Roadmovie mit Jack Nicholson in der Rolle eines pensionierten Versicherungsagenten aus Omaha, der nach dem Tod seiner Frau nach dem Sinn des Lebens sucht. Eine denkwürdige Szene in einem Warmwasserbecken trug dazu bei, dass Kathy Bates als beste Nebendarstellerin für den Oscar nominiert wurde. Im Mittelpunkt des preisgekrönten *Sideways* (2004) standen ein gescheiterter Romancier und sein bester Freund, ein Schürzenjäger, die in den Weinanbaugebieten Kaliforniens für Aufregung sorgen. Spätestens seit diesem Film gilt Payne als inoffizieller Kopf einer locker miteinander verbundenen Truppe, zu der seine Freunde David O. Russell und Spike Jonze zählen, die auch dem Trostlosen komische Seiten abzugewinnen vermögen. Gemeinsam mit seinem Drehbuchpartner Jim Taylor hat sich Payne auf jene Sorte unglückseliger Verlierertypen und gescheiterter Existenzen – ob Mann oder Frau – spezialisiert, denen es gelingt, sowohl Indie-Puristen als auch ein breites Publikum anzurühren. Mit seiner Fähigkeit, aus traurigen Geschehnissen eine bittersüße Komödie zu zaubern, steht Payne in der Tradition von Billy Wilders Klassiker *Das Appartement* (*The Apartment*, 1960). Die herzerweichende Szene in *Sideways*, in der Virginia Madsen als reizende Schönheit Maya das Altern mit dem Reifen einer Pinot-noir-Traube vergleicht und damit die Zuneigung des glücklosen Schreibers Miles (Paul Giamatti) gewinnt, gehört zu jenen herausragenden Momenten, die dazu beitrugen, dass der Film mit dem Oscar für das beste Drehbuch ausgezeichnet wurde. Paynes jüngstes Werk *14th arrondissement* ist einer von 20 Kurzfilmen für *Paris, je t'aime* (2006), ein Projekt, für das jeder der beteiligten Filmemacher seinen Beitrag über einen der 20 Pariser Stadtbezirke beigesteuert hat.

Après avoir fait ses premières armes comme *script-doctor* chez Universal, Alexander Payne écrit et réalise *Citizen Ruth* (1995), production indépendante et satire sociale, avec Laura Dern en sniffeuse de colle enceinte qui se laisse embarquer dans la lutte anti-avortement. Nouvelle satire qui a permis à Reese Witherspoon de devenir une star, *L'Arriviste* (*Election*, 1999) raille la vie et la politique au sein d'un lycée. Jack Nicholson incarne le rôle-titre de *Monsieur Schmidt* (*About Schmidt*, 2002) ; dans ce road movie, un courtier en assurances à la retraite cherche le sens de la vie après le décès de son épouse. Kathy Bates a remporté l'oscar du meilleur second rôle pour une scène de bain mémorable. Un écrivain raté et son meilleur ami très donjuanesque sèment le chaos dans les vignobles californiens dans *Sideways* (2004), film récompensé qui confirme que Payne est à la tête d'un mouvement informel de cinéastes adeptes de l'humour très noir, réunissant ses amis David O. Russell et Spike Jonze. Avec son scénariste Jim Taylor, Payne a un faible pour les perdants malheureux dont les échecs drolatiques font d'eux (et d'elles, car leurs personnages féminins sont tout aussi riches) des personnages qui plaisent aux cinéphiles purs et durs comme au grand public. Le cinéaste est l'héritier du Billy Wilder de *La Garçonnière*, par sa manière de créer une comédie aigre-douce à partir d'éléments dramatiques. Dans une scène déchirante de *Sideways*, la belle et attachante Maya (Virginia Madsen) compare la vieillesse au pinot noir et enflamme le cœur de Miles, l'écrivain malchanceux (Paul Giamatti). Payne a signé *14e Arrondissement*, l'un des épisodes du film à sketches *Paris, je t'aime* (2006), dans lequel vingt cinéastes proposent leur vision des arrondissements parisiens.

FILMS →
1995 *Citizen Ruth* **1999** *Election* **2002** *About Schmidt* **2004** *Sideways* **2006** *Paris, je t'aime: 14th arrondissement*

About Schmidt
Monsieur Schmidt

"My method of writing is rather simple. I read a book; once I'm done reading it, I throw it away. I then create my own version of the book. And that's how I write a script."

„Mein Vorgehen beim Schreiben ist ganz einfach. Ich lese ein Buch, und wenn ich mit der Lektüre durch bin, schmeiße ich es weg. Dann verfasse ich meine eigene Version der Geschichte. So schreibe ich ein Drehbuch."

«Ma façon d'écrire est simple. Je lis un livre. Quand je l'ai fini, je le jette. Et puis, je crée ma propre version du livre. Voilà comment j'écris un scénario.»

Jack Nicholson is retired widower Warren Schmidt, who embarks on a cross-country odyssey to attend his daughter's wedding, and begins to live for the first time. Bottom right: Nicholson and Alexander Payne.

Jack Nicholson spielt den pensionierten Witwer Warren Schmidt, der sich zu einer Odyssee kreuz und quer durch die USA auf den Weg macht, um zur Hochzeit seiner Tochter zu fahren. Zum ersten Mal lebt er wirklich auf. Unten rechts: Nicholson und Alexander Payne.

Veuf en retraite, Warren Schmidt (Jack Nicholson) part pour un long périple afin d'assister au mariage de sa fille et découvre enfin la vie. En bas, à droite: Nicholson et Alexander Payne.

Sideways

A failed writer and his philandering best friend hit the Californian wine country with farcical and bittersweet results. Bottom left: The main delight of the film is seeing the fragile romance between Miles (Paul Giamatti) and Maya (Virginia Madsen) develop despite their mutual reticence.

Ein gescheiterter Schriftsteller und sein ständig schäkernder bester Freund suchen die Weinbaugebiete Kaliforniens heim – mit grotesken und bittersüßen Auswirkungen. Unten links: Zu beobachten, wie sich die zarte Romanze zwischen den beiden zurückhaltenden Figuren Miles (Paul Giamatti) und Maya (Virginia Madsen) entwickelt, ist der vergnüglichste Genuss, den dieser Film bietet.

Un écrivain raté et son meilleur ami donjuanesque parcourent le vignoble californien, avec humour mais non sans amertume. En bas, à gauche : La fragile histoire d'amour qui naît entre Miles (Paul Giamatti) et Maya (Virginia Madsen), malgré leur réticence mutuelle, fait le principal délice du film.

Paris, je t'aime: 14th arrondissement

Paris, je t'aime : 14e arrondissement

Payne directed the closing installment of this omnibus film about the distinctive numbered neighborhoods in the City of Lights. American Margo Martindale is a middle-aged letter carrier on vacation in Paris who walks around the 14ème Arrondissement.

Beim letzten Beitrag dieses Episodenfilms mit Geschichten aus den durchnummerierten Bezirken der Lichterstadt führte Payne Regie. Die Amerikanerin Margo Martindale spielt eine Briefträgerin mittleren Alters, die in Paris Urlaub macht und durch das 14. Arrondissement streift.

Payne a signé le dernier volet de ce film à sketchs, consacré aux arrondissements de la Ville lumière. Une factrice américaine (Margo Martindale) en vacances arpente le 14e Arrondissement.

Born 3 April 1967 in Bucharest, Romania

The national cinema that can be declared overwhelmingly RIGHT NOW is the new wave of Romanian filmmakers, lead by Bucharest's Cristi Puiu, which stormed the Cannes Film Festival beginning in 2005, when Puiu's second feature, *The Death of Mister Lazarescu* (*Moartea domnului Lazarescu*, 2005) won the Un Certain Regard. The following year, two more strongly received Romanian films premiered at Cannes, including Corneliu Porumboiu's *12:08 East of Bucharest* (*A fost sau n-a fost?*, 2006), which won the Camera d'Or. Puiu's mordant film tells the story of the retired engineer and widower Dante Remus Lazarescu, an aging alcoholic living in seclusion with his three cats in a dour Bucharest apartment where he suffers from headaches. After repeated calls for an ambulance, thinking his condition grave, Lazarescu is finally picked up by medics but spends the night getting ferried around to several hospitals where he is refused admittance, ultimately dying alone – the long night of the soul in a Romanian emergency room. Puiu tracks Lazarescu's slow fade into nothingness with a trenchant dark humor that the director says was inspired by the television show *ER* (since 1994), as well as by Eric Rohmer, whose *Six Moral Tales* prompted him to envision a series of answer films, *Six Stories from the Bucharest Suburbs*, of which *The Death of Mister Lazarescu* addresses "the love of humanity," or, in the case of Dante Lazarescu, the lack thereof. His first feature, the road movie *Stuff and Dough* (*Marfa si banii*, 2001) debuted in the Director's Fortnight program of the Cannes Film Festival in 2001.

Wenn ein nationales Kino mit Fug und Recht als überzeugend zeitgenössisch bezeichnet werden kann, dann das junge rumänische Kino, zu dessen führenden Vertretern der aus Bukarest stammende Cristi Puiu gehört. Seit dem Festival von Cannes 2005, auf dem Puius zweiter Spielfilm *Der Tod des Herrn Lazarescu* (*Moartea domnului Lazarescu*, 2005) preisgekrönt wurde, sorgt die rumänische Filmszene für Furore. Im Jahr darauf erregten zwei weitere rumänische Filme, die in Cannes Premiere feierten, noch größere Aufmerksamkeit, darunter der ebenfalls mit einem Preis bedachte Corneliu Porumbois *12:08, East of Bucharest* (*A fost sau n-a fost?*, 2006). Puius sarkastischer Film erzählt die Geschichte des pensionierten Ingenieurs und Witwers Dante Remus Lazarescu, eines alternden Alkoholikers, der mit seinen drei Katzen zurückgezogen in einer finsteren Bukarester Wohnung lebt und an Kopfschmerzen leidet. Nachdem er mehrfach einen Krankenwagen gerufen hat, weil er seinen Zustand als ernst einschätzt, wird Lazarescu endlich von Sanitätern abgeholt, im Laufe der Nacht jedoch von einem Hospital zum anderen gekarrt, weil man sich überall weigert, ihn aufzunehmen. Schließlich stirbt er ganz alleine – eine einsame Seele in einer rumänischen Notaufnahme. Puiu verfolgt Lazarescus langsames Hinübergleiten in das Nichts mit bissigem schwarzem Humor. Seine Inspirationen seien, so der Regisseur, sowohl die Fernsehserie *Emergency Room – Die Notaufnahme* (*E. R.*, seit 1994) als auch Eric Rohmer. Auf dessen *Sechs moralische Erzählungen* wolle er mit *Six Stories from the Bucharest Suburbs* eine Serie von sechs Entgegnungen drehen. Als eine dieser Geschichten behandelt *Moartea domnului Lazarescu* die „Liebe zu den Menschen", im Falle des Dante Lazarescu das Fehlen dieser Liebe. Puius erster Spielfilm, das Roadmovie *Stuff and Dough* (*Marfa si banii*, 2001), wurde im Rahmen des Director's-Fortnight-Programms des Filmfestivals von Cannes 2001 präsentiert.

S'il existe une nouvelle vague aujourd'hui, elle se trouve en Roumanie, avec à sa tête Cristi Puiu, lauréat du prix un Certain Regard en 2005 avec son deuxième film, *La Mort de Dante Lazarescu* (*Moartea domnului Lazarescu*, 2005). L'année suivante, deux autres films roumains sont encore mieux accueillis à Cannes, dont *12 h 08 à l'est de Bucarest* (*A fost sau n-a fost*) de Corneliu Porumboiu, lauréat de la caméra d'or. Sur un ton mordant, le film de Puiu raconte l'histoire de Dante Remus Lazarescu, ingénieur veuf à la retraite, alcoolique vieillissant qui vit reclus avec ses trois chats, dans un appartement sinistre de Bucarest où il souffre de migraines. Après avoir plusieurs fois appelé une ambulance, se croyant gravement malade, il est enfin secouru par des médecins qui l'emmènent d'un hôpital à un autre, sans qu'il y soit jamais admis. Il finit par mourir seul, durant une longue nuit aux urgences. Puiu retrace le lent passage au néant de Lazarescu avec un humour noir cinglant, qui lui a été inspiré par la série *Urgences* (*E. R.*) autant que par Éric Rohmer dont les *Six Contes moraux* l'ont incité à tourner des «réponses», *Six Histoires des quartiers de Bucarest*. *La Mort de Dante Lazarescu* en est le volet «amour de l'humanité» ou, en l'occurrence, son absence totale. Son tout premier film, *Le Matos et la thune* (*Marfa si banii*, 2001), avait été présenté à la Quinzaine des Réalisateurs en 2001.

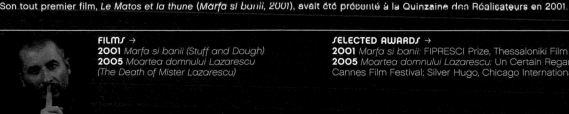

FILMS →
2001 *Marfa si banii* (Stuff and Dough)
2005 *Moartea domnului Lazarescu*
(The Death of Mister Lazarescu)

SELECTED AWARDS →
2001 *Marfa si banii*: FIPRESCI Prize, Thessaloniki Film Festival
2005 *Moartea domnului Lazarescu*: Un Certain Regard Award,
Cannes Film Festival; Silver Hugo, Chicago International Film Festival

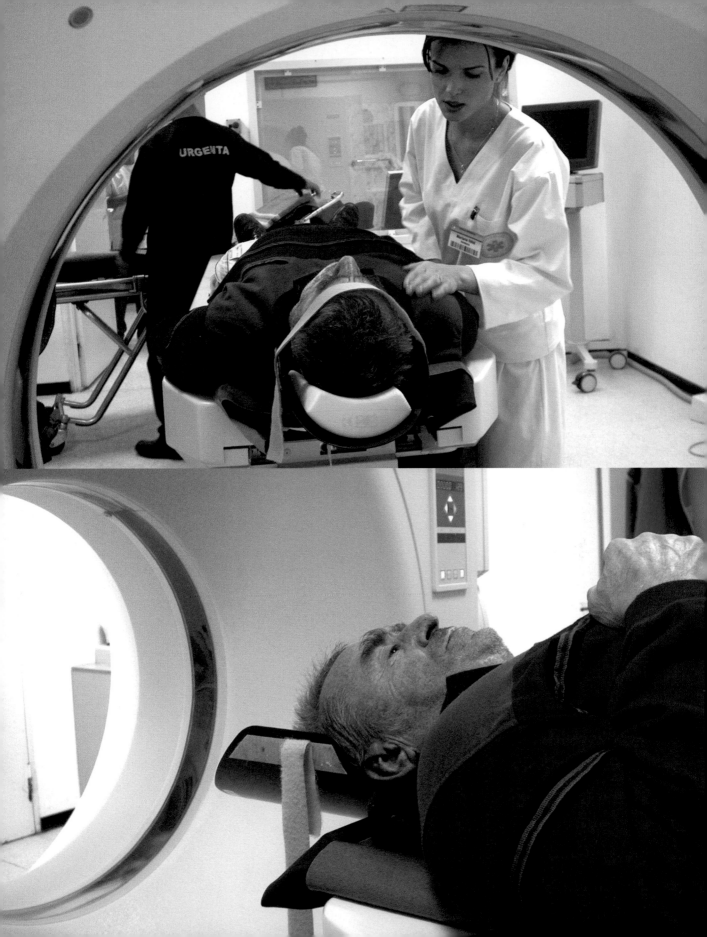

Moartea domnului Lazarescu

The Death of Mister Lazarescu / Der Tod des Herrn Lazarescu / La Mort de Dante Lazarescu

In Cristi Puiu's mordantly bleak feature, Ion Fiscuteanu stars as 62-year-old Dante Remus Lazarescu, whose head and stomach pains result in a nocturnal odyssey through four frenzied Bucharest hospitals.

In Cristi Puius sarkastisch-düsterem Film spielt Ion Fiscuteanu den 62-jährigen Dante Remus Lazarescu, der über Kopf- und Magenschmerzen klagt und daraufhin eine nächtliche Odyssee durch vier chaotische Bukarester Krankenhäuser erleiden muss.

Dans le film à la noirceur mordante de Cristi Puiu, Ion Fiscuteanu incarne Dante Remus Lazarescu (62 ans), dont les céphalées et les douleurs abdominales l'entraînent dans une tournée nocturne de quatre hôpitaux en déréliction de Bucarest.

"The stories I have in my mind and would like to tell are all linked to suffering."

„Alle Geschichten, die mir im Kopf herumschwirren und die ich gerne erzählen würde, haben etwas mit Leiden zu tun."

«Les histoires que j'ai en tête et que j'aimerais raconter sont toutes liées à la souffrance.»

PEN-EK RATANARUANG

Born 8 March 1962 in Bangkok, Thailand

Part of the new wave of Thai auteurs including Apichatpong Weerasethakul and Wisit Sasanatieng, Pen-ek Ratanaruang directed a pair of crime romances, *Fun Bar Karaoke* (*Fan ba karaoke*, 1996/97) and *6ixtynin9* (*Ruang talok 69*, 1999) that gained him a following in Southeast Asia. After the frothy Thai country-music curio *Transistor Love Story* (*Monrak Transistor*, 2001), Ratanaruang turned to more serious fare, including his international breakthrough *Last Life in the Universe* (*Ruang rak noi nid mahasan*, 2003), written in collaboration with the Thai novelist Prabda Yoon and photographed by the Australian-born cinematographer and Wong Kar-wai mainstay Christopher Doyle. A melancholy love story starring Japanese actor Tadanobu Asano as a suicidal librarian living in exile in Thailand who mistakenly kills a yakuza and finds love with a woman who has also killed somebody, *Last Life in the Universe* was an international festival favorite examining themes of alienation, interconnectedness and existential malaise, featuring a cameo performance by Takashi Miike as a yakuza. *Invisible Waves* (2005/06), another collaboration with Yoon, Doyle and Asano, is a film noir about a Japanese hit man (Asano) moonlighting as a chef in Macau who is hired to kill his boss's wife, with whom he is having an affair. Ratanaruang's latest feature is *Ploy* (2007).

Pen-ek Ratanaruang, der gemeinsam mit Apichatpong Weerasethakul und Wisit Sasanatieng zu den Autorenfilmern des jungen thailändischen Kinos zählt, hat mit zwei Kriminalromanzen, *Fun Bar Karaoke* (*Fan ba karaoke*, 1996/97) und *6ixtynin9* (*Ruang talok 69*, 1999), in Südostasien eine Schar von Anhängern gefunden. Nach der seichten *Transistor Love Story* (*Monrak Transistor*, 2001), einem Thai-Countrymusic-Kuriosum, wandte er sich ernsthafteren Themen zu und drehte *Last Life in the Universe* (*Ruang rak noi nid mahasan*, 2003). Das Drehbuch zu diesem Film schrieb er zusammen mit dem thailändischen Romancier Prabda Yoon, für die Kamera zeichnete der in Australien geborene Christopher Doyle verantwortlich, einer der wichtigsten Mitarbeiter Wong Kar-wais. *Last Life in the Universe* ist eine melancholische Liebesgeschichte zwischen einem zum Selbstmord neigenden japanischen Bibliothekar (Tadanobu Asano) im thailändischen Exil, der in seiner Wohnung unfreiwillig ein Yakuza-Mitglied ermordet, und einer Frau, die ebenfalls jemanden getötet hat. Der Film über Themen wie Entfremdung, Kontaktmangel und existenzielle Nöte, in dem Takashi Miike eine winzige Nebenrolle als Yakuza spielt, fand auf internationalen Festivals viel Zuspruch. *Invisible Waves* (2005/06), bei dem Ratanaruang wieder mit Yoon, Doyle und Asano zusammenarbeitete, ist ein Film noir über einen japanischen Killer (Asano), der illegal als Koch in Macau arbeitet und von seinem Boss angeheuert wird, dessen Ehefrau, mit der er selbst eine Affäre hat, umzulegen. Ratanaruangs jüngster Film ist *Ploy* (2007).

Membre de la nouvelle vague des auteurs thaïs, avec Apichatpong Weerasethakul et Wisit Sasanatieng, Pen-ek Ratanaruang a réalisé deux histoires sentimentalo-criminelles, *Fun Bar Karaoke* (*Fan ba karaoke*, 1996/97) et *6ixtynin9* (*Ruang talok 69*, 1999), très appréciées en Asie du Sud-Est. Après *Monrak Transistor* (2001), curiosité autour de la musique country version thaïe, Ratanaruang revient aux choses sérieuses et perce sur la scène internationale avec *Last Life in the Universe* (*Ruang rak noi nid mahasan*, 2003), coécrit avec l'écrivain thaï Prabda Yoon et photographié par le chef opérateur d'origine australienne Christopher Doyle, collaborateur régulier de Wong Kar-wai. Le comédien japonais Tadanobu Asano incarne un bibliothécaire suicidaire, exilé en Thaïlande, qui tue un yakuza par erreur et connaît une histoire d'amour mélancolique avec une femme qui a également tué. Chouchou des festivals internationaux, ce film aborde les thèmes de l'exclusion, du lien social et du malaise existentiel. L'acteur Takashi Miike y fait une apparition remarquée dans le rôle du yakuza. Nouvelle collaboration avec Yoon, Doyle et Asano, pour *Vagues invisibles* (*Invisible Waves*, 2005/06) qui est un film noir dans lequel un tueur japonais (Asano), qui travaille au noir comme cuisinier à Macao, est engagé pour tuer la femme de son patron, avec laquelle il a une liaison amoureuse. Le tout dernier opus de Ratanaruang est intitulé *Ploy* (2007).

FILMS →
1996/97 *Fan ba karaoke (Fun Bar Karaoke)*
1999 *Ruang talok 69 (6ixtynin9)* **2001** *Monrak Transistor (Transistor Love Story)* **2003** *Ruang rak noi nid mahasan (Last Life in the Universe)* **2005/06** *Invisible Waves* **2007** *Ploy*

SELECTED AWARDS →
2000 *Ruang talok 69*: FIPRESCI Prize, Hong Kong International Film Festival; Don Quixote Award – Special Mention, Berlin International Film Festival **2002** *Monrak Transistor*: Asian Trade Winds Award, Seattle International Film Festival **2004** *Ruang rak noi nid mahasan*: FIPRESCI Prize, Bangkok International Film Festival

Invisible Waves

Vagues invisibles

"Each project that I work on is just a combination of what I want to say at the time, what question I have in life, what I'm obsessed with at the time, plus, things that are forced upon me. And then I combine them, and see what I come up with. And that's the way I make films."

„Jedes Projekt, an dem ich arbeite, ist einfach nur eine Kombination dessen, was ich gerade ausdrücken will: der Fragen, die mir das Leben stellt, der Themen, die mich zu jenem Zeitpunkt beschäftigen, und der Dinge, die mir aufgezwungen werden. Dann versuche ich, alle Aspekte miteinander zu verbinden, um zu sehen, was dabei herauskommt. So entstehen meine Filme."

«Chacun des projets sur lesquels je travaille est un mélange de ce que je veux dire à ce moment-là, de mes interrogations et obsessions du moment, et de choses qui me sont imposées. Je mélange tout et je vois ce que cela donne. Voilà comment je fais des films.»

With cinematography by Australian Christopher Doyle and a central performance by Japanese matinee idol Tadanobu Asano, the second feature by the Thai stylist Pen-ek Ratanaruang is a film noir set in Macau and Phuket.

Schauplätze des zweiten Spielfilms des stilprägenden Thailänders Pen-ek Ratanaruang sind Macau und Phuket. Die Hauptrolle in diesem Film noir spielt das japanische Kinoidol Tadanobu Asano, für die Kamera zeichnete der Australier Christopher Doyle verantwortlich.

Pen-ek Ratanaruang signe un film noir d'un grand stylisme, qui se déroule à Macao et à Phuket, interprété par la vedette japonaise Tadanobu Asano. On doit la photographie à l'Australien Christopher Doyle.

NICOLAS WINDING REFN

Born 29 September 1970 in Copenhagen, Denmark

The years that came between the first and last installments of Nicolas Winding Refn's searing, unrepentant *Pusher* trilogy (1996–2005), examining the Copenhagen drug trade with the handheld verisimilitude of docudrama, were erratic ones for the Danish-born, American-educated son of director Anders Refn. After studying acting in New York City, Refn *fils* returned to Denmark and captured, in his debut feature *Pusher* (1996), the day-to-day struggles of the small-time drug dealers Frank and Tonny, played by Kim Bodnia and Mads Mikkelsen, generating popular acclaim for the film's unsentimentalized depiction of dealers living on the edge. Refn moved to Los Angeles for two years to collaborate with underground author Hubert Selby Jr. on the script for his third feature, *Fear X* (2003), a Lynchian psychological thriller starring John Turturro. He rebounded with successive *Pusher* sequels, *With Blood on My Hands: Pusher II* (2004) and *I'm the Angel of Death: Pusher III* (2005), widening his saga to include Tonny's struggle to survive in the shadow of his powerful gangster father and showing the aging Serbian drug lord Milo (Zlatko Buric) as he takes on rival Albanian dealers. Dark, moody and unstylized in its depiction of the power struggles, violent retribution and ensuing addiction in the drug underworld, the *Pusher* movies were superior urban dramas that earned Refn an international following among extreme action-thriller devotees.

Die Jahre zwischen der Fertigstellung des ersten und des letzten Teils seiner als wirklichkeitsnahes Dokudrama gedrehten, eindringlichen und gnadenlosen *Pusher*-Trilogie (1996–2005) über den Drogenhandel in Kopenhagen waren für Nicolas Winding Refn, den in Dänemark geborenen und in den USA aufgewachsenen Sohn des Regisseurs Anders Refn, schwierige Zeiten. Nach seinem Studium der Schauspielerei in New York City kehrte Refn junior nach Dänemark zurück und zeichnete in seinem ersten Spielfilm *Pusher* (1996) den täglichen Überlebenskampf der von Kim Bodnia und Mads Mikkelsen verkörperten Gelegenheitsdealer Frank und Tonny nach. Für seine unsentimentale Darstellung von Dealerexistenzen am Rande der Gesellschaft fand der Film großen Beifall. Für seinen dritten Spielfilm *Fear X* (2003), einen mit John Turturro besetzten Psychothriller im Stile David Lynchs, zog Refn für zwei Jahre nach Los Angeles, um gemeinsam mit dem Underground-Autor Hubert Selby jr. das Drehbuch auszuarbeiten. Dann wandte er sich mit *With Blood on My Hands: Pusher II* (2004) und *I'm the Angel of Death: Pusher III* (2005) dem zweiten und dritten Teil seiner Trilogie zu. Der zweite Teil der Saga erzählt von Tonnys Überlebenskampf im Schatten seines mächtigen Vaters, eines Gangsterbosses, der dritte kreist um den alternden serbischstämmigen Drogenbaron Milo (Zlatko Buric), der sich mit einer albanischen Bande auseinandersetzen muss, die ihm sein Geschäft streitig macht. Die *Pusher*-Filme, überragende städtische Dramen mit düsteren, deprimierenden und ungeschönten Schilderungen von Machtkämpfen, gewalttätiger Vergeltung und zwangsläufiger Sucht in der Unterwelt des Drogenhandels, haben Refn unter den Freunden extremer Actionthriller zu einer internationalen Anhängerschaft verholfen.

Entre 1996 et 2005, Nicolas Winding Refn, fils du cinéaste Anders Refn, réalise les trois volets de la trilogie *Pusher*, consacrée au trafic de drogue à Copenhague et réalisée avec la vraisemblance d'un docu-fiction. C'est une période instable pour le réalisateur danois qui a fait ses études en Amérique. Après des cours d'art dramatique à New York, Refn retourne au Danemark et filme, dans le premier *Pusher* (1996), la lutte quotidienne des petits dealers que sont Frank et Tonny (Kim Bodnia et Mads Mikkelsen). Ce film est salué pour son portrait très nature de dealers toujours sur la brèche. Refn s'installe à Los Angeles pendant deux ans pour écrire, avec l'écrivain Hubert Selby Jr, le scénario de son troisième film, *Inside Job* (*Fear X*, 2003), thriller psychologique à la David Lynch, avec John Turturro. Puis, avec *With Blood on My Hands: Pusher II* (2004) et *I'm the Angel of Death: Pusher III* (2005), la saga se développe : Tonny tente de survivre dans l'ombre de son père, chef de gang, et en remontre au Serbe Milo (Zlatko Buric), seigneur de la drogue vieillissant, en s'en prenant à une bande rivale de dealers albanais. Sombre, sans fioritures dans la description du milieu de la drogue, de ses rapports de force, de la violence et de la dépendance, la série des *Pusher* est un excellent drame urbain qui a valu à Refn la reconnaissance internationale chez les fans de thrillers extrêmes.

FILMS →
1996 *Pusher*
1999 *Bleeder*
2003 *Fear X*
2004 *With Blood on My Hands: Pusher II*
2005 *I'm the Angel of Death: Pusher III*

SELECTED AWARDS →
2000 *Bleeder:* FIPRESCI Prize, Sarajevo Film Festival

Pusher II

With Blood on My Hands: Pusher II

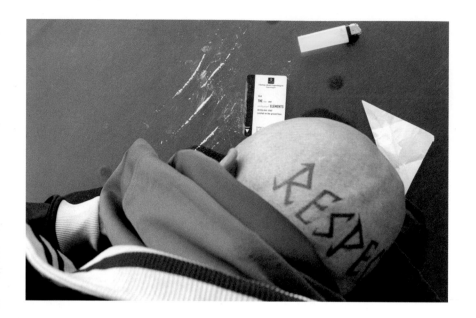

In the second installment of Refn's drug-dealing trilogy, Mads Mikkelsen stars as Tonny, released from prison and determined to gain the respect of his criminal father. Right: Nicolas Winding Refn directs.

Im zweiten Teil von Refns Trilogie über den Drogen-handel spielt Mads Mikkelsen den aus dem Ge-fängnis entlassenen Tonny, der endlich den Respekt seines kriminellen Vaters gewinnen will. Rechts: Nicolas Winding Refn bei der Arbeit.

Dans le deuxième volet de la trilogie de Refn, Mads Mikkelsen interprète Tonny, dealer libéré de prison et bien décidé à obtenir le respect de son père criminel. À droite : Nicolas Winding Refn au travail.

Pusher III

I'm the Angel of Death: *Pusher III*

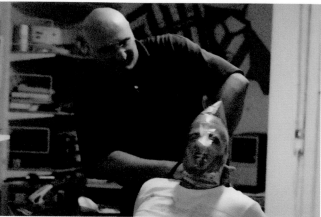

"Like all art forms, film is a media as powerful as weapons of mass destruction; the only difference is that war destroys and film inspires."

„Wie jede Kunstform ist auch das Medium Film so wirkungsvoll wie Massenvernichtungswaffen.
Der einzige Unterschied – Kriegswaffen zerstören, Film inspiriert."

«Comme toutes les formes d'expression artistique, le cinéma est un moyen aussi puissant que les armes de destruction massive,
à cette différence que la guerre détruit et que le cinéma inspire.»

Violence and bloodshed reaches a fever pitch as the aging drug lord Milo (Zlatkó Buric, left) tries to sell 10,000 tabs of Ecstasy, whilst dealing with his daughter's birthday and a takeover bid from Albanian drug dealers.

Als der alternde Drogenbaron Milo (Zlatko Buric, links) versucht, zehntausend Ecstasypillen zu verkaufen, und sich gleichzeitig noch um den Geburtstag seiner Tochter und ein Übernahme-angebot albanischer Drogenhändler kümmern muss, erreichen Gewalt und Blutvergießen den Höhepunkt.

Violence et hémoglobine sont à leur comble lorsque Milo (Zlatko Buric, à gauche), trafiquant de drogue vieillissant, tente de vendre 10 000 comprimés d'ecstasy, tout en s'occupant de l'anniversaire de sa fille et d'une OPA lancée sur lui par des dealers albanais.

CARLOS REYGADAS

Born 10 October 1971 in Mexico City, Mexico

A rising star of New Mexican Cinema, Carlos Reygadas discovered Tarkovsky's films at sixteen before embarking on a career in international law that sent him to London in his early twenties for a Masters program in the study of armed conflict. He toiled briefly in the Mexican foreign service before abandoning law for a career in filmmaking that led to his first feature *Japón* (2001), an auspicious debut shown in Cinema-Scope with almost no dialogue that tracked a Mexico City artist on a symbolic journey through a rugged landscape toward a remote canyon where the man plans to commit suicide. He undergoes a spiritual awakening in the home of a pious old widow, after a vivid lovemaking session with the matron, illuminating Reygadas's conjoined themes of sex, death and religion among the spiritually addled. His sex scenes, featuring unconventional body types, including fat women and the elderly, figure in both of his features. The filmmaker's controversial *Battle in Heaven* (*Batalla en el cielo*, 2005) built on those same themes in the subjectively focused story of a military chauffeur atoning for various sins including kidnapping, infidelity and murder. The film opened with a scene of fellatio that was bathed in heavenly light. Casting non-professionals in the style of Bresson – in some cases random people plucked directly off the street – and employing external spaces and architecture as poetic visual metaphors for his characters' anguished inner states (in *Battle in Heaven* the vast sprawl of Mexico City directly corresponds with the protagonist Marcos' inner turmoil), Reygadas creates philosophical marvels about the human condition that have earned him an international following. His latest film is *Silent Light* (*Stellet Licht*, 2007).

Als Carlos Reygadas, eines der aufstrebenden Talente des neuen mexikanischen Kinos, 16 Jahre alt war, entdeckte er für sich die Filme Tarkowskis. Doch zunächst ging er mit Anfang zwanzig nach London, wo er seinen Magister mit einer Untersuchung über bewaffnete Konflikte machte, und begann dann eine Karriere als Völkerrechtler. Nach einer kurzen Beschäftigung im auswärtigen Dienst Mexikos gab er die Rechtswissenschaften auf, um sich fortan dem Filmemachen zu widmen. Sein erster Spielfilm *Japón* (2001), ein vielversprechendes, in Cinemascope vorgeführtes Debüt, das fast ohne Dialoge auskommt, folgt einem Künstler aus Mexiko-Stadt auf eine symbolische Reise durch zerklüftete Landschaften zu einem abgelegenen Canyon, wo sich der Protagonist das Leben nehmen will. Doch im Hause einer frommen alten Witwe hat er, nach einem munteren Liebesakt mit der Matrone, ein spirituelles Erweckungserlebnis. So umriss Reygadas schon in diesem Film seine sich vor einem Hintergrund geistiger Desorientierung entwickelnden Themen Sex, Tod und Religion. Sexszenen mit unkonventionellen Typen – dicken Frauen etwa oder Alten – sind in beiden bislang vorliegenden Filmen des Regisseurs zu sehen. Reygadas kontrovers diskutierter Film *Battle in Heaven* (*Batalla en el cielo*, 2005) kreist um die gleichen Themen, konzentriert sich jedoch auf die subjektive Geschichte eines Militärchauffeurs, der für seine Sünden wie Kidnapping, Untreue und Mord büßen will. Der Film setzt mit einer in ein geradezu entrücktes Licht getauchten Fellatioszene ein. Wie Bresson sucht sich Reygadas Amateurschauspieler, manchmal entdeckt er seine Darsteller zufällig auf der Straße. Durch die Art und Weise, wie er Außenwelt und Architektur zu visuellen poetischen Metaphern der inneren Leiden seiner Charaktere stilisiert (in *Battle in Heaven* entspricht die wuchernde Ausbreitung von Mexiko-Stadt dem aufgewühlten Zustand des Protagonisten Marco), gelingen Reygadas philosophische Wunderwerke über das menschliche Dasein, die ihm eine internationale Anhängerschar sichern. Sein neuer Film heißt *Stilles Licht* (*Stellet Licht*, 2007).

Étoile montante du nouveau cinéma mexicain, Carlos Reygadas découvre, à 16 ans, les films de Tarkovsky, avant d'entreprendre une carrière dans le droit international. Âgé d'une vingtaine d'années, il fait une maîtrise sur les conflits armés, à Londres. Après un bref passage aux Affaires étrangères mexicaines, il renonce au droit pour le cinéma et tourne son premier film – très prometteur –, *Japón* (2001) : c'est le voyage symbolique, en cinémascope et presque sans dialogues, d'un artiste de Mexico à travers un paysage d'une grande désolation, jusqu'au canyon isolé où il compte se suicider. Chez une vieille veuve, avec laquelle il fait l'amour intensément, il connaît une révélation spirituelle. Tous les thèmes de Reygadas sont présents : le sexe, la mort, la religion chez des personnage à l'esprit confus. Son film montre des corps qui échappent aux conventions – femmes obèses, vieillards. Très controversé, *Bataille dans le ciel* (*Batalla en el cielo*, 2005) repose sur les mêmes thèmes, du point de vue d'un chauffeur de l'armée qui se rachète de divers péchés, dont l'enlèvement, l'infidélité et le meurtre. Le film s'ouvre sur une scène de fellation baignée de lumière céleste. À la manière de Bresson, Reygadas tourne avec des acteurs amateurs, parfois choisis au hasard dans la rue ; l'espace et l'architecture lui servent de métaphores poétiques des angoisses de ses personnages. Dans *Bataille dans le ciel*, la mégalopole de Mexico est le reflet des tourments intérieurs de Marco. Reygadas est l'auteur de prodiges philosophiques sur la condition humaine, appréciés dans le monde entier. *Lumière silencieuse* (*Stellet Licht*, 2007) est son dernier film en date.

FILMS →
2001 *Japón*
2005 *Batalla en el cielo (Battle in Heaven)*
2007 *Stellet Licht (Silent Light)*

SELECTED AWARDS →
2002 *Japón*: Golden Camera – Special Mention, Cannes Film Festival; New Director's Award, Edinburgh International Film Festival; Best Director, Thessaloniki Film Festival
2004 *Japón*: Silver Ariel: Best First Work, Best Screenplay, Ariel Awards
2007 *Stellet Licht*: Jury Prize, Cannes Film Festival

Japón

"Hope is the most important feeling we can have."

„Hoffnung ist das wichtigste Gefühl, das wir haben."

« L'espoir est le sentiment le plus important dont nous disposions. »

A vagabond painter (Alejandro Ferretis) travels to a remote canyon to commit suicide, experiencing en route a spiritual transformation that proves both earthly and divine. Left: Reygadas and his crew.

Ein umherziehender Maler (Alejandro Ferretis) macht sich zu einem einsam gelegenen Canyon auf, um Selbstmord zu begehen. Unterwegs hat er, sowohl in irdischer als auch in spiritueller Hinsicht, ein Erweckungserlebnis. Links: Reygadas und seine Crew.

Un peintre vagabond (Alejandro Ferretis) se rend dans un canyon isolé pour se suicider, mais connaît une transformation spirituelle qui s'avérera à la fois bien concrète et divine. À gauche : Reygadas et son équipe.

Reygadas cast non-professional actors: a family friend, Alejandro Ferretis, plays the despairing, suicidal and nameless protagonist; Magdalena Flores plays the elderly widow Ascen, a surprising figure in the artist's masturbatory dreams.

Reygadas sucht sich Laiendarsteller: Ein Freund der Familie, Alejandro Ferretis, spielt den verzweifelten, selbstmordgefährdeten und namenlosen Protagonisten; Magdalena Flores verkörpert die ältere Witwe Ascen, die überraschenderweise in den Masturbationsfantasien des Künstlers auftaucht.

Reygadas a fait jouer des non-professionnels : Alejandro Ferretis, un ami de la famille, incarne le héros désespéré, suicidaire et anonyme ; Magdalena Flores interprète Ascen, la veuve âgée, figure étonnante des rêves onanistes de l'artiste.

Residents from the Mexican state of Hidalgo were cast for all the roles, giving natural, unaffected performances. Right: The cast and crew battled the environment and the elements to make one of the greatest film debuts in the history of cinema.

Alle Rollen wurden mit Bewohnern des mexikanischen Bundesstaates Hidalgo besetzt, die sich als Darsteller natürlich und ungekünstelt geben. Rechts: Darsteller und Crew hatten bei der Entstehung eines der bemerkenswertesten Debüts der Filmgeschichte mit den landschaftlichen Gegebenheiten und den Elementen zu kämpfen.

Jouant tous les rôles, des habitants de l'État mexicain d'Hidalgo donnent des interprétations naturelles et sans affectation. À droite : l'équipe et les acteurs se sont confrontés à l'environnement naturel pour créer l'un des premiers films les plus réussis de l'histoire du cinéma.

Batalla en el cielo

Battle in Heaven / Bataille dans le ciel

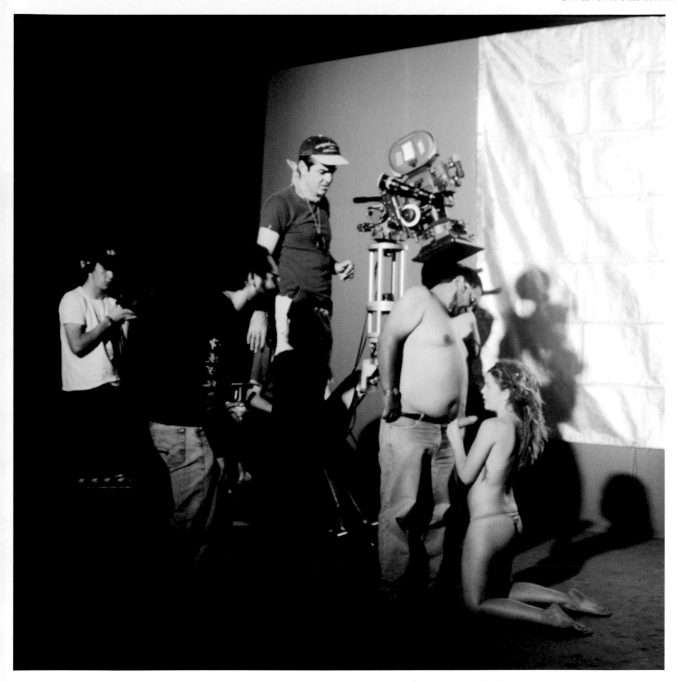

An explicit sex scene opens *Battle in Heaven*, which recounts the existential crises of the Mexico City chauffeur Marco (Marcos Hernández) and the general's daughter (Anapola Mushkadiz) who soothes him. Above: Carlos Reygadas directs.

Battle in Heaven wird mit einer expliziten Sexszene eröffnet. Der Film schildert die existenziellen Krisen des als Chauffeur in Mexico City arbeitenden Marcos (Marcos Hernández) und der ihn tröstenden Generalstochter (Anapola Mushkadiz). Oben: Carlos Reygadas bei der Regiearbeit.

Ce film s'ouvre sur une scène de sexe explicite qui évoque les crises existentielles de Marco (Marcos Hernández), chauffeur militaire de Mexico, et de la fille du général (Anapola Mushkadiz) qui l'apaise. Ci-dessus : Carlos Reygadas au travail.

Spiritual malaise and sexual release are recurring themes in *Battle in Heaven*. Marco views the general's daughter with rose-colored glasses, but she is as tainted as he is – he is a kidnapper, she is a prostitute.

Spirituelle Orientierungslosigkeit und die Befriedigung sexueller Bedürfnisse sind die Grundthemen in *Battle in Heaven*. Marcos sieht die Tochter des Generals durch die rosarote Brille, doch wie er hat auch sie keine weiße Weste – er ist ein Kidnapper, sie eine Prostituierte.

Malaise spirituel et apaisement sexuel sont les thèmes récurrents de *Bataille dans le ciel*. Marco voit la fille du général avec des lunettes roses. Mais elle est aussi souillée que lui : lui ravisseur, elle prostituée.

Like Federico Fellini and Robert Bresson before him, Reygadas casts people off the street based on how they look. Among them is Bertha Ruiz (top left), a police commissioner's wife, who played Marco's wife.

Wie Federico Fellini und Robert Bresson vor ihm sucht sich Reygadas seine Darsteller auf der Straße. Dabei interessiert ihn vor allem das Erscheinungsbild der Figuren. Zu ihnen gehört auch Bertha Ruiz (oben links). Die Ehefrau eines Polizeikommissars verkörperte im Film Marcos' Frau.

Comme Federico Fellini et Robert Bresson avant lui, Reygadas choisit ses acteurs dans la rue selon leur physique. Parmi ceux-ci, Bertha Ruiz (ci-contre, en haut), épouse de commissaire de police, qui interprète de la femme de Marco.

To pay for his sins (adultery, kidnapping, murder) Marco undertakes an act of extreme humility and self-flagellation, resulting in a religious catharsis.

Um für seine Sünden (Ehebruch, Kidnapping, Mord) zu büßen, unternimmt Marcos einen Akt extremer Demut und Selbstzüchtigung, der schließlich in einer religiösen Katharsis mündet.

Pour se racheter de ses péchés (adultère, rapt, meurtre), Marco se livre à un acte d'humilité absolue et d'autoflagellation se soldant pas une catharsis religieuse.

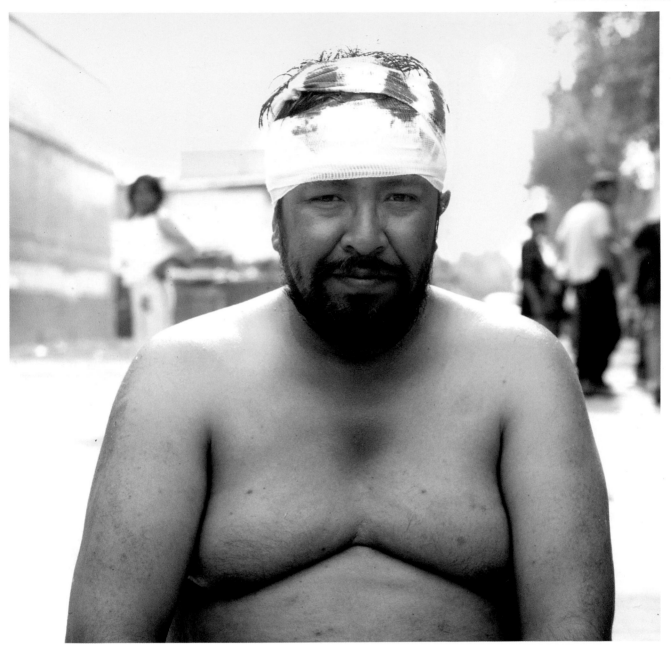

Stellet Licht

Silent Light / Stilles Licht / Lumière silencieuse

Silent Light explores the repercussions of an extra-marital affair on a close-knit Mennonite community in northern Mexico; Reygadas shot his third feature in the Manitoba colony in Cuauhtemoc, Chihuahua, Mexico.

Stilles Licht untersucht die Auswirkungen einer außerehelichen Beziehung auf die eng miteinander verbundenen Mitglieder einer Mennonitengemeinde im nördlichen Mexiko. Seinen dritten Spielfilm drehte Reygadas in der Manitoba-Kolonie in Cuauhtemoc, Chihuahua, Mexiko.

Lumière silencieuse s'intéresse aux répercussions d'une liaison extraconjugale sur l'unité d'une communauté mennonite du Nord du Mexique. Reygadas a tourné son troisième film dans la colonie Manitoba de Cuauhtemoc, dans l'État mexicain de Chihuahua.

JOÃO PEDRO RODRIGUEſ

Born 1966 in Liſbon, Portugal

In only two features the Portuguese punk melodramatist João Pedro Rodrigues has succeeded in channeling the obsessive desire of Alfred Hitchcock's *Vertigo* (1958) and Douglas Sirk's *Magnificent Obsession* (1954) and the barely contained hysteria of early Almodóvar and Waters into standout works that rank him among Europe's most fascinating and unpredictable young directors – one could die of arrhythmia wondering what he'll conjure up next. In the deliciously sordid and over-the-top *Phantom* (*O Fantasma*, 2000), Rodrigues served up a sex-obsessed young sanitation worker (played by non-actor Ricardo Meneses) on the prowl in Lisbon whose animalistic lust results in bouts of wall licking, crotch sniffing, cop stalking and a final act of depravity in a garbage dump that is both unsettling and hilarious. Whereas *Phantom* featured sparse dialogue and a soundtrack comprised mainly of barking dogs, its successor contained some of the best use of music in movies today – including a children's choir rendition of 'Smells Like Teen Spirit.' *Two Drifters* (*Odete*, 2005), which takes its English title from the opening lyrics of Henry Mancini's 'Moon River,' tells the story of a mentally unstable supermarket worker (Ana Cristina de Oliveira) who believes she is pregnant with the child of her dead gay neighbor, a car accident victim whose garish final breath in his lover's arms haunts the film's opening scene – it's a screen kiss like no other. As the titular Odete plummets further into madness and obsession, confounding her neighbors, Rodrigues ratchets up his deranged melodramatics with an implied transmigration of souls and climactic three-way sex scene that threatens to change forever the way you listen to 'Moon River.'

Mit nur zwei Spielfilmen ist es dem portugiesischen Punk-Melodramatiker João Pedro Rodrigues gelungen, der obsessiven Begierde aus Alfred Hitchcocks *Vertigo – Aus dem Reich der Toten* (*Vertigo*, 1958) und Douglas Sirks *Die wunderbare Macht* (*Magnificent Obsession*, 1954) sowie der kaum verhüllten Hysterie der frühen Filme von Almodóvar und Waters in seinen herausragenden Arbeiten zu neuer Geltung zu verhelfen, sodass man ihn zu den faszinierendsten und unberechenbarsten jungen europäischen Regisseuren zählen muss. Man wird schon ganz unruhig bei dem Gedanken, was er wohl als Nächstes hervorzuzaubern mag. In seinem herrlich verkommen und übertrieben dargebotenen *Phantom* (*Fantasma*, 2000) streift ein (von dem Amateurschauspieler Ricardo Meneses verkörperter) sexbesessener junger Müllwerker durch Lissabon und lässt seiner animalischen Lust freien Lauf: In regelrechten Anfällen leckt er Wände, schnüffelt am Schritt anderer, stellt Polizisten nach und lässt uns schließlich an einem irritierenden und zugleich urkomischen letzten Akt der Verdorbenheit auf einer Mülldeponie teilhaben. Während *O Fantasma* nur spärliche Dialoge bietet und der Soundtrack sich im Wesentlichen in Hundegebell erschöpft, glänzt sein folgendes Werk durch den Einsatz von Musik – darunter eine von einem Kinderchor gesungene Version von „Smells Like Teen Spirit" –, wie man ihn sich für einen Film kaum besser vorstellen kann. *Two Drifters – Odete* (*Odete*, 2005), dessen englischer Titel den ersten Zeilen von Henry Mancinis „Moon River" entstammt, erzählt die Geschichte einer psychisch labilen Supermarktangestellten (Ana Cristina de Oliveira), die sich einbildet, sie sei von ihrem schwulen Nachbarn, der bei einem Verkehrsunfall ums Leben kam, geschwängert worden. Mit dessen heftigen letzten Atemzügen in den Armen seines Geliebten – und einem Kuss, wie man ihn bislang noch nicht auf der Leinwand geboten bekam – setzt der Film ein. Als die Titelheldin immer verrückter und besessener wird und nicht einmal mehr ihre Nachbarn auseinanderhalten kann, gibt Rodrigues seinem aus den Fugen geratenden Melodram noch einen Schub – mit einer angedeuteten Seelenwanderung und dem Höhepunkt einer Sexszene zu dritt, nach deren Genuss man als Zuschauer „Moon River" vermutlich nie wieder so hören wird wie zuvor.

Il a suffi de deux films à João Pedro Rodrigues, représentant du mélodrame punk, pour figurer au rang des jeunes cinéastes européens les plus passionnants et les plus imprévisibles. Ses œuvres réunissent les désirs obsédants de *Sueurs froides* d'Hitchcock et du *Secret magnifique* de Douglas Sirk tout comme l'hystérie à peine contenue des premiers films d'Almodóvar et de Waters. On se demande bien ce qu'il va nous concocter désormais ! Délicieusement sordide et outré, *O Fantasma* (2000) suit l'itinéraire d'un jeune éboueur obsédé par le sexe (l'acteur amateur Ricardo Meneses) qui arpente Lisbonne. Son désir animal l'amène à lécher des murs, sentir des entrejambes, suivre un policier et se livrer, dans une décharge, à un dernier acte de perversion, suscitant rire et malaise. Si la bande-son se résume à de rares dialogues et à de nombreux aboiements de chien, celle de son film suivant témoigne d'une des meilleures utilisations de la musique dans le cinéma d'aujourd'hui, notamment grâce à l'interprétation par un chœur d'enfants de *Smells Like Teen Spirit* de Nirvana. *Odete* (2005), dont le titre anglais *The Drifters* fait référence à la chanson *Moon River* d'Henry Mancini, est l'histoire d'une employée de supermarché psychologiquement instable (Ana Cristina de Oliveira), persuadée d'être enceinte de son défunt voisin homosexuel. Mort dans un accident de voiture, ce dernier a rendu son dernier soupir entre les bras de son amant, dans un baiser de cinéma impitoyable et inédit, comme le montre la scène d'ouverture. Déconcertant ses voisins, Odete plonge toujours plus loin dans la folie et l'obsession. À cette histoire de fous, Rodrigues ajoute implicitement une transmigration des âmes et une scène d'ébats sexuels à trois qui pourrait changer à tout jamais la perception qu'on a de *Moon River*.

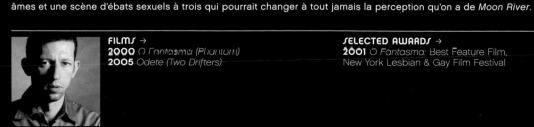

FILMſ →
2000 *O Fantasma (Phantom)*
2005 *Odete (Two Drifters)*

ſELECTED AWARDſ →
2001 *O Fantasma*: Best Feature Film,
New York Lesbian & Gay Film Festival

O Fantasma
Phantom

"Through life there is a path, and though we may not take it, sometimes in dreams, we're able to see it.
And beyond this path, we can see strange pictures, fragments, pieces, like visions of another life we might somewhere lead."

„Es gibt einen Pfad, der durchs Leben führt, und auch wenn wir ihn nicht einschlagen, so können wir ihn doch manchmal in unseren Träumen erkennen. Und am Ende dieses Pfads sehen wir seltsame Bilder, Fragmente, Elemente, die wie Visionen von einem anderen Leben wirken, das wir irgendwo führen könnten."

«Un chemin traverse la vie. Bien qu'on ne l'emprunte pas forcément, on le voit parfois en rêve. Au-delà de ce chemin, nous voyons d'étranges images, fragments et morceaux, vision d'une autre vie que nous connaîtrons peut-être ailleurs.»

Sérgio (Ricardo Meneses), an insatiable Lisbon sanitation worker, descends into sexual degradation and animalistic lust in *O Fantasma*, the feature debut from Portuguese bad boy João Pedro Rodrigues.

In *O Fantasma*, dem ersten Spielfilm des portugiesischen Bad Boy João Pedro Rodrigues, gibt sich der unersättliche Sergio (Ricardo Meneses), ein Müllmann aus Lissabon, sexueller Erniedrigung und animalischer Lust hin.

Sérgio (Ricardo Meneses), insatiable éboueur, tombe dans l'avilissement sexuel et le désir bestial dans *O Fantasma*, premier film du mauvais garçon portugais João Pedro Rodrigues.

Odete

Two Drifters / Two Drifters – Odete

In this dark comic melodrama, a young supermarket clerk (left) develops a hysterical pregnancy in the aftermath of a gay man's sudden and violent death (right).

In dieser melodramatischen schwarzen Komödie bildet sich eine junge Supermarktangestellte (Ana Cristina de Oliveira, links) nach dem plötzlichen und gewaltsamen Tod eines schwulen Mannes (João Carreira, rechts) ein, sie wäre von ihm schwanger.

Dans ce mélodrame tragicomique, une jeune employée de supermarché (à gauche) connaît une grossesse nerveuse, à la suite de la mort soudaine et violente d'un homosexuel (à droite).

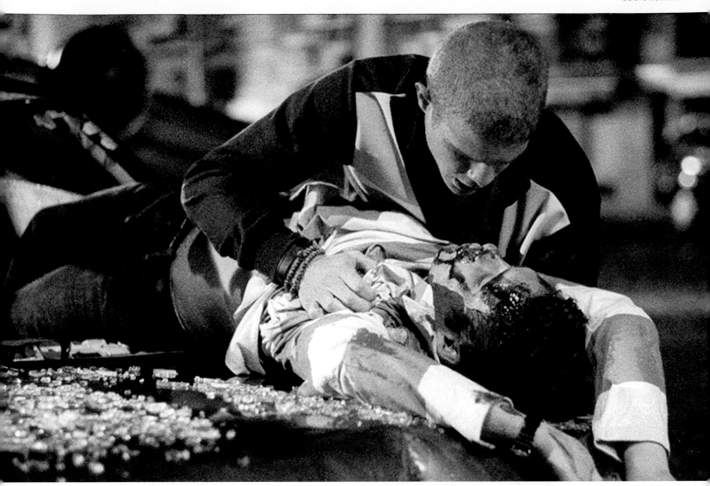

ROBERT RODRIGUEZ

Born 20 June 1968 in San Antonio, USA

The self-professed "rebel without a crew" shot action and horror movies on video as a child before creating a daily comic strip during his adolescence followed by a first feature in his early twenties, the notorious *El Mariachi* (1992), made for $7,000, much of which was raised from Rodriguez's participation in medical research studies. A rousing hit at the Sundance Film Festival, where it won the Audience Award and resulted in a studio distribution deal through Columbia Pictures, *El Mariachi* put the Austin, Texas-based one-man crew on the independent film map, where he was embraced by the same movie geek contingent that helped turned his friend and fellow B-movie obsessive, Quentin Tarantino, into a cause célèbre. The two kindred spirits would go on to work together in various capacities over the years, culminating in the exploitation double-header *Grindhouse* (2007), to which Rodriguez contributed the zombie horror opus *Planet Terror*. After a string of studio projects, including the blockbuster *Spy Kids* trilogy (2001–2003) and two *Mariachi* sequels, *Desperado* (1995) and *Once Upon a Time in Mexico* (2003), Rodriguez unleashed his most impressive feat to date, an adaptation of Frank Miller's graphic novel *Sin City* (2005), featuring a rogue's gallery of villains and vixens, some of the most visceral screen violence in memory, and a digitally-enhanced veneer that gave the film a kinetic visual edge over countless comic-book competitors. A multi-hyphenate known for his "Mariachi-style" low-budget, no-nonsense, do-it-yourself method of filmmaking, Rodriguez has worked (often all at once) as producer, director, writer, editor, camera operator, musical score composer, production designer and sound editor. His next two features are *Sin City* sequels.

Der selbst ernannte „rebel without a crew" drehte als Kind Action- und Horrorfilme auf Video, als Jugendlicher produzierte er einen täglich fortgesetzten Comicstrip und im Alter von 24 Jahren seinen ersten Spielfilm, den berüchtigten *El Mariachi* (1992), der mit einem Budget von nur 7000 Dollar entstand, die sich Rodriguez zum Teil als Testperson für Medikamente verdiente. Mit *El Mariachi*, der auf dem Sundance Film Festival begeistert aufgenommen, mit dem Publikumspreis ausgezeichnet und danach von Columbia Pictures in die Kinos gebracht wurde, gelang es dem in Austin, Texas, lebenden Ein-Mann-Unternehmen, sich einen Namen in der Independent-Szene zu machen und von den gleichen Kinobesessenen mit offenen Armen aufgenommen zu werden, die auch schon seinem Freund und B-Movie-Verrückten Quentin Tarantino zu Berühmtheit verholfen hatten. Die beiden Brüder im Geiste arbeiteten fortan bei den verschiedensten Projekten zusammen, eine Kooperation, die in dem als Doppel-Feature geplanten *Grindhouse* (2007) gipfelte, zu dem Rodriguez das Zombie-Horror-Opus *Planet Terror* beisteuerte. Nach einer Reihe von Studioproduktionen – darunter die Blockbuster-Trilogie *Spy Kids* (2001–2003) sowie *Desperado* (1995) und *Irgendwann in Mexiko* (*Once Upon a Time in Mexico*, 2003), der zweiten und dritten Folge der *Mariachi*-Trilogie – wartete Rodriguez mit seinem bislang beeindruckendsten Werk auf, *Sin City* (2005), einer Adaption von Frank Millers Comicvorlage. Mit Bösewichten und Flintenweibern wie aus einem Verbrecheralbum, einigen der brutalsten Szenen, die je auf der Leinwand zu sehen waren, und einer digital aufgemotzten Optik bot der Film eine überlegene kinetisch-visuelle Qualität, die ihn weit über die zahllosen Comicverfilmungen hinaushebt. Rodriguez, den man als Filmemacher für seinen „Mariachi-Stil", im Do-it-yourself-Verfahren realisierte No-Nonsense- und Low-Budget-Produktionen nur mit Bindestrich-Konstruktionen zu beschreiben vermag, hat als Produzent, Regisseur, Autor, Cutter, Kameramann, Filmmusikkomponist, Setdesigner und Soundeditor gearbeitet – und oft genug alles alleine und gleichzeitig gemacht. Seine nächsten beiden Spielfilme sind Fortsetzungen von *Sin City*.

Celui qui s'autoproclame « rebelle solitaire » a tourné, dans son enfance, des films d'action et d'horreur en vidéo, a dessiné une BD quotidiennement pendant son adolescence, et signé son premier long métrage la vingtaine venue, le célèbre *El Mariachi* (1992), tourné avec 7 000 dollars recueillis grâce à sa participation en tant que cobaye à la recherche médicale. Prix du public au Festival Sundance, distribué par Columbia, ce film impose le solitaire d'Austin sur la carte du cinéma indépendant, salué par les cinglés de cinoche qui avaient fait une célébrité de son ami Quentin Tarantino, amateur, comme lui, de séries B. Nos deux potes allaient ensuite travailler ensemble au fil des ans, à des titres divers, en particulier pour le tout récent *Grind House* (2007), dont Rodriguez a réalisé l'épisode des zombies de « Planet Terror ». Après une série de productions hollywoodiennes, dont la trilogie à succès des *Spy Kids* (2001–2003) et deux suites d'*El Mariachi* – *Desperado* (1996) et *Il était une fois au Mexique* (*Once Upon a Time in Mexico* (2003) –, Rodriguez signe son plus grand exploit à ce jour, l'adaptation du roman graphique de Frank Miller, *Sin City* (2005). On y voit une galerie de portraits de méchants et de mégères, des scènes de violence parmi les plus crues du cinéma, le tout sous un vernis numérique qui donne au film une longueur d'avance sur les innombrables adaptations de BD. Abonné aux petits budgets, adepte du travail sérieux et de la débrouillardise façon *El Mariachi*, Rodriguez a été (parfois simultanément) producteur, réalisateur, scénariste, monteur, cameraman, compositeur, décorateur et monteur son. Ses deux prochains films seront des suites de *Sin City*.

FILMS →
1992 *El Mariachi* **1995** *Desperado* **1996** *From Dusk Till Dawn* **1998** *The Faculty* **2001** *Spy Kids* **2002** *Spy Kids 2: Island of Lost Dreams* **2003** *Once Upon a Time in Mexico* **2003** *Spy Kids 3-D: Game Over* **2005** *The Adventures of Sharkboy and Lavagirl 3-D* **2005** *Sin City* **2007** *Grindhouse: Planet Terror* **2007/08** *Sin City 2*

SELECTED AWARDS →
1993 *El Mariachi:* Audience Award, Sundance Film Festival; Audience Award, Deauville Film Festival **1994** *El Mariachi:* Best First Feature, Independent Spirit Awards **1996** *From Dusk Till Dawn:* Silver Scream Award, Amsterdam Fantastic Film Festival **1999** Berlinale Camera, Berlin International Film Festival **2005** *Sin City:* Technical Grand Prize, Cannes Film Festival

Desperado

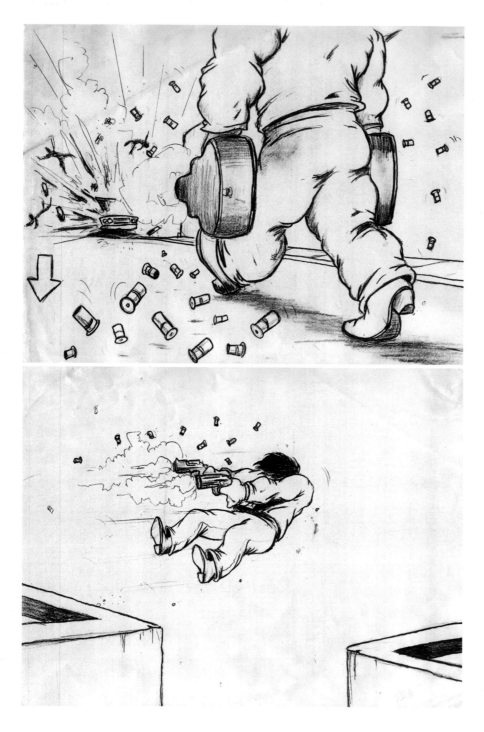

Above: Storyboards from the spaghetti western hom- age *Desperado*, featuring the gun-slinging singing pistolero protagonist from the trilogy that began with *El Mariachi* and concluded with *Once Upon a Time in Mexico* (right).

Oben: Storyboards zur Spaghetti-Western-Hommage *Desperado*. Im Mittelpunkt dieses zweiten Films einer Trilogie, die mit *El Mariachi* begann und mit *Irgendwann in Mexiko* (rechts) endete, steht ein mit Waffen fuchtelnder singender Pistolero (Antonio Banderas).

Ci-dessus : Story-boards de *Desperado*, hommage aux westerns spaghetti, avec le pistolero chantant, à la gachette facile, né avec *El Mariachi* et que l'on retrouve ensuite dans *Il était une fois au Mexique* (à droite).

Once Upon a Time in Mexico

Irgendwann in Mexiko / Il était une fois au Mexique

Spy Kids 3-D: Game Over
Mission 3D / Mission 3D Spy Kids 3

The Adventures of Sharkboy and Lavagirl 3-D

Die Abenteuer von Sharkboy und Lavagirl in 3-D / Les Aventures de Shark Boy et Lava Girl

"Video technology puts filmmaking back in the hands of the people. That's how I learned how to make movies – making movies at home."

„Mit der Videotechnik wird das Filmemachen wieder für jeden möglich. So habe ich es gelernt – indem ich zu Hause Filme gedreht habe."

«La vidéo remet le cinéma à la portée de tout le monde. C'est comme ça que j'ai appris à faire des films, en les faisant chez moi.»

Rodriguez' grasp of the economics and range of green-screen technology has resulted in some way cool kid flicks. Above: With co-screenwriters and cast members Rebel and Rodriguez on the set of *The Adventures of Sharkboy and Lavagirl in 3D*.

Rodriguez wusste die Möglichkeiten der Green-screen-Technik geschickt zu nutzen. So entstanden ein paar ziemlich coole Filme für Jugendliche. Oben: Mit den Koautoren und Darstellern Rebel und Marcel Rodriguez am Set von *Die Abenteuer von Shark Boy und Lava Girl in 3 D*.

La maîtrise de «l'écran vert» par Rodriguez donne des images très léchées. Ci-dessus: Coscénaristes et interprètes: Rodriguez et son fils Rebel sur le plateau des *Aventures de Shark Boy et Lava Girl*.

Sin City

Right: Rodriguez transformed Frank Miller's popular graphic novel *Sin City* into an equally popular graphic film, co-directing with Frank Miller (right), and on set with Bruce Willis (below).

Rechts: Rodriguez setzte Frank Millers populäre Comicgeschichte *Sin City* in eine ebenso erfolgreiche Comicverfilmung um. Gemeinsam mit Miller (rechts) führte er Regie, Bruce Willis (unten, Rodriguez mit dem Schauspieler am Set) wirkte als Darsteller mit.

À droite : Rodriguez a transposé à l'écran *Sin City*, la bande dessinée très populaire de Frank Miller, pour en faire un film tout aussi populaire, coréalisé avec Miller (à droite). Ci-dessous : Rodriguez et Bruce Willis sur le plateau.

PAVEL RUMINOV

Born 25 November 1974 in Vladivostok, Russia

Maverick in the making (he has likened himself to Kubrick, Spielberg and Shyamalan) or world cinema's answer to Terence Trent D'Arby ("I'm a genius. Point fucking blank."), the Russian provocateur Pavel Ruminov began drawing attention to his third feature, the garish low-budget horror film *Dead Daughters* (*Myortvye docheri*, 2006) through a highly effective series of Internet teasers that established a rich mythology behind the film before it even started production. Internet blogs like the influential genre news site *Twitch* picked up on the haunting teasers and word of mouth spread for both the film and Ruminov, who had already been hailed as "the future of Russian cinema" by influential entertainment weekly *Afisha*, after two previous features barely created a ripple outside Russia. With a background in music videos and commercials, a predilection for Japanese and Korean horror films and a self-confidence that commands attention, Ruminov barely wrapped *Dead Daughters* before an American production company snapped up remake rights. Set in present-day Moscow, *Dead Daughters* – which Ruminov wrote, directed, edited, art directed, scored and executive produced for under $1 million – follows the ghosts of three young girls killed by their insane mother as they haunt five randomly selected people for several days, after which time the targets are killed via telekinesis if their moral standards are not up to snuff. An object lesson in how buzz is built and disseminated through the Internet blogosphere, *Dead Daughters* is also a fascinating example of how genre films transmogrify from nation to nation, creating new permutations out of familiar stories. J-horror, K-horror and now R-horror – if Ruminov and *Dead Daughters* succeed in living up to their own gargantuan hype.

Ist der russische Provokateur Pavel Ruminov ein einzelgängerischer Filmemacher (er hat sich selbst mit Kubrick, Spielberg und Shyamalan verglichen) oder die Antwort des Weltkinos auf Terence Trent D'Arby („Ich bin ein Genie. So verdammt einfach ist das")? Die Aufmerksamkeit für seinen dritten Spielfilm, den schrillen Low-Budget-Horrorfilm *Dead Daughters* (*Myortvye docheri*, 2006), weckte er durch eine höchst effektive Serie von Internet-Kostproben, die den Film schon mit einem Mythos umgaben, bevor er überhaupt produziert wurde. Internet-Blogs wie die einflussreichen Genrenachrichten *Twitch* griffen diese Kostproben und Gerüchte über den Film und über Ruminov auf, der nach seinen beiden ersten Spielfilmen, die außerhalb Russlands kaum Aufmerksamkeit erregten, von der viel beachteten Unterhaltungs-Wochenzeitschrift *Afisha* bereits als „Zukunft des russischen Films" bejubelt wurde. Ruminov, der mit Musikvideos und Werbespots begann, eine Vorliebe für japanische und koreanische Horrorfilme hat und mit einem Selbstbewusstsein ausgestattet ist, das Beachtung einfordert, hatte *Dead Daughters* kaum abgedreht, da sicherte sich eine amerikanische Produktionsgesellschaft bereits die Rechte für ein Remake. Für *Dead Daughters*, den Ruminov für weniger als eine Million Dollar produzierte, zeichnete der Regisseur auch als Drehbuchautor, Cutter, Ausstatter, Soundtrack-Komponist und ausführender Produzent verantwortlich. Die im Moskau unserer Tage angesiedelte Geschichte erzählt von den Geistern dreier von ihrer geistesgestörten Mutter umgebrachter Mädchen, die für einige Tage fünf zufällig ausgewählte Personen heimsuchen, sie beobachten und telekinetisch töten, sobald sie sich einer moralischen Verfehlung schuldig machen. *Dead Daughters* ist nicht nur ein Lehrstück, wie ein Film über Internet-Blogs bekannt gemacht werden kann, sondern auch ein faszinierendes Beispiel dafür, wie sich Genrefilme durch immer neue Wandlungen vertrauter Geschichten von Nation zu Nation verändern. Da gibt es den J-Horror, den K-Horror und nun offenbar auch den R-Horror – vorausgesetzt, Ruminov und *Dead Daughters* überleben den gewaltigen, selbst inszenierten Hype.

Myortvye docheri

Dead Daughters

In Russian upstart Pavel Ruminov's atmospheric chiller *Dead Daughters*, a deranged man tells of a madwoman killed by the ghosts of her slain children.

In *Dead Daughters*, dem atmosphärisch dichten Horrorfilm des russischen Senkrechtstarters Pavel Ruminov, erzählt ein verwirrter Mann die Geschichte einer geistesgestörten Frau, die von den Geistern ihrer von ihr ermordeten Kinder getötet wird.

Dans le film très troublant du nouveau venu Pavel Ruminov, un homme dérangé parle d'une folle tuée par les fantômes de ses enfants qu'elle a assassinés.

"I think I could shoot a movie with a boot."

„Ich glaube, ich könnte einen Film auch über einen Stiefel drehen."

«Je me sens capable de tourner un film avec une botte.»

DAVID O. RUSSELL

Born 20 Augu/t 1958 in new York City, U/A

A modern-day master of the screwball comedy, this American writer-director rose to prominence with his dark indie comedy *Spanking the Monkey* (1993), about a medical student who spends his summer vacation taking care of his depressed and overbearing convalescent mother. The film won the Audience Award at the Sundance Film Festival, launching Russell's career in tandem with a new wave of acerbic comedy mavericks including Alexander Payne, Todd Solondz and Spike Jonze. With the farcical ensemble *Flirting with Disaster* (1996) Russell introduced his penchant for multiple characters engaging in rambunctious, often bumbling behavior, a comic blend deliciously served in his masterpiece, *Three Kings* (1999), a combat farce set during the first Gulf War that wasn't a huge hit during its initial release, but resulted in movie stardom for George Clooney. The prescient *Three Kings* was re-released in 2004, earning Russell renewed admiration for his astute depiction of embedded reporters, looted artifacts and cocksure American soldiers that would become hallmarks of the second Gulf War. His slapstick existential farce *I ♥ Huckabees* (2004) was Russell's most personal film, a meta screwball comedy encapsulating everything from Eastern and Western philosophy and French nihilism to environmental activism, consumer branding and, of all things, the plight of Sudanese lost boys repatriated into suburban American Christian families. Featuring Dustin Hoffman and Lily Tomlin as a pair of zany existential detectives and Jude Law and Naomi Watts as corporate drones sleepwalking through the American dream, *I ♥ Huckabees* earned both fans and detractors for its metaphysical philosophizing on materialism and interconnectedness.

Dieser amerikanische Autor und Filmemacher, ein zeitgenössischer Meister der Screwball-Komödie, kam mit seiner Indie-Produktion *Spanking the Monkey* (1993) zu Ruhm. Der von schwarzem Humor geprägte Film über einen Medizinstudenten, der seine Sommerferien opfern muss, um seine depressive und herrische Mutter zu pflegen, die krank und bettlägerig ist, gewann beim Sundance Film Festival den Publikumspreis. So entwickelte sich Russells Karriere im Sog einer neuen Welle bissiger Komödien von Regie-Einzelgängern wie Alexander Payne, Todd Solondz und Spike Jonze. Mit der Groteske *Flirting with Desaster – Ein Unheil kommt selten allein* (*Flirting with Disaster*, 1996) deutete Russell seine Vorliebe für multiple Charaktere an, die durch lärmendes, oft schusseliges Verhalten auffallen, eine schräge Mischung, die in seinem Meisterstück *Three Kings – Es ist schön, König zu sein* (*Three Kings*, 1999) vorzüglich zur Geltung kommt. Dieser Kriegsfarce, die während des ersten Golfkriegs spielt, war anfangs zwar kein allzu großer Erfolg beschieden, für George Clooney jedoch sollte sie sich als Sprungbrett zum Starruhm erweisen. 2004 lief *Three Kings* erneut an und brachte Russell Bewunderung ein für seine vorausschauende, scharfsinnige Darstellung mitreisender Kriegsreporter, der Plünderung von Artefakten und des arroganten Auftretens amerikanischer Soldaten, wie sie für den jüngsten Golfkrieg so bezeichnend waren. Die slapstickartige existenzielle Farce *I ♥ Huckabees* (2004) ist Russells bislang persönlichster Film. In dieser Meta-Screwball-Komödie wird von östlicher und westlicher Philosophie, von französischem Nihilismus und Umweltaktivismus über die Beeinflussung von Konsumverhalten bis zum Kummer sudanesischer Waisenknaben, die in christlichen Familien amerikanischer Vorstädte Aufnahme fanden, so ziemlich alles zur Sprache gebracht. Sowohl Fans als auch böse Zungen ergötzten sich an Russells metaphysischem Philosophieren über Materialismus und menschliches Miteinander, das Dustin Hoffman und Lily Tomlin als durchgeknalltes existenzialistisches Detektivpärchen und Jude Law und Naomi Watts als Schmarotzer, die gemeinsam durch den amerikanischen Traum schlafwandeln, in *I ♥ Huckabees* zelebrierten.

Maître de la comédie débridée moderne, ce scénariste et réalisateur américain s'est fait remarquer avec *Spanking the Monkey* (1993), une comédie noire dans laquelle un étudiant en médecine passe ses vacances avec sa mère possessive, en convalescence d'une dépression. Lauréat du prix du public au Festival Sundance, Russell se fait un nom en même temps que d'autres auteurs de comédies acerbes, comme Alexander Payne, Todd Solondz et Spike Jonze. *Flirter avec les embrouilles* (*Flirting with Disaster*, 1996) témoigne du penchant de son auteur pour les foules de personnages truculents et empotés, veine comique au cœur de son chef-d'œuvre *Les Rois du désert* (*Three Kings*, 1999). Cette farce qui se déroule au lendemain de la première guerre du Golfe n'a pas été un succès immédiat, mais a valu à George Clooney d'accéder au rang de star. Grâce à ce film prémonitoire, ressorti en 2004, Russell est l'objet d'une nouvelle admiration pour sa description des journalistes « embarqués », des objets pillés et des soldats américains trop sûrs d'eux, si caractéristiques de la seconde guerre du Golfe. *J'adore Huckabees* (*I ♥ Huckabees*, 2004) est une comédie burlesque existentielle et le film le plus personnel de Russell, où tout y passe : philosophies orientales et occidentales, nihilisme français, militantisme écologique, marques commerciales et même le drame de jeunes Soudanais perdus, rapatriés dans des familles américaines chrétiennes BCBG. Dustin Hoffman et Lily Tomlin y incarnent deux détectives existentialistes cinglés, tandis que Jude Law et Naomi Watts sont des robots somnambules du capitalisme en plein rêve américain. Le discours métaphysique sur le matérialisme et le lien social de *J'adore Huckabees* enthousiasme ou exaspère.

FILM/ ›
1993 *Spanking the Monkey*
1996 *Flirting with Disaster*
1999 *Three Kings*
2004 *I ♥ Huckabees*

/ELECTED AWARD/ →
1994 *Spanking the Monkey:* Audience Award, Sundance Film Festival
1995 *Spanking the Monkey:* Best First Feature, Best First Screenplay, Independent Spirit Awards

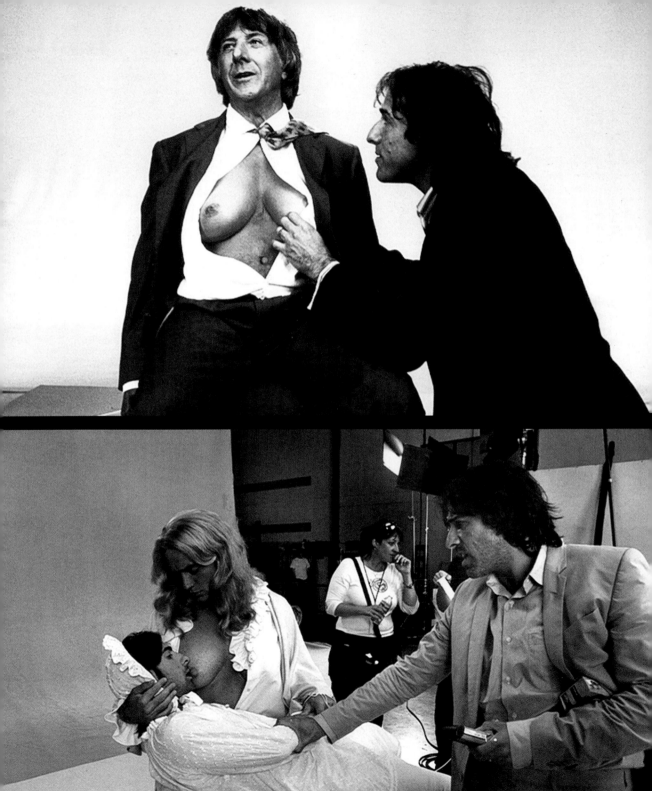

Three Kings

Three Kings – Es ist schön, König zu sein / Les Rois du désert

"A Zen monk once said to me, 'If you're not laughing, then you're not getting it.'"

„Ein Zen-Mönch hat mir mal gesagt: ‚Wenn du nicht lachen kannst, begreifst du nichts.'"

« Une fois, un moine zen m'a dit: « Si tu ne ris pas, c'est que tu n'as rien compris. »

David O. Russell directing the first Gulf War heist comedy *Three Kings*, a prescient political commentary on American imperialism co-starring George Clooney, Mark Wahlberg, Ice Cube and Spike Jonze.

David O. Russell bei der Arbeit an *Three Kings – Es ist schön, König zu sein*. Die gegen Ende des zweiten Golfkriegs spielende Militärfarce mit George Clooney, Mark Wahlberg, Ice Cube und Spike Jonze erwies sich als vorausschauender Kommentar zur amerikanischen Weltmachtpolitik.

David O. Russell sur le tournage des *Rois du désert*, aventure comique sur fond de première guerre du Golfe et commentaire politique prémonitoire sur l'impérialisme américain. Avec George Clooney, Mark Wahlberg, Ice Cube et Spike Jonze.

I ♥ Huckabees

J'♥ Huckabees

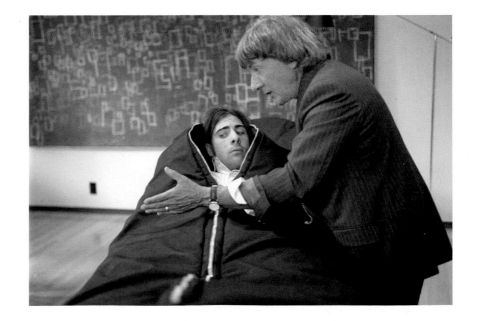

Dustin Hoffman is an existential detective hired by environmental activist Jason Schwartzman in Russell's metaphysical comedy I ♥ Huckabees.

In Russells metaphysischer Komödie I ♥ Huckabees spielt Dustin Hoffman einen existenzialistischen Detektiv, der von Jason Schwartzman, einem Umweltaktivisten, angeheuert wird.

Un détective tourmenté par des questions existentielles (Dustin Hoffman) est engagé par un militant écologiste (Jason Schwartzman) dans cette comédie métaphysique.

ᗑATE ЅHORTLAND

Born 10 August 1968 in Temora, Australia

With the lyrical coming-of-age drama *Somersault* (2004), which swept the Australian Film Institute Awards in 2004, winning thirteen prizes, writer-director Cate Shortland made an auspicious feature debut, eliciting breakthrough performances by Abbie Cornish and Sam Worthington as anguished young paramours in a faded Australian ski town. As Heidi, a 16-year-old girl who skips out on her home life after making moves on her mother's boyfriend, Cornish intuits the psychological complexities of a young woman who means well but doesn't grasp the ramifications of her budding sexuality. Arriving off-season in the desolate resort town, Heidi finds work at a petrol station and a surrogate mother in the form of Irene, a lonely woman who gives Heidi lodging. But she slips back into her self-destructive patterns of drinking and promiscuity after falling for the handsome but repressed son of a wealthy local farmer, whose own sexual awakening is just as messy. Shot with a handheld camera in and around the Lake George area of New South Wales, *Somersault* comes alive through director of photography Robert Humphreys' wintry, monochromatic images of Heidi rushing into the cold chill of adulthood, with its nuanced sexuality and frequent disappointments. Cornish, who was 20 when the film was shot, and the first to audition for the role of Heidi, delivers a revelatory performance; she seems to be discovering life's uncomfortable pull in tandem with the character she plays.

Mit *Somersault – Wie Parfum in der Luft* (*Somersault*, 2004), einem lyrischen Drama über das Erwachsenwerden, das 2004 bei den Australian Film Institute Awards 13 Preise abräumte, gelang der Autorenfilmerin Cate Shortland ein vielversprechendes Debüt, das zudem Abbie Cornish und Sam Worthington, die ein in einem abgelegenen australischen Skiort aufeinandertreffendes Pärchen eingeschüchterter junger Liebender spielen, den Durchbruch als Schauspieler brachte. In der Rolle der Heidi, eines 16-jährigen Mädchens, das ihr Zuhause verlässt, nachdem es dem Freund ihrer Mutter nachgestellt hat, zeigt sich Cornishs intuitives Verständnis für die psychischen Probleme einer Heranwachsenden, die es eigentlich gut meint, die Konsequenzen ihrer aufblühenden Sexualität aber nicht in den Griff bekommt. So landet Heidi in einem öden Ferienort, wo sie einen Job an einer Tankstelle findet und in Irene, einer einsamen Frau, die ihr Unterkunft gewährt, eine Art Ersatzmutter. Doch als sie sich in den gut aussehenden, aber verklemmten Sohn eines reichen Farmers verliebt, der mit seiner aufkeimenden Sexualität ebenso wenig zurechtkommt, verfällt sie wieder den selbstzerstörerischen Mechanismen von Alkohol und Promiskuität. Der in der Gegend um den Lake George in New South Wales mit einer Handkamera gedrehte Film verdankt seine Wirkung auch den eisigen, monochromen Bildern des Kameramanns Robert Humphreys, der die Kälte des von betonter Sexualität und wiederholten Enttäuschungen geprägten Erwachsenenlebens, in das Heidi sich stürzt, einzufangen wusste. Cornish, die als Erste für die Rolle der Heidi vorgesprochen hatte und bereits zwanzig war, als der Film gedreht wurde, liefert eine aufschlussreiche Darbietung. Es sieht so aus, als entdecke sie die unangenehmen Seiten des Lebens gleichzeitig mit der Entwicklung der Figur, die sie spielt.

En 2005, *Somersault*, récit lyrique d'un passage à l'âge adulte, remporte treize récompenses de l'Australian Film Institute. Sa réalisatrice, Cate Shortland, fait un début prometteur avec ce film, interprété par des nouveaux venus à l'écran, Abbie Cornish et Sam Worthington, dans le rôle de jeunes amants angoissés dans une station de sport d'hiver australienne défraîchie. À 16 ans, Heidi (Abbie Cornish) renonce à la vie familiale, après avoir fait des avances au petit copain de sa mère. La comédienne sait suggérer les complications psychologiques d'une jeune femme pleine de bonnes intentions, mais maladroite quant à sa sexualité naissante. Heidi débarque dans la station désolée, trouve du travail dans une station-service, ainsi qu'une mère de substitution en Irene, une femme seule qui accepte de l'héberger. Mais elle replonge dans une sexualité et un alcoolisme autodestructeurs, après être tombée amoureuse du fils séduisant, mais coincé, d'un riche fermier, dont la sexualité en éveil n'est pas moins tourmentée. Filmées caméra à l'épaule dans la région du lac George en Nouvelle-Galles-du-Sud, les images monochromes et hivernales de Robert Humphreys illustrent le portrait d'une jeune femme se précipitant dans les frimas de la vie d'adulte, à la sexualité nuancée et aux déceptions fréquentes. Première à se présenter à l'audition pour le rôle, âgée de 21 ans lors du tournage, Cornish est une révélation : elle semble découvrir l'attirance incommode de la vie en même temps que son personnage.

FILMЅ →
2004 *Somersault*

ЅELECTED AWARDЅ →
2004 *Somersault*: Best Film, Best Direction, Best Original Screenplay, Best Lead Actor, Best Lead Actress, Australian Film Institute Awards; Best Feature Film, Best Direction, Best Script, Best Cinematography, Best Actress, IF Awards Australia **2005** *Somersault*: Special Mention (Best Dramatic Feature – World Cinema Competition: Breakthrough Awards), Miami Film Festival

Somersault

Somersault – Wie Parfum in der Luft

"Fairy tales have an awful underlying violence to them.
I think women relate to them because walking through the streets at night, you often feel scared. In fairy tales women are always pursued, or they're lost and they have to be rescued. They have this real erotic, dark element that was really influential when we looked at the film.
It wasn't on the page, it was something we created."

„Märchen sind von einer fürchterlichen, unterschwelligen Gewalt geprägt. Ich glaube, Frauen haben zu ihnen deshalb eine besondere Beziehung, weil sie diese Angstgefühle kennen, wenn sie nachts alleine durch die Straßen gehen. In Märchen werden Frauen immer verfolgt, oder sie sind verloren und müssen gerettet werden. Als wir uns den fertigen Film ansahen, zeigte sich genau diese wirklich erotische, dunkle Seite der Märchen. Das war so nicht geplant, wir haben diese Atmosphäre geschaffen."

«Les contes de fée comportent une affreuse violence sous-jacente. Je crois que les femmes les comprennent parce qu'on a souvent peur quand on est dans la rue la nuit. Dans les contes de fées, les femmes sont toujours pourchassées, ou bien elles sont perdues et doivent être sauvées. Il y a un côté érotique et sombre qui a pris beaucoup d'importance quand on a vu le film. Ce n'était pas dans le scénario, c'est nous qui l'avons créé.»

Heidi (Abbie Cornish) is a 16-year-old runaway in Cate Shortland's multiple-award-winning *Somersault*, a sexual awakening drama set in a ski resort in southeastern Australia.

Heidi (Abbie Cornish), die 16-jährige Ausreißerin, ist Hauptfigur in Cate Shortlands mit mehreren Preisen ausgezeichnetem Film *Somersault – Wie Parfum in der Luft*, einem in einem Skiort im südöstlichen Australien angesiedelten Drama um das sexuelle Erwachen von Jugendlichen.

Dans ce film, plusieurs fois récompensé, de Cate Shortland, Heidi (Abbie Cornish) est une adolescente fugueuse de 16 ans, dont la sexualité s'éveille dans une station de sports d'hiver du Sud-Est de l'Australie.

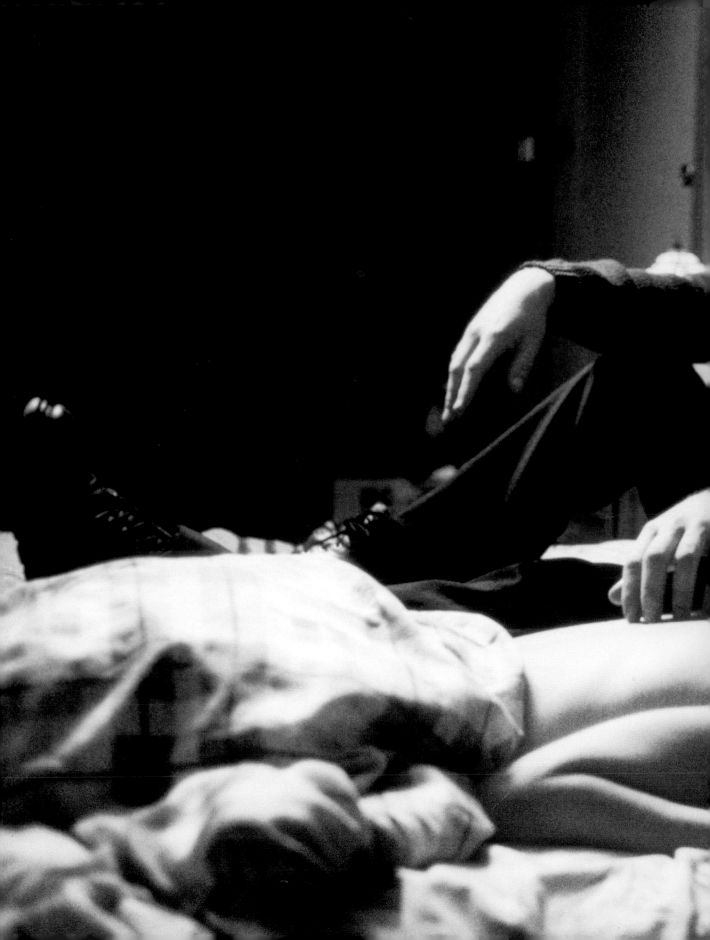

JOHNNIE TO

Born 22 April 1955 in Hong Kong, China

The Hong Kong action director Johnnie To Kei-fung, known as Johnnie To to his worldwide fans, began his career as an assistant television director during the Shaw Studios era of low-budget martial arts films that would later be fetishized in the works of Quentin Tarantino, Ang Lee and Zhang Yimou. To's first box-office hit was the action vehicle *All About Ah Long* (*You jian A Lang*, 1989), starring a young Chow Yun-Fat. To directed comedies and romances for a decade before hitting paydirt with a series of high-octane thrillers that, alongside the work of his contemporaries Tsui Hark and Ringo Lam, ushered in a golden age of Hong Kong action flicks – *The Mission* (*Cheung fo*, 1999), *Fulltime Killer* (*Chuen jik sat sau*, 2001) and *PTU* (2002/03) being To's most popular titles. He ascended to loftier heights with his internationally acclaimed, *Godfather*esque series of Triad movies beginning with *Election* (*Hak se wui*, 2005) and continuing with *Election 2* (*Hak se wui yi wo wai kwai*, 2006), both featuring large-ensemble casts and delving into the intricate and violent political maneuverings of the Wo-Sing organized-crime family, operating amid the precarious dilemma of Hong Kong's post-1997 return to Chinese sovereignty. Low on bullets and chopsocky, the *Election* movies opted instead for baroque, cerebral renderings of influence peddling, bribery and uneasy alliances among rival Triad societies that made the Corleone family's machinations seem trivial by comparison. Brilliantly conceived and executed, *Election* and its darker, more historically dense sequel were both shown at the Cannes Film Festival during successive years and hinted at future installments from To and his mighty Wo-Sing Triad. To's latest feature is *Exiled* (*Fong juk*, 2006), another contemporary action thriller.

Der Hongkonger Actionregisseur Johnnie To Kei-fung, seinen Fans in der ganzen Welt als Johnnie To bekannt, startete seine Karriere als Regieassistent beim Fernsehen während jener Ära der Shaw Studios, in der die Low-Budget-Kampfkunstfilme gedreht wurden, die später durch die Werke von Quentin Tarantino, Ang Lee und Zhang Yimou Kultstatus erlangten. Tos erster Kassenknüller war das Actionspektakel *All About Ah Long* (*You jian A Lang*, 1989) mit dem jungen Chow Yun-Fat in der Hauptrolle. Ein Jahrzehnt lang führte To bei Komödien und Romanzen Regie, bis er mit einer Serie explosiver Thriller – darunter die populärsten Titel *The Mission* (*Cheung fo*, 1999), *Fulltime Killer* (*Chuen jik sat sau*, 2001) und *PTU* (2002/03) – gemeinsam mit Werken seiner Kollegen Tsui Hark und Ringo Lam das goldene Zeitalter des Hongkonger Actionkinos einleitete. Mit seiner auch international mit großem Beifall aufgenommenen Serie von Triadenfilmen, die an den *Paten* erinnern, setzte er schließlich zu einem Höhenflug an: *Election* (*Hak se wui*, 2005) und *Election 2* (*Hak se wui yi wo wai kwai*, 2006) schildern mit einem Großaufgebot an Darstellern die intriganten politischen Machenschaften des organisierten Gangsterclans der Wo-Sing, der sich die schwierige Lage Hongkongs nach der 1997 erfolgten Rückgabe der einstigen Kronkolonie an China zunutze macht. In den *Election*-Filmen gibt es relativ wenig Schießereien und Kampfsportszenen, stattdessen wird in barocker und intellektueller Manier ein kompliziertes Spiel um Einfluss, Bestechung und Allianzen zwischen rivalisierenden Triaden dargestellt, gegen das die Machtmechanismen innerhalb der Corleone-Familie vergleichsweise blass wirken. *Election* und der düsterere, historisch noch dichtere *Election 2*, beide brillant erdacht und ausgeführt, wurden in aufeinanderfolgenden Jahren beim Filmfestival von Cannes aufgeführt und ließen die Hoffnung aufkeimen, dass To uns noch weitere Folgen mit Geschichten um seine mächtige Wo-Sing-Triade bieten könnte. Auch Tos jüngster Spielfilm *Exiled* (*Fong juk*, 2006) ist ein zeitgenössischer Actionthriller.

Le réalisateur de films d'action de Hong Kong, Johnnie To Kei-fung, connu dans le monde entier sous le nom de Johnnie To, a d'abord été assistant-réalisateur à la télévision, au temps des films d'art martiaux à petit budget produits par les studios Shaw, fétichisés depuis par Tarantino, Ang Lee et Zhang Yimou dans leurs films. Son premier succès est le film d'action *All about Ah Long* (*You jian a Lang*, 1989), avec Chow Yun-fat. Pendant dix ans, To réalise des comédies et des histoires d'amour, puis exploite le filon des thrillers haletants qui, avec ceux de ses confrères Tsui Hark et Ringo Lam, inaugurent l'âge d'or des films d'action de Hong Kong : *The Mission* (*Cheung feng*, 1999), *Fulltime Killer* (*Chuen jik sat sau*, 2001) et *PTU* (2002/03) sont les films les plus populaires de To. La qualité de ses films augmente avec *Election* (*Hak se wui*, 2005) et *Election 2* (*Hak se wui yi wo wai kwai*, 2006), deux films qui rappellent *Le Parrain*, autour des mafieux de la Triade, salués par la critique internationale. Interprétés par une pléiade d'acteurs, ils nous font pénétrer dans la complexité et la violence des intrigues politiques de la famille Wo Shing, clan de gangsters en action durant les lendemains précaires de la rétrocession de Hong Kong à la Chine, en 1997. Ces deux films délaissent les coups de feu et les chinoiseries, au profit d'une description baroque et intellectuelle des luttes d'influence, de la corruption et des mésalliances entre sociétés rivales, à faire pâlir la famille Corleone. Conçus et mis en scène avec brio, *Election* et sa suite, plus dense du point de vue historique, ont été lancés à Cannes deux années de suite et on peut s'attendre à de nouveaux épisodes des aventures de la famille Wo Shing. *Exilé* (*Fang ju*, 2006) est le dernier film d'action en date de To.

SELECTED FILMS →
1993 *Dung fong saam hap (The Heroic Trio)*
1998 *Chan sam ying hung (A Hero Never Dies)*
1999 *Am zin (Running Out of Time)* **1999** *Cheung fo (The Mission)* **2001** *Chuen jik sat sau (Fulltime Killer)* **2002/03** *PTU* **2003** *Daai chek liu (Running on Karma)* **2004** *Daai si gin (Breaking News)* **2004** *Yau doh lung fu bong (Throw Down)* **2005** *Hak se wui (Election)* **2006** *Hak se wui yi wo wai kwai (Election 2)* **2006** *Fong juk (Exiled)*

SELECTED AWARDS →
2000 *Cheung fo*: Best Director, Hong Kong Film Awards
2003 *PTU*: Asian Trade Winds Award, Seattle International Film Festival
2004 *PTU*: Best Director, Hong Kong Film Awards
2006 *Hak se wui*: Best Director, Hong Kong Film Awards

Hak se wui

Election

Johnnie To's intricately woven dual Triad crime thrillers examine a power struggle inside the Wo Shing organized crime family, incorporating Hong Kong's volatile and restless relations with mainland China.

In den beiden komplex strukturierten Kriminalthrillern Johnnie Tos über die Machenschaften von Triaden geht es um Machtkämpfe innerhalb des organisierten Gangsterclans der Wo-Sing. Dabei spielt auch die prekäre Beziehung der einstigen Kronkolonie Hongkong zu China eine Rolle.

Ces deux films criminels aux intrigues complexes autour de la Triade racontent les luttes de pouvoir au sein de la famille de mafieux Wo Shing, tout en y intégrant les relations volatiles entre Hong Kong et la Chine continentale.

Hak se wui yi wo wai kwai

Election 2

Fong juk
Exiled / Exilé

"In the shadow of this ambiguous giant called China, what does it mean to be a Hong Kongese?"

„Was es wohl bedeuten mag, als Hongkonger im Schatten dieses ehrgeizigen Riesen China leben zu müssen?"

« À l'ombre de ce géant ambigu qu'est la Chine, que signifie être de Hong Kong ? »

Set in teeming Macau but rooted in the spaghetti western tradition of Sergio Leone, with its baroquely choreographed shootouts, To's *Exiled* centers on four gangsters sent by a crime boss to kill a family man.

Tos *Exiled* ist zwar im vor Menschen wimmelnden Macau angesiedelt, bezieht sich jedoch auf die Tradition der Spaghetti-Western eines Sergio Leone mit ihren ausladend choreografierten Schießereien. Die Geschichte kreist um vier Kriminelle, die ein Gangsterboss beauftragt hat, einen Familienvater zu töten.

Quatre gangsters sont chargés par un chef de gang de liquider un père de famille, dans le Macao surpeuplé. Dans une ambiance à la Sergio Leone, les fusillades sont chorégraphiées de manière baroque.

TSAI MING-LIANG

Born 27 October 1957 in Kuching, Malaysia

One of the major names in New Taiwanese Cinema, along with Hou Hsiao-hsien and Edward Yang, Tsai Ming-liang specializes in static depictions of urban alienation featuring minimal dialogue, long fixed shots and sudden bursts of surreal humor courtesy of impassive actor Lee Kang-sheng, who has appeared in all of the director's features. Floods, incessant rain and leaks figure prominently in both *The Hole / The Last Dance* (*Dong*, 1998), a love story set in a quarantined Taipei about two neighbors who fall in love through a hole separating their apartments, and *Goodbye, Dragon Inn* (*Bu San*, 2003), set inside a dying movie temple on the eve of its closure, as lonely souls (both living and dead) wander its faded interior starved for connection. Water is scarce in Tsai's subsequent feature *The Wayward Cloud* (*Tian bian yi duo yun*, 2004/05), in which a porn actor (Lee) falls in love with a museum tour guide during a drought in which citizens are encouraged to consume watermelons in lieu of water. Like *The Hole*, it featured campy musical numbers and concluded with an extended long take that can be read as a kind of symbolic orgasm between its disconnected protagonists. Tsai's most recent feature, the aptly titled *I Don't Want to Sleep Alone* (*Hei yan quan*, 2006) is a tragicomedy about a group of laborers who enjoy watching Bollywood movies, a Chinese-Indonesian girl who works in Kuala Lumpur, a man wandering in the streets without an identity and a mysterious mattress abandoned by a rich man.

Tsai Ming-liang, der neben Hou Hsiao-hsien und Edward Yang zu den wichtigsten Repräsentanten des neuen taiwanesischen Kinos zählt, ist bekannt für seine in langen Einstellungen festgehaltenen, sehr ruhigen Beschreibungen der Isolation von Stadtbewohnern. Dabei kommt er mit einem Minimum an Dialogen aus, die aber immer wieder unvermittelt von einem surrealen Humor aufgebrochen werden, der seinem wie unbeteiligt wirkenden Schauspieler Lee Kang-sheng zu verdanken ist, der bislang in allen Filmen des Regisseurs agierte. Fluten, unaufhörliche Regengüsse und Lecks spielen in gleich zwei Filmen eine besondere Rolle: In *Der letzte Tanz* (*Dong*, 1998), einer Liebesgeschichte im unter Quarantäne gestellten Taipeh, kommunizieren zwei Nachbarn über ein Loch im Fußboden zwischen den beiden Wohnungen und verlieben sich ineinander. Der Schauplatz von *Goodbye, Dragon Inn* (*Bu San*, 2003) ist ein alter Kinopalast, in dem die letzten Vorstellungen gegeben werden und in dessen abgewracktem Ambiente einsame, nach Kontakten hungernde Seelen (sowohl lebende als auch tote) herumirren. In Tsais nächstem Spielfilm *The Wayward Cloud* (*Tian bian yi duo yun*, 2004/05) ist Wasser allerdings knapp. Ein Pornodarsteller (Lee) verliebt sich in einer extremen Trockenperiode, in der die Bürger aufgefordert werden, statt Wasser Wassermelonen zu konsumieren, in eine Museumsführerin. Wie in *Der letzte Tanz* gibt es auch in diesem Film immer wieder grelle Musicalsequenzen, und er endet mit einer ungewöhnlich langen Einstellung, die als eine Art symbolischer Orgasmus zwischen den beiden vereinzelten Protagonisten interpretiert werden kann. Tsais jüngster Film mit dem passenden Titel *I Don't Want to Sleep Alone* (*Hei yan quan*, 2006) ist eine Tragikomödie über eine Gruppe von Arbeitern, die gerne Bollywood-filme sehen, ein chinesisch-indonesisches Mädchen, das in Kuala Lumpurs Chinatown arbeitet, einen Mann ohne Identität, der durch die Straßen irrt, und eine mysteriöse Matratze, die ein reicher Mann zurückgelassen hat.

Avec Hou Hsiao-hsien et Edward Yang, Tsaï Ming-liang est l'un des grands noms du nouveau cinéma taïwanais. Son cinéma se caractérise par la description statique de l'isolement en milieu urbain, les dialogues rares, de longs plans fixes et des explosions d'humour surréaliste, grâce à l'acteur Lee Kang-sheng, au visage impassible, qui joue dans tous les films de Tsaï. Inondations, pluies incessantes et fuites d'eau sont les éléments principaux de *The Hole* (*Dong*, 1998), dans lequel deux voisins, vivant dans un Taipei mis en quarantaine, tombent amoureux par un trou entre leurs appartements, et *Goodbye, Dragon Inn* (*Bu San*, 2003), qui se déroule dans un cinéma, à la veille de sa fermeture définitive, où des âmes solitaires (vivantes et mortes) errent dans un décor défraîchi, en quête de relations. Il en est tout autrement dans *La Saveur de la pastèque* (*Tian bian yi duo yun*, 2004/05), où l'eau se fait rare : un acteur porno (Lee) tombe amoureux d'une guide de musée, lors d'une période de sécheresse pendant laquelle les habitants sont invités à consommer des pastèques pour pallier le manque d'eau. Comme dans *The Hole*, des numéros musicaux décalés ponctuent le film qui s'achève par un long plan-séquence, sorte d'orgasme symbolique entre les deux personnages déconnectés l'un de l'autre. Judicieusement intitulé *Je ne veux pas dormir seul* (*Hei yan quan*, 2006), le tout dernier film de Tsaï est une tragicomédie qui réunit un groupe d'ouvriers fans de films de Bollywood, une Sino-Indonésienne travaillant dans le quartier chinois, un homme errant sans identité et un mystérieux matelas abandonné par un homme riche.

FILMS →
1992 *Ch'ing shaonien na cha (Rebels of the Neon God)* **1994** *Aiqing wansui (Vive l'Amour)* **1997** *He liu (The River)* **1998** *Dong (The Hole / The Last Dance)* **2001** *Ni neiban jidian / Et là-bas, quelle heure est-il? (What Time Is It There?)* **2002** *Tianqiao bu jianle (The Skywalk Is Gone)* **2003** *Bu San (Goodbye, Dragon Inn)* **2004/05** *Tian bian yi duo yun (The Wayward Cloud)* **2006** *Hei yan quan (I Don't Want to Sleep Alone)*

SELECTED AWARDS →
1994 *Aiqing wansui:* Golden Lion, Venice Film Festival **1997** *He liu:* Silver Bear (Special Jury Prize), Berlin International Film Festival; Silver Hugo (Special Jury Prize), Chicago International Film Festival; Channel 4 Director's Award – Special Mention, Edinburgh International Film Festival **1998** *Dong:* FIPRESCI Prize, Cannes Film Festival; Gold Hugo, Best Film, Chicago International Film Festival **2001** *Ni neibian jidian:* Silver Hugo, Grand Jury Prize, Best Director, Chicago International Film Festival **2003** *Bu San:* FIPRESCI Prize, Venice Film Festival **2005** *Tian bian yi duo yun:* Alfred Bauer Award, FIPRESCI Prize; Silver Bear (Outstanding Artistic Achievement), Berlin International Film Festival

He liu

The River / Der Fluss / La Rivière

"When I can use one shot, I won't use a second one."

„Wenn ich mit einer Einstellung auskomme, brauche ich keine zweite."

«Si je peux me contenter d'un seul plan, je n'en fais pas un deuxième.»

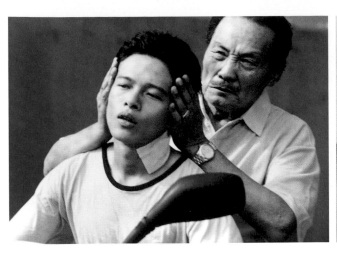

Recurring Tsai Ming-liang player Lee Kang-sheng stars as Xiao-kang, a sometime actor who suffers from a chronic neck pain and clashes with his tortured father (Miao Tien) in the existential comedy-drama *The River*.

Lee Kang-sheng, der in Tsai Ming-liangs Filmen immer wieder Rollen übernimmt, spielt in der existenzialistisch-dramatischen Komödie *Der Fluss* einen Gelegenheitsschauspieler, der unter chronischen Nackenschmerzen leidet und mit seinem geplagten Vater (Miao Tien) aneinandergerät.

Acteur fétiche de Tsaï Ming-liang, Lee Kang-sheng incarne Xiao-kang, comédien occasionnel souffrant d'un torticolis chronique, en butte à un père torturé (Miao Tien) dans *La Rivière*, tragicomédie existentielle.

Dong

The Hole I The Last Dance / Der letzte Tanz / The Hole

Tsai muse Lee Kang-sheng returns in *The Hole*, a bleak musical romance set in Taipei during a mysterious quarantine, in which neighboring apartment dwellers fall in love through a hole in the floor resulting from a plumbing mishap.

Auch in *Der letzte Tanz* ist Tsais männliche Muse wieder dabei. Die düstere Musical-Romanze spielt in Taipei, das unter eine geheimnisvolle Quarantäne gestellt wird. Über ein Loch im Fußboden, das durch einen Wasserschaden entstanden ist, verlieben sich die Bewohner zweier Nachbarswohnungen ineinander.

Lee Kang-sheng est l'interprète principal de *The Hole*, sombre histoire d'amour musicale qui se déroule à Taïpei lors d'une étrange mise en quarantaine. Les occupants de deux appartements voisins tombent amoureux l'un de l'autre, à travers un trou dû à un accident de plomberie.

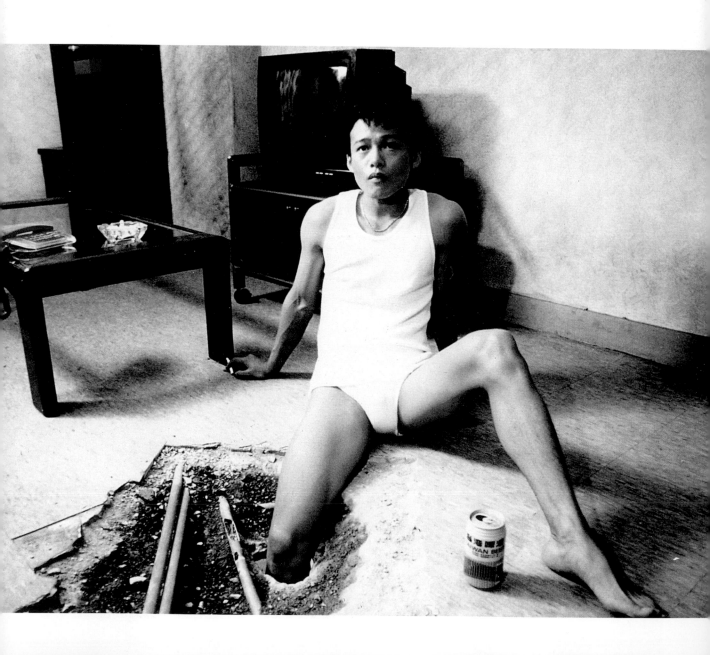

Ni neibian jidian

What Time Is It There? / Et là-bas, quelle heure est-il ?

Quiet contemplation and the inability to connect
haunt the minimalist dysfunctional family drama
What Time is it There?, starring recurring players Lee
Kang-sheng and Miao Tien as son and dead father.

Kontemplative Ruhe und die Unfähigkeit zu kommunizieren bestimmen die Atmosphäre des minimalistischen Dramas um eine Problemfamilie. Auch in
What Time Is It There? gehören Lee Kang-sheng und
Miao Tien wieder zur Besetzung, diesmal als Sohn
und toter Vater.

Contemplation et incommunicabilité sont les thèmes
de ce récit minimaliste autour d'une famille à
problèmes. Avec, de nouveau, Lee Kang-sheng et
Miao Tien, respectivement fils et père défunt.

Above and right: Chen Shiang-chyi visits Paris and is the unwitting object of Lee Kang-sheng's affections after he sells her a watch. Left: Tsai directs street musicians in Paris.

Oben und rechts: Chen Shiang-chyi besucht Paris. Nachdem Lee Kang-sheng ihr eine Uhr verkauft hat, wird sie zum ahnungslosen Objekt seiner Zuneigung. Links: Tsai gibt Straßenmusikern in Paris Regieanweisungen.

Ci-dessus et ci-contre : Durant une visite à Paris, une femme (Chen Shiang-chyi) devient l'objet involontaire de l'affection d'un homme (Lee Kang-sheng), après que ce dernier lui a vendu une montre. À gauche : Tsaï dirige des musiciens de rues à Paris.

Tianqiao bu jianle
The Skywalk Is Gone / La Passerelle disparue

The Skywalk is Gone is a 25-minute short coda to *What Time is it There?*, where Lee Kang-sheng and Chen Shiang-chyi cross paths in Taiwan but fail to recognize each other.

In *The Skywalk Is Gone* (2002), einer 25-minütigen Coda zu *What Time Is It There?*, laufen sich Lee Kang-sheng und Chen Shiang-chyi in Taiwan über den Weg, erkennen einander aber nicht.

La Passerelle disparue est un épilogue de 25 minutes à *Et là-bas, quelle heure est-il?* Les chemins de Lee Kang-sheng et de Chen Shiang-chyi se croisent à Taïwan, mais ils ne se reconnaissent pas.

Bu San

Goodbye, Dragon Inn

A torrential downpour soaks the streets of Taipei on the closing night of the Fu-Ho movie palace that is the setting for the ghostly, melancholy *Good Bye, Dragon Inn*, widely regarded as Tsai's masterpiece.

Ein stürmischer Regenguss setzt die Straßen Taipeis ausgerechnet an jenem Abend unter Wasser, an dem im Fu-Ho-Kinopalast die letzte Vorstellung gegeben wird. Das alte Kino ist Schauplatz des geisterhaften, melancholischen Films *Goodbye, Dragon Inn*, der allgemein als Tsais Meisterwerk angesehen wird.

Une pluie torrentielle balaie les rues de Taipei le soir de la fermeture définitive du cinéma Fu-Ho, décor de ce film fantômatique et mélancolique, considéré comme le chef-d'œuvre de Tsaï.

Tian bian yi duo yun

The Wayward Cloud / La Saveur de la pastèque

Outrageously garish musical interludes are a highlight of the deadpan comedy *The Wayward Cloud*, a sequel to *What Time is it There?*, featuring Lee Kang-sheng and his thwarted lover Chen Shiang-chyi.

Zu den Höhepunkten von *The Wayward Cloud*, einer Komödie mit trockenem Humor, die als Fortsetzung von *What Time Is It There?* wieder mit Lee Kang-sheng und seiner verhinderten Geliebten Chen Shiang-chyi aufwartet, gehören ausnehmend schrille Musikeinlagen.

Les interludes musicaux très colorés sont les clous de cette comédie pince-sans-rire, suite d'*Et là-bas, quelle heure est-il?*, avec Lee Kang-sheng et Chen Shiang-chyi, son amante contrariée.

Lee Kang-sheng is a pornographic actor in several over-the-top sex scenes, one of which memorably involves a watermelon. Bottom right: Tsai Ming-liang.

Lee Kang-sheng spielt einen Pornodarsteller, der in einigen überkandidelten Sexszenen – denkwürdig die Szene mit der Wassermelone – zu sehen ist. Unten rechts: Tsai Ming-liang.

Lee Kang-sheng incarne un acteur porno dans plusieurs scènes de sexe, dont l'une comprend une pastèque comme partenaire. En bas, à droite : Tsaï Ming-liang.

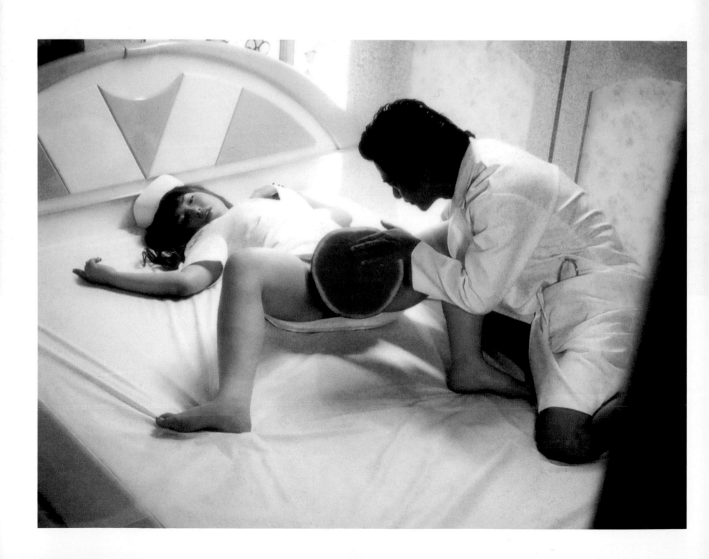

Hei yan quan

I Don't Want to Sleep Alone / Je ne veux pas dormir seul

Set in Tsai's native Malaysia, *I Don't Want To Sleep Alone* reunites Lee Kang-sheng and Chen Shiang-chyi in a minimalist romance, filmed in an abandoned factory in Kuala Lumpur.

I Don't Want to Sleep Alone ist in Tsais Geburtsland Malaysia angesiedelt. Auch in dieser minimalistischen Romanze, die in einer stillgelegten Fabrik in Kuala Lumpur gedreht wurde, agieren Lee Kang-sheng und Chen Shiang-chyi wieder zusammen.

Tourné dans une usine abandonnée de Kuala Lumpur, ce film, qui se déroule dans la Malaysia natale de Tsaï, réunit à nouveau Lee Kang-sheng et Chen Shiang-chyi dans une histoire d'amour minimaliste.

TOM TYKWER

Born 23 May 1965 in Wuppertal, Germany

Contemporary German cinema's favorite son began his career in film as a Berlin projectionist before he began making short films. In 1994, he formed the X Filme Creative Pool, a loose-knit gaggle of filmmakers including Stefan Arndt, Wolfgang Becker and Dani Levy, whose breakout production was Tykwer's debut feature *Winter Sleepers* (*Winterschläfer*, 1997), which drew raves for its breathtaking camera moves and vibrant film score wrapped around a tragic story of five characters united by coincidence and fate as they grapple with generational malaise. Tykwer's unique visual style exploded on the international film scene with *Run Lola Run* (*Lola rennt*, 1998), a hyperkinetic triptych of stories employing alternate versions of the same frenzied scenario in which a young German woman (played by Franka Potente, in a starmaking role) has twenty minutes to track down some missing cash before her desperate boyfriend robs a bank. With its flashy production values incorporating elements of video game play and music video cutting, *Run Lola Run* catapulted Tykwer to the top of the heap of European visual stylists. After the indifferently received *Heaven* (2001/02), based on a script by the late Polish maverick Krzysztof Kieslowski, Tykwer returned to form with *Perfume: The Story of a Murderer* (*Das Parfum – Die Geschichte eines Mörders*, 2006), the long-gestating adaptation of Patrick Süskind's international bestseller about a young man in 18th-century France who concocts a fragrance containing the essence of nubile young virgins. The handsomely mounted English-language period psychodrama starred newcomer Ben Whishaw as the creepily enigmatic Jean-Baptiste Grenouille. But once again it was Tykwer's hypnotic technical mastery that permeated the atmospheric chiller, yielding riveting suspense out of the unwieldy narrative device of a young man's malevolent and murderous sense of smell.

Der Liebling des zeitgenössischen deutschen Kinos arbeitete zu Beginn seiner Karriere als Filmvorführer in Berlin und drehte schließlich Kurzfilme. 1994 schloss er sich mit Filmemachern wie Stefan Arndt, Wolfgang Becker und Dani Levy zur Produktionsfirma X-Filme Creative Pool zusammen, die mit Tykwers Spielfilmdebüt *Winterschläfer* (1997) ihren Durchbruch erlebte. Für seine atemberaubenden Kamerafahrten und die dynamische Musik erhielt der Film, der die tragische Geschichte von fünf Menschen und ihre oft generationsbedingten Probleme erzählt und in der die Figuren durch Zufälle und schicksalhafte Fügungen miteinander verbunden sind, begeisterte Kritiken. *Lola rennt* (1998) brachte Tykwers einzigartigen visuellen Stil auf furiose Weise auf internationale Bühnen. In diesem hyperkinetischen Triptychon, in dem dasselbe ungestüme Szenario in drei verschiedenen Versionen erzählt wird, bleiben einer jungen Frau (die Rolle machte Franka Potente zum Star) nur 20 Minuten, um eine hohe Geldsumme aufzutreiben, die ihr verzweifelter Freund einem Autoschieber schuldet. *Lola rennt*, mit seinem ungewöhnlichen gestalterischen Mix, der Elemente von Videospielen und Schnitttechniken von Musikvideos einbezieht, katapultierte Tykwer an die Spitze stilbildender europäischer Filmemacher. Nach dem eher indifferent aufgenommenen *Heaven* (2001/02), der auf der Grundlage eines Drehbuchs entstand, das der polnische Einzelgänger Krzysztof Kieslowski in seinen letzten Lebensjahren verfasst hatte, lief Tykwer mit *Das Parfum – Die Geschichte eines Mörders/Perfume: The Story of a Murderer* (2006) wieder zu Hochform auf. Die lang erwartete Verfilmung des internationalen Bestsellers von Patrick Süskind erzählt die Geschichte eines jungen Mannes, der einen Duft aus der Essenz hübscher Jungfrauen komponiert. In dem aufwendig ausgestatteten historischen Psychodrama spielt der Newcomer Ben Whishaw die Rolle des gruselig-rätselhaften Jean-Baptiste Grenouille. Doch wieder einmal gelang es Tykwer, die atmosphärische Schauergeschichte technisch meisterlich zu inszenieren und die schwierige erzählerische Vorgabe um die Heimtücke und den mörderischen Geruchssinn Grenouilles in fesselnder Spannung umzusetzen.

Le fils chéri du cinéma allemand contemporain débute dans le cinéma comme projectionniste à Berlin, puis réalise des courts métrages. En 1994, il fonde le groupe informel de cinéastes qui rassemble Stefan Arndt, Wolfgang Becker et Dani Levy, X Filme Creative Pool. Leur première production est aussi le premier film de Tykwer, *Les Rêveurs* (*Winterschläfer*, 1997), salué pour ses étonnants mouvements de caméra et une musique saisissante qui raconte l'histoire tragique de cinq personnages réunis par le destin, aux prises avec le malaise de leur génération. Le style de Tykwer conquiert la scène internationale avec *Cours Lola, cours* (*Lola rennt*, 1998), triptyque effréné, fondé sur trois versions du même scénario haletant dans lequel une jeune Allemande (Franka Potente, devenue une vedette grâce à ce rôle) a vingt minutes pour se procurer une grosse somme d'argent avant que son copain ne cambriole une banque par désespoir. Très léché, composé d'éléments empruntés aux jeux vidéo, monté comme un clip, *Cours Lola, cours* fait de Tykwer l'un des grands stylistes européens. Tourné d'après un scénario du regretté cinéaste polonais Krzysztof Kieslowki, *Heaven* (2001/02) connaît un accueil indifférent. Tykwer revient à son goût de la forme avec *Le Parfum, histoire d'un meurtrier* (*Perfume: The Story of a Murderer*, 2006), adaptation longtemps attendue du best-seller éponyme de l'écrivain allemand Patrick Süskind : quelque part au XVIIIe siècle en France, un jeune homme concocte un parfum contenant l'essence de jeunes vierges nubiles. Ben Wishaw, nouveau venu à l'écran, interprète l'énigmatique et inquiétant Jean-Baptiste Grenouille, dans ce superbe psychodrame en costumes, tourné en anglais. Tykwer envoûte par sa maîtrise technique et crée une ambiance d'épouvante, d'où sourd un suspense captivant autour de l'histoire complexe d'un jeune homme et de son odorat malveillant et assassin.

SELECTED FILMS →
1997 *Winterschläfer (Winter Sleepers)* **1998** *Lola rennt (Run Lola Run)* **2000** *Der Krieger und die Kaiserin (The Princess and the Warrior)* **2001/02** *Heaven* **2006** *Perfume: The Story of a Murderer / Das Parfum – Die Geschichte eines Mörders*

SELECTED AWARDS →
1997 *Winterschläfer*: Audience Award, FIPRESCI Prize, Thessaloniki Film Festival **1999** *Lola rennt*: Audience Award, Sundance Film Festival; Film Award in Gold (Outstanding Achievement: Direction), German Film Awards **1999** Emerging Masters Showcase Award, Seattle International Film Festival **2000** *Lola rennt*: Best Foreign Film, Independent Spirit Awards **2006** *Perfume*: Bambi (Film – National), Bambi Awards **2007** *Perfume*: Bavarian Film Award (Best Director), Bavarian Film Awards

Perfume/Das Parfum

Perfume: The Story of a Murderer / Das Parfum – Die Geschichte eines Mörders / Le Parfum, histoire d'un meurtrier

There's this saying in German – *ich kann dich nicht riechen* – I can't smell you, or I don't like smelling you, which means I don't like you. Sympathy and smell and acceptance and smell and all these things have a strong and a close relation to each other in our own idea. This whole idea of saying identity and smell is deeply connected makes total sense.

„Im Deutschen gibt es die Redewendung ‚Ich kann dich nicht riechen', was ja bedeutet ‚Ich mag dich nicht'. Sympathie und Geruch oder Akzeptanz und Geruch sind eng miteinander verbunden. Dieser Grundgedanke, dass Identität und Geruch eines Menschen fest zusammengehören, erscheint mir völlig logisch."

«En allemand, quand on dit «je ne peux pas te sentir», cela signifie que je ne t'aime pas. La sympathie et l'odeur, le consentement et l'odeur sont très intimement liés. Cette étroite relation entre identité et odeur est très juste.»

An international cast highlights Tom Tykwer's adaptation of the bestselling novel *Perfume: The Story of a Murderer*, including Dustin Hoffman as the parfumier Giuseppe Baldini and Alan Rickman as the provincial merchant Antoine Richis.

Tom Tykwers Adaption des Bestsellerromans „Das Parfum. Die Geschichte eines Mörders" (1985) zeichnet sich durch eine internationale Starbesetzung aus: Dustin Hoffman spielt den Parfümeur Giuseppe Baldini und Alan Rickman den Provinzhändler Antoine Richis.

L'adaptation par Tom Tykwer du best-seller *Le Parfum, histoire d'un meurtrier* bénéficie d'un casting international, avec notamment Dustin Hoffman dans le rôle du parfumeur Giuseppe Baldini et Alan Rickman dans celui du marchand de province Antoine Richis.

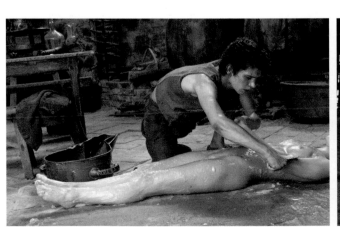

Ben Whishaw is the parfumier-cum-serial killer Jean-Baptiste Grenouille, whose heightened olfactory sense results in the killing of several nubile young women.

Ben Whishaw verkörpert den Parfümeurlehrling und Serienmörder Jean-Baptiste Grenouille, der einen besonders ausgeprägten Geruchssinn besitzt und mehrere Jungfrauen tötet.

Ben Whishaw incarne Jean-Baptiste Grenouille, parfumeur et tueur en série, que son odorat exceptionnel amène à tuer plusieurs jeunes femmes nubiles.

GUS VAN SANT

Born 24 July 1952 in Louisville, USA

A pioneer of American independent film and New Queer Cinema in the 1980s, the Portland, Oregon-based Van Sant made his name with a run of gritty underbelly dramas featuring provocative outsider male protagonists, including the narcoleptic street hustler in *My Own Private Idaho* (1991) – an iconic role for the late actor River Phoenix – and the prescription medication hustler in *Drugstore Cowboy* (1989), which re-energized Matt Dillon's then-moribund career. Van Sant next catapulted Joaquin Phoenix and Nicole Kidman to stardom in the prescient media satire *To Die For* (1995) before directing the formulaic Miramax drama *Good Will Hunting* (1997), which turned Matt Damon and Ben Affleck into Oscar-winning overnight sensations. Van Sant toiled in Hollywood for several years, churning out his *Psycho* remake in 1998 and the urban tear-jerker *Finding Forrester* two years later before returning to his indie roots with the stunning trifecta of *Gerry* (2001), *Elephant* (2003) and *Last Days* (2005), all three odes to the Hungarian minimalist Béla Tarr, with their long takes, minimalist dialogue and unconventional narrative strategies. The best of these, *Elephant*, a meditation on the Columbine high school massacre, won two major prizes at Cannes in 2003, restoring Van Sant's reputation as one of independent film's most enduring mavericks. He deconstructed the Kurt Cobain mythos in *Last Days*, eliciting a great performance by slovenly indie pin-up Michael Pitt. Van Sant served as executive producer on two films from up-and-coming young gay indie directors Jonathan Caouette (*Tarnation*, 2003) and Cam Archer (*Wild Tigers I Have Known*, 2005), both of whom were discovered at the Sundance Film Festival. His next feature is the Portland, Oregon skateboarding drama *Paranoid Park* (2007), starring a cast of unknown teenagers.

Van Sant, einer der Pioniere des amerikanischen Independent-Films und des New Queer Cinema der 1980er-Jahre, hat sich mit einer Reihe schonungslos offener Filme über die Schattenseiten der Gesellschaft einen Namen gemacht. In seinen Dramen stehen provokante männliche Außenseiter im Mittelpunkt, wie der narkoleptische Straßenstricher aus *My Private Idaho* (*My Own Private Idaho*, 1991) – eine Rolle wie maßgeschneidert für den früh verstorbenen Schauspieler River Phoenix – oder der Drogenabhängige in *Drugstore Cowboy* (1989) – ein Part, der Matt Dillons daniederliegender Karriere wieder einen Schub gab. Anschließend verhalf Van Sant mit der prophetischen Mediensatire *To Die For* (1995) Joaquin Phoenix und Nicole Kidman zu Starruhm und übernahm dann die Regie für das formelhafte Miramax-Drama *Good Will Hunting* (1997), mit dem Matt Damon und Ben Affleck einen sensationellen Erfolg als Oscar-Gewinner feierten. Ein paar Jahre lang rackerte Van Sant in Hollywood und brachte 1998 sein *Psycho*-Remake heraus und zwei Jahre später die Stadtlebenschnulze *Forrester – Gefunden!* (*Finding Forrester*, 2000), bevor er mit dem überwältigenden Hattrick *Gerry* (2001), *Elephant* (2003) und *Last Days* (2005) wieder zu seinen Indie-Wurzeln zurückkehrte. Alle drei Filme sind mit ihren langen Einstellungen, knappen Dialogen und unkonventionellen Erzählstrategien Oden an den ungarischen Minimalisten Béla Tarr. Das beste dieser drei Werke, *Elephant*, das die Hintergründe des Massakers an der Columbine-Highschool zu beleuchten versucht, wurde 2003 in Cannes mit zwei Hauptpreisen bedacht und stellte Van Sants Ruf als einer der konsequentesten Einzelgänger des Independent-Kinos wieder her. In *Last Days* nahm er den Mythos um Kurt Cobain auseinander und entlockte dabei dem schlampigen Indie-Pin-up Michael Pitt eine herausragende Darbietung. Als ausführender Produzent betätigte sich Van Sant bei zwei Filmen der beiden aufstrebenden jungen, schwulen Indie-Regisseure Jonathan Caouette (*Tarnation*, 2003) und Cam Archer (*Wild Tigers I Have Known*, 2005), die auf dem Sundance Film Festival entdeckt wurden. Der nächste Film des Regisseurs, *Paranoid Park* (2007), spielt in der Welt der Skateboarder und wurde mit unbekannten Teenagern als Darstellern in Portland, Oregon, gedreht.

Pionnier du cinéma américain indépendant et du nouveau cinéma *queer* dans les années 1980, Van Sant s'est fait un nom avec plusieurs films très crus, peuplés de personnages masculins marginaux, comme le prostitué narcoleptique de *My Own Private Idaho* (1991) – rôle emblématique du feu River Phoenix – ou l'escroc aux ordonnances médicales de *Drugstore Cowboy* (1989), qui a permis à Matt Dillon de relancer sa carrière moribonde. Van Sant fait ensuite de Joaquin Phoenix et de Nicole Kidman des stars avec une satire prémonitoire des médias, *Prête à tout* (*To Die For*, 1995). Il tourne ensuite un film conventionnel pour Miramax, *Will Hunting* (*Good Will Hunting*, 1997), pour lequel Matt Damon et Ben Affleck remportent chacun un oscar. Van Sant travaille à Hollywood pendant plusieurs années, où il réalise un remake de *Psychose* en 1998 et un drame sentimental, *À la rencontre de Forrester* (*Finding Forrester*, 2000), avant de revenir à ses racines du cinéma indépendant avec la splendide trilogie constituée par *Gerry* (2002), *Elephant* (2003) et *Last Days* (2005). Ces trois odes au minimaliste hongrois Béla Tarr sont faites de longs plans-séquences, de dialogues réduits et de stratégies narratives originales. *Elephant*, le meilleur des trois, est une réflexion sur le massacre du lycée de Columbine et a remporté deux prix importants à Cannes en 2003, ranimant ainsi la réputation de Van Sant d'être un authentique indépendant. Dans *Last Days*, il déconstruit le mythe de Kurt Cobain, grâce à l'interprétation volontairement négligée de Michael Pitt, vedette du cinéma indépendant. Van Sant est le producteur exécutif de deux jeunes cinéastes gays, Jonathan Caouette *(Tarnation)* et Cam Archer *(Wild Tigers I Have Known)*. De même que Van Sant avec son premier film *Mala Noche* (1985), ils ont tous deux été découverts au Festival Sundance. Il tourne *Paranoid Park* (2007) avec des adolescents inconnus, dans le milieu des skaters de Portland, ville de l'Orégon, où il s'est établi.

FILMS →
1985 *Mala Noche* **1989** *Drugstore Cowboy* **1991** *My Own Private Idaho* **1993** *Even Cowgirls Get the Blues* **1995** *To Die For* **1997** *Good Will Hunting* **1998** *Psycho* **2000** *Finding Forrester* **2001** *Gerry* **2003** *Elephant* **2005** *Last Days* **2007** *Paranoid Park*

SELECTED AWARDS →
1990 *Drugstore Cowboy:* Best Screenplay, Independent Spirit Awards **1991** *My Own Private Idaho:* Critics Award, Deauville Film Festival **1992** *My Own Private Idaho:* Best Screenplay, Independent Spirit Awards **2002** *Gerry:* Visions Award – Special Citation, Toronto International Film Festival **2003** *Elephant:* Golden Palm, Best Director, Cannes Film Festival **2007** *Paranoid Park:* 60th Anniversary Award, Cannes Film Festival

My Own Private Idaho

My Private Idaho

"I'm really going in a weird I-don't-know-where direction.
I prefer it to anything like what standardized filmmaking has
become."

„Ich bewege mich in eine seltsame Ich-weiß-nicht-wohin-Richtung.
Das ist mir aber allemal lieber als irgendeine standardisierte Filmemacherei."

«Je suis dans une phase où je ne sais pas où je vais.
Et je préfère cela à ce que le cinéma conventionnel est devenu.»

Left: Gus Van Sant on the set of *My Own Private Idaho* with cast members River Phoenix and Keanu Reeves, starring as itinerant Pacific Northwest male hustlers.

Links: Gus Van Sant mit River Phoenix und Keanu Reeves, die vagabundierende Stricher spielen, am Set von *My Private Idaho*.

À gauche : Gus Van Sant sur le tournage de *My Own Private Idaho*, avec River Phoenix et Keanu Reeves, interprétant deux prostitués qui parcourent le Nord-Ouest de la côte Pacifique des États-Unis.

Gerry

Casey Affleck and Matt Damon star in Van Sant's minimalist drama *Gerry*, recalling the works of Béla Tarr and Samuel Beckett, a story of two loquacious wanderers adrift in a desert wasteland.

Casey Affleck und Matt Damon gehören zur Besetzung von Van Sants minimalistischem Drama *Gerry*, das an Werke von Béla Tarr und Samuel Beckett erinnert. Es erzählt die Geschichte zweier redseliger Vagabunden, die in einer Wüstenei herumirren.

Casey Affleck et Matt Damon sont les interprètes de *Gerry*, drame minimaliste qui rappelle les œuvres de Béla Tarr et de Samuel Beckett, histoire de deux jeunes hommes bavards à la dérive dans le désert.

Elephant

Van Sant scoured his home base of Portland, Oregon for the cast of unknown and non-professional young actors for *Elephant*, the director's artful re-imagining of the Columbine high school massacre.

Für die Besetzung von *Elephant*, seine kunstvoll inszenierte Version des Massakers an der Columbine High School, sah sich der Regisseur in seiner Heimatstadt Portland, Oregon, nach unbekannten Darstellern und Laienschauspielern um.

C'est dans sa ville de Portland, dans l'Oregon, que Van Sant a trouvé les jeunes acteurs amateurs et inconnus d'*Elephant*, reconstitution imaginaire du massacre du lycée de Columbine.

Last Days

Michael Pitt stars as a fictitious American rock star loosely based on Kurt Cobain, whiling away his final hours in Van Sant's meditative, naturalist drama *Last Days*.

In Van Sants meditativem, naturalistischem Drama *Last Days* spielt Michael Pitt einen fiktiven amerikanischen Rockstar, der die letzten Stunden seines Lebens verbringt. Die Figur orientiert sich in groben Zügen an Kurt Cobain.

Michael Pitt incarne un chanteur de rock américain, librement inspiré de Kurt Cobain, qui vit comme il peut ses dernières heures, dans *Last Days*, drame naturaliste et méditatif.

Set predominantly inside a rambling mansion, the minimalist drama *Last Days* traces the events leading up to the suicide of a rock star, including the comings and goings of several visitors.

Das minimalistische Drama *Last Days*, dessen Schauplatz im Wesentlichen ein weitläufiges Gebäude ist, schildert die Ereignisse, die zum Selbstmord des Rockstars führen. Auch das Kommen und Gehen verschiedener Besucher spielt dabei eine Rolle.

Œuvre minimaliste, *Last Days* se déroule pour l'essentiel dans un manoir décati et retrace les événements, parmi lesquels la visite de plusieurs personnages, qui conduisent au suicide d'une star du rock.

APICHATPONG WEERASETHAKUL

Born 16 July 1970 in Bangkok, Thailand

The director with the unpronounceable name (just call him Joe) and several uncategorizable films is the critical darling of the Thai New Wave whose breakthrough feature *Tropical Malady* (*Sud pralad*, 2004) won the Jury Prize at the Cannes Film Festival. The film opens with an epigram, encapsulating a major theme of Weerasethakul's work: "All of us by nature are wild beasts. Our duty as human beings is to become like trainers who keep their animals in check and even teach them to perform tasks alien to their bestiality." Weerasethakul throws conventional narrative structures out the window, requiring his audience to think and see in wholly new ways. Like his second feature, *Blissfully Yours* (*Sud sanaeha*, 2002), *Tropical Malady* takes a sudden detour into the primitive realm, shifting abruptly from a playful gay love story about an ice cutter and a soldier who fall in love in the city to a Thai folk story set in the jungle about a shaman tiger spirit world. For Weerasethakul, love transcends space and time, seeping into the spirit world – think of his films as bifurcated fever dreams that take giant leaps into the unknown. Operating outside the strict Thai studio system, Weerasethakul's peculiar style of filmmaking defies easy description, though he's managed to put Thai filmmaking on the international map, with the help of his compatriots Wisit Sasanatieng and Pen-ek Ratanaruang. His latest feature, *Syndromes and a Century* (*Sang sattawat*, 2006), is a tribute to his doctor parents before they were lovers, as perceived by Weerasethakul in two separate architectural spaces, from the vantage point of both past and present.

Dieser Regisseur mit dem unaussprechlichen Namen, der einige kaum einzuordnende Filme gedreht hat, ist der Kritikerliebling unter den Filmemachern des neuen thailändischen Kinos. Seinen Durchbruch feierte er mit dem Spielfilm *Tropical Malady* (*Sud Pralad*, 2004), der beim Filmfestival von Cannes mit dem Preis der Jury ausgezeichnet wurde. Der Film wird mit einem Epigramm, das eines der zentralen Themen Weerasethakuls fasst, eingeleitet: „Wir alle sind von Natur aus wilde Tiere. Unsere Pflicht als menschliche Wesen besteht darin, das Tier in uns wie ein Dompteur in Schach zu halten und es sogar zu lehren, Dinge zu tun, die seinem tierischen Wesen fremd sind." Weerasethakul wirft sämtliche konventionelle Erzählstrukturen über Bord und verlangt dem Zuschauer die Bereitschaft ab, sich auf völlig neue Denk- und Sehgewohnheiten einzulassen. Wie sein zweiter Spielfilm *Blissfully Yours* (*Sud sanaeha*, 2002) wendet sich *Tropical Malady* dem Reich des Primitiven zu, als er die spielerische schwule Liebesgeschichte zwischen einem Eisschneider und einem Soldaten, die sich in der Stadt ineinander verlieben, fallen lässt und abrupt in die Welt thailändischer Folklore wechselt, zu einer im Dschungel angesiedelten Geschichte um einen Schamanen, der sich nachts in einen Tiger verwandelt. Nach Weerasethakuls Überzeugung transzendiert die Liebe Raum und Zeit und dringt in die Welt der Geister vor – man sollte die Filme dieses Regisseurs als fiebrige Traumsequenzen sehen, die mit Riesenschritten ins Unbekannte streben. Weerasethakul arbeitet außerhalb des strikt organisierten thailändischen Studiosystems. Sein ganz besonderer Stil entzieht sich nicht nur jeder einfachen Beschreibung, gemeinsam mit seinen Landsleuten Wisit Sasanatieng und Pen-ek Ratanaruang ist es ihm auch gelungen, dem thailändischen Film einen Platz auf der internationalen Landkarte zu sichern. Sein jüngster Spielfilm *Syndromes and a Century* (*Sang sattawat*, 2006) ist ein Tribut an das Leben seiner Eltern, eines Ärztepaars, bevor sie sich ineinander verliebten. Weerasethakul betrachtet, wie sich diese Geschichte, sowohl von der Vergangenheit als auch der Gegenwart aus gesehen, in zwei verschiedenen räumlichen Umgebungen abspielt.

Le cinéaste au nom imprononçable par une langue occidentale et aux films inclassables est le chouchou de la nouvelle vague thaïe. *Tropical Malady* (*Sud pralad*, 2004), le film qui l'a révélé, a remporté le prix du jury à Cannes. L'épigramme qui ouvre le film résume l'un des thèmes principaux de l'œuvre de Weerasethakul : « Nous sommes tous, par nature, des bêtes sauvages. Notre devoir d'êtres humains est de devenir des sortes de dresseurs qui domptent leurs animaux et leur apprennent même à effectuer des tâches étrangères à leur bestialité. » Tournant le dos aux structures narratives conventionnelles, le cinéaste demande à ses spectateurs de réfléchir d'une manière entièrement nouvelle. De même que son deuxième film *Blissfully Yours* (*Sud sanaeha*, 2002), *Tropical Malady* nous emmène dans le monde primitif, en passant soudainement d'une gentille amourette homosexuelle, entre un tailleur de glace et un soldat qui tombent tous les deux amoureux de la grande ville, au monde spirituel du tigre shaman d'un conte populaire thaï. Pour Weerasethakul, l'amour transcende l'espace et le temps et s'immisce dans le monde spirituel. Ses films sont des rêves fiévreux aux chemins qui bifurquent et font des pas de géant dans l'inconnu. Hors du fonctionnement strict des studios thaïs, le cinéma si personnel de Weerasethakul défie toute description facile. Pourtant, c'est ainsi qu'il impose la Thaïlande dans le cinéma mondial, avec ses compatriotes Wisit Sasanatieng et Pen-ek Ratanaruang. Son dernier film en date, *Syndromes and a Century* (*Sang sattawat*, 2006), sont les souvenirs d'enfance du réalisateur auprès de ses parents médecins. Le cinéaste se place dans deux espaces architecturaux distincts, dans le passé et le présent.

FILMS →
2000 *Dokfa nai meuman (Mysterious Object at Noon)* **2002** *Sud sanaeha (Blissfully Yours)* **2003** *Hua jai tor ra nong (The Adventures of Iron Pussy)* **2004** *Sud pralad (Tropical Malady)* **2005** *Worldly Desires* [short] **2006** *Sang sattawat (Syndromes and a Century)* **2006** *FAITH* [video installation]

SELECTED AWARDS →
2002 *Sud sanaeha:* Un Certain Regard Award, Cannes Film Festival; Golden Alexander Award – Best Film, Thessaloniki Film Festival; Grand Prize, TOKYO FILMeX **2003** *Sud sanaeha:* KNF Award, Rotterdam International Film Festival **2004** *Sud pralad:* Jury Prize, Cannes Film Festival; Grand Prize, TOKYO FILMeX **2006** *Sang sattawat:* Best Film, Deauville Asian Film Festival; Best Editor, Asian Film Award

Sud sanaeha

Blissfully Yours

"Film is a drug.
It is a shelter when you cannot deal with reality."

„Film ist eine Droge. Er ist eine Zuflucht, wenn man mit der Wirklichkeit draußen nicht zurechtkommt."

«Le cinéma est une drogue, mais c'est un refuge, lorsque l'on n'arrive pas à faire face à la réalité.»

During a forest picnic, nature envelops the three characters. This is the story of two women (Kanokporn Tongaram and Jenjira Jansuda) caring for a Burmese migrant worker (Min Oo).

Während eines Picknicks im Wald werden die drei Charaktere von der Natur umschlossen. Es ist die Geschichte zweier Frauen (Kanokporn Tongaram und Jenjira Jansuda), die sich um einen buddhistischen Wanderarbeiter (Min Oo) kümmern.

La nature enveloppe les trois personnages d'un pique-nique en forêt : deux femmes (Kanokporn Tongaram et Jenjira Jansuda) prennent en charge un ouvrier birman immigré (Min Oo).

Sud pralad

Tropical Malady

Left: The natural world once again plays a prominent role in a love story involving a shy country boy and a Thai soldier. Above: A second story shows a soldier hunting an animal spirit in the forest – Weerasethakul makes visual and allegorical parallels between the stories.

Links: Auch in dieser Liebesgeschichte zwischen einem schüchternen Jungen vom Lande und einem Soldaten der thailändischen Armee spielt die Natur eine herausragende Rolle. Oben: Entlang eines zweiten Handlungsfadens wird von einem Soldaten erzählt, der im Dschungel einen Tiergeist jagt – Weerasethakul lässt zwischen den Geschichten sowohl visuelle als auch allegorische Parallelen aufscheinen.

Ci-contre: La nature joue à nouveau un rôle clé dans une histoire d'amour entre un timide garçon de la campagne et un soldat thaï. Ci-dessus: Dans une seconde intrigue, un soldat chasse un esprit animal dans la forêt. Weerasethakul crée des échos visuels et allégoriques entre les deux histoires.

Worldly Desires

The director describes this 42-minute film as "a simulation of filmmaking manners, dedicated to my memories of the jungle during the period 2001–2005." Bottom Right: Weerasethakul mans the camera.

Für Weerasethakul ist dieser 42-minütige Kurzfilm auch „eine nostalgische Erinnerung an meine Dreharbeiten im Dschungel in den Jahren 2001 bis 2005." Unten rechts: Weerasethakul an der Kamera.

Le réalisateur décrit ce film de 42 minutes comme « une simulation de manières de tourner, dédiée à mes souvenirs de jungle pendant la période de 2001 à 2005. » En bas, à droite : Weerasethakul à la caméra.

Sang sattawat
Syndromes and a Century

Nantarat Sawaddikul stars as Dr. Toey in Weerasethakul's cryptic fifth feature *Syndromes and a Century*, set amid patients and doctors at a provincial hospital and a city hospital.

In Weerasethakuls kryptischem fünften Spielfilm *Syndromes and a Century* (*Sang sattawat*, 2006), der unter Patienten und Ärzten in zwei thailändischen Krankenhäusern spielt, verkörpert Nantarat Sawaddikul die Rolle des Dr. Toey.

Dans le cinquième film à clé de Weerasethakul, *Syndromes and a Century*, Nantarat Sawaddikul interprète le docteur Toey, qui évolue parmi les patients et les médecins de deux hôpitaux, l'un situé en province, l'autre dans une grande ville.

FAITH

Commissioned by the Liverpool Biennial in 2006, Weerasethakul's abstract, science-fiction-themed art installation 'FAITH' documents his feelings during the making of his most recent feature, *Syndromes and a Century*.

Mit seiner abstrakten, sich thematisch mit Science-Fiction auseinandersetzenden Kunstinstallation, die 2006 auf der Biennale in Liverpool präsentiert wurde, dokumentiert Weerasethakul seine Empfindungen während der Dreharbeiten an seinem jüngsten Spielfilm *Syndromes and a Century*.

Commande de la Biennale de Liverpool en 2006, l'installation *FAITH* – abstraction inspirée par la science-fiction – permet à Weerasethakul d'évoquer ses sentiments durant le tournage de *Syndromes and a Century*.

WONG KAR-WAI

Born 1958 in Shanghai, China

The dull ache of stolen moments and passing time weighs heavily on the Hong Kong art-house sensualist Wong Kar-wai, whose Proust-like evocations of memory and regret have attained the status of fetish objects among his slavish international fan base. Central among these is *In the Mood for Love* (*Fa yeung nin wa*, 2000), the melancholy swoon starring Maggie Cheung and Tony Leung as thwarted lovers in circa 1962 Hong Kong containing some of the most gorgeous moments on celluloid, including a scene of Cheung ascending a staircase in a cheongsam dress that encapsulates Wong's obsession with unattainable female beauty. *In the Mood for Love* is the second installment of an informal trilogy that stands as Wong's masterpiece, beginning with his second feature *Days of Being Wild* (*A Fei jing juen*, 1990), and concluding – if such a thing is possible in Wong's work – with *2046* (2004), picking up where its predecessor left off. All three films feature the intoxicating cinematography of Christopher Doyle and a cast of Chinese and Hong Kong icons including Leslie Cheung, Carina Lau, Andy Lau, Faye Wong, Gong Li – and of course Leung and Cheung, Wong's own Bogey and Bacall – each adrift in an ephemeral fog of heartbreak, nostalgia and regret and enslaved by clocks, cigarettes and Nat King Cole. Next up for Wong, notorious for taking his time directing films – the production of *2046* stretched out into five years – is his English-language debut, *My Blueberry Nights* (2007), a road movie starring Jude Law and American jazz chanteuse Norah Jones that was inspired by the Cat Power album *The Greatest*.

Der dumpfe Schmerz über verpasste Augenblicke und das Verrinnen der Zeit sind die bevorzugten Themen von Wong Kar-wai, dem Hongkonger Schöpfer sinnlicher Filmkunst. Seine an Proust gemahnenden, von Gefühlen der Reue geprägten Beschwörungen von Erinnerungen genießen inzwischen innerhalb einer hingebungsvollen internationalen Fangemeinde Kultstatus. Im Mittelpunkt dieser Verehrung steht der um 1962 in Hongkong spielende, geradezu betörend melancholische Film *In the Mood for Love* (*Fa yeung nin wa*, 2000) mit Maggie Cheung und Tony Leung als verhinderte Liebende. Dieser Film bietet einige der hinreißendsten Momente, die je auf Zelluloid gebannt wurden, darunter eine Szene, in der Cheung, in ein Cheongsam gekleidet, eine Treppe emporsteigt und emblematisch Wongs Obsession für unerreichbare weibliche Schönheit verkörpert. *In the Mood for Love* ist der bisherige Höhepunkt von Wongs Karriere und der zweite Teil einer lockeren Trilogie, die mit seinem zweiten Spielfilm, *Days of Being Wild* (*A Fei jing juen*, 1990), beginnt und mit *2046* (2004), der da einsetzt, wo der zweite endet, abschließt – sofern man bei Wongs Gesamtwerk überhaupt davon reden kann. Alle drei Filme leben auch von der berauschenden Kameraführung Christopher Doyles und ihrer Besetzung mit chinesischen und Hongkonger Ikonen des Kinos, darunter Leslie Cheung, Carina Lau, Andy Lau, Faye Wong, Gong Li und natürlich auch Maggie Cheung und Tony Leung, für Wong ein Paar wie Bogart und Bacall. Jeder von ihnen treibt, willenlos dem Ticken der Uhr, Zigaretten und der Musik von Nat King Cole ausgeliefert, verloren in einem kurzlebigen Nebel aus Herzschmerz, Sehnsucht und Reue. Wongs neues Werk – der Regisseur ist dafür berüchtigt, dass er sich Zeit nimmt, die Produktion von *2046* zog sich fünf Jahre lang hin – ist sein erster in englischer Sprache gedrehter Film, *My Blueberry Nights* (2007), ein von Cat Powers Album *The Greatest* inspiriertes Roadmovie mit Jude Law und der amerikanischen Jazzsängerin Norah Jones.

Le cinéma de Wong Kar-wai est marqué par la douleur sourde des moments volés et du temps qui passe, dans des évocations proustiennes du souvenir et du regret, devenues objets d'un culte aveugle pour des fans du monde entier. Œuvre centrale, *In the Mood for Love* (*Fa yeung nin wa*, 2000), est un film mélancolique à se pâmer, avec Maggie Cheung et Tony Leung en amants contrariés, dans le Hong Kong de 1962. On peut y voir certains des plus beaux moments de cinéma, notamment l'ascension d'un escalier par Maggie Cheung, vêtue d'une robe *cheongsam*, condensé de l'obsession du cinéaste pour la beauté féminine inaccessible. *In the Mood for Love* est le deuxième volet d'une trilogie magistrale de Wong, entamée avec *Nos années sauvages* (*A Fei jing juen*, 1990), son deuxième film, et s'achève – si le mot a un sens chez lui – avec *2046* (2004), dont le point de départ est la fin d'*In the Mood for Love*. L'image enivrante de ces trois films est due à Christopher Doyle et le casting réunit des stars du cinéma chinois et de Hong Kong : Leslie Cheung, Carina Lau, Andy Lau, Faye Wong, Gong Li et, bien sûr, Leung et Cheung, les Bogart et Bacall de Wong, à la dérive dans une brume éphémère de peines sentimentales, de nostalgie et de regret, esclaves de la pendule, de la cigarette et de Nat King Cole. Cinéaste qui prend son temps – la réalisation de *2046* lui a pris cinq ans –, Wong tourne pour la première fois un film en anglais, *My Blueberry Nights*, en 2007, road movie inspiré par l'album de Cat Power *The Greatest*, avec Jude Law et la chanteuse américaine Norah Jones.

Fa yeung nin wa

In the Mood for Love

Wong's elegant, rapturous period drama stars Tony Leung as a journalist and Maggie Cheung as his married lover in this intoxicating love story set in Hong Kong circa 1962.

In Wongs ebenso elegantem wie begeisterndem Drama, einer betörenden Liebesgeschichte, die um 1962 in Hongkong spielt, wirken Tony Leung als verheirateter Journalist und Maggie Cheung als dessen ebenfalls verheiratete Geliebte mit.

Un journaliste (Tony Leung) et sa maîtresse, une femme mariée (Maggie Cheung), vivent une histoire d'amour enivrante à Hong Kong vers 1962, dans ce film d'une élégance à ravir.

2046

"I used to recall, back in those days, the sun was brighter, the air fresher, with distant noises from wireless sets flowing down the streets. One felt so good it was almost like a dream."

„Ich musste immer wieder daran denken, dass die Sonne früher strahlender schien, die Luft frischer war, während irgendwo aus der Ferne Musik aus dem Radio die Straßen erfüllte. Man fühlte sich so wohl, es war fast wie in einem Traum."

«À l'époque, je me souviens, le soleil était plus lumineux, l'air était plus frais, le son des TSF flottait dans les rues. On se sentait si bien que c'était presque comme un rêve.»

Tony Leung returns as a writer in Wong's sensual memory piece, co-starring a bevy of immaculate Asian actresses including Faye Wong, Zhang Ziyi (above), Carina Lau, Gong Li (right) and Wong muse Maggie Cheung.

Auch in Wongs sinnlichem Werk *2046* ist Tony Leung wieder dabei. Diesmal spielt er – neben einer Schar makelloser asiatischer Schauspielerinnen wie Faye Wong, Zhang Ziyi (oben), Carina Lau, Gong Li (rechts) und Wongs Muse Maggie Cheung – einen Schriftsteller.

Tony Leung est l'acteur principal de ce film sensuel sur la mémoire, signé Wong. À ses côtés, une escouade d'impeccables comédiennes chinoises : Faye Wong, Zhang Ziyi (ci-dessus), Carina Lau, Gong Li (ci-contre) et Maggie Cheung, actrice fétiche de Wong.

ZHANG YIMOU

Born 14 November 1950 in Xi'an, China

The most celebrated of contemporary Chinese directors learned his trade at the state-sponsored Beijing Film Academy, specializing in cinematography. In the 1980s he became an integral force in the Fifth Generation of filmmakers, including Chen Kaige and Tian Zhuangzhuang, who began making films after the Cultural Revolution (1966–1976), when art was a political instrument of propaganda. Zhang's feature debut, *Red Sorghum* (*Hong gao liang*, 1987), a visually stunning romantic melodrama filmed in CinemaScope, introduced Gong Li to Western audiences in a story of an arranged marriage between a poor farm girl and a leper set during the 1920s and 1930s. The film won the top prize at the Berlin Film Festival and was the first modern Chinese work to be released in the United States. Zhang's subsequent works included a trilogy of historical dramas centering on female sexuality, all starring Gong Li. Two of these films, *Raise the Red Lantern* (*Da hong deng long gao gao gua*, 1991) and *Ju Dou* (1990) were censored for their frank depictions of sexuality. For the third film, *The Story of Qiu Ju* (*Qiu Ju da guan si*, 1992), Zhang employed hidden cameras to film in the streets of modern-day China, his first departure from the period drama. Ten years later, Zhang returned to China's past with the lush martial arts epic *Hero* (*Ying xiong*, 2002), starring Jet Li, Zhang Ziyi and Maggie Cheung. With gorgeous cinematography by Christopher Doyle and a cast of thousands, Zhang repeated *Hero*'s formula in two more lavish *wuxias*, *House of Flying Daggers* (*Shi mian mai fu*, 2004) and his latest feature, *Curse of the Golden Flower* (*Man cheng jin dai huang jin jia*, 2006), which marked Gong Li's return to Zhang's work.

Der berühmteste aller zeitgenössischen chinesischen Regisseure erlernte sein Handwerk an der auf Kameraarbeit spezialisierten staatlichen Beijing Film Academy. In den 1980er-Jahren gehörte er, gemeinsam mit Chen Kaige und Tian Zhuangzhuang, zum Kern der „Fünfte Generation" genannten Filmemacher, die zum ersten Mal seit der Kulturrevolution (1966–1976), während der alle Kunst der Propaganda untergeordnet war, wieder Spielfilme drehten. Zhangs Erstlingswerk *Rotes Kornfeld* (*Hong gao liang*, 1987), ein in Cinemascope gedrehtes, visuell überwältigendes romantisches Melodram, schildert die arrangierte Ehe zwischen einem armen Bauernmädchen und einem Aussätzigen im China der 1920er- und 1930er-Jahre. Mit diesem Film, der auf den Berliner Filmfestspielen den Goldenen Bären erhielt, wurde auch Gong Li einem westlichen Publikum bekannt. Zugleich war es das erste moderne chinesische Filmkunstwerk, das in den USA in die Kinos kam. Zu Zhangs anschließenden Filmen gehört auch eine Trilogie historischer Dramen mit Gong Li in der Hauptrolle, in denen die weibliche Sexualität im Mittelpunkt steht. Zwei dieser Filme, *Rote Laterne* (*Da hong deng long gao gao gua*, 1991) und *Judou* (1990), wurden in China wegen allzu freizügiger Darstellung von Sexualität zensiert. Für den dritten Film, *Die Geschichte der Qiu Ju* (*Qiu Ju da guan si*, 1992), nutzte Zhang den Einsatz versteckter Kameras, um Bilder von den Straßen des modernen China einfangen zu können. Damit rückte er zum ersten Mal von rein historischen Dramen ab. Zehn Jahre später setzte sich Zhang mit dem üppigen Kampfkunstepos *Hero* (*Ying xiong*, 2002), in dem Jet Li, Zhang Ziyi und Maggie Cheung auftraten, wieder mit Chinas Vergangenheit auseinander. In zwei noch verschwenderischer inszenierten, von Kameramann Christopher Doyle großartig fotografierten *Wuxia*-Dramen, *House of Flying Daggers* (*Shi mian mai fu*, 2004) und seinem jüngsten Spielfilm *Der Fluch der goldenen Blume* (*Man cheng jin dai huang jin jia*, 2006), in dem auch Gong Li wieder eine Rolle spielt, nahm Zhang die Grundstrukturen von *Hero* auf.

Le réalisateur chinois contemporain le plus célèbre a appris le métier de chef opérateur à l'école d'État du cinéma de Pékin. Dans les années 1980, il anime, avec Chen Kaige et Tian Zhuangzhuang, la cinquième génération de cinéastes de l'après-Révolution culturelle (1966–1976), période où l'art était une arme de propagande. Le premier film de Zhang est *Le Sorgho rouge* (*Hong gao liang*, 1987), mélodrame romantique resplendissant, en cinémascope. Histoire d'un mariage arrangé entre une pauvre fermière et un lépreux, dans les années 1920 et 1930, ce film révèle Gong Li au public occidental. Ours d'or à Berlin, *Le Sorgho rouge* est le premier film chinois contemporain à avoir été distribué aux États-Unis. Parmi les films suivants, on compte une trilogie de reconstitutions historiques autour de la sexualité féminine, tous les premiers rôles féminins étant interprétées par Gong Li. Deux de ces films, *Épouses et concubines* (*Da hong deng long gao gao gua*, 1991) et *Ju Dou* (1990), ont été censurés pour la crudité des scènes de sexe. Pour *Qiu Ju, une femme chinoise* (*Qiu Ju da guan si*, 1992), Zhang filme en caméra cachée les rues de la Chine d'aujourd'hui, abandonnant le film en costumes. Dix ans plus tard, il revisite le passé national avec un splendide film d'arts martiaux, *Hero* (*Ying xiong*, 2002), avec Jet Li, Zhang Ziyi et Maggie Cheung. En collaboration avec le chef opérateur Christopher Doyle et des milliers de figurants, il reprend la formule de *Hero* dans deux autres superbes *wu xia pian* (genre à part entière du cinéma chinois), *Le Secret des poignards volants* (*Shi mian mai fu*, 2004) et son tout dernier film, *La Cité interdite* (*Man cheng jin dai huang jin jia*, 2007), qui marque le retour de Gong Li dans le cinéma de Zhang.

SELECTED FILMS →
1991 *Da hong deng long gao gao gua (Raise the Red Lantern)* **1992** *Qiu Ju da guan si (The Story of Qiu Ju)* **1994** *Huozhe (To Live)* **1995** *Yao a yao yao dao waipo qiao (Shanghai Triad)* **1999** *Wo de fu qin mu qin (The Road Home)* **1999** *Yi ge dou bu neng shao (Not One Less)* **2002** *Ying xiong (Hero)* **2004** *Shi mian mai fu (House of Flying Daggers)* **2005** *Qian li zou dan ji (Riding Alone for Thousands of Miles)* **2006** *Man cheng jin dai huang jin jia (Curse of the Golden Flower)*

SELECTED AWARDS →
1991 *Da hong deng long gao gao gua:* Silver Lion, Venice Film Festival **1992** *Qiu Ju da guan si:* Golden Lion, Venice Film Festival **1993** *Da hong deng long gao gao gua:* Best Film not in the English Language, BAFTA Awards **1994** *Huozhe:* Grand Prize of the Jury, Cannes Film Festival **1995** *Yao a yao yao dao waipo qiao:* Technical Grand Prize, Cannes Film Festival **1999** *Yi ge dou bu neng shao:* Golden Lion, Venice Film Festival **2000** *Wo de fu qin mu qin:* Silver Bear, Prize of the Ecumenical Jury, Berlin International Film Festival **2001** *Wo de fu qin mu qin:* World Cinema Audience Award, Sundance Film Festival **2003** *Ying xiong:* Alfred Bauer Award, Berlin International Film Festival

Qian li zou dan ji

Riding Alone for Thousands of Miles / Pour un fils

"For thousands of years, there's been a tradition of teaching us in China to think in terms of the collective experience, so we are rarely able to act in accordance with personal desires or emotions. Now young people, especially under Western influences, have become much more interested in themselves and their own values."

„Seit Tausenden von Jahren wird uns Chinesen traditionell beigebracht, in Begriffen kollektiver Erfahrung zu denken. Deshalb sind wir selten in der Lage, in Übereinstimmung mit unseren persönlichen Wünschen und Gefühlen zu handeln. Die jüngeren Leute sind inzwischen, vor allem durch Einflüsse westlicher Ideen, sehr viel mehr an ihrer eigenen Person und ihren persönlichen Werten interessiert."

«Pendant des milliers d'années, en Chine, on nous a appris à penser en fonction du collectif. Nous sommes donc rarement capables d'agir en accord avec nos émotions ou nos désirs personnels. Aujourd'hui, les jeunes, surtout sous l'influence de l'Occident, s'intéressent de plus en plus à eux-mêmes et à leur propre valeur.»

A village fisherman (Ken Takakura) returns to Tokyo to make peace with his estranged, terminally ill son in Zhang Yimou's quiet respite between the second and third works in his lavish action trilogy.

Ein zurückgezogen lebender Fischer (Ken Takakura) macht sich auf nach Tokio, um sich mit seinem unheilbar kranken Sohn auszusöhnen, mit dem er sich zerstritten hatte. Zhang Yimou drehte diesen ruhigen Film gewissermaßen zur Entspannung zwischen dem zweiten und dem dritten Teil seiner schwelgerischen Actiontrilogie.

Un modeste pêcheur (Ken Takakura) regagne Tokyo pour faire la paix avec son fils, qu'il a quitté et qui vit ses derniers jours. Ce film constitue un répit entre les deux derniers volets de la trilogie de films d'action de Zhang.

Man cheng jin dai huang jin jia

Curse of the Golden Flower / Fluch der goldenen Blume / La Cité interdite

Following *Hero* and *House of Flying Daggers*, Zhang's third foray into the wu xia martial-arts film stars Chow Yun-Fat and Gong Li in a lavish Tang Dynasty palace drama.

Nach *Hero* und *House of Flying Daggers* ist der Film Zhangs dritter Abstecher ins Wuxia-Kampfkunst-Genre. In dem Palastdrama, das während der Tang-Dynastie spielt, sind Chow Yun-Fat und Gong Li mit von der Partie.

Après *Hero* et *Le Secret des poignards volants*, Zhang fait une troisième incursion dans le genre *wu xia pian* du film d'arts martiaux. Chow Yun-fat et Gong Li sont les interprètes principaux de ce film somptueux qui se déroule à la cour de la dynastie Tang.

Film Festivals

This is a selection of the major international film festivals and their top prizes. Visit their websites for more detailed information on past winners, dates and locations.

BANGKOK INTERNATIONAL FILM FESTIVAL

www.bangkokfilm.org
Established: 2002
Description: Organized to coincide with the Bangkok Film Market
Location: Bangkok, Thailand
Date: July 2007, but usually late January
Films shown/emphasis: 150 international films
Programs: International Competition, ASEAN Competition (films from Brunei, Darussalam, Cambodia, Indonesia, Laos, Malaysia, Myanmar, The Philippines, Singapore, Thailand and Vietnam), Reel World, New Voices, Asian-Short Films, Windows on the World
Competitive: Yes
Top Prizes: Golden Kinnaree, Best Picture, Best Director and Best Documentary

Golden Kinnaree, Best Picture
2006 *Water*, Deepa Mehta (Canada/India)
2005 *Mar adentro (The Sea Inside)*, Alejandro Amenábar (Spain/France/Italy)

Golden Kinnaree, Best Director
2006 Park Chan-wook, *Chin-jeol-han Geum-ja-ssi (Lady Vengeance)* (South Korea)
2005 (tie) Christophe Barratier, *Les Choristes (The Chorus)* (France/Switzerland/Germany); Park Chan-wook, *Oldboy* (South Korea)

Golden Kinnaree, Best Documentary
2006 *Rize*, David LaChapelle (USA/UK)
2005 *Born Into Brothels*, Zana Briski & Ross Kauffman (India/USA)

Golden Kinnaree, Best Actor
2006 Presley Chweneyagae, *Tsotsi* (UK/South Africa)
2005 Javier Bardem, *Mar adentro (The Sea Inside)* (Spain/France/Italy)

Golden Kinnaree, Best Actress
2006 Felicity Huffman, *Transamerica* (USA)
2005 (tie) Annette Bening, *Being Julia* (Canada/USA/Hungary/UK); Anna Geislerová, *Zelary* (Czech Republic/Slovakia/Austria)

BERLIN INTERNATIONAL FILM FESTIVAL

www.berlinale.de
Established: 1951
Description: Berlin's largest cultural event and one of the most important dates on the international film industry's calendar, with 16,000 industry professionals and 3,600 journalists from 80 countries present at the festival
Location: Berlin, Germany
Date: Early February
Films shown/emphasis: 350 international films; a showcase for world cinema and European premieres of Hollywood prestige titles
Programs: Competition, Panorama, Generation (children's festival), Perspektive Deutsches Kino, International Forum of New Cinema, Retrospective
Competitive: Yes
Top Prizes: Golden Berlin Bear, Best Film; Silver Berlin Bear, Best Director

Golden Berlin Bear, Best Film
2007 *Tuya de hun shi (Tuya's Marriage)*, Quanan Wang (China)
2006 *Grbavica (Grbavica: The Land of My Dreams)*, Jasmila Zbanic (Austria/Bosnia-Herzegovina/Germany/Croatia)
2005 *U-Carmen eKhayelitsha*, Mark Dornford-May (South Africa)

Silver Berlin Bear, Best Director
2007 Joseph Cedar, *Beaufort* (Israel)
2006 Michael Winterbottom & Mat Whitecross, *The Road to Guantanamo* (UK)
2005 Marc Rothemund, *Sophie Scholl – Die letzten Tage (Sophie Scholl – The Final Days)* (Germany)

Silver Berlin Bear, Best Actor
2007 Julio Chávez, *El otro (The Other)* (Argentina/France/Germany)
2006 Moritz Bleibtreu, *Elementarteilchen (The Elementary Particles)* (Germany)
2005 Lou Taylor Pucci, *Thumbsucker* (USA)

Silver Berlin Bear, Best Actress
2007 Nina Hoss, *Yella* (Germany)
2006 Sandra Hüller, *Requiem* (Germany)
2005 Julia Jentsch, *Sophie Scholl – Die letzten Tage (Sophie Scholl – The Final Days)* (Germany)

BUTT-NUMB-A-THON

Established: 1999
Description: *Ain't It Cool News*' guru Harry Knowles' all-night film festival at the Alamo Draft House in celebration of his birthday; program revealed day of event; twelve films back-to-back with filmmaker/actor Q&As, short subjects and vintage and current trailers interspersed
Location: Austin, Texas, USA
Date: Early December
Films shown/emphasis: Previews of studio tentpoles, genre discoveries, classics, Asian extreme cinema; vintage, forgotten and overlooked B movies
Programs: n/a
Competitive: No
Top Prizes: n/a

2006 Program
Black Snake Moan, Craig Brewer (USA)
Dreamgirls, Bill Condon (USA)
Once Upon a Girl (1976), Don Jurwich (USA)
Inherit the Wind (1960), Stanley Kramer (USA)
Rocky Balboa, Sylvester Stallone (USA)
Knocked Up, Judd Apatow (USA)
Zwartboek (Black Book), Paul Verhoeven (Netherlands/Belgium/UK/Germany)
The Informer (1935), John Ford (USA)
Raw Force (1982), Edward D. Murphy (USA/Philippines)
Smokin' Aces, Joe Carnahan (UK/France/USA)
300, Zack Snyder (USA)

2005 Program
The Most Dangerous Game (1932), Irving Pichel, Ernest B. Schoedsack (USA)
King Kong, Peter Jackson (New Zealand/USA)
Footlight Parade (1933), Lloyd Bacon (USA)
Masters of Horror: Sick Girl, Lucky McKee (USA) (TV)
Chin-jeol-han Geum-ja-ssi (Lady Vengeance), Park Chan-wook (South Korea)

Le Professionnel (The Professional) (1981),
Georges Lautner (France)
Banlieue 13 (District 13) (2004), Pierre Morel
(France)
The Descent, Neil Marshall (UK)
Stunt Rock (Sorcery) (1978), Brian Trenchard-
Smith (Australia/Netherlands)
Drum (1976), Steve Carver (USA)
V for Vendetta, James McTeigue (UK/USA/
Germany))

CAIRO INTERNATIONAL
FILM FESTIVAL

www.cairofilmfest.org
Established: 1976
Description: Large general-interest film
festival; one of the twelve largest 'A-status'
international film festivals, as recognized
by the International Federation of Film Pro-
ducers Association; the first film festival in
the Middle East
Location: Cairo, Egypt
Date: Late November
Films shown/emphasis: International titles
and films from the Arab diaspora
Programs: Competition, Official Selection:
Out of Competition, Arabs in World Cinema,
New Arab Cinema, Golden Pyramid, Festival
of Festivals
Competitive: Yes
Top Prizes: Golden Pyramid, Best Film, Best
Director

Golden Pyramid, Best Film
2006 *Fang xiang zhi lu (The Road)*, Zhang
Jiarui (China)
2005 *Äideistä parhain (Mother of Mine)*,
Klaus Härö (Finland/Sweden)

Silver Pyramid, Best Director
2006 Khosro Masoumi, *Jayee Dar Dour-Dasti
(Somewhere Too Far)* (Iran)
2005 Kujtim Çashku, *Syri magjik (Magic Eye)*
(Albania/Germany)

CINEVEGAS

www.cinevegas.com
Established: 1998
Description: 'One of the hottest and fastest-
growing film festivals in the world,' with

Dennis Hopper as Chairman of the Board
and Sundance Programmer Trevor Groth in
charge of the films, including 'world premiere
films and unique independent cinema'
Location: Las Vegas, Nevada, USA
Date: Early June
Films shown/emphasis: American indies
(including Sundance faves), studio previews,
raucous evening parties and celebrity trib-
utes abound
Programs: Jackpot Premieres, Vegas Uncov-
ered, Sure Bets, Diamond Discoveries, Shorts
Programs, Nevada Filmmaking Features
Competitive: Yes
Top Prizes: Jury Award, Best Film; Audience
Award

Jury Award, Best Film
2006 *G. I. Jesus*, Carl Colpaert (USA)
2005 *In Memory of My Father*, Christopher
Jaymes (USA/Austria)

Audience Award
2006 *Park*, Kurt Voelker (USA)
2005 *Buy It Now*, Antonio Campos (USA)

EDINBURGH INTERNATIONAL
FILM FESTIVAL

www.edfilmfest.org.uk
Established: 1947
Description: The longest continually running
film festival in the world; began as a docu-
mentary-based festival established in the
wake of World War Two
Location: Edinburgh, Scotland
Date: Mid-August
Films shown/emphasis: New cinema from
around the world is showcased, with an
emphasis on works from the United Kingdom
Programs: Animation, Black Box, British Gala,
Directors' Showcase, Document, Late Night
Romps, Reel Life, Retrospective, Shorts Pro-
gramme
Competitive: Yes
Top Prizes: Audience Award; Best New British
Feature

Audience Award
2006 *Clerks II*, Kevin Smith (USA)
2005 *Tsotsi*, Gavin Hood (UK/South Africa)

Best New British Feature
2006 *Brothers of the Head*, Keith Fulton &
Louis Pepe (UK)
2005 *Tsotsi*, Gavin Hood (UK/South Africa)

New Director's Award
2006 Paul Andrew Williams, *London to
Brighton* (UK)
2005 Mike Mills, *Thumbsucker* (USA)

FESTIVAL DE CANNES/
CANNES FILM FESTIVAL

www.festival-cannes.fr
Established: 1947
Description: The mother of all international
film festivals, comprising the sprawling
Marché du Film and two parallel sidebar
programs, International Critic's Week and
Director's Fortnight
Location: French Riviera, France
Date: Mid-May
Films shown/emphasis: 930 feature films
(including market titles) and 51 short films,
comprising Hollywood studio tentpoles, world
cinema mavericks and international discover-
ies as well as unsold titles from around the
world seeking distribution in the Marché du
Film
Programs: Main Competition, Un Certain
Regard, Out of Competition
Competitive: Yes
Top Prizes: Palme d'Or, Best Picture

Palme d'Or, Best Picture
2007 *4 Luni, 3 Saptamini si 2 Zile (4 Months,
3 Weeks and 2 Days)*, Cristian Mungiu
(Romania)
2006 *The Wind That Shakes The Barley*,
Ken Loach (Germany/Italy/Spain/France/
Ireland/UK)
2005 *L'Enfant (The Child)*, Jean-Pierre &
Luc Dardenne (Belgium/France)

Un Certain Regard
2007 *California Dreamin' (Nesfarsit)
(California Dreaming [Endless])*,
Cristian Nemescu (Romania)
2006 *Jiang cheng xia ri (Luxury Car)*,
Wang Chao (France/China)
2005 *Moartea Domnului Lazarescu*

Film Festivals

(The Death of Mister Lazarescu), Cristi Puiu (Romania)

Camera d'Or, Best First Film
2007 *Meduzot (Jellyfish)*, Etgar Keret and Shira Geffen (France/Israel)
2006 *A fost sau n-a fost? (12:08 East of Bucharest)*, Corneliu Porumboiu (Romania)
2005 (tie) *Sulanga Enu Pinisa (The Forsaken Land)*, Vimukthi Jayasundara (France/Sri Lanka); *Me and You and Everyone We Know*, Miranda July (USA)

KARLOVY VARY INTERNATIONAL FILM FESTIVAL
www.kviff.cz
Established: 1946; celebrated annually since 1994
Description: From 1960 to 1992 it alternated years with the Moscow Film Festival
Location: Karlovy Vary, Czechoslovakia
Date: Late June, early July
Films shown/emphasis: 242 feature-length films from dozens of countries around the world in 2005 festival.
Programs: Official Selection, Competition and Out of Competition, Documentary Films in Competition, East of the West, Horizons, Forum of Independents, Another View, Sundance at Karlovy Vary, Focus on British Films, Midnight Screenings, Treasures from the National Film Archive
Competitive: Yes
Top Prizes: Crystal Globe

Crystal Globe, Best Film
2006 *SherryBaby*, Laurie Collyer (USA)
2005 *Mój Nikifor (My Nikifor)*, Krzysztof Krauze (Poland)

Best Director
2006 Joachim Trier, *Reprise* (Norway)
2005 Krzysztof Krauze, *Mój Nikifor (My Nikifor)* (Poland)

LOCARNO INTERNATIONAL FILM FESTIVAL
http://jahia.pardo.ch
Established: 1948

Description: Ranked a 'Category A' festival by the FIAPF, making it one of the Big Twelve international film festivals; known for its popular outdoor screenings at the Piazza Grande, featuring a 26 m x 14 m outdoor screen, one of the biggest in the world
Location: Locarno, Switzerland
Date: Early August
Films shown/emphasis: 407 feature films screened in the 2006 festival. Video competition, video art, major auteur works, independent and foreign discoveries
Programs: International Competition, Piazza Grande, Filmmakers of the Present, Leopards of Tomorrow, Play Forward, Retrospective, Open Doors, Critic's Week
Competitive: Yes
Top Prizes: Golden Leopard, Best Film; Special Jury Prize, Best Director

Golden Leopard, Best Film
2006 *Das Fräulein*, Andrea Staka (Germany/Switzerland/Bosnia-Herzegovina)
2005 *Nine Lives*, Rodrigo García (USA)

Special Jury Prize, Best Director
2006 Laurent Achard, *Le dernier des fous (Demented)* (France)
2005 Nobuhiro Suwa, *Un couple parfait* (Japan/France)

Audience Award
2006 *Das Leben der Anderen (The Lives of Others)*, Florian Henckel von Donnersmarck (Germany)
2005 *Zaïna, cavaliere de l'Atlas (Zaina: Rider of the Atlas)*, Bourlem Guerdjou (France/Germany)

THE TIMES BFI LONDON FILM FESTIVAL
www.lff.org.uk
Established: 1956
Description: Festival of festivals, showcasing the best new films from around the world, with an emphasis on films never before screened in the UK
Location: London, UK
Date: Mid-October
Films shown/emphasis: 200 feature films

making their UK premieres and emphasizing world cinema, new UK cinema and hits from other festivals
Programs: Galas & Special Screenings, Film on the Square, New British Cinema, French Revolutions, Cinema Europa, World Cinema, Experimenta, Treasures from the Archives, Short Cuts and Animation
Competitive: Yes
Top Prizes: Sutherland Trophy 'for most original and imaginative first feature'

Sutherland Trophy
2006 *Red Road*, Andrea Arnold (UK/Denmark)
2005 *Eläville ja kuolleille (For the Living and the Dead)*, Kari Paljakka (Finland)

LOS ANGELES FILM FESTIVAL
www.lafilmfest.com
Established: 1994
Description: Formerly the IFP/West Film Festival, this large general-interest festival now claims 60,000 annual attendance
Location: Los Angeles, California, USA
Date: Late June
Films shown/emphasis: 175 narrative features, documentaries, shorts and music videos; the best of American and international cinema
Programs: Dark Wave, Documentary Competition, Family Screenings, Future Filmmakers Showcase, Galas, Guilty Pleasures, International Showcase, Music Video Showcase, Narrative Competition, Shorts, Special Screenings, Spotlight, Summer Previews, Tribute Screenings
Competitive: Yes
Top Prizes: Target Filmmakers Award, Best Narrative Feature, Best Documentary Feature; Audience Award, Best Narrative Feature

Target Filmmakers Award, Best Narrative Feature
2006 *Gretchen*, Steve Collins (USA)
2005 *Jellysmoke*, Mark Banning (USA)

Target Filmmakers Award, Best Documentary Feature
2006 *Deliver Us From Evil*, Amy Berg (USA)
2005 *Everyone Their Grain of Sand*, Beth Bird (Mexico/USA)

Audience Award, Best Narrative Feature
2006 *Ira & Abby*, Robert Cary (USA)
2005 *Me and You and Everyone We Know*, Miranda July (USA)

MAR DEL PLATA INTERNATIONAL FILM FESTIVAL

www.mardelplatafilmfest.com
Established: 1954
Description: Category A festival – one of the 'Big Twelve,' among the largest international film festivals; unspools 400 km from the city of Buenos Aires on the Atlantic Coast. Average annual audience of 150,000 spectators; vanished for 25 years after 1970 but was revived in 1996
Location: Mar del Plata, Argentina
Date: Early March
Films shown/emphasis: Hundreds of features, shorts and docs screened; a noticeable lack of Hollywood and American films in general
Programs: Point of View (world cinema), LatinAmerica Sidebar, Women and Film, Heterodoxy (experimental cinema), Narrative Competition
Competitive: Yes
Top Prizes: Golden Ástor, Best Film

Golden Ástor, Best Film
2007 *Ficció (Fiction)*, Cesec Gay (Spain)
2006 *Noticias lejanas (News From Afar)*, Ricardo Benet (Mexico)
2005 *Le grand voyage*, Ismaël Ferroukhi (France/Morocco)

Silver Astor, Best Director
2007 (tie) Marina Spada, *Come l'ombra (As the Shadow)* (Italy); Sang-soo Hong, *Haebyonui yoin (Woman on the Beach)* (South Korea)
2006 Marco Martins, *Alice* (Portugal)
2005 Yasmine Kassari, *L'Enfant endormi (The Sleeping Child)* (Belgium/Morocco)

MONTREAL WORLD FILM FESTIVAL

www.ffm-montreal.org
Established: 1976
Description: The only competitive event in North America recognized by the FIAPF
Location: Quebec, Montreal, Canada

Date: Late August, early September
Films shown/emphasis: 215 features and 194 short and medium-length films from 76 countries in the 2006 festival; emphasis on world cinema and Canadian works
Programs: World Competition, First Films World Competition, Hors Concours (World Greats, out-of-competition), Focus on the World Cinema (Americas, Europe, Asia, Africa, Oceana), Documentaries of the World, Tributes, Cinema Under the Stars, Canadian Student Film Festival
Competitive: Yes
Top Prizes: Grand Prix of the Americas, Best-Film; Golden Zenith for Best Feature Film

Grand Prix of the Americas, Best Film
2006 (tie) *Nagai sanpo (A Long Walk)*, Eiji Okuda (Japan); *O maior amor do mundo (The Greatest Love of All)*, Carlos Diegues (Brazil)
2005 *Off Screen*, Pieter Kuijpers (Netherlands/Belgium)

Golden Zenith for Best First Feature Film
2006 *Más que a nada en el mundo (More Than Anything in the World)*, Andrés León Becker & Javier Solar (Mexico)
2005 *Ang Pagdadalaga ni Maximo Oliveros (The Blossoming of Maximo Oliveros)*, Auraeus Solito (Philippines)

Audience Award for Best Film
2006 *Les Filles du botaniste (The Chinese Botanist's Daughters)*, Dai Sijie (France/Canada)
2005 *Kamataki*, Claude Gagnon (Canada/Japan)

MOSCOW INTERNATIONAL FILM FESTIVAL

www.moscowfilmfestival.ru
Established: 1935
Description: Designated a Class A festival by the FIAPF in 1972 — one of the Big Twelve international film festivals; celebrated annually since 1995, before that the festival was biannual, alternating with the Karlovy Vary International Film Festival
Location: Moscow, Russia
Date: Late June, early July

Films shown/emphasis: World Cinema
Programs: Main Competition, Russian Program, Out-of-Competition Screenings, Perspectives (world cinema program)
Competitive: Yes
Top Prizes: Golden St. George, Best Film

Golden St. George, Best Film
2006 *Om Sara*, Karim Othman (Sweden)
2005 *Kosmos kak predchuvstvie (Dreaming of Space)*, Aleksei Uchitel (Russia)

Silver St. George, Best Director
2006 Bertrand Blier, *Combien tu m'aimes? (How Much Do You Love Me?)* (Italy/France)
2005 Thomas Vinterberg, *Dear Wendy* (Denmark/France/Germany/UK)

NEW YORK FILM FESTIVAL

www.filmlinc.com/nyff
Established: 1962
Description: Prestigious annual festival organized by the Film Society of Lincoln Center; films selected by a panel of several major critics
Location: New York, New York, USA
Date: Early October
Films shown/emphasis: Average of 28 feature films & 12 shorts selected each year, showcasing 'inspiring and provocative cinema by emerging talents and first-rank international artists'
Programs: Main Selection, Views from the Avant-Garde
Competitive: No
Top Prizes: None

Selected Highlights

2006
The Queen, Stephen Frears (UK/France/Italy)
Little Children, Todd Fields (USA)
49 Up, Michael Apted (UK)
Sang sattawat (Syndromes and a Century), Apichatpong Weerasethakul (Thailand/France/Austria)
Inland Empire, David Lynch (USA/Poland/France)

Film Festivals

2005

Good Night, and Good Luck., George Clooney (USA)

Breakfast on Pluto, Neil Jordan (Ireland/UK)

Caché (Hidden), Michael Haneke (France/Austria/Germany/Italy)

L'Enfant (The Child) Luc & Jean-Pierre Dardenne (Belgium/France)

Les Amants réguliers (Regular Lovers), Philippe Garrel (France)

PUSAN INTERNATIONAL FILM FESTIVAL

www.piff.org

Established: 1995

Description: Largest film festival in Asia

Location: Pusan, South Korea

Date: Mid-October

Films shown/emphasis: 245 films from 63 countries, with an emphasis on new Asian works seeking distribution

Programs: A Window on Asia. New Currents, Korean Cinema Today, Korean Cinema Retrospective, World Cinema, Wide Angle, Open Cinema, Critic's Choice, Special Programs in Focus, Midnight Passion

Competitive: Yes

Top Prizes: New Currents Award

New Currents Award, Best Asian Film

2006 (tie) *Binglang (Betelnut)*, Heng Yang (China); *Love Conquers All*, Chui Mui Tan (Netherlands/Malaysia)

2005 *Mang zhong (Grain in Ear)*, Zhang Lu (China/South Korea)

Audience Award, New Currents Program

2006 *Ao lua ha dong (The White Silk Dress)*, Huynh Luu (Vietnam)

2005 *Yongseobadji mothan ja (The Unforgiven)*, Jong-bin Yun (South Korea)

INTERNATIONAL FILM FESTIVAL ROTTERDAM

www.filmfestivalrotterdam.com

Established: 1971

Description: Massive festival (358,000 admissions in 2006) offering 'a quality selection of worldwide independent, innovative and experimental cinema and visual arts'; runs concurrently with CineMart, the largest co-production market for film projects in the world

Location: Rotterdam, The Netherlands

Date: Late January

Films shown/emphasis: Hundreds of features and shorts from every corner of the globe

Programs: Tiger Awards Competition (First or Second Feature Films), Tiger Awards Competition for Short Films, Cinema of the Future, Cinema of the World, Maestros (auteur classics), Cinema Regained, Exploding Cinema

Competitive: Yes

Top Prizes: Tiger Award, Best First or Second Film; three prizes awarded

VPRO Tiger Award, Best First or Second Film

2007

AFR, Martin Hartz Kaplers (Denmark)

Baixio das Bestas, Cláudio Assis (Brazil)

Love Conquers All, Chui Mui Tan (Netherlands/Malaysia)

Die Unerzogenen, Pia Marais (Germany)

2006

Lai xiao zi (Walking on the Wild Side), Han Jie (China)

La perrera (Dog Pound), Manuel Nieto Zas (Uruguay/Argentina/Canada/Spain)

Old Joy, Kelly Reichardt (USA)

2005

Nemmeno il destino (Changing Destiny), Daniele Gaglianone (Italy)

4, Ilya Khrjanovsky (Russia)

El cielo gira (The Sky Turns), Mercedes Álvarez (Spain)

Tiscali Audience Award

2006 *Eden*, Michael Hofmann (Germany/Switzerland)

2005 *Lakposhtha hâm parvaz mikonand (Turtles Can Fly)*, Bahman Ghobadi (Iran/France/Iraq)

RIO DE JANEIRO INTERNATIONAL FILM FESTIVAL

www.festivaldorio.com.br

Established: 1999

Description: Considered the largest and most important film festival in South America

Location: Rio de Janeiro, Brazil

Date: Late September

Films shown/emphasis: 400 films screened in 2006 festival; emphasis on world cinema and Latin American Cinema

Programs: World Panorama, Brazil Premieres, Latin Premieres, Midnight Movies, Documentaries

Competitive: Yes

Top Prizes: Best Brazilian Feature

Best Fiction Feature, Brazil

2006 *O Ano em que Meus Pais Saíram de Férias (The Year My Parents Went on Vacation)*, Cao Hamburger (Brazil)

2005 *Cidade Baixa (Lower City)*, Sérgio Machado (Brazil)

Audience Award

2006 *Fabricando Tom Zé (Fabricating Tom Zé)*, Décio Matos Júnior (Brazil)

2005 *A Máquina (The Machine)*, João Falcão (Brazil)

SAN FRANCISCO INTERNATIONAL FILM FESTIVAL

www.sffs.org

Established: 1957

Description: America's oldest and longest-running film festival, celebrating its 50th anniversary in 2007; the first USA festival to showcase international films

Location: San Francisco, California, USA

Date: Late April

Films shown/emphasis: 200 films from 50 countries, highlighting current trends in international film and video production with an emphasis on work that has not secured US distribution

Programs: Big Nights, Documentaries, Live & Onstage, New Directors, Shorts Programs, Spotlight: Family Films, World Cinema

Competitive: Yes

Top Prizes: SKYY Prize for First-Time Film-maker; Virgin Megastore Audience Award, Narrative Feature

SKYY Prize, First-Time Filmmaker
2006 Ying Liang, *Bei yazi de nanhai (Taking Father Home)* (China)
2005 Miranda July, *Me and You and Everyone We Know* (USA)

Virgin Megastore Audience Award, Narrative Feature
2006 *Look Both Ways*, Sarah Watt (Australia)
2005 *Me and You and Everyone We Know*, Miranda July (USA)

SAN FRANCISCO INTERNATIONAL LGBT FILM FESTIVAL

www.frameline.org
Established: 1976
Description: The world's oldest and largest lesbian, gay, bisexual and transgendered film festival, with 62,000 annual attendees; presented by Frameline, a non-profit media organization dedicated to the support, development and promotion of queer visibility through media arts
Location: San Francisco, California, USA
Date: Mid-June
Films shown/emphasis: 260 features and short films screened, including gay-themed features, documentaries and short subjects from around the world
Programs: USA Features, World Cinema, Documentaries, Shorts, Family Films
Competitive: Yes
Top Prizes: Audience Award, First Feature Award

First Feature Award
2006 *Pusang gala (Stray Cats)*, Ellen Ongkeko-Marfil (Philippines)
2005 *Gypo*, Jan Dunn (UK)

Audience Award
2006 *The Gymnast*, Ned Farr (USA)
2005 *Transamerica*, Duncan Tucker (USA)

SHANGHAI INTERNATIONAL FILM FESTIVAL

www.siff.com
Established: 1993; celebrated biannually until 2001
Description: Huge, non-specialized, general international festival showcasing Asian films; the only annual film-world gathering in the Chinese market
Location: Shanghai, China
Date: Mid-June
Films shown/emphasis: 959 official films from 60 countries; emphasis on Asian films from the Chinese marketplace
Programs: International Film Panorama
Competitive: Yes
Top Prizes: Golden Goblet (JinJue); Best Film, Best Director

Golden Goblet, Best Film
2006 *Vier Minuten (Four Minutes)*, Chris Kraus (Germany)
2005 *Mura no shashinshuu*, Mitsuhiro Mihara (Japan)

Golden Goblet, Best Director
2006 Fabienne Godet, *Sauf le respect que je vous dois (Burnt Out)* (France)
2005 Rumle Hammerich, *Unge Andersen (Young Andersen)* (Denmark/Norway/Sweden)

SLAMDANCE

www.slamdance.com
Established: 1995
Description: First and biggest of the parallel festivals that sprung up in Park City, Utah in tandem with the Sundance Film Festival; originally conceived as a *salon des réfusés* showcasing films rejected by Sundance, with which Slamdance has no affiliation
Location: Park City, Utah, USA
Date: Mid-January
Films shown/emphasis: Emerging American independent filmmakers not quite ready for or rejected by Sundance
Programs: Unknown
Competitive: Yes
Top Prizes: Grand Jury Sparky Award, Best Film; Audience Sparky Award, Best Narrative Feature

Grand Jury Sparky Award, Best Film
2007 *Tijuana Makes Me Happy*, Dylan Verrechia (Mexico)
2006 *We Go Way Back*, Lynn Shelton (USA)

Audience Sparky Award, Best Narrative Feature
2007 *Murder Party*, Jeremy Saulnier (USA)
2006 *The Sasquatch Dumpling Gang*, Tim Skousen (USA)

SUNDANCE FILM FESTIVAL

http://festival.sundance.org
Established: 1981; previously the US Film Festival
Description: 'The premier showcase for American and international independent film'
Location: Park City, Utah, USA
Date: Mid-January
Films shown/emphasis: American independent and world cinema discoveries; documentaries
Programs: Independent Film Competition: Documentary, Independent Film Competition: Dramatic, World Cinema Competition: Documentary, World Cinema Competition: Dramatic, Premieres, Spectrum, Park City at Midnight, Frontier, From the Collection, Animation Spotlight, Shorts Program
Competitive: Yes
Top Prizes: Grand Jury Prize, Directing Prize, Audience Award

Grand Jury Prize
2007 *Padre Nuestro*, Christopher Zalla (USA)
2006 *Quinceañera*, Richard Glatzer & Wash Westmoreland (USA)

Directing Prize
2007 Jeffrey Blitz, *Rocket Science* (USA)
2006 Dito Montiel, *A Guide To Recognizing Your Saints* (USA)

Audience Award
2007 *Grace Is Gone*, James C. Strouse (USA)
2006 *Quinceañera*, Richard Glatzer & Wash Westmoreland (USA)

Film Festivals

THESSALONIKI INTERNATIONAL FILM FESTIVAL

www.filmfestival.gr
Established: 1960
Description: The Balkans' primary showcase for the work of new and emerging filmmakers from around the world
Location: Thessaloniki, Greece
Date: Mid-November
Films shown/emphasis: n/a
Programs: International Competition, Panorama of Greek Cinema, Independence Days, Balkan Survey
Competitive: Yes
Top Prizes: Golden Alexander, Best Film; Audience Award, International Competition

Golden Alexander, Best Film

2006 *Gajokeui tansaeng (Family Ties)*, Kim Tae-yong (South Korea)
2005 *Een Ander zijn geluk (Someone Else's Happiness)*, Fien Troch (Belgium/Netherlands)

Audience Award, International Competition

2006 *Gajokeui tansaeng (Family Ties)*, Kim Tae-yong (South Korea)
2005 *Man Push Cart*, Ramin Bahrani (USA/Iran)

TOKYO INTERNATIONAL FILM FESTIVAL

www.tiff-jp.net
Established: 1985
Description: One of the world's twelve largest international film festivals, as established by the International Federation of Film Producers Association (FIAPF); Japan's only approved international film festival
Location: Tokyo, Japan
Date: Mid-October
Films shown/emphasis: Asian discoveries and highlights, new Japanese works
Programs: Competition, Special Screenings, Winds of Asia, Japanese Eyes
Competitive: Yes
Top Prizes: Tokyo Sakura Grand Prize, Best Film; Best Director; Audience Award

Tokyo Sakura Grand Prize

2006 *OSS 117: Le Caire nid d'espions (OSS 117: Cairo Nest of Spies)*, Michel Hazanavicius (France)
2005 *Yuki ni negau koto (What the Snow Brings)*, Kichitaro Negishi (Japan)

Best Director

2006 Jonathan Dayton & Valerie Faris, *Little Miss Sunshine* (USA)
2005 Kichitaro Negishi, *Yuki ni negau koto (What the Snow Brings)* (Japan)

Audience Award

2006 *Little Miss Sunshine*, Jonathan Dayton & Valerie Faris
2005 *Yuki ni negau koto (What the Snow Brings)*, Kichitaro Negishi (Japan)

TORONTO INTERNATIONAL FILM FESTIVAL

www.torontointernationalfilmfestival.ca
Established: 1970
Description: Huge North American general-interest festival attracting 280,000 spectators and a phalanx of celebrities, buyers, publicists and journalists
Location: Toronto, Canada
Date: Early September
Films shown/emphasis: 335 films from 52 countries in 2005; world premieres of studio Oscar hopefuls, North American premieres of international festival darlings, Canadian independents, midnight discoveries
Programs: Canada First!, Gala Presentations, Mavericks, Sprockets Family Zone, Visions, Contemporary World Cinema, Discovery, Masters, Midnight Madness, Real to Reel, Special Presentations, Vanguard, Wavelengths
Competitive: Yes
Top Prizes: People's Choice Award, Discovery Award, Best Canadian Feature Film

People's Choice Award

2006 *Bella*, Alejandro Gomez Monteverde (Mexico/USA)
2005 *Tsotsi*, Gavin Hood (UK/South Africa)

Discovery Award

2006 *Reprise*, Joachim Trier (Norway)
2005 *Look Both Ways*, Sarah Watt (Australia)

Best Canadian Feature Film

2006 *Sur la trace d'Igor Rizzi (On the Trail of Igor Rizzi)*, Noël Mitrani (Canada)
2005 *C. R. A. Z. Y.*, Jean-Marc Vallée (Canada)

VENICE INTERNATIONAL FILM FESTIVAL

www.labiennale.org/en/cinema/
Established: 1932
Description: One of Europe's oldest and most prestigious festivals, known officially as the Mostra Internazionale d'Arte Cinematographica
Location: Venice, Italy
Date: Late August, early September
Films shown/emphasis: World cinema; latest work from the world's top international auteurs
Programs: Venizia (competition films), Out of Competition (star-driven premieres), Ozizzonti (new trends in cinema), Corto Cortissimo (international short film competition)
Competitive: Yes
Top Prizes: Golden Lion, Best Picture; Silver Lion, Best Director

Golden Lion, Best Picture

2006 *Sanxia haoren (Still Life)*, Zhangke Jia (China/Hong Kong)
2005 *Brokeback Mountain*, Ang Lee (USA)

Silver Lion, Best Director

2006 Alain Resnais, *Cœurs (Private Fears in Public Places)* (France/Italy)
2005 Philippe Garrel *Les Amants réguliers (Regular Lovers)* (France)

Best Actor

2006 Ben Affleck, *Hollywoodland* (USA)
2005 David Straithairn, *Good Night, and Good Luck.* (USA)

Best Actress

2006 Helen Mirren, *The Queen* (UK/France/Italy)
2005 Giovanna Mezzogiorno, *La bestia nel cuore (Don't Tell)* (Italy/UK/France/Spain)

Websites

This is a selection of notable English-language websites.

AIN'T IT COOL NEWS
www.aintitcool.com

Long-running website run by Austin, Texas-based Harry Knowles, catering to fanboys and movie geeks and specializing in guerrilla movie reviews of major studio test screenings posted by anonymous spies months before movies are released in theaters, instilling fear in the hearts of nervous studio executives beholden to the bottom line. Helped turn the Internet (not to mention Knowles's fanboy contingent) into a major force in word-of-mouth marketing of studio motion pictures, spawning its own film festival, the annual Butt-Numb-a-Thon, in which Knowles screens a dozen movies during a 24-hour-period, some of them world premieres, including *The Passion of the Christ* (2003/04), which Mel Gibson sneak previewed for festivalgoers in 2003.

ANIME NEWS NETWORK
www.animenewsnetwork.com

Billed 'the Internet's most trusted anime news source,' this frequently updated, meticulously organized news site is chock full of information on – but not confined to – the Japanese animation scene, including manga (graphic novels) and anime (animated films). Includes features, interviews, editorials, reviews, convention reports, staff and industry blogs, interactive forums and an exhaustive encyclopedia compiling 7,000 anime titles, 6,000 production companies and a handy lexicon for neophytes who still live in the land of cartoons and comic books.

BOLLYWOOD WORLD
www.bollywoodworld.com

Bollywood, a term combining Bombay and Hollywood, is the Mumbai-based Hindi language film industry in India specializing in melodramatic productions with Indian stars that often feature musical numbers, three-hour running times and spicy thrills, hence the nickname "masala movie." Bollywood World bills itself 'India's premiere Bollywood portal' and 'the most trusted name in Bollywood,' with its news, reviews, trailers, celebrity gossip and fan forums. Be sure and read the site's introductory primer, 'What is Bollywood?,' located on the site's table of contents.

BOX OFFICE GURU
www.boxofficeguru.com

Maintained by the indefatigable Gitesh Pandya, this box-office numbers site is the best of its kind for anyone obsessed with the Hollywood numbers game, i.e. the weekend box-office numbers that can make or break a film, director, actor, and sometimes even an entire movie studio. Pandya writes thoughtful, meticulous weekend reports, identifying a film's target audience and its projected weekend haul, then provides the requisite numbers as they become available on Sunday afternoon. A database contains comprehensive box office data on motion pictures released between 1989 and the present. The site also features a release schedule and a list of top-grossing films ranked by season.

CINEMASCOPE
www.cinema-scope.com

This bimonthly Toronto-based print and web publication, edited by Mark Peranson, is the *Cahiers du cinéma* of its day for its savvy intellectual voice and mostly young and open-minded writing staff. Featuring reviews, festival reports and interviews by correspondents from around the world, this is some of the most astute film writing on the scene today, if your taste lies in the direction of Olivier Assayas, Jia Zhangke and Apichatpong Weerasethakul.

CINEUROPA
www.cineuropa.org

Dubbed 'the portal of European Cinema,' this industry news site is dedicated to tracking the moves of European actors, filmmakers, professionals, producers, distributors, sales agents, screenwriters via news items, features and interviews. Published in French, English, Italian and Spanish by a consortium of European companies and government bureaus, Cineuropa is an indispensable resource for production company contact information and breaking European film news. The site's country profiles section examines the movie-going habits of specific European countries.

DAVE KEHR
www.davekehr.com

This DVD columnist for *The New York Times* is a superb writer and seems to possess an encyclopedic knowledge for classic film lore, making him an ideal chronicler of forgotten films of the past repackaged on DVD for a new generation – film noir is a particular strong point for Kehr but his blog also includes festival reports, obituaries and the odd critical rant, making his message board a must-read among the haute film criticism cognoscenti.

FILMLAND DICTIONARY OF FILM, AUDIO AND VIDEO TERMINOLOGY
www.filmland.com/glossary/Dictionary.html

Indispensable on-line film terms dictionary that's uncomplicated, uncluttered and keeps its definitions as concise as possible for easier retention. Emphasizes production and post-production terms, so if you're looking for a definition of film noir or Hammer Horror, head over to www.greencine.com/static/primers/index.jsp for detailed genre descriptions and movie recommendations. This one's on the technical side, but haven't you ever wondered what a Foley artist does?

DVD BEAVER
www.dvdbeaver.com

Hardcore film aficionados comb the Internet for the best deals (and even more important, the best transfers) on new and classic DVD releases from around the world, to be lovingly inserted into their region-free DVD players and enjoyed in surround sound on their 66-inch rear-projection television set. That said, *DVD Beaver* provides DVD release information and technical specifications for discerning cinephiles who might not know that the UK version of Fritz Lang's *M* (1931) is infinitely

Websites

better in sound and quality than the Region One Criterion Collection version available exclusively in the US – and which can only be played on Region One DVD players. Specializing in foreign, independent and classic films, covering all six DVD regions, Gary W. Tooze's informative site features astute feedback from 130 contributing writers around the world, making the complicated world of region-coded DVDs that much easier to navigate.

INDIEWIRE
www.indiewire.com

The indefatigable Eugene Hernandez, along with his loyal sidekick and cohort Brian Brooks, have been documenting the independent film scene around the world for ten years via this industry-related site filled with production news, festival reports, filmmaker interviews, contributor blogs and more. While not as well funded as the on-line versions of its trade rivals *Variety*, *The Hollywood Reporter* or *Screen International*, *indieWIRE* is nevertheless the plucky little engine that could, outclassing its rivals with its fierce dedication to covering every corner of independent film. From small regional film festivals to Cannes, Sundance and the Independent Spirit Awards, chances are strong that someone from *indieWIRE* is there for the party.

FILM COMMENT
www.filmlinc.com/fcm/fcm.htm

The house publication of New York's highbrow Film Society of Lincoln Center is one of the last few monthly publications in America to focus on foreign films and film culture in general, but it's still a vital read, despite the magazine's recent foray into A-list celebrity cover stars, including Kirsten Dunst, Keanu Reeves and Dustin Hoffman. Featuring news, reviews and features from the old guard of American film writers, including Amy Taubin and Dave Kehr, as well as young turks like Kent Jones and Nathan Lee, *Film Comment* is as close as the USA will ever get to having a *Cahiers du cinéma* of its own.

FILM FESTIVALS
www.filmfestivals.com

There are now more than 2,000 major film festivals in existence around the world, from Beirut to Palm Springs to San Sebastian and all points in between – this site will tell you which films screened where, what won the Grand Jury Prize and where you might stay or eat if you go to the Edinburgh Film Festival next year. Featuring daily festival reports (including videoblogs!), breaking festival news, an awards database and a Professional section with advice for filmmakers on submitting their work to festivals, this is one-stop surfing for filmmakers and festivalgoers who might not know the tricks of an increasingly frenzied and very global trade.

FILMMAKER MAGAZINE
www.filmmakermagazine.com

The web companion to the print version of the bible of independent filmmaking in the USA includes on-line versions of much of *FilmMaker*'s print content, including filmmaker interviews, technical reviews, festival reports and set visits, in addition to the magazine's annual '25 Faces to Watch,' which is ground zero for the next wave of indie talent. Editors Scott Macauley, Matthew Ross and Peter Bowen provide erudite updates to the site's blog, which is a must-read for anyone tracking the New York independent film scene.

FILM THREAT
www.filmthreat.com

Once the *enfant terrible* of USA film publications, *Film Threat* – like its patron saint John Waters — has matured into an almost mainstream entity while still preserving its rebellious undercurrent and biting commentary. This renegade force now exists only on-line but the general mission is the same: to champion the increasingly popular explosion of independent and underground films. The merciless reviews have been replaced by more subdued commentary but this is still the best place to find out about the next generation's Kuchar Brothers and where you might be able to obtain that bootleg copy of

the 1980 punk rock movie *Ladies and Gentlemen, The Fabulous Stains* (1981), starring a 15-year-old Diane Lane. The site also sells DVDs released under the *Film Threat* label, including the notoriously foul-mouthed underground classic *Red* (1992), directed by the publication's founder and editor, Chris Gore.

HOLLYWOOD REPORTER
www.hollywoodreporter.com

The website for this second-fiddle Hollywood trade paper (the wider-read and more informative *Variety* is its rival and principal competitor) features breaking news, reviews, box office figures and columns, including the must-read Risky Business blog by seasoned entertainment reporter Anne Thompson. Chief critic Kirk Honeycut writes the most insightful movie reviews on the site, which offers full access to magazine content as part of its premium service, available at a cost of approximately $20 a month.

INTERNET MOVIE DATABASE
www.imdb.com

The Internet's premier movie reference site is an exhausting compendium of every motion picture ever filmed, including hyperlinks to cast and crew, reader commentary, links to external reviews, and much, much more. Supplementary information, like film festival award winners, for example, aren't always accurate or up to date, but you can usually count on finding the key facts here, like the original Thai title for Apichatpong Weerasethakul's *Tropical Malady* (*Sud pralad*, 2004); who played Mrs. Chasen in Hal Ashby's *Harold and Maude* (1971) (Vivian Pickles); or the US box-office gross for Harmony Korine's *Gummo* (1997) (approximately $20,000), with information easily accessible through a search engine that categorizes by title, person, company or event. Indispensable.

LIGHT SLEEPER
www.lightsleepercinemag.com

Billing itself 'late night writings on cinema,' *Light Sleeper* is an erudite and informative on-line film journal that stands out after only two issues in as many years. Featuring mostly academic-related articles on 'past, classic, cult and obscure cinema,' including the recent 'Innocent Incest and Other Displacements: Re-Dreaming Bertolucci's *The Dreamers*,' – not nearly as dry as it sounds – this meaty, well-organized web journal is an inauspicious labor of movie love. *Light Sleeper* kicks off its shoes for its DVD reviews, many of which analyze films sorely overlooked or ignored, including *Cisco Pike*, Bill L. Norton's forgotten 1971 gem starring Kris Kristofferson as a peripatetic singer-songwriter grappling with a serious Sixties hangover.

MAƒTERƒ OF CINEMA
www.mastersofcinema.org
Movie love at its most collaborative and gregarious, this web journal was founded in 2001 by five friends in opposite corners of the globe, joined together in cyberspace through their love of world cinema and auteurs like Bresson, Dreyer, Ozu and Tarkovsky, for whom they have constructed separate sites through *Masters of Cinema*, serving as a clearinghouse for information and news related to each respective maverick filmmaker. The main site aims to collate and disseminate information for discerning cinephiles the world over via news items, a worldwide DVD release calendar and in-house articles like 'The Polarizing, Magnificent Cinema of Bruno Dumont,' replete with footnotes running down the right for easier access. Academic in tone but never preachy, *Masters of Cinema* is a wise, crackling good read. The quintet has even joined with the Eureka! UK DVD label to release a Masters of Cinema line of DVDs, including the recent box set *The Complete Buster Keaton Short Films* (1917–1923).

MIDNIGHT EYE
www.midnighteye.com
Billed 'the latest and best in Japanese cinema,' this site is edited by the Paris-based author Tom Mes, whose recent books on Takashi Miike and Shinya Tsukamoto have established him as one of the foremost

experts on contemporary Japanese film. *Midnight Eye* contains features, interviews, film reviews, book reviews and a calendar of events, including international release dates of DVDs. Stone Bridge Press published *The Midnight Eye Guide to New Japanese Film*, a collaboration between Mes and co-editor Jasper Sharp, in December 2006.

MOVIE CITY NEWƒ
www.moviecitynews.com
The best of the Hollywood news blogs, this site run by David Poland is rife with links to breaking news, the latest box-office figures and various columns, including Mr. Poland's own The Hot Button, which is often more insightful and probing than any print alternative – including the industry bible *Daily Variety*. It's Poland's insider's perspective (which pulls no punches), combined with a genuine passion for films and filmmaking that makes The Hot Button and its companion blog a must-read for Hollywood watchers. Even when Poland rants, he's onto something, to wit his slamming of *Marie Antoinette*: 'I don't think Sofia Coppola needs to be beheaded for this effort, but there is no doubt she lost her head. Young girl queen trapped by her position acts out and is fabulous. And that is beautifully rendered for 40 minutes or so. And then, Sofia loses interest in storytelling, just as Marie loses interest in the monarchy.' No print journalist could get away with saying that in this day and age.

ROUGE
www.rouge.com.au
This decidedly minimalist academic film journal published sporadically in Australia since 2003 has nine scant issues to its name, though each one is so rewarding and rich with information that it will take you months to sift through its many rarefied treasures. The site's design is refreshingly low on bells and whistles, lending it a patina of elegance and simplicity – even when its articles verge on the arcane. Featuring scholarly writing from the likes of Raymond Durgnat, Serge Daney and Nicole Brenez, among others, *Rouge* helps you to see cine-

ma through more reflective eyes; many of its writers possess PhDs but their criticism is surprisingly devoid of pretension. Don't miss *Los Angeles Plays Itself* director Thom Andersen's sublime take on Warhol's cinematic oeuvre in 'The '60s Without Compromise: Watching Warhol's Films,' a highlight of *Rouge 8*.

ƒIGHT & ƒOUND
www.bfi.org.uk/sightandsound
This monthly print publication of the British Film Institute remains a must-read for world cinephiles but for those outside the UK who can't afford an international subscription or the hefty cover price, the magazine's web presence is the next best thing. Featuring selected articles and reviews, the *Sight & Sound* site also provides links to the BFI's extensive film & T. V. database. You can also browse the holdings for the BFI National Library, offering hours of escape for the discerning cinema addict.

ƒCREEN DAILY
www.screendaily.com
The web presence of the European trade bible *Screen International* features breaking news on European productions and major acquisitions and distribution deals, international box office figures and reviews from most major film festivals. Most of the information can be accessed for a monthly charge, though some content is free, including a daily e-mail digest of the latest Euro-centric film world headlines.

ƒENƒEƒ OF CINEMA
www.sensesofcinema.com
This online journal devoted to the serious and eclectic discussion of cinema is an indispensable resource for its database of great director past and present, including detailed articles on maverick filmmakers by some of the best academic writers in the world. But it also features engrossing, analytical articles on a variety of film-related topics, including festival reports and book and DVD reviews. Though based in Australia, its contributors are far-reaching, lending *Senses*

Websites

of Cinema a truly international flair. Recent
articles include such varied topics as heroines in the works of Hayao Miyazaki and
the use of opera music as dramatic form in
Woody Allen's *Match Point* (2005), from the
perspective of a composer and musicologist.

TWITCH

www.twitchfilm.net

Todd Brown's *Twitch* site is everything a movie
news and information site should be in this
day and age, with its keen, discriminating
eye for news on independent cult, foreign
and genre films from around the world, many
of which you're unlikely to have heard of –
though probably will hear about in due time,
considering Todd's impressive eye for the
next big thing in, say, Russian horror films,
Thai slashers or Spanish television commercial directors bent on feature filmmaking
careers. Featuring breaking news, festival
reviews and DVD information, among other
tidbits, this is the best blog on the web for
staying abreast on genre films, burgeoning
mavericks, the latest and coolest trailers,
the hottest horror directors and much, much
more. With correspondents around the world,
Brown's built up a loyal readership hungry
for his frequent updates.

VARIETY

www.variety.com

The premier resource for breaking news in
the motion picture industry and its ancillary offshoots, this web site for the industry
trade paper *Daily Variety* is free for print
subscribers but costs in the vicinity of $20
a month for everyone else – but it's worth
every penny. The site features breaking
production and casting news, box office
figures and reviews of virtually any film
released in theaters or screened at a major
festival in the USA and abroad – Todd
McCarthy's insightful reviews of major releases are often the first out of the gate among
rival outlets and can affect a movie's perception in the marketplace, for better or worse:
such is *Variety*'s power. Grady Hendrix's
Variety-hosted blog *Kaiju Shakedown* is a
daily must-read for Asian film devotees; and

the weekly editorials by powerful editor
Peter Bart often course through the motion
picture industry like the aftershocks of a
strong earthquake. There's a reason why
everyone in the film world reads *Variety*
before any other publication – its coverage
of motion pictures is all-encompassing,
from pre-production to box-office post-
mortem.

YESASIA!

www.yesasia.com

Asian cinephiles need look no further than
this vast on-line outlet – modeled after
Amazon.com, with simple navigation and
customer feedback – for the latest in DVDs,
music, anime, books, collectibles, toys and
electronics from Korea, Japan and China,
replete with free international shipping. Get
the lowest prices on region-free DVD players,
then stock up on Asian DVDs that often show
up on this site before they are released in
the Western world. So determined was I to
see Wong Kar-wai's ravishing *2046* (2004)
before it was released in the States, I ordered
a copy from the site expecting a sub-par
transfer with negligible subtitles but I was
delighted to receive a crisp transfer in addition to a copy of the film's elegant soundtrack at no additional charge. While there's
no substitute for *2046*, *Hero* (*Ying xiong*,
2002) or *Casshern* (2004) on the big
screen, there's something to be said about
beating cautious distributors to the punch
and watching recent Asian fare in your own
home. Still, it's sites like *YesAsia* that are
contributing to the decline of theatrical
exhibition of foreign films around the world –
think about this the next time you skip the
latest Tsai Ming-Liang opus at your local art
house because you can get it for $14.99 here.

Awards

This is a selection of the major international awards ceremonies and selected recent winners. Visit their websites for more detailed information on past winners, dates and locations.

ACADEMY AWARDS

www.oscar.com

Description: The bulwark of televised movie awards attracts more than a billion viewers around the world each year
Host Institution: Academy of Motion Picture Arts & Sciences
Top Prizes: Oscar, Best Picture
Location: Kodak Theater, Hollywood, USA
Date: Late February

Selected Winners

2007

Best Picture: *The Departed*, Graham King (Producer) (USA/Hong Kong)
Best Director: Martin Scorsese, *The Departed* (USA/Hong Kong)
Best Foreign Film: *Das Leben der Anderen (The Lives of Others)*, Florian Henckel von Donnersmarck (Germany)

2006

Best Picture: *Crash*, Paul Haggis & Cathy Schulma (Producers) (USA/Germany)
Best Director: Ang Lee, *Brokeback Mountain* (USA)
Best Foreign Film: *Tsotsi*, Gavin Hood (UK/South Africa)

ARIEL AWARDS

www.academiamexicana.com

Description: The official national film award of Mexico
Host Institution: Academia Mexicana de Artes y Ciencias Cinematograficas A. C.
Top Prizes: Golden Ariel, Best Film
Location: Mexico City, Mexico
Date: Mid-March

Selected Winners

2007

Golden Ariel, Best Film: *El laberinto del fauno (Pan's Labyrinth)*, Guillermo del Toro (Mexico/Spain/USA)
Silver Ariel, Best Director: Guillermo del Toro, *El laberinto del fauno (Pan's Labyrinth)* (Mexico/Spain/USA)
Silver Ariel, Best First Work: *El violin (The Violin)*, Francisco Vargas (Mexico)

2006

Golden Ariel, Best Film: *Mezcal*, Ignacio Ortiz (Mexico)
Silver Ariel, Best Director: Felipe Cazals, *Las vueltas del citrillo (The Citrillo's Turn)* (Mexico) Silver Ariel, Best First Work: *Noticias lejanas (News From Afar)*, Ricardo Benet (Mexico)

AUSTRALIAN FILM INSTITUTE AWARDS

www.afi.org.au

Description: Australia's official national film awards, presented by the country's foremost screen culture organization
Host Institution: Australian Film Institute
Top Prizes: AFI Award, Best Film
Location: Melbourne, Australia
Date: Early December

Selected Winners

2006

AFI Award, Best Film: *Ten Canoes*, Julie Ryan (Producer), Rolf de Heer (Australia)
AFI Award, Best Direction: Rolf de Heer, *Ten Canoes* (Australia)

THE ORANGE BRITISH ACADEMY FILM AWARDS

www.bafta.org

Description: The official national film awards of Great Britain, commonly known as the BAFTAs. Awards excellence in the artforms of the moving image.
Host Institution: British Academy of Film and Television
Top Prizes: The Alexander Korda Award for the Outstanding British Film of the Year
Location: London, UK
Date: Mid-February

2007

The Alexander Korda Award, Outstanding British Film: *The Last King of Scotland*, Andrea Calderwood, Lisa Bryer, Charles Steel, Peter Morgan & Jeremy Brock (Producers); Kevin Macdonald (UK)
Best Film: *The Queen*, Stephen Frears (UK/France/Italy)
The David Lean Award, Achievement in Direction: Paul Greengrass, *United 93* (France/UK/USA)
Best Film not in the English Language: *El Laberinto del Fauno (Pan's Labyrinth)*, Guillermo del Toro (Mexico/Spain/USA)

2006

The Alexander Korda Award, Outstanding British Film: *Wallace & Gromit: The Curse of the Were-Rabbit*, Claire Jennings, David Sproxton, Nick Park, Steve Box, Mark Burton & Bob Baker (Producers) (UK)
Best Film: *Brokeback Mountain*, Diana Ossana & James Schamus (Producers) (USA)
The David Lean Award, Achievement in Direction: Ang Lee, *Brokeback Mountain* (USA)
Best Film not in the English Language: *De battre mon cœur s'est arrêté (The Beat That My Heart Skipped)*, Pascal Caucheteux (Producer); Jacques Audiard (France)

BRITISH INDEPENDENT FILM AWARDS

www.bifa.org.uk

Description: Celebrates merit and achievement in independently funded British filmmaking; commonly known as the BIFAs
Host Institution: Raindance
Top Prizes: BIFA, Best British Independent Film
Location: London, UK
Date: Late November

Selected Winners

2006

Best British Independent Film: *This Is England*, Shane Meadows (UK)
Best Director of a British Independent Film: Kevin Macdonald, *The Last King of Scotland* (UK)

Awards

CÉSAR AWARDS

www.lescesarducinema.com
Description: The main national film awards of France
Host Institution: L'Académie des Arts et Techniques du Cinéma
Top Prizes: César, Best French Film
Location: Paris, France
Date: Late February

Selected Winners

2007

Best French Film: *Lady Chatterley*, Pascale Ferran (Belgium/France/UK)
Best Director: Guillaume Canet, *Ne le dis à personne (Tell No One)* (France)
Best First Film: *Je vous trouve très beau*, Isabelle Mergault (France)

2006

Best French Film: *De battre mon cœur s'est arrêté (The Beat That My Heart Skipped)*, Jacques Audiard (France)
Best Director: Jacques Audiard, *De battre mon cœur s'est arrêté (The Beat That My Heart Skipped)* (France)
Best First Film: *Le Cauchemar de Darwin/ Darwin's Nightmare*, Hubert Sauper (Austria/Belgium/France/Canada/Finland/Sweden)

DAVID DI DONATELLO AWARDS

www.daviddidonatello.it
Description: The main national film award of Italy
Host Institution: Accademia del Cinema Italiano
Top Prizes: David, Best Film
Location: Rome, Italy
Date: Late April

Selected Winners

2006

Best Film: *Il caimano (The Caiman)*, Angelo Barbagallo (Producer); Nanni Moretti (Italy/France)
Best Director: Nanni Moretti, *Il caimano (The Caiman)* (Italy/France)

Best European Film: *Match Point*, Woody Allen (UK/France/Luxembourg)
Best Foreign Film: *Crash*, Paul Haggis (USA/Germany)

2005

Best Film: *Le conseguenze dell'amore (The Consequences of Love)*, Domenico Procacci & Nicola Giuliano (Producers); Paolo Sorrentino (Italy)
Best Director: Paolo Sorrentino, *Le conseguenze dell'amore (The Consequences of Love)* (Italy)
Best European Film: *Mar adentro (The Sea Inside)*, Alejandro Amenábar (Spain/France/Italy)
Best Foreign Film: *Million Dollar Baby*, Clint Eastwood (USA)

EUROPEAN FILM AWARDS

www.europeanfilmacademy.org
Description: Celebrating excellence in films from the European Union and beyond
Host Institution: European Film Academy
Top Prizes: Best European Film
Location: Varies (2006 Awards in Warsaw, Poland)
Date: Early December

Selected Winners

2006

Best European Film: *Das Leben der Anderen (The Lives of Others)*, Florian Henckel von Donnersmarck (Germany)
Best European Director: Pedro Almodóvar, *Volver* (Spain)
Best Non-European Film: No award given

2005

Best European Film: *Caché (Hidden)*, Michael Haneke (France/Austria/Germany/Italy)
Best European Director: Michael Haneke, *Caché (Hidden)* (France/Austria/Germany/Italy)
Best Non-European Film: *Good Night, and Good Luck.*, George Clooney (USA)

FILMFARE AWARDS

www.filmfare.com
Description: India's equivalent to the Oscars,

rewarding excellence in Bollywood filmmaking
Host Institution: FilmFare Magazine
Top Prizes: FilmFare Award, Best Film; Best Director
Location: Mumbai, India
Date: Late February

Selected Winners

2007

Best Film: *Rang De Basanti (Paint It Yellow)*, Rakesh Omprakash Mehra (India)
Best Director: Rakesh Omprakash Mehra, *Rang De Basanti (Paint It Yellow)* (India)

2006

Best Film: *Black*, Sanjay Leela Bhansali (India)
Best Director: Sanjay Leela Bhansali, *Black* (India)

GERMAN FILM AWARDS

www.deutscher-filmpreis.de
Description: Main national film award in Germany; nicknamed the Lolas, after various film characters played by Marlene Dietrich, Barbara Sukowa and Franka Potente
Host Institution: Deutsche Filmakademie
Top Prizes: Lola, Outstanding Feature Film; Best Direction
Location: Berlin, Germany
Date: Mid-May

Selected Winners

2006

Outstanding Feature Film: *Das Leben der Anderen (The Lives of Others)*, Quirin Berg & Max Wiedemann (Producers); Florian Henckel von Donnersmarck (Germany)
Best Direction: Florian Henckel von Donnersmarck, *Das Leben der Anderen (The Lives of Others)* (Germany)

2005

Outstanding Feature Film: *Alles auf Zucker! (Go for Zucker)*, Manuela Stehr (Producer); Dani Levy (Germany)
Best Direction: *Alles auf Zucker! (Go for Zucker)*, Dani Levy (Germany)

GOLDEN HORSE AWARDS

www.goldenhorse.org.tw

Description: Considered the most prestigious national film awards for Chinese-language films made outside the People's Republic of China; awards are voted on by a selected jury and presented at the close of the Taipei Golden Horse Film Festival, showcasing the nominated works

Host Institution: Golden Horse Film Festival

Top Prizes: Golden Horse Award, Best Film, Best Director

Location: Taiwan, China

Date: Late November

Selected Winners

2006

Best Picture: *Fu zi (After This Our Exile)*, Patrick Tam (Hong Kong)

Best Director: Peter Chan, *Ruguo Ai (Perhaps Love)* (China/Malaysia/Hong Kong)

2005

Best Picture: *Kung fu (Kung Fu Hustle)*, Stephen Chow (China/Hong Kong)

Best Director: Stephen Chow, *Kung fu (Kung Fu Hustle)* (China/Hong Kong)

GOLDEN TRAILER AWARDS

www.goldentrailer.com

Description: Recognizing the creative people who make movie trailers; judged by film industry notables

Host Institution: Golden Trailer Awards

Top Prizes: Golden Trailer, Best Action, Best Drama, Best Comedy

Location: New York, New York, USA

Date: Early June

Selected Winners

2006

Best Action: *Mission: Impossible III*, Paramount Pictures, Trailer Park (Producer) (USA)

Best Drama: *Good Night, and Good Luck.*, Warner Independent Pictures, Hammer Creative (Producer) (USA)

Best Comedy: *Wedding Crashers*, New Line Cinema, mOcean (Producer) (USA)

2005

Best Action: *War of the Worlds*, Paramount Pictures, Trailer Park (Producer) (USA)

Best Drama: *Collateral*, DreamWorks SKG, The Cimarron Group (Producer) (USA)

Best Comedy: *Napoleon Dynamite*, Fox Searchlight, mOcean (Producer) (USA)

GOYA AWARDS

www.sie.es/pgoya

Description: The main national film awards of Spain

Host Institution: Academia de las Artes y las Ciencias Cinematograficas de España

Top Prizes: Goya, Best Film, Best Director

Location: Madrid, Spain

Date: Late January

Selected Winners

2007

Best Film: *Volver*, Pedro Almodóvar (Spain)

Best Director: Pedro Almodóvar, *Volver* (Spain)

Best European Film: *The Queen*, Stephen Frears (UK/France/Italy)

2006

Best Film: *La vida secreta de las palabras/ The Secret Life of Words*, Isabel Coixet (Spain)

Best Director: Isabel Coixet, *La vida secreta de las palabras (The Secret Life of Words)* (Spain)

Best European Film: *Match Point*, Woody Allen (UK/France/Luxembourg)

GRAND BELL AWARDS

www.daejongsang.com

Description: Official film awards of South Korea; also known as the Daejong Film Festival

Host Institution: Unknown

Top Prizes: Grand Bell Award

Location: Seoul, South Korea

Date: Mid-July

Selected Winners

2006

Best Film: *Chin-jeol-han Geum-ja-ssi (Lady Vengeance)*, Park Chan-wook (South Korea)

Best Director: Lee Jun-ik, *Wang-ui namja (The King and the Clown)* (South Korea)

HONG KONG FILM AWARDS

www.hkfaa.com

Description: The main film award in Hong Kong

Host Institution: Hong Kong Film Society

Top Prizes: Hong Kong Film Award, Best Picture, Best Director

Location: Hong Kong

Date: Early April

Selected Winners

2006

Best Picture: *Hak se wui (Election)*, Johnnie To (Hong Kong)

Best Director: Johnnie To, *Hak se wui (Election)* (Hong Kong)

Best Asian Film: *Kekexili (Kekexili: Mountain Patrol)*, Chuan Lu (China/Hong Kong)

2005

Best Picture: *Kung fu (Kung Fu Hustle)*, Stephen Chow (China/Hong Kong)

Best Director: Yee Tung-shing, *Wong gok hak yau (One Night in Mongkok)* (Hong Kong)

Best Asian Film: *Oldboy*, Park Chan-wook (South Korea)

INDEPENDENT SPIRIT AWARDS

www.filmindependent.org

Description: The Oscars of the American independent film scene, organized by a non-profit organization 'dedicated to helping independent filmmakers get their films made, building the audience for independent film, and increasing diversity in the film industry'

Host Institution: Film Independent

Top Prizes: Independent Spirit Award, Best Feature, Best Director

Location: Santa Monica, California, USA

Date: Early March

Selected Winners

2007

Best Feature: *Little Miss Sunshine*, Marc

Awards

Turtletaub, David T. Friendly, Peter Saraf, Albert Berger & Ron Yerxa (Producers); Jonathan Dayton & Valerie Faris (USA)
Best Director: Jonathan Dayton & Valerie Faris, *Little Miss Sunshine* (USA)
Best First Feature: *Sweet Land*, Ali Selim (USA)
Best Foreign Film: *Das Leben der Anderen (The Lives of Others)*, Florian Henckel von Donnersmarck (Germany)

2006

Best Feature: *Brokeback Mountain*, James Schamus, Diana Ossana (Producers); Ang Lee (USA)
Best Director: Ang Lee, *Brokeback Mountain* (USA)
Best First Feature: *Crash*, Paul Haggis (USA/ Germany)
Best Foreign Film: *Paradise Now*, Hany Abu-Assad (Palestine/France/Germany/Netherlands/Israel)

JAPANESE ACADEMY AWARDS

www.japan-academy-prize.jp
Description: The main national film awards of Japan
Host Institution: Unknown
Top Prizes: Award of the Japanese Academy, Best Picture, Best Director
Location: Tokyo, Japan
Date: Late February

Selected Winners

2007

Best Picture: *Hula gâru (Hula Girls)*, Sang-il Lee (Japan)
Best Director: Sang-il Lee, *Hula gâru (Hula Girls)* (Japan)

2006

Best Picture: *Always san-chôme no yûhi (Always – Sunset on Third Street)*, Takashi Yamazaki (Japan)
Best Director: Takashi Yamazaki, *Always san-chôme no yûhi (Always – Sunset on Third Street)* (Japan)

NIKA AWARDS

www.kinonika.com
Description: Main national film award in Russia
Host Institution: Russian Academy of Cinema Arts and Sciences
Top Prizes: Nika, Best Picture, Best Director
Location: Moscow, Russia
Date: March

Selected Winners

2006

Best Picture: *9-ya Rota (The 9th Company)*, Yelena Yatsura, Sergei Melkumov & Alexandr Rodnyansky (Producers); Fyodor Bondarchuk (Finland/Russia/Ukraine)
Best Director: Alexei A. German Jr., *Garpastum* (Russia)

OPHIR AWARDS

Description: Main national film award in Israel; the trophy (known as the Ophir) was named for the late actor Shaike Ophir; also known as the Award of the Israeli Film Academy
Host Institution: Israel Film Academy
Top Prizes: Ophir, Best Picture, Best Director
Location: Tel Aviv, Israel
Date: Late August

Selected Winners

2006

Best Picture: (tie), *Aviva Ahuvati (Aviva, My Love)*, Eitan Evan (Producer) (Israel); *Adama Meshuga'at (Sweet Mud)*, Sharon Shamir, Edgard Tenenbaum & Philippa Kowarsky (Producers); Dror Shaul (Israel/Germany/ Japan)
Best Director: Shemi Zarhin, *Aviva Ahuvati (Aviva, My Love)* (Israel)

POLISH FILM AWARDS

www.pnf.pl
Description: The main national film awards of Poland
Host Institution: Polish Ministry of Culture
Top Prizes: Eagle, Best Film and Director
Location: Warsaw, Poland
Date: Late February

Selected Winners

2007

Best Film: *Plac Zbawiciela (Saviour Square)*, Joanna Kos & Krzysztof Krauze (Poland)
Best Director: Joanna Kos & Krzysztof Krauze, *Plac Zbawiciela (Saviour Square)* (Poland)
Best European Film: *Volver*, Pedro Almodóvar (Spain)

2006

Best Film: *Komornik (The Collector)*, Janusz Morgenstern (Producer); Feliks Falk (Poland)
Best Director: Feliks Falk, *Komornik (The Collector)* (Poland)
Best European Film: *My Summer of Love*, Pawil Pawlikowski (UK)

RAZZIE AWARDS

www.razzies.com
Description: Alternative industry awards celebrating the worst Hollywood filmmaking in a given year
Host Institution: Golden Raspberry Award Foundation
Top Prizes: Razzie, Worst Picture
Location: Ivar Theater, Hollywood, California, USA
Date: Early March

Selected Winners

2007

Worst Picture: *Basic Instinct 2*, Michael Caton-Jones (USA)
Worst Director: M. Night Shyamalan, *Lady in the Water* (USA)

2006

Worst Picture: *Dirty Love*, John Mallory Asher (USA)
Worst Director: John Mallory Asher, *Dirty Love* (USA)

Index of Films — Filmindex — Index des films

Index of Films — Filmindex — Index des films

Photo Credits — Fotonachweis — Crédits photographiques

We would like to thank all the individual directors, production companies and distributors who placed photographs and information at our disposal for CINEMA NOW./Unser Dank gilt allen Regisseuren, Produzenten und Verleihern, die großzügig Bildmaterial und Informationen für CINEMA NOW zur Verfügung gestellt haben./Nous remercions tous les cinéastes, producteurs et distributeurs qui ont mis gracieusement à la disposition de CINEMA NOW leurs documentations, images et informations.

Imprint — Impressum — Imprint

p. 1 Still from *Red Road* (2006) (director: Andrea Arnold)
pp. 2/3 Pedro Almodóvar on the set of *La mala educación* (*Bad Education*, 2004)
pp. 4/5 Still from *Qian li zou dan ji* (*Riding Alone for Thousands of Miles*, 2005) (director: Zhang Yimou)
pp. 6/7 Still from *Somersault* (2004) (director: Cate Shortland)
pp. 8/9 Still from *Batalla en el cielo* (*Battle in Heaven*, 2005) (director: Carlos Reygadas)
pp. 10/11 Still from *Oldboy* (2003) (director: Park Chan-wook)
pp. 12/13 Still from *Man cheng jin dai huang jin jia* (*Curse of the Golden Flower*, 2006) (director: Zhang Yimou)
pp. 18/19 Rehearsal photo for *Miami Vice* (2006) (director: Michael Mann)
p. 576 Still from *Gerry* (2001) (director: Gus Van Sant)

Endpapers:
Still from *Boksuneun naui geot* (2001/02) (director: Park Chan-wook)
Still from *Perfume/Das Parfüm* (2006) (director: Tom Tykwer)

To stay informed about upcoming TASCHEN titles, please request our magazine
at www.taschen.com/magazine or write to TASCHEN, Hohenzollernring 53, D-50672 Cologne,
Germany, contact@taschen.com, Fax: +49-221-254919. We will be happy to send you
a free copy of our magazine which is filled with information about all of our books.

© 2007 TASCHEN GmbH
Hohenzollernring 53, D–50672 Köln
www.taschen.com

Editor/Picture Research/Layout: Paul Duncan/Wordsmith Solutions
Editorial Coordination: Martin Holz, Cologne
Technical Editing: David Gaertner and Jörn Hetebrügge, Berlin
Production Coordination: Horst Neuzner, Cologne
German Translation: Egbert Baqué, Berlin
French Translation: Jean-François Cornu, Nantes
Cover and Typeface Design: Sense/Net, Andy Disl and Birgit Reber, Cologne

Printed in Spain
ISBN 978-3-8228-5636-9